THE RED FORT OF SHAHJAHANABAD

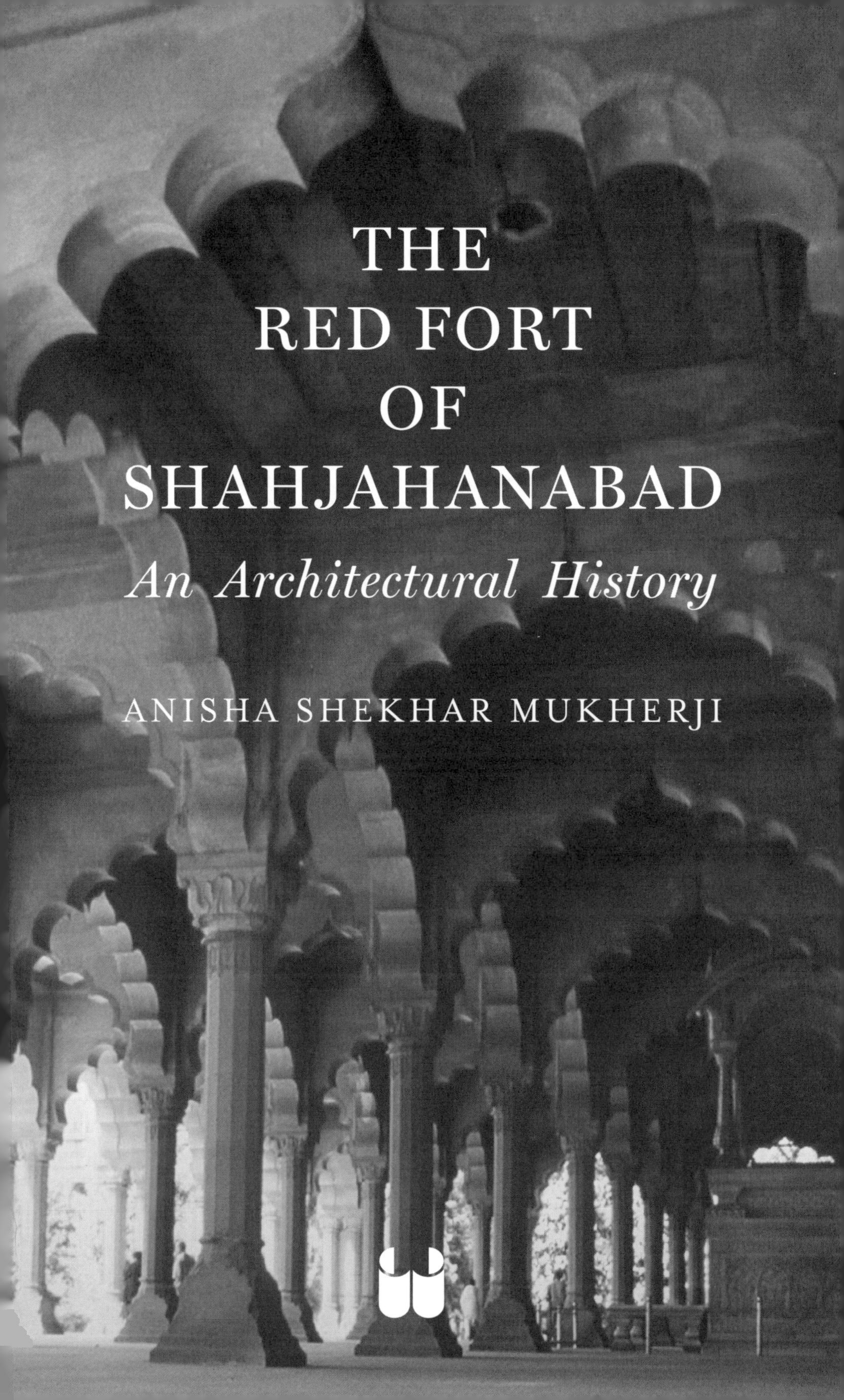

THE RED FORT OF SHAHJAHANABAD

An Architectural History

ANISHA SHEKHAR MUKHERJI

First published by Oxford University Press in 2003

Published by Westland Non-Fiction, an imprint of Westland Books, a division of Nasadiya Technologies Private Limited, in 2024

No. 269/2B, First Floor, 'Irai Arul', Vimalraj Street, Nethaji Nagar, Alapakkam Main Road, Maduravoyal, Chennai 600095

Westland, the Westland logo, Westland Non-Fiction and the Westland Non-Fiction logo are the trademarks of Nasadiya Technologies Private Limited, or its affiliates.

ISBN: 9789360455743

10 9 8 7 6 5 4 3 2 1

Typeset by Jojy Philip, New Delhi
Printed at Thomson Press (India) Ltd.

To

Mrs Aruna Shekhar and

Lieutenant General Chandra Shekhar (PVSM, AVSM)

The author gratefully acknowledges the following for permissions to reproduce copyright material and for help in accessing archival material: Oriental and India Office Collections, British Library; Bodelian Library, University of Oxford; Deutsche Forschungsgemeinschaft (DFG) Geographische Institute der Universität Bonn; National Archives of India; Archaeological Survey of India; Survey of India; Shri D.N. Chaudhuri; Shri E. Alkazi; and the estate of Anjali Chanda; Delhi Archives, D.C. Office Records, New Delhi; ASI Central Photographic Section; ASI Central Library; India International Centre Library, New Delhi; Map Section and the Royal Commonwealth Society, Cambridge University Library, Cambridge; Oriental and India Office Collections, British Library, London; Chester Beatty Library, Dublin.

The computer-generated analytical drawings of the Red Fort have been specially prepared for this book, and are based on a combined analysis of a number of visual and written sources including primary surveys and measurements carried out during the author's research on the Fort. In the instances that drawings are reproduced directly from any source, they are done so with copyright permission.

I'd especially like to thank Karthika V.K., Saurabh Garge, Sonia Madan, Sanjana T., Jojy Philip and everyone at Westland for all the work they have done and the care they have taken to bring this second edition to life.

CONTENTS

PREFACE

Any book is a long journey. For this book, with the vast and vastly transformed Red Fort as its subject, the journey from the first nebulous stirrings of perplexity to a partially assuaged curiosity about this unique Fort, has been accomplished with the help of a great number of people. It is simultaneously gratifying and humbling that, despite no direct stake in my project, individuals and institutions within and outside this country, have been almost uniformly appreciative and helpful.

I would like to thank previous writers, historians, recorders and researchers—especially Louise Nicholson, whose book on the Red Fort spurred my interest in it. Without their effort it would not have been possible to research this subject further, or indeed write the book. Some of these inputs include historical and spatial records and their analysis, both of which have served as invaluable supplements to primary information. They are reproduced in the book, wherever possible and necessary.

Other valuable inputs have come from the work of archaeologists, geologists and geophysicists. Though not strictly part of a conventional historical study, their work was necessary to provide a holistic background to the architectural discussion attempted in this book. Along with the occasional healthy scepticism, invaluable help was also rendered by many individuals in and around the Red Fort. This help was so extensive that it would take many lines to record its various forms. Though the constraints of space do not allow a detailed enumeration, I thank everybody who has assisted me—the soldiers who accompanied me on my circuits of the Fort walls, those who helped me gain admittance into various parts of the Fort and into relevant libraries, friends who surveyed with me the Fort's remnants in the blazing summer sun of Delhi and the officials who assisted me in identifying voluminous records at the Archives.

At the Red Fort, Colonel Fogart extended his help at the very beginning of my endeavour. Dr Judith Roberts at Delhi, and later at the Centre for Conservation Studies, De Montfort University, Leicester, energetically supported the idea of the spatial conservation of the Red Fort. I would also like to record my appreciation of John Stanley, Tim Abbot and David Watt of De Montfort University, for their constructive discussions, Stuart Tappin for his insight into a structural attitude to conservation, Gordon Cain, for generously sharing with me his time as well as his experience in conservation projects and Gillian Dawson at Aberdeen University, for voluntarily hunting out rare editions of books on Indian history.

I am grateful that there have been—and continue to be—individuals and institutions committed to the memory of past generations and their art. If I have felt some incongruity and dismay in the contrast between the unmistakably Indian records and their foreign settings, it has been quickly replaced by gratitude for the existence of these settings. Nonetheless, it is ironic and inescapably sad that these records are more easily accessible to foreign researchers for whom they do not constitute a living direct memory, than for Indians for whom they do.

At the India Office Collections, London, Dr J.P. Losty, Curator of Prints, Drawings, and Records, and his colleagues Rod Hamilton and Linda Raymond, helped me greatly with information on the Red Fort on my repeated visits there as a student. I am especially grateful to Dr Losty for his continued encouragement. Dr Andrew Cook, Curator of Maps at the same institution, lent his scholarship to clarify sources on the Fort. Dr Eckart Ehlers and Dr Thomas Krafft of the University of Bonn, Germany, gave encouragement and information that was extremely helpful to my project and Sinead Ward and Dr Elaine Wright of the Chester Beatty Library, Dublin, and Terri Barringer of the Royal Commonwealth Society, Cambridge University Library, were very cooperative in helping to identify sources from their collections. I greatly appreciate Dr Doris Johnson's help with the permissions regarding the material of the Bodleian Library Collections.

At the Archaeological Survey of India (ASI) Central Photographic Library, I would especially like to thank J.D. Namala, I.M. Tikoo, Ravindra Singh and Komal Singh for being unfailingly efficient and helpful, all the staff at the India International Centre Library and at the ASI Delhi Circle Library, Poornima Ray for her kindness and courtesy. At the Reading Room, National Archives of India, P.K. Roy and Jaya Ravindran helped me in tracking down references to the Red Fort, while Dr P.C. Pradhan and Jagmohan Singh eased the process of obtaining reproductions of historical maps.

I am indebted to the Team for Engineering Architecture and Management (TEAM) for logistic support, invigorating company and innumerable cups of lemon tea; Shri K. Karuppuchamy for assistance in keying in the text; Colonel V.K. Narula for help with acquiring and digitising a great deal of material; Colonel S.K. Mohan for images of the Rang Mahal, Allahabad; Dr Narayani Gupta for useful suggestions despite her own very busy schedule. I thank Dr Jagatpati Joshi, former Director General of the ASI, for his encouragement and for providing useful information Dr Yunus Jaffery, who spared time to clarify the meaning and sources of Persian and Urdu words, and talk of many interesting aspects of Shahjahanabad and Shri Ebrahim Alkazi and Shri D.N. Chaudhuri for generously allowing me to use rare photographs from their private collections. My period of interaction with the ASI as their conservation consultant for the Fort gave me the opportunity to detail out some of my ideas. I am grateful to Mrs Komal Anand, former Director General of the ASI, for initiating such an interaction.

The book would have been much reduced in scope but for Squadron Leader Rana Chinna's loan of his rare books as well as Adit Pal and Ritika Prasad's loan of more such books. I thank Sophie Noble for helping to make my stay in England a pleasurable experience; Lieutenant Amit Sharma for literally opening many doors in the Fort, Romi Khosla for good advice, Jenelle Bonner, who despite a brief acquaintance, took the trouble to send me her photographs on Isfahan, Soutrik Das for his enthusiasm and his photographs and Danny Cherian and Nikhil Joshi for help with the drawings.

Finally, I thank Lt. General Chandra Shekhar and Mrs Aruna Shekhar for their continual guidance and Snehanshu Mukherjee, without whose presence and encouragement, the conception and the realisation of this book would not have been possible. The book itself is an acknowledgement to the creators of the Red Fort—named and unnamed—in the hope that the appreciation of their work will be finally reflected in a sustained conservation of its spirit.

WHOSE FORT IS IT ANYWAY?

PREFACE TO THE SECOND EDITION

There are many reasons for publishing a second edition of a book that was brought out almost exactly twenty years ago. Though the book has been out of print for long and there have been sustained requests over the years for it to be reprinted, the foremost reason for me is that, despite the amount of information that is now publicly available on the Red Fort of Shahjahanabad and its huge national importance, there is still insufficient understanding and appreciation of its essential qualities—and a continuing degradation of its built form and appropriation of its symbolic value. While much has changed, much remains the same.

From the controversy some years ago over the proposal for a private organisation to partner in the conservation of the Red Fort, to its identification with certain episodes in the history of the sub-continent, to wild imaginings about its establishment and use, to selective make-overs of some of its parts, the Fort is almost constantly in the news. But surfeit does not always imply sufficiency, or veracity.

To come to any reasonable conclusion about all this information on the Fort, it is necessary to understand its story, and why this story is both different from, and also similar to, any other monument. The first thing to realise is that actually the Red Fort encompasses within itself not one, but many stories. Some of these have gained centre-stage, such as the one which links the Red Fort with our independence movement. The first Prime Minister of free India started the tradition of Independence Day Speeches from the ramparts of the Fort. His decision to come here after the formal declaration of Independence at Parliament Hall on 15 August 1947, overturned the actual schedule of the official Independence Parade to be held on Kingsway (Rajpath/Kartavyapath) on the lines of the Victory Parade that had been held after the Second World War. Pandit Jawaharlal Nehru was probably influenced by the multitude of associations of the Fort—with the 'Dilli Chalo' slogan of Subhash Chandra Bose, with the Siege and Defence of Delhi in 1857, and with his own involvement in the defence of officers of the Indian National Army at their trial here by the British after the Second World War.

This story is extremely important, but we cannot stop at it. Neither can we tell it appropriately unless we realise why, in the first place, the Fort is such a potent symbol of our identity as an independent nation. Indeed, the wall in front of the Lahori Gate, routinely printed on the front pages of our newspapers every 15 August, blocks our view of the Fort's interiors, and is the very opposite of its original appearance. It is literally 'a veil upon the face of the Fort', as the ailing Shah Jahan, imprisoned at the Agra Fort, wrote in a letter to his son, Aurangzeb, on whose orders this wall was constructed.

Metaphorically too, when we narrow our vision to just this image of the Fort or to one event in its history, we fail to see its pivotal and least understood story—the value of its original form and use. All we know about this part of the story is that the Red Fort was established during the time of the fifth Mughal emperor, Shah Jahan. We are not told that the Fort was built with the active involvement of an array of craftspeople, whose tremendous aesthetic and technical skill was integral to its conception and creation. That they did not just implement instructions, but were collaborators in a project that brought together people from all over the Mughal Empire. That they worked in a decentralised way—an extension of the Indian way of life. That court histories record that in the inauguration celebrations, 'artisans of wondrous talent and magical skill' were publicly honoured by Shah Jahan in the Diwan-i-Am. That the Red Fort's design and construction represents not just the sense and sensibilities of its patron, but also those of all the people who worked on the Fort. All of them, in a sense, were its custodians.

Since we do not know all this, it is scarcely surprising that we fail to appreciate how beautiful its proportions and decoration were, comparable to those we still see at the Taj Mahal. Or how perfectly the Fort was planned, so that its construction along with its contemporary city of Shahjahanabad was accomplished in a little over nine years. Or how their fame rivalled that of Isfahan, established by the Safavid Emperor Shah Abbas. Or that 200 years after being visited by artists, ambassadors, imitators and invaders from all over the world, the pioneering British historian James Fergusson in his monumental *History of Eastern and Indian Architecture* came upon the remnants of the Fort and termed it 'The Most Magnificent Palace in the East—perhaps in the World'.

But the Red Fort was much more than just a palace. This multifaceted complex was the urban focus of Shahjahanabad, the first and last resort for the residents of the entire empire, their administrative and political core, a centre of the highest levels of art and music. It was virtually a miniature city—with imperial pavilions, gardens, audience halls, *karkhanas*, markets, attendants' houses, stables, quarters for the Mughal army. Fergusson himself compared it to the Escorial near Madrid, one of the few renaissance royal palaces built on the scale of a small city, which was still a fraction of the Red Fort. To put this in today's context, the Fort optimised space in an incredibly efficient way to combine within it the range of activities now carried out in the Rashtrapati Bhawan, North and South Block, Lok Sabha, Rajya Sabha, cantonment, Mandi House, Crafts Museum, etc. It cannot, thus, be seen as just any Fort or merely branded as 'Mughal'. It exemplifies the Indian way of life and design, which it further evolved to even greater refinement, inspiring art and architecture within and beyond the sub-continent.

It is difficult to read these chapters of the stories of the Red Fort today. There are literally big chunks of the Fort missing—the result of a radical transformation 160 years ago, during and after the Great War of 1857. As the seat of Badshah Bahadur Shah Zafar, the Red Fort was the focus of 1857. In the battles between the Indians and the British to gain control over this decisive rallying point, many sections of the Fort were damaged. And after the victory of the British, there was wholesale plunder of its precious stone-inlay, carved marble panels, gilded copper domes, artefacts and art. In 1860, orders were passed to deliberately demolish everything within the distance of 500 yards around the Fort, and more than 85 per cent of its internal buildings, courtyards and gardens. Barracks for the British army were constructed on the cleared areas after 'this fearful piece of Vandalism', as Fergusson put it. Instead of the principle of coexistence of different kinds of people accommodated within the Fort, only one use was made of it—that of a British garrison, insulated from and barred to Indians.

So, what we see today are the very few Mughal structures that escaped this demolition. They have lived through years of desecration; used by the British as prisons, canteens, hospitals, mess-rooms, ammunition-depots. From the early twentieth century, they have also gone through cycles of restoration that began with their presentation as showpieces to British royalty such as King George V, who visited Delhi in 1911 for the Coronation Durbar.

Why is it that most of us who visit the Fort do not know this? It is because we are not given any clues about this part of the story. To unearth these clues on our own is difficult. We would need to piece together available fragments from many different sources that illustrate some parts of this vast Fort—official court chronicles, miniatures, archival paintings, travelogues, photographs, drawings, etc., and most importantly, the few Mughal buildings that still exist in the Fort. That is what I began to do twenty years ago.

It was only when I did so that I could visualise the Fort's original form and function. It was then that I realised how imperative it is that each part of what exists of this unique design—mere shadows as they are of their former selves—still have immeasurable value, and have to be looked after with the greatest thought and care. And how equally imperative it is to give sufficient information at site, to involve visitors in all the facets of all the stories latent in the Fort. For this, it is necessary to have a clear understanding of its historical layers, as well as its defining attributes, so that we do not destroy them in however well-meaning a way. This, in essence, is what I tried to share through the book.

However, it seemed to me that more people needed to know these stories of the Fort, since subsequent acts over the past decades even in the name of conservation have reduced its historic value. In many parts it appears that the Fort's maintenance and interpretation has gone from bad to worse. Rare remnants of its original decoration and proportions have been effaced. Conjectural and ill-advised interventions above and below-ground have been inserted. Finely worked remains of craftsmanship in the imperial pavilions have been replaced by crude restoration. Entrance to these fragile and rare buildings has been blocked by barriers of untidy ropes, rusted pipes propped up against stairs, taciturn and impatient guards.

The colonial model of keeping the natives out is still followed, with authorities and agencies remaining tight-lipped about their plans to conserve the Fort. This is especially ironical, given the Fort's symbolic value as a national icon of independent India and its soubriquet of 'The Fortress of Freedom'. The insistence on viewing the Fort as a monument with no real interaction with people is, in a sense, no different from its use by the British as their garrison. People are not just kept out literally from parts of the Fort, but also from its decision-making process. This is why we can only react retrospectively every time a fresh disaster strikes the Fort. One such time in the Red Fort's recent history was when a Public Interest Litigation (PIL) was filed in 2003 to protect the Fort against further degradation. It was only after part of the renovation work by the ASI was already done that it came to the notice of vigilantes, who were able to demonstrate the inappropriateness of this work through a record of the Fort prior to this intervention and the evidence in the *The Red Fort of Shahjahanabad* published earlier in the same year. Though they were successful in obtaining a decision to review and direct, to some extent, the Fort's future conservation, there has been no real change subsequently in how it is viewed or interpreted.

I would argue that it is not enough to form more committees and authorities or promulgate evermore rules and policies. Seventy-five years after Independence is enough time to stop regarding our monuments as fiefdoms of either official or private agencies. We need a fundamental change in attitude to evaluate what should be *the objectives* of the custodianship of our heritage. Should we still be seeking ratification for our past from elsewhere in the world? Should we be trying to get 'World Heritage' tags, or concentrating our efforts to make our heritage relevant to our own people? Is it enough to involve only professionals within these domains, whose 'disabling effect' as the Austrian philosopher, Ivan Illich terms it, works on a principle of exclusion and monopoly? Should we not let citizens have a say in the planning of our cities, whether related to monuments, roads or infrastructure?

What would such a process have meant for the Fort? It means we could have guided, through appropriate conservation norms, the continued presence of the Indian Army to keep alive one of the historical uses of the Fort and to contribute to better security integral to its conception and maintenance. It means we could have reinstated the attribute of the ecologically appropriate orchards that originally surrounded the Fort, instead of making swathes of water-guzzling lawns ringed by high metal fences. It means we could have integrated the economic and social well-being of the people living and working around the Fort by including them as skilled guides and representatives of our cultural heritage. It means we could have made it a truly national symbol, with the possibility of engaging resources from any member of our nation who wished to contribute their money, expertise or ideas. It means we need not have given anybody the freedom to jeopardise its physical and historic presence, whether official custodians or powerful business interests. It means we need to remind ourselves about the pertinence of the question: 'Whose Fort is it anyway'?*

This is true not just for the Fort. Other, less complex sites, which have seen smaller amounts of transformation, will also have many stories individual and unique to them, even if perhaps not as many as the Red Fort. They will also need to be interpreted and integrated with people around them. Let us take this opportunity to own our right and our responsibility for the custody of our heritage. So far, we have interpreted 'custody'—whose dictionary meanings are both 'protective care' and 'imprisonment'—within meanings that see people as interlopers. We need to now see custodianship as protective care, both for the monuments we profess to conserve and the people whom we ostensibly conserve them for. But the duty or right to take care of something can only be effective or justified if we have sufficient knowledge of and empathy with what we are taking care of. It is my hope that the second edition of *The Red Fort of Shahjahanabad*, which also includes some updates from the first edition, and in a format and size that is easy to carry and to assimilate, will help in some measure toward doing that.

* This was also the title of a piece contributed by the author, first published in *The Indian Express*, 3 June 2018. You can read more about it here: https://indianexpress.com/article/express-sunday-eye/whose-fort-is-it-anyway-red-fort-controversy-5200389/.

1

OF TIME AND SPACE

'It is in short, in the Buildings, and in them only, so far as regards long periods, that the history of India can be satisfactorily read, whilst from them at all periods, is derived a most vivid picture of her arts, her civilization and her position relatively to the rest of the world.'

Extract from an address to the Secretary of State, 22 July 1873,
signed by a body of noblemen and gentlemen of England,
urging the necessity of preserving Monuments in India.[1]

One of the important buildings—or more appropriately, collection of buildings—that encapsulates a long period of Indian history and its arts is the Red Fort in Delhi. This was the only palace complex under the enlightened patronage of the powerful Mughal dynasty to be conceived and built as a complete entity along with its supporting city.[2]

As a highly visible imperial construction famed for its regal splendour, order and aesthetic standards, the Fort exercised enormous influence. This influence extended not only to kings and noblemen who sought to emulate the emperor, but also to envoys and visitors from various parts of the country and other countries as well as hundreds of inhabitants of the Mughal empire. Reinterpreted prolifically, but not unrecognisably, the Fort's image largely formed the inspiration for what is called the 'provincial Mughal Style' that spread to different parts of

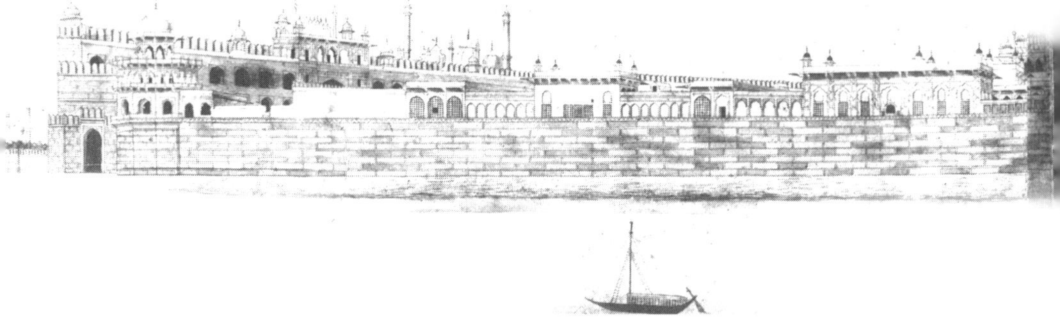

The Palace at Delhi (F 7/8 and 7/9, NAI)

India in the seventeenth, eighteenth and nineteenth centuries—a potent memorial to the mystique of 'the Great Mughal' long after he himself had passed away.[3]

Over the years, this mystique has dimmed into a blurred picture of the Fort's life in those times. However, its mystery has increased. Why did Shah Jahan, with his ostensible passion for symmetry, establish a Fort that was asymmetrical? What impelled him to create an entirely new city? How did the inmates of the huge Fort use its different areas? Where did the emperor eat, bathe, escape into solitude from his numerous courtiers, attendants, women and children? What were the systems of security, water supply and sewage? Such questions are not easy to answer. Much of the Red Fort's overall layout as conceived at its founding is either destroyed or obscured. Only its outer walls remain today along with a handful of the numerous pavilions, courts, gardens, colonnades, houses, markets and workshops that virtually constituted a city within the Fort.

Available written and pictorial information on these aspects of the Fort is limited. Shah Jahan did not, unlike earlier Mughal emperors such as Jahangir and Babur, write his own biography. However, he did commission court histories. Based on documents that recorded day-to-day events in his court as well as in other parts of the Mughal empire, and illustrated with miniature paintings from the best painters of the imperial atelier, they offer exhaustive information—but not an insight into his mind or actions.

Of the four major Persian court histories of his reign, two exist as unpublished manuscripts and the other two are in a partially published form. The first two, each called the *Badshah Nama (Padshah Nama)*, are by Mirza Jalala Tabataba'i and by Mohammed Amina Qazwini, respectively, and are incomplete, seemingly prey to the fickleness of imperial whim. Of the remaining two, the combined work of Abdul Hamid Lahori and his pupil and collaborator, Mohammed Waris (who is recorded to

have completed at least part of the third volume of the court history independently after Lahori's ill health and subsequent death in 1654 CE)—also called *Badshah Nama* (*Padshah Nama*)—has been translated and published only in part.[4]

The fourth history, the *Shah Jahan Nama* by Mohammed Salih Kambo, known as *Amal-i-Salih* or the work of Salih,[5] has been published, but only in the original Persian and in an Urdu translation.[6] Though a recasting of material from the earlier official histories, it is believed to contain some important additions, especially of events during and after the war of succession (1657–1660 CE) between Shah Jahan's sons. It is also more authentic in its divisions of the first decade of Shah Jahan's reign on the basis of solar years, as compared to the lunar year divisions retrospectively adopted in Lahori's work.

Apart from these, a fifth work is a summary of the huge, three-volume official court history of Lahori and Waris, written by Inayat Khan—appointed superintendent of Shah Jahan's royal library in 1657. Entitled *Mulakhkhas,* literally 'the abridgement', and translated and published in English in the nineteenth century, it is also known today as *Shah Jahan Nama*. Its updated version under the title of *The Shah Jahan Nama of Inayat Khan* has additional information culled from the Lahori and Waris court history as well as that of Kambo's, and has served as a valuable reference of Shah Jahan's reign for this book.

These works by rival authors, though backed by their personal interpretation and written in different styles based on the changing demands of the emperor, are based on the same source material and contain overlapping references to a similar range of events arranged according to each regnal year—milestones in the emperor's life and that of his family, ceremonial public activities and celebrations, major military campaigns, transcripts of orders, important architectural episodes. As the official court histories were finalised only after being scrutinised first by high officials and then Shah Jahan himself, they also contain implicit and explicit information about what the emperor considered important to be recorded for posterity. However, since Shah Jahan was deposed barely ten years after he inaugurated the Red Fort, his court histories could not reach their natural conclusion in Delhi. The politically turbulent period that followed his removal from the throne, coupled with the disposition of his immediate successor, Aurangzeb, shifted the emphasis of actual activities as well as written memoirs away from architecture. Even the daily records and detailed documents stored in the Mughal imperial records office which formed the basis for these histories were, for the most part, lost during the disordered reigns of the later Mughal rulers.

Thus, in the court histories, specific information related to the Red Fort at Shahjahanabad—inaugurated in the twenty-first year of Shah Jahan's reign—is limited, and is largely to do with costs of construction and descriptions of the imperial buildings of the Fort at the time of establishment. Events when Shah Jahan and his court were at Shahjahanabad are also recorded. However, these are only a few, since it is not as if the remaining part of Shah Jahan's reign was spent entirely in the Red Fort; the Mughal emperors moved frequently between different parts of their huge empire. Nonetheless, such references as they are, as well as accounts of Shah Jahan's activities in the other forts at Agra and Lahore, are useful in generating an overall picture of the use and form of imperial architecture.

To give some idea of the emperor's routine: barely five months after the inauguration of the Red Fort, Shah Jahan proceeded on a month-long hunting excursion to Safidun with his imperial camp. On his return, after spending just about a month at the Red Fort, he left for Lahore and Kabul to oversee the imminent threat of invasion of Qandahar by Shah Abbas, the ruler of Iran. It was more than a year later that he returned to Shahjahanabad, before setting off again the next year—this time for Kashmir, Lahore and Kabul. It was almost two years before he came back to Shahjahanabad. The emphasis of the court histories was naturally on documenting the emperor's activities at the imperial court, which moved with him.

Accounts of the Fort are also available in the writing of various travellers. These have their own limitations, since the travellers were often from an alien culture, debarred from entering certain private domains

Eastern face of the Red Fort, early 1858
(Photo: J. Murray, 1858, Murray Collection, 52/28, OIOC, BL)

of the court, and insensible to many subtleties of Mughal custom. Their representations of the Red Fort are from a time when it had already begun transforming from its original appearance and their own cultural and personal perceptions inevitably intrude on their accounts. One of the earliest visitors to the Mughal imperial court at Delhi, who was privileged to visit many (though not all) parts of the Fort, was the French traveller, Francois Bernier. The English translation of his book by Archibald Constable containing a detailed record of his experiences, titled *Travels in the Mogul Empire AD 1656-68*, was first published in 1891. It is one of the main European sources referred to in this work.

A number of pictorial representations of the Red Fort were made by Indian as well as foreign artists. The works by Indian artists include formal stylised paintings commissioned to depict specific buildings or events in the Fort, as well as less detailed views covering a larger area, perhaps drawn on the artists' own initiative. As the residence of the Mughal emperors, the Fort also came in for its fair share of visual representation by European visitors. Of these, perhaps the first professional artist to tour India extensively (from 1780 to 1783 CE) was William Hodges, about 130 years after the establishment of the Fort.

Photographic images of the Fort from the mid-nineteenth-century onwards—a time when it was already 200 years old—documenting various periods of its later existence are available as well. Perhaps more objective as historical documents than hand-drawn paintings, they too are insufficient in themselves to generate a complete understanding of the Fort. Most parts of the inner palace at the time of the earliest photographs were still inaccessible to visitors. Thus, these photographs

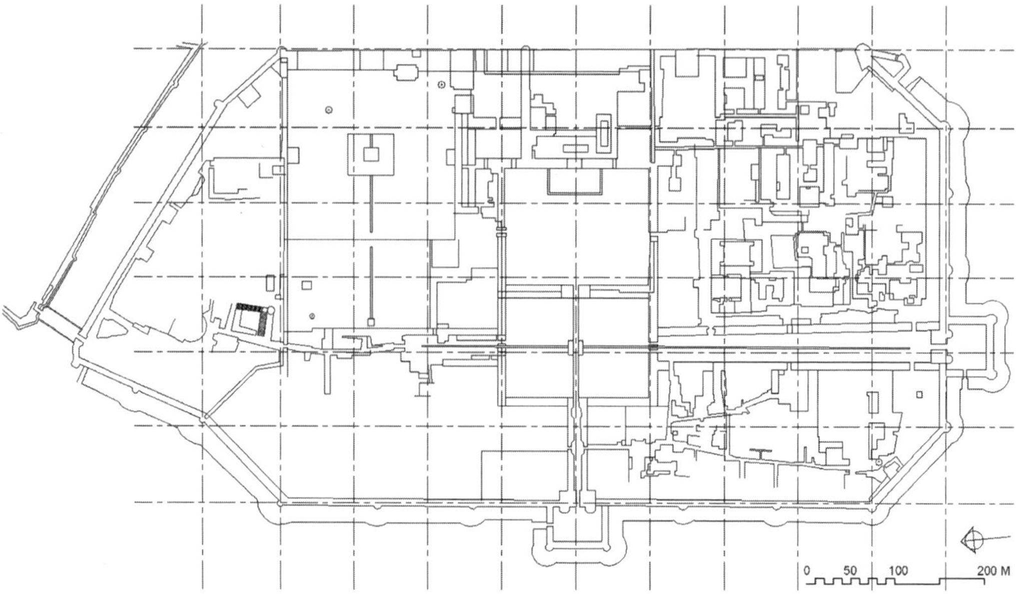

Plan of the Fort before demolition by the British
(Drawing: N. Joshi, Author, based on Map 15/9, ASI Delhi Circle Archives)

are mainly confined to the public areas of the Fort and are incomplete as records.[7]

As for maps, the earliest surviving map of any part of Shahjahanabad, as researched by Susan Gole, appears to be a small plan of the Red Fort in the Jaipur collection dating from the mid-eighteenth-century. However, the most detailed extant map of Shahjahanabad is from the mid-nineteenth-century.[8] Though the more famous version of this map is with the Oriental and India Office Collections (OIOC) in London,[9] an almost identical version is also in the possession of the Archaeological Survey of India (ASI).

The more widely known OIOC version has been referred to in the discussion in this book. Rightly recognised as 'an indispensable source for reconstructing the morphology of Shahjahanabad',[10] the information offered in it, however, needs to be considered keeping in mind two main issues. To begin with, 200 years separate the Fort's establishment and the making of this map. Thus, the representations in it need to be carefully sifted and interpreted in the context of the possible changes that may have occurred over this period in order to distinguish the original spatial elements from later-date interventions. The second issue is that of accuracy. Though rich in presentation and dense in detail, this map is not an exact rendition of the proportions and size of either

Shahjahanabad in c.1846-47 (X/1659, OIOC, BL)

the overall dimensions of the Fort or its internal arrangement. In fact, different historical plans of the Fort, despite some basic similarities, differ substantially from each other.

An important visual document that helps clarify key dimensions is a plan of the Fort dated 1904. This plan, not generally considered in discussions on the Fort, was discovered and identified in the ASI archives by the author, during her appointment as a conservation consultant to the ASI.[11] The plan, though it does not contain any detailed profiles, is

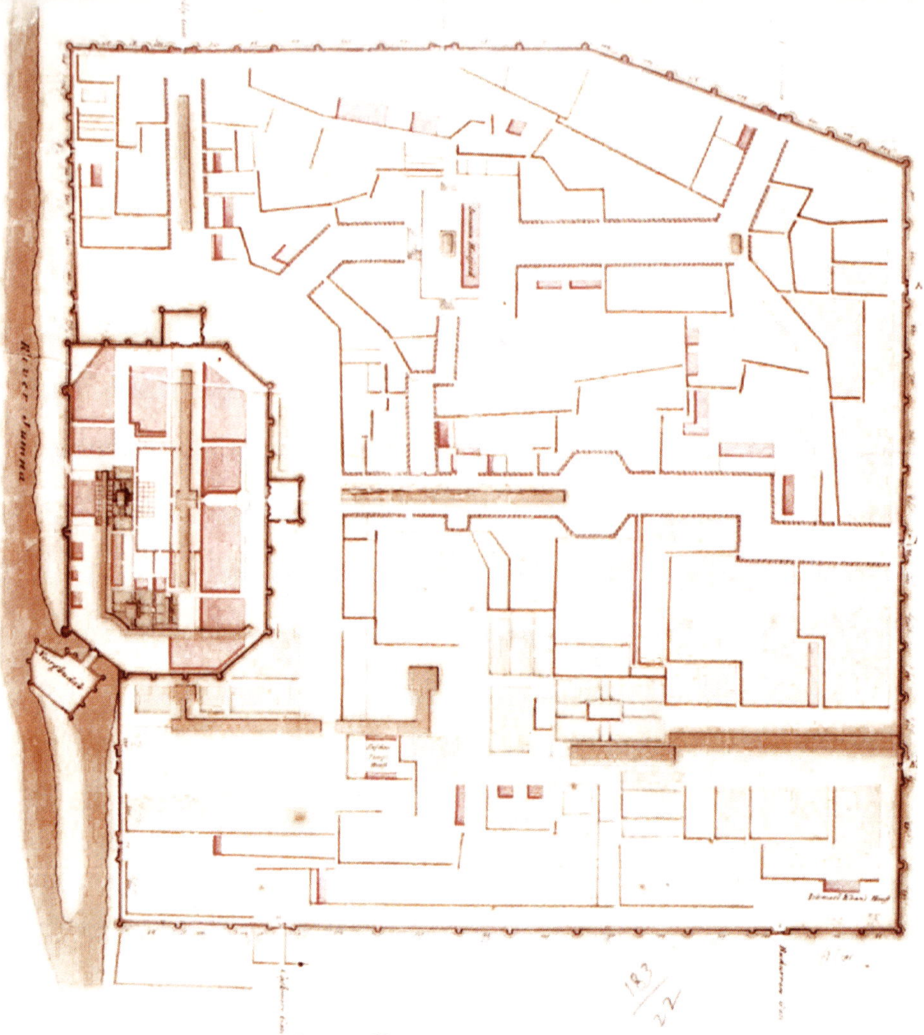

Plan of Dehly from a Hindustani Map
(F 181/22, NAI)

invaluable in that it records overall measurements of many—though not all—Mughal courts and buildings demolished or planned to be demolished by the British. It makes available, for the first time, the proportions of original architectural elements no longer extant today, documented by the people who destroyed them.

The foregoing brief enumeration indicates the fragmentary nature of the actual and recorded remains of the Red Fort. Thus, the only way to configure its original appearance and use, as well as the location and function of its spaces, is by investigating, both individually and as a whole, its actual extant built fragments as seen in conjunction with its recorded

Plan of Red Fort, eighteenth century (Add.Or. 1790, OIOC, BL)

history. Apart from the sources already mentioned, other available written and visual accounts contemporary with the establishment of the Red Fort and its city, and their later such representations, offer important supplementary information. References to earlier Mughal palaces are also useful in clarifying the customs and the practical uses of different buildings and spaces within the Red Fort. However, given the scarcity of primary material and the subjective nature of the secondary sources, it must be clarified that such an analysis can only be interpretive.

It is well-known that written accounts or drawings often employ artistic license. Thus, identifiable architectural structures in some of the beautiful Mughal miniature paintings, otherwise rendered with skill and faithful attention to detail, may bear transposed brackets or roof types seemingly from other buildings. For instance, the painting titled 'Shah Jahan's Ceremonial Reunion with the Princes Dara Shikoh, Shah Shuja and Aurangzeb in the Hall of Public Audience of Akbarabad Fort on 1 Rajab 1037 (7 March 1628 AD)' from the illustrated *Padshah Nama* in the Windsor Library, instead of showing the throned balcony in the Diwan-i-Am in Akbarabad or Agra Fort, appears to actually depict the one in the Lahore Fort![12]

Other paintings, while truthfully showing architectural details, sometimes depict objects within them which could not have been physically present at the date at which these paintings were executed. Such is the case in a Mughal miniature in the Chester Beatty Collection in Dublin. It dates from 1839 and depicts the last Mughal king Bahadur Shah II enthroned within the Red Fort on the Peacock Throne. However, the original Peacock Throne, a fabled possession of the Mughal dynasty, had been lost a century ago to invading armies.[13] Other such examples—though not of the Red Fort—are Thomas and William Daniells' late eighteenth and early nineteenth century aquatints of various parts of India, an important reference for life in those years (1795–1803 CE). In the book *India, Yesterday and Today: Aquatints by Thomas and William Daniell*, the revisited sites of these sketches have been photographed from the same position as those of the original aquatints.[14] These photographs clearly show that elements of the natural and built landscape have been played up in the Daniells' sketches—sometimes substantially—to achieve greater dramatic or compositional effect.

Even if there is no deliberate attempt at dramatising a space, any account or representation is inevitably an individual perception which can never be completely objective.[15] The selective nature of perception and memory is illustrated in many of the numerous drawings of the Red Fort and Shahjahanabad by both Indian and European artists in which the inner features of the Fort and sometimes even its outer profile are completely transformed. Since the Fort was a complex construction—of a vast size with many facades, and comprising many pavilions, gateways, colonnades and courtyards—it is not surprising that its depictions vary considerably between one representation and another. Thus, in some of the maps of the city, the complex profile and functions of the Red Fort have been simplified into more geometrical subdivisions or with only the external elements inserted. One such example dates from the early nineteenth century titled 'Plan of Dehly from a Hindustani map', in the National Archives of India. Another is a map from the eighteenth century in the OIOC collection.[16]

Most sketches by European artists choose a different method of simplification. They reduce the Fort's sequence of numerous single-storey pavilions connected by colonnades and courts, to just a couple of towering and isolated buildings. Two representative examples of such sketches clarify this assertion. Situated at the end of a wide-open space or a driveway flanked by trees and shrubbery in the manner of a stately English mansion, and capped by many bulbous domes, these do not tally with photographs of the area taken during the same time period or with later depictions by the ASI based on consolidated evidence from old maps, drawings and archaeological investigations. Even the extant Mughal monuments within the Fort today are either omitted altogether or are almost unrecognisable in these sketches.

The proliferation of the onion domes in these sketches may have been due to their reassuring charm as exotic cousins of the more prosaic domes used extensively in formal religious, institutional and residential Western architecture. While the reasons for such depictions of the Fort are not relevant within the scope of the present discussion, it seems apparent that no single version of its recorded images can be relied upon as an accurate rendition of its parts.

Therefore, all the above sources—including the writing and research of other scholars on Mughal history who work under similar constraints of information—have been used to derive an integrated analysis of the geometrical form, the functional use as well as the symbolism of individual and combined spaces of the Red Fort. And in doing so, to extend the understanding of Mughal architecture through one of its pre-eminent examples. The analysis in the following sections leads back through time into the spaces of the Fort as they may have appeared when Shah Jahan inhabited them. But the peculiar freedom invested by the passage of time also makes it possible to view these spaces simultaneously

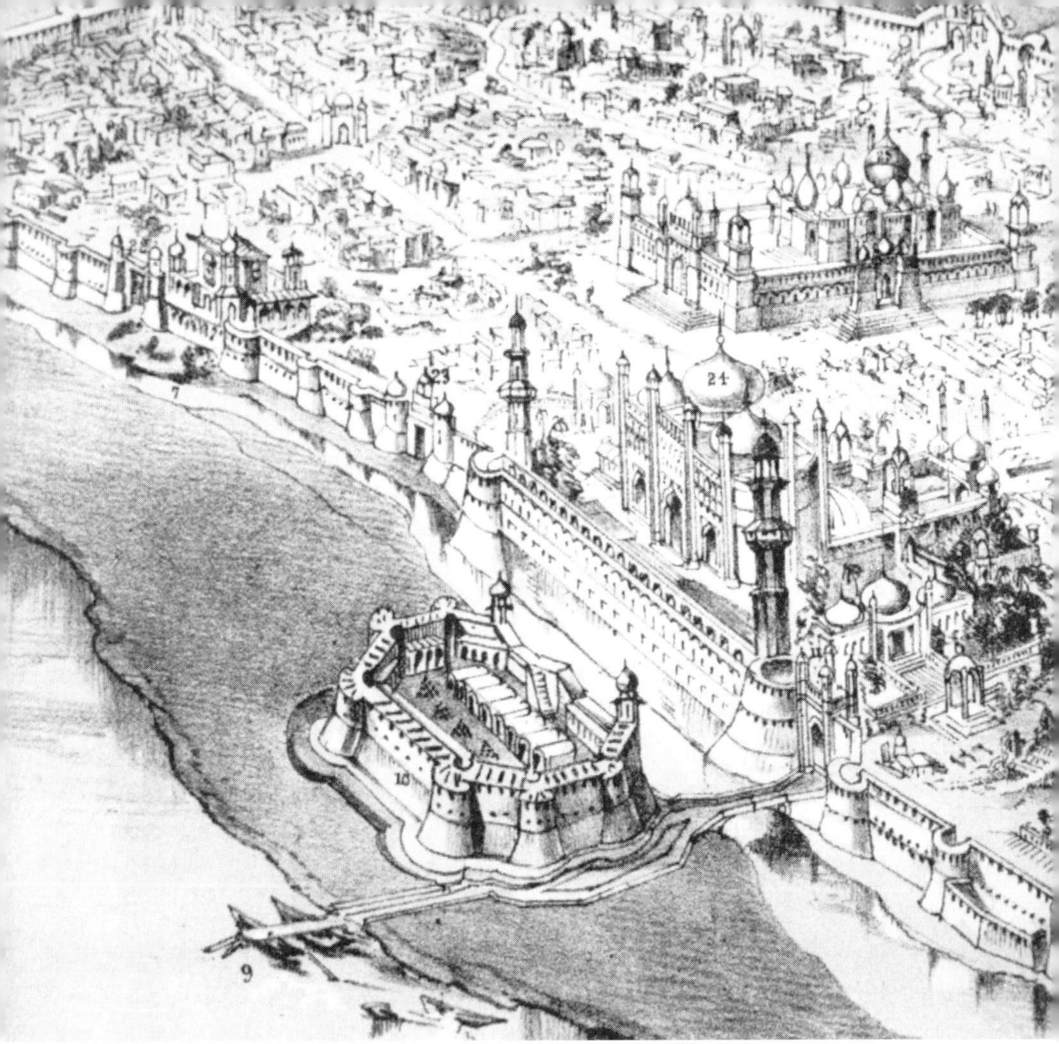

Delhi and surrounding countryside, 1857
(A. Maclure, P 137, OIOC, BL)

'as they are', contrasted with 'as they were' in order to communicate the transformation in the Fort and to generate a picture of it as created for Shah Jahan.

Such a study also allows back-and-forth movement through macro and micro views. Thus, while the overall planning principles are investigated before examining individual spaces, some indication of these spaces is included right at the outset, with the imperial parts of the Fort discussed at length. Portions of these are still extant, and they have also been recorded more extensively than other parts of the Fort. They are unique in that they represent the culmination of the experiments in space, form and decoration by the Mughal emperors, of whom Count H.A. Keyserling, the nineteenth-century German philosopher and traveller, wrote:

Delhi before the siege, 1857
(John Luard, private collection)

> It goes hard to judge rightly here, but today it seems to me as if the great ones among the Grand Moghuls, were as types, the greatest rulers which mankind has produced. They were men of vehement temperament ... refined diplomats, experienced connoisseurs of men, and simultaneously sages, architects and dreamers. Such a constellation has never occurred in the West, at any rate to no good purpose.[17]

The Red Fort was the outcome of the combined vision of a skilled team of artists and their patron, Emperor Shah Jahan, arguably the most imaginatively gifted of the Mughal emperors. The construction and the design of this Fort, though not as universally recognised as the Taj Mahal—another of Shah Jahan's incomparable acts of patronage—represents an architectural feat that is unrivalled in scale and imagination perhaps anywhere in the world. The resolution of built and open space in the design of the Fort, while being appropriate to its own era, transcends time and continues to be valid even today. This enduring quality can perhaps best be communicated by a general observation of Rabindranath

Tagore, whose own prodigiously creative output eminently qualifies him as a sage, architect and dreamer.

> All organic beings live like a flame, a long way beyond themselves. They have thus a smaller and a larger body. The former is visible to the eye; it can be touched, captured and bound. The latter is indefinite; it has no fixed boundaries, but is widespread both in space and time.[18]

2

THE MOST MAGNIFICENT PALACE IN THE EAST

'The palace at Delhi, is, or rather was, the most magnificent palace in the East—perhaps in the world—and the only one, at least in India, which enables us to understand what the arrangements of a complete palace were when deliberately undertaken and carried out on one uniform plan.'

James Fergusson, *The History of Indian and Eastern Architecture*

Around 350 years after its founding by Emperor Shah Jahan, the palace at Delhi still forms one of the most compelling memories of the city. These memories owe more to the sight of its powerful expanse than to any sustained association with its past, which is half-forgotten. This is perhaps an inevitable consequence of a long existence, and as true for a place as for a people. However, the particular mix of symbolic and actual historical events that have taken place in the palace and the sweeping transformations that have been wrought to its form and function make its image more enigmatic than many other structures of its age. The loss and replacement of so many of its original architectural and spatial elements make it difficult to separate or even recognise the shifting layers of the palace's earlier historical existences.

As seen today, the majestic outer walls and the moat running along them remain much as originally designed, strengthening the illusion of a

Western facade, Red Fort (Photo: D.N. Chaudhuri, 1960)

complete, unharmed palace within. However, beyond the entrance gates and the covered entrance arcade, this strong enclosure gives way to a confused mixture of structures—a legacy of its turbulent history. Airy Mughal pavilions in exquisitely carved red sandstone and marble, partially obscured by abundant tree growth, sit uncomfortably in the shadow of tall barracks. Flamboyant arched gateways are set in prim green lawns. Tarred roads insolently touch beautifully ornamented plinths. This strange cohabitation, in the absence of sufficient information and interpretation, is perceived in different ways, depending on the spirit, orientation and expectation of its visitors, but rarely recognised as the remnant of 'the most magnificent palace in the East'.

Though known as an architectural symbol of the Mughal dynasty—one of the most dynamic political and cultural reigns of its time—the palace today is seen rather more simply as an urban landmark. Its red walls loom large on the crowded horizon of one of the main transport routes of Delhi, their cusped battlements and domed corners offering a relieving counterpoint to the monotony of modern facades in the city. Originally termed the Qila-u-Mubarak[1] (the Fortunate or Exalted Citadel), the vast circuit of its red sandstone walls that once served as battlements has led to its being termed Lal Qila or the Red Fort.

The Red Fort has an immediate political and national significance all over India. It is both a symbol and setting of events that shape India's national identity. It continues to be the focus of the annual Independence Day celebrations, and the final destination of the festive parade to mark the founding of the Indian Republic. The Fort is also unfailingly associated with stories of the last stand, tragic as it was, against the relentless mind and hand of the British. The most enduring of these stories, perhaps, is that of the white-bearded King Bahadur Shah Zafar who composed poetry in his translucent marble rooms, before assuming briefly the spirit of his commanding ancestors over the battlements of his red citadel. The story ends with the killing of the king's sons and his own banishment to a distant land from the gardens, river and Fort where he spent nearly all his life.

Other stories refer to a time almost a hundred years later when young men were brought into alien structures within the familiar red walls to face a judge and jury from whose race they were trying to reclaim what remained of their own spirit; of the fate that followed them, and the day that marked the independence of their people. This is perhaps the most dominant theme in the perception of the palace today, kept alive each year in ceremonies that reaffirm national identity. Seen in this context, it is natural that the symbolic importance of the Red Fort in the sub-continent's freedom struggle against British rule has focused interest away from its design. This design, a unique combination of architecture and urban planning, invested with the aura of the Mughals, made the Fort an object of admiration for travellers and even rival rulers.

It was 'on the night of Friday, the 25th of Zi'l-Hijja … corresponding to 1048 (29 April 1639) [CE]' that the Red Fort's foundations are recorded to have been marked out and 'the night of Friday, the 9th of Muharram 1049, (12 May 1639) [CE]' when the foundation stone was laid.[2] In the more than 380 years that have elapsed since then, the Red Fort and its city of Shahjahanabad have altered greatly. The way of life of people has also changed. The river Yamuna, on whose banks the city was located, has shrunken manifold and moved far away. The Ring Road—originally termed the Lower Bela Road from the word *bela*[3] or sandy land adjoining a river—runs over its former course. The river's once sandy bank was, for a time, an unfrequented no-man's land

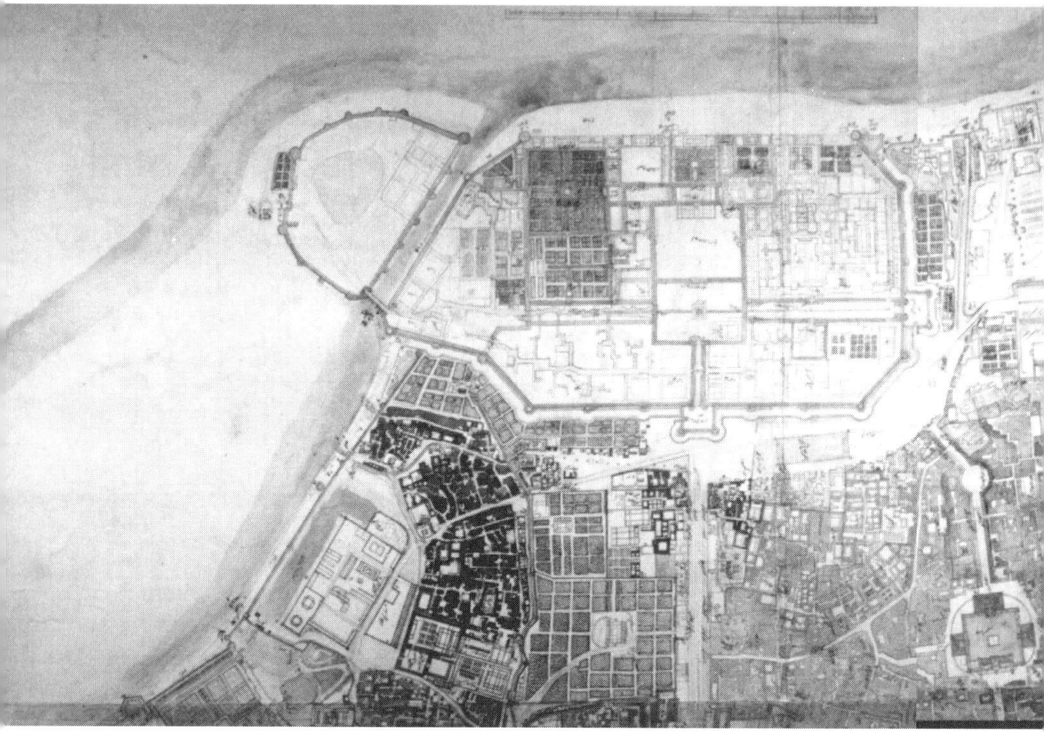

The Red Fort on the banks of the Yamuna (X/1659, OIOC, BL)

peppered with squat public urinals. Its transformation into a vibrant open-air market on the Sunday of each week is now overtaken by a wave of gentrification in the form of a dreary municipal park. Of the multitude of gardens that characterise Shahjahanabad and formed a vivid foreground to the Fort, barely one or two remain. The others have been usurped by buildings, roads and fenced lawns. Begum Bagh, its main public garden, re-invented by the British as the 'Queen's Gardens', has contracted further in its present avatar of the Mahatma Gandhi Bagh. The area of the gardens that Shah Jahan had established in front of the Fort[4] is used occasionally for festivals and Independence Day celebrations. The Red Fort now lies like an island, surrounded by a wide confluence of roads that link Shahjahanabad to other parts of Delhi—south to British imperial[5] and post-Independence New Delhi, north to the old cantonment and Delhi University, and west and east to the newest concentrations of urban growth in the national capital. The central line of trees and fountains that cooled the main streets of

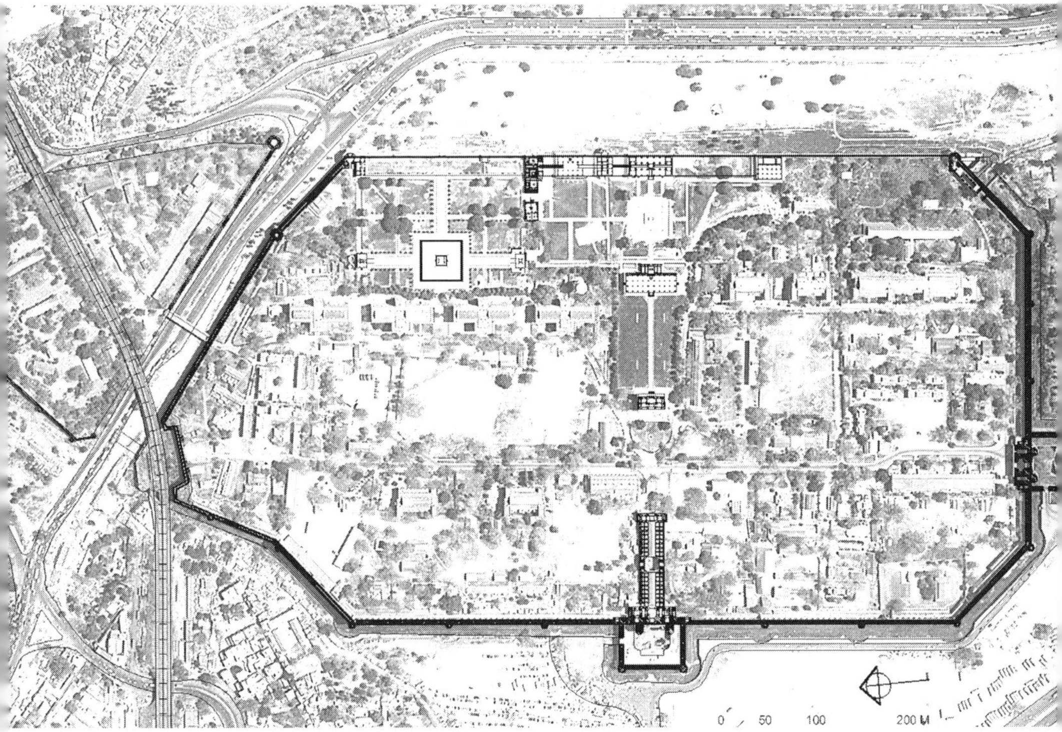

The Red Fort and the present position of the Yamuna (Drawing: Author, N. Joshi, D. Cherian; based on an aerial photograph, courtesy VCOAS Sectt. and NRSA)

Shahjahanabad no longer exist. The green fields, smaller settlements, and scrub forests of the surrounding suburbs where Shah Jahan hunted, camped and travelled en route to other parts of his empire, have almost disappeared. Encompassed in the increasing pressure of sustained migration, Shahjahanabad is now just one part of Delhi.

When Shahjahanabad was founded, the road sequence outside the Fort consisted primarily of two principal streets, which in turn linked up with the two important road systems of medieval north India.

> [These] two principal streets of the city ... may be five and twenty or thirty ordinary paces in width. They run in a straight line nearly as far as the eye can reach; but the one leading to the Lahor gate is much the longer ... there are arcades on both sides ... The houses of the merchants are built over the warehouses at the back of the arcades, they look handsome enough from the street and appear tolerably commodious.[6]

One of these streets went south through the city's Delhi or Akbarabadi Gate—so named because this gate linked Shahjahanabad with the older

Eastern face of the Fort, 1820 (Add.OR.540, OIOC, BL)

cities of Delhi: Firoz Shah Kotla, Indraprastha, Siri, Tughlakabad, and further on to Agra or Akbarabad, the city of Akbar as it was then called. The other principal street ran westwards to the city's Lahori Gate, and linked up with the Grand Trunk Road to Multan and Lahore. Outside the city walls, these roads were no longer bounded by arcades but ran through scrubland or pockets of trees with habitation confined to small isolated areas. Though resting-houses, milestones, fields and occasional gardens bordered these roads, the ordered streets of the city bisected by canals and fountains must have offered an agreeable contrast to travellers entering the city. And the main entrance gates of the Fort, rearing up at the end of the straight avenues visible from the main Delhi and Lahori Gates of Shahjahanabad, would have presented both a reassuring and awesome sight.

These entrance gates of the Fort, also called the Lahori and the Delhi Gates, still exist as do some of the other city gates. However, only a very small portion of the walls that linked the gates remain today, though their memory lives on in the title of 'The Walled City' that Shahjahanabad continues to be referred to. The absence of the city walls reduces the functional connection between the gates of the Fort and the city to one that is merely symbolic. The Fort gates also function somewhat differently from the time of the Mughals. The Delhi Gate is now mainly used for official purposes. The only public entrance is the Lahori Gate, which faces the main thoroughfare of Shahjahanabad—the east-west avenue now termed the Chandni Chowk.

However, the view of the Gate from Chandni Chowk is partially blocked by high battlemented walls.[7] The Fort and Chandni Chowk are

separated today by tarred roads of immense breadth interspersed with open ground. A steady stream of visitors passes in to the Fort across these roads, and through a slightly circuitous sequence of a bridge and a smaller gateway leading to the Lahori Gate itself.

This bridge, the smaller gateway and the wall in front of the Lahori Gate did not exist in the original conception of the Red Fort. Before the smaller gateway was added, Shahjahanabad's east-west avenue led straight through a bridge over a moat into the Fort's Lahori Gate from a great *chowk*. Rose and grape gardens formed a green border on either side of the chowk. It was in this chowk that the Rajput nobles aligned to the Mughals,[8] encamped when it was their turn to mount guard for the

View of Salimgarh, Red Fort and Nigambodh Ghat along the banks of the Yamuna (Delhi, Vol. 4, 919-21, no. 230, e-397, ASI PL)

Eastern face of the Fort, 1997 (Photo: Author)

emperor. It was also here that during the war of 1857, the cavalry camp of the Indian soldiers, who pledged renewed allegiance to the Mughal ruler, was located.[9] Looking back over the chowk towards the city, the Rajahs in the seventeenth century and the soldiers in the nineteenth century would have seen a red mosque, the Fatehpuri Masjid, sitting across the far end of the main street.

The chowk does not exist anymore, though the Fatehpuri Masjid still does. However, it is not easily visible with the growth of newer buildings and the increase in traffic. In Mughal times, the Masjid's presence could not be ignored despite the wide range of activity in the areas preceding it—*Katra Neel,* the indigo-quarter; *Bagh-i-Begum,* the Queen's garden; *Kucha-i-Patua,* the quarter of embroiders; *Chabutra Johar Bazar*, the square of the jewellery bazaar; *Chabutra Kotwali,* the square of the police headquarters; *Kucha-i-Chooriwala,* the banglemakers' street; interspersed with areas named after important and influential residents such as *Haveli Haider Quli Khan, Kucha-i-Jeevandas, Kucha-i-Haveli Rajah Jugal Kishore* and *Kucha-i-Chowdhary Hukum Das.*[10] The uninterrupted visual and spatial axis that existed through the Lahori Gate from the city into the Fort and vice versa was later interrupted by the addition of the barbicans.

This interruption is, however, not perceived as an intrusion. Indeed, the barbicans topped by grassy embankments comprise one of the recurring images of the Red Fort. It is from here that the Prime Minister addresses the country each 15 August to mark Independence Day. Apart from their manifest defensive function, the barbicans also impart greater privacy to the interior of the Fort. Before their construction, the direct axis into the Fort would have meant that imperial ceremonial activities were almost on public display—a situation comparable to the front door of a house, and those of its hall and its living rooms, being all flung wide open!

The smaller red sandstone gateway to the north of the Lahori Gate provides an indirect entrance to the Fort. In the space between the Lahori Gate and its barbican, steps and semi-circular arches (added by the British) climb up high embankments on two sides towards an unevenly enclosed sky. Even amidst the surging crowds that move almost unpunctuatedly towards the massive Lahori Gate, this space has an elusive sense of a sanctuary. The Gate, its rows of minarets and *chattris* crowning a soaring many-cusped arch, effortlessly dominates over the later construction around it. An intricately worked metal door set within the arch echoes the scale of the huge Gate and gives access into the vaulted street of the *Chatta Bazaar*, the covered market. High pursed-up niches contradict the partially obscured liveliness of the Chatta Bazaar's lower arcades behind signboards, colourful wares and insistently echoing shopkeepers' voices. The *Chatta Chowk*, a central octagonal open-to-sky court located in the middle of this arcade, lets light into the Bazaar.

Termed the *Bazaar-i-Musaqqaf* when constructed in the seventeenth century, the Chatta Bazaar was the first example of such a covered street in India. Then, as now, it had an unmistakably commercial function, described as 'a long and tolerably wide street, which has a divan on both sides bordered by shops instead of arcades ... this street is a bazaar.'[12] Its high walls were originally decorated with painted floral designs in many colours, lighted by the sun during the day and perhaps camphor candles during the night. From this octagonal court, open archways perpendicular to the market street led into gardens.

Today, these side archways lead into bare land stretching out to the inner face of the Fort walls. There are no gardens to be seen, though the power of the straight, vaulted street is so potent that rarely is a glance directed away from its axis. Ahead of the Chowk, the clamour of the Chatta

Bazaar continues till it leads out through another arched gateway into an open space. A British barrack looms up immediately to the north of the gateway and some temporary structures nestle to its south, presenting a perplexing picture to an uninitiated visitor.

Entrance routes through this Bazaar would have originally opened out into a very different scene. In a painting by Mazhar Ali Khan, an artist of the nineteenth century, the long market street broadens out into a paved rectangular forecourt bounded by red sandstone arcades. Minor officials are said to have occupied these arcades for administrative transactions. The forecourt with noblemen, soldiers, elephants and horses passing to and fro through tall sandstone gateways set into the boundary of its arcaded walls is depicted with an air of serenity around its central water tank. During the events of the war of 1857, the same space was the scene of tumultuous activity, including the tragic killing of some Europeans.[13]

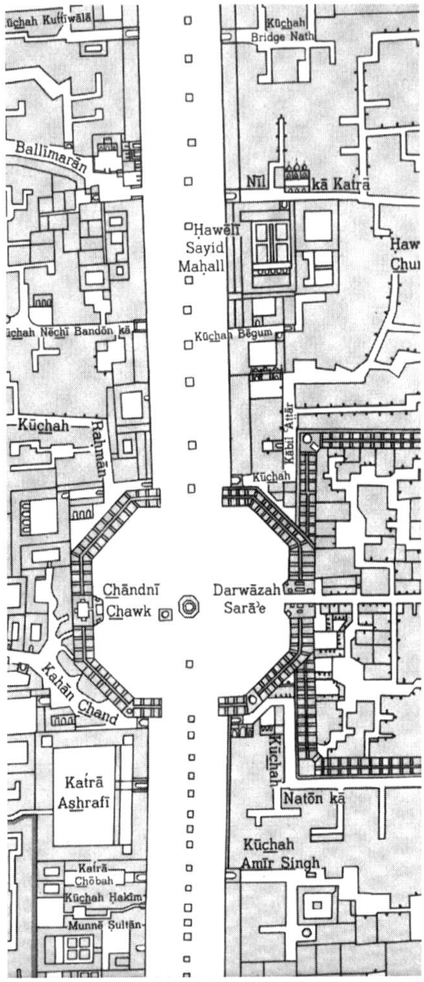

Chandni Chowk, Detail
(Based on X/1659, OIOC, BL)

Though the gateways in the forecourt rose in the centre of all its four sides, the main movement path was eastwards through the tallest and most ornate of them,

The Kotwali, Chandni Chowk (e-409, Delhi Museum, Vol. 1, 1911-12)

the *Naqqar Khana* (also called the *Naubat Khana*) or the Drum House. The Naqqar Khana gave entrance to the *Diwan-i-Am*, the Hall of Public Audience.

The smaller gateways of the forecourt formed a secondary movement route from Delhi Gate to the old sixteenth-century citadel of Salimgarh, used as an occasional prison for rebellious kin and courtiers. Though Delhi Gate was also used as a public entrance into the Fort, the main sequence of movement was from Lahori Gate and Chatta Chowk, continuing through the forecourt and under the Naqqar Khana to the Diwan-i-Am.

This system of the western parts of the Fort containing public functions and progressing to private areas on the eastern side still exists today, though in a diluted way. The Naqqar Khana now stands alone. There are no subsidiary arcades, no forecourt, no sign of the other three gateways to proclaim its importance as the final ceremonial gateway of the Fort. The first sight of this red sandstone building from the Chatta Chowk is obscured amidst tall trees. It is flanked by fences and foliage that draw attention away from the scarred side walls, evidence of the dismembering of its connecting arcades. The central arched double-height gateway of the Naqqar Khana is entered by way of steps leading up to a plinth. Arched windows within sandstone panels float silently above the gateway.

These windows would have originally been in the form of open archways within a covered verandah, the sound of music rolling out sonorously through them. It was in a central chamber within the verandah that the court musicians marked time with the emperor's appearance. Ceremonial music with twenty pairs of *nakkarahs* or kettle drums, four pairs of *karranas* and three pairs of cymbals in brass or iron, is recorded to have rung out at different times of the day from the Naqqar Khana.[14] On Sundays, the music was kept up all day because it was a day sacred to the sun and the same honour was paid to the day of the week on which the emperor was born.

The arched entrance gateway of the Naqqar Khana, earlier level with the forecourt, marked the transition into the imperial presence. As the gateway between the inner and outer parts of the Fort, strict rules governed its use. Though no one was barred entry, only the emperor and his kin were privileged to ride beyond this archway. All others had to dismount under pain of death. During the reign of later emperors, this regulation continued to be observed as a mark of respect. But one day, Francis Hawkins, the British Resident at Delhi, 'a gentleman whose energy went beyond his discretion',[15] unaffected by such a memory or tradition, rode in. The emperor at that time, dependent on a British pension and re-titled the king of Delhi, was unable to retaliate in a manner his ancestors would have deemed fit. Bereft of power, yet reluctant to relinquish all semblance of it, he protested strongly. This breach of custom was regarded seriously enough to transfer the palace affairs from the jurisdiction of the Resident to that of the Magistrate of Delhi.[16]

Almost a century before the infringement of these rules resulted in a setback for Hawkins, the Naqqar Khana was recorded as the scene of fatal attacks on two emperors. In the eighteenth century, Emperor Jahandar Shah (who ruled from 1712–13) and Emperor Farukhsiyar (who succeeded him till 1719) are believed to have been killed[17] in this building by their ministers.

The Naqqar Khana gateway still functions as a point of transition, though distinctions of royalty are invalid in a democracy, and the possibility of anyone riding in any mode of transport is now ruled out by the raised plinth. The archway is accessible to anyone with an entrance ticket. A niche on the building's western facade once served as the public face of the custodians of this part of the Fort, the Archaeological Survey of India (ASI), their offices located in side rooms hidden behind rough curtains and rectangular doors set into delicately cusped archways.

Framed through the Naqqar Khana archway is a large red sandstone pavilion at the end of a lawn. This, the Diwan-i-Am pavilion, is reached via a central paved path. Immaculately proportioned and supported by

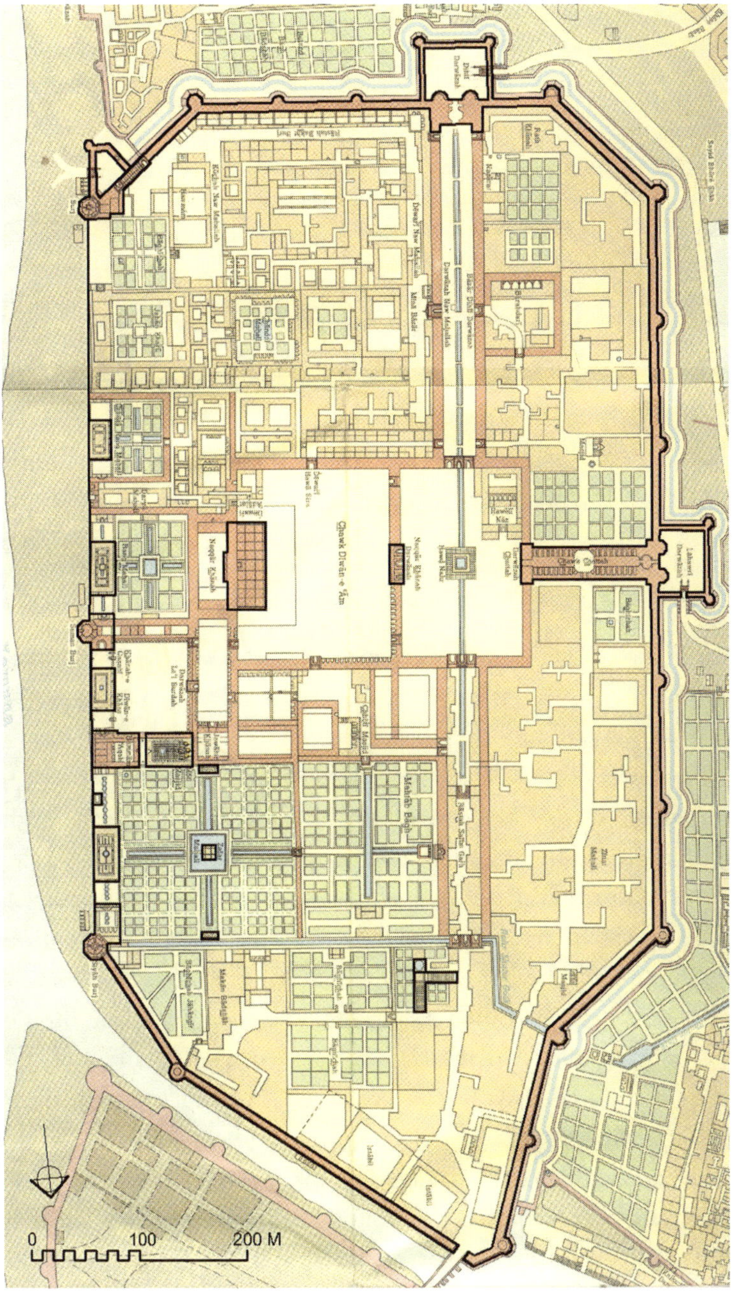

The buildings within the Red Fort, mid-nineteenth century (with the extant structures outlined in black) (Based on X/1659, OIOC, BL and the translated map redrawn by courtesy of the British Library, Oriental and India Office Collections, from the original manuscript in the India Office Records, eds: E. Ehlers, T. Krafft and J. Malik, University of Bonn, 1992)

Shops in Khas Bazaar (e-402, Delhi Museum, Vol. 2, 1911-12)

three rows of stately carved columns, it conveys an imperial authority echoed by a central white marble canopy inlaid with precious stones. A shadowed masonry wall on the pavilion's fourth side forms a resplendent backdrop to the Imperial Throne, whose celebrated mosaic of birds and flowers in semi-precious stones is more clearly revealed at closer quarters.

In the seventeenth century, when Francois Bernier visited the Mughal Court, the appearance of the building was markedly different. Bernier describes the Diwan-i-Am as 'a large and magnificent hall, decorated with several rows of pillars, which, as well as the ceiling, are all painted and overlaid with gold'.[18] This pavilion, always embellished lavishly, was especially decorated at the inauguration of the Fort when it was the centre of celebrations. As is recorded, the hall was surrounded by a golden railing, a canopy was erected around it on silver poles, its arcades were hung with velvet and silk from China, finely embroidered carpets were spread and the throne was provided with a special canopy fringed with pearls.

Chatta Bazaar, 1846
(Panorama by Mazhar Ali Khan, Add.Or 4126, OIOC, BL)

Chatta Bazaar, 1997 (Photo: Author)

Naqqar Khana, 1858 (Photo: J. Murray, 52/29, OIOC, BL)

Apart from being the centre of ceremonial public celebrations, the Diwan-i-Am formed the setting for the daily *durbar* or court assembly. Non-attendance of this durbar by the courtiers—tantamount to a slight to the emperor—was to invite imperial displeasure, as the nobleman Khan Jahan Lodi discovered. His omission to present himself at the durbar, following an attempt to take over the province of Malwa, was deemed suspicious conduct, for which he subsequently had to beg forgiveness.[19] Tavernier, a French jeweller who came to the Mughal court in the middle of the seventeenth century, also noted that from the time that the emperor seated himself on the throne till he rose, no one was allowed to leave the palace.[20]

Today, visitors walk down a narrow central path and come to a final inexorable stop at the Diwan-i-Am, no longer overlaid with gold or painted but still large and magnificent. Around and beyond the concentrated attention that the Diwan-i-Am evokes, unusual fragments intrude upon the skyline. These include the sharply dipping roofs of grey British military barracks and uneven masses of shrubs, bushes and trees. All these have to be erased from sight and mind to realise that the space

Naqqar Khana, 1997 (Photo: Author)

occupied by the lawn in front of the Diwan-i-Am was originally in the shape of a rectangular red forecourt.

This forecourt was subdivided by railings and awnings into rectangular areas. These were graded into different areas of importance depending on their distance from the Imperial Throne. The nearest area was obviously reserved for the most influential members of the court, but even they had to approach it with due ceremony and the rules for accessing the forecourt continued to be followed strictly even after Shah Jahan's reign. Court chronicles record that in 1668 CE, when the expelled king of Kashgar came to Delhi, he was allowed to ride till the doors of the forecourt, but only on horseback. He then alighted from horseback to mount a palanquin till he reached the area immediately around the Hall, which was shaded by an awning and enclosed by a red sandstone barrier. From here, he ascended the steps to the pavilion on foot, and arrived at the inner bays demarcated by a silver railing. Finally, he sat down near the golden railing that separated the throne from the rest of the Hall and partook of the emperor's bread and water.[21]

Diwan-i-Am forecourt and adjoining buildings, Agra Fort (I 319/1919-20, ASI PL)

Diwan-i-Am forecourt, Red Fort, 1858 (Photo: J. Murray, 53/17, OIOC, BL)

Diwan-i-Am area, Red Fort, 1997 (Photo: S. Mukherjee, 1997)

The forecourt of the Diwan-i-Am also marked the furthest limit to which most citizens would have been allowed access within the Fort. On occasion, special arrangements were made in this forecourt for the well-being of the emperor's subjects. For instance, after the 60th birthday of Shah Jahan in 1650 CE, it was decreed that His Majesty would give funds for charity in lieu for observing the Ramzan fast and 'every night during this sacred month all kinds of foodstuffs and sweetmeats were to be laid out in the Forty Pillared Hall (Chihil-Sutun) in the court of public audience, so that famishing and destitute people might appease their hunger'.[22]

Beyond this forecourt and its boundary of red arcaded cells interrupted by a few gateways was the private part of the palace. This consisted of the emperor's own living quarters and that of his family. Here, only a privileged few were allowed restricted access. Trusted courtiers were permitted to enter the Hall of Private Audience, *Diwan-i-Khas.* They entered its precinct through a gate in the northeast wall of the Diwan-i-Am forecourt. Another gate on this forecourt's southeast wall led into the royal seraglio—a part of the palace particularly susceptible to intrigues. In addition to these entrances, two more gates on the forecourt's south and north walls led to the public part of the seraglio and the imperial kitchens respectively.

Today, none of these remain. The seraglio, the state robe-chambers and the kitchens that surrounded the forecourt have also disappeared, along with any indication of the forecourt. Furtive paths now circuit the Diwan-i-Am. Following their lead, past shoulder-high shrubs, one reaches an open expanse divided by lawns and paths. Several white buildings are disposed around the lawns and on a raised marble terrace beyond. The closest of these is a pavilion directly behind the Diwan-i-Am—the *Rang Mahal.* This, inevitably, is the pavilion first approached.

To the right of the Rang Mahal is a solitary white plastered building; to its left are a series of pavilions in different configurations, finally stepping down to the bulbous domes of a small mosque within an enclosing wall. These isolated buildings constitute the remnants of the inner palace—the part of the Fort inhabited by the Mughal emperor and his family. Designed as its most private part:

Diwan-i-Am, c.1840 (Add.Or 4668, OIOC, BL)

Diwan-i-Am, 1997 (Photo: Author, 1997)

> ... the whole of the area between the central range of buildings to the south and eastward from the bazaar, measuring about thousand feet each way, was occupied by the haram and private apartments of the palace, covering, consequently, more than twice the area of the Escurial, or in fact, of any palace in Europe.[23]

The construction of the Escorial, one of the largest palaces in Europe commissioned by King Philip II in the mountains above Madrid, was begun in 1563, almost 100 years before the Red Fort. At about 206 by 161 metres (675 by 528 feet), its size made it closer than most other Renaissance royal buildings to the scale of a small city. Yet, it was more than five times smaller in plan area than just the inner palace of the Red Fort.

Originally, each of the pavilions within the inner palace of the Red Fort were constructed with their own individual courts separated by arcades, colonnades and buildings, through which there were limited points of entry and exit. Movement was planned and organised carefully in this part of the palace which was reserved solely for Shah Jahan and his numerous wives whom he wed in the polygamous tradition of the Mughals. In addition, the Mughal seraglio was also the residence of the emperor's female relatives and concubines and their attendants. The Mughal emperors only occasionally gave their daughters in marriage to foster political alliances, ostensibly since no man was considered good enough to marry a Mughal princess,[24] but more probably to limit contenders for the throne.

Outsiders were therefore forbidden to enter this part of the palace, both to ensure the emperor's safety and to prevent the large number of royal women in the seraglio from contracting any misalliances. The strict practice of segregation of the inner palace was aided by its maze-like quality with shifting axes and protected entry points. Nevertheless, it is said that some ingenious and daring young men did manage to enter this area, aided by the women within. An old woman, a half-caste Portuguese who was a slave in the seraglio, apparently related one such story to Bernier, as recorded in his memoirs.[25]

> One day during the reign of Emperor Aurangzeb, a young man was secretly smuggled into the inner part of the Red Fort, with the help of some of the inmates. The object of his visit was the emperor's younger sister, Roshanara Begum. The princess, after contriving to keep the youth hidden in her part of the palace for some days, entrusted him to her personal attendants to lead him out of the Fort in safety. Promising faithfully to do so, the attendants guided the youth out from the seraglio under cover of darkness.
>
> But, before they could even lead him out of the inner palace, the women fled, perhaps for fear of discovery. The youth, terrified and lost,

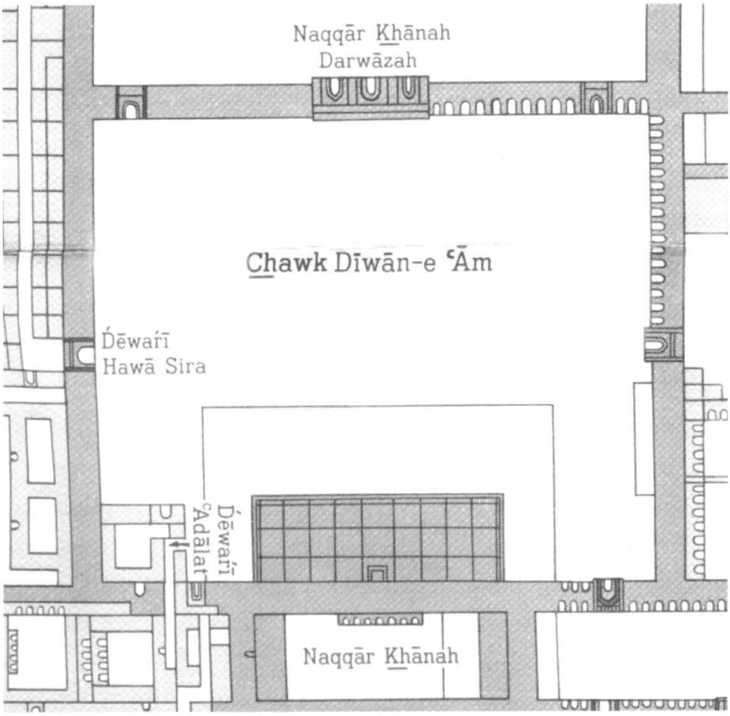

Diwan-i-Am forecourt with its entrance gateways, 1840s
(Based on X/1659, OIOC)

tried all night to find a way out. In the morning, he was discovered, still wandering in the maze of passages and gardens. The presence of a strange man in the seraglio was a serious matter, and he was summarily brought into Aurangzeb's presence. Well aware what an admission of his presence in the royal seraglio might result in, the youth insisted even on repeated questioning, that he had merely scaled the high walls of the Fort on the riverbank and gained entry into the Imperial Quarter. The sceptical emperor ordered him to descend in the same way. And the palace eunuchs, in an excess of zeal, threw the young man down a height of sixty feet on the river-bank.

The final fate of Roshanara's unfortunate suitor is not recorded, though it is unlikely that he would have successfully survived such a descent from the Fort walls. This news must have increased the vigilance of the eunuch guards (who were, it seems, punished severely for this security lapse) as well as discouraged prospective visitors to the seraglio. Such visitors were naturally enough, debarred from using the more prosaic and securely guarded entrances and exits into the inner palace which led off from the Diwan-i-Am forecourt and from its adjoining courts.

For the emperor, there was a separate and private entrance route through a door immediately behind the throne, which connected it to a chamber on the Diwan-i-Am's east face. Through this chamber, the emperor descended a staircase into a small court through arcaded verandahs, which led to the garden of the Rang Mahal, reputedly the chief building of the seraglio. The garden of the Rang Mahal was divided into four quadrants with a fountain at the centre, and was bounded by a range of arcades on its south and north. The emperor, as he came out into the verandah behind his throne chamber, would have thus had a central view of this pavilion and its garden arranged symmetrically on the axis linking the Lahori Gate and the Diwan-i-Am. Today, the emperor's door to the staircase behind the throne is kept locked and the connecting courtyards and their surrounding colonnades do not exist. Instead, one large space separates the Diwan-i-Am and the Rang Mahal. This space, different in size and detail from the original layout, is now organised as a type of Mughal garden in its divisions, though not in its scheme of planting.

The Rang Mahal exists as a pillared hall flanked by a set of more opaque chambers. Its garden and what is now the rear of the Diwan-i-Am are visible through the open arches of the hall. On the other side of the hall, five arched windows overlook a river of traffic and a dense network of roads. Within, an empty marble channel runs down the entire

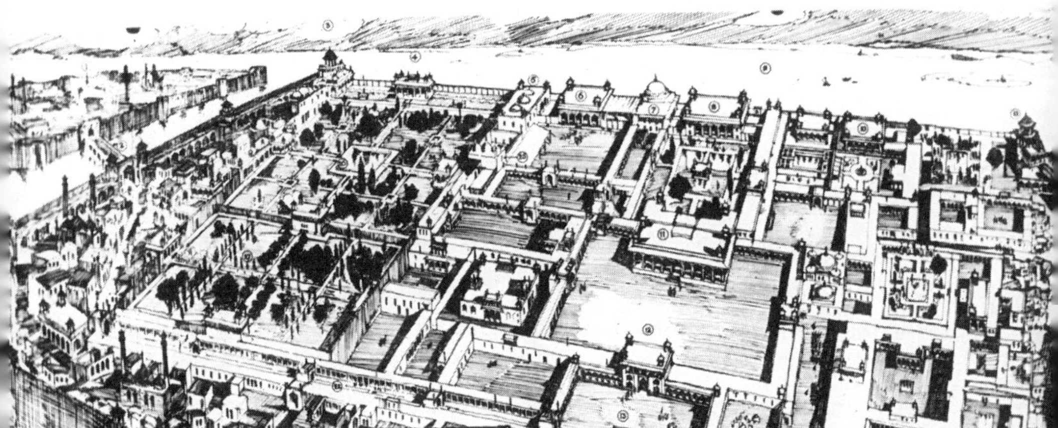

Inner Palace, conjectural view (G. Sanderson, Vol. 12, 102/99, 1931-32, ASI PL)

length of the pavilion, momentarily lingering to form a flower-shaped central fountain basin still inlaid in parts with coloured precious stones. A single arched vista towards the north of the Rang Mahal gives a view of a marble terrace. A pavilion sits on the terrace, its carved arches and screens glowing delicately. In contrast, the vista to the south yields a view of a rundown grass terrace and a white plastered building.

When Shah Jahan inhabited these pavilions, cool water flowed in the shallow marble channel through the length of the Rang Mahal. Termed the *Nahr-i-Bahist,* literally the river of paradise, the water channel led into the central fountain-basin. The swirls and ebbs of the water, from all accounts, gave an almost life-like impression to the stone flowers and leaves inlaid within the basin. During the day, vividly coloured glass, said to have been used in the imperial pavilions, let in concentrated spots of colour amidst the patterned sunlight and the river breezes filtering in through the wall screens. Standing close to these delicate marble screens, the royal inmates, themselves shadowy silhouettes even to the most prying eyes, could have gazed outside at the clear flowing waters of the Yamuna, the dark, gorgeously attired elephants stirring up sand on the riverbanks and the green fields beyond.

At night, the interiors of the pavilion must have appeared even more beautiful in the soft light of candles set in its wall-niches, reflecting off the profuse gold decoration on the ceiling and arches and in the water in the channel. Mirrors inlaid in the wall-plaster in the side rooms would have broken these up into myriad points of light, even as their remnants do. Framed views through the arches north and south from the Rang Mahal would have yielded glimpses of the Nahr-i-Bahist—dappled and shimmering in the day, and dark and gleaming during the night—running on the translucent white terrace into the shadowed marble pavilions beyond.

These adjoining pavilions, reached through two equal courts flanking the Rang Mahal on the terrace, were part of the emperor's living quarters and his seraglio respectively. The courts were protected by intricately patterned screens and arcades on their eastern and western boundaries, which also imparted privacy to the emperor as he moved from one pavilion to another on the marble terrace under thick awnings. The screens would have granted the emperor comparative seclusion to enjoy the cool river

Rang Mahal, fountain basin (32572/97, Vol. 12, Delhi, 1931, ASI PL)

Rang Mahal, east face, c.1820 (F 7/9, NAI)

breezes as well as an aesthetic experience that changed along with the pattern of shifting shadows on the floors and the water channels.

Today, the terrace court is no longer edged by screens, and iron rings under the cornice of the pavilions are the only remnant of the awnings under which Shah Jahan walked. The marble terrace throws back the heat of a sky, dusty white for most of the year. A dome surmounts the east corner of a pavilion to the north of the Rang Mahal at the end of a marble arcaded verandah. Despite hurried steps and eyes screwed to lessen the blinding onslaught of light, the carved and cusped outlines of the arcade are startlingly clear even today. Within it, filtered light reveals the remains of stone inlay and painted patterns on the walls and ceilings.

A walk through this verandah leads the visitor to a central open chamber. Within this chamber, an elaborate screen, its silhouette surmounted by the carved scales of justice, quietly and translucently overshadows the patterned ceilings and floors as well as the marble channel that it spans. The chamber is flanked by two rooms, one on either side, their ceilings faintly glittering with fragments of glass inset in plaster. The room on the east leads into an octagonal chamber, projecting out over the red boundary wall of the Fort. Visible through a central tiny balcony and the geometrical marble screens on four sides of this chamber are parts of the marble terrace and the Rang Mahal, as well as open land and the Ring Road below. In contrast, the room on the west ends in a largely opaque

Rang Mahal, west face, 1990 (Photo: 454/96, ASI PL)

wall, under which steps lead down to the very edge of the Fort. Beyond the thick metal railings that border the pavilion and these steps, crowds of visitors drift past on sand-strewn paths, catching only brief glimpses of its decorated interiors.

This complex pavilion, termed the *Khas Mahal* or Special Palace, formed the emperor's personal living quarters. Its verandahs and chambers had different functions that were reflected in their names—the *Khwabgah*, the House of Dreams or, more prosaically, the Sleeping Chamber; the *Tasbih Khana* or the Chamber of Telling Beads; the *Toshakhana* or the *Baithak Khana*, the Robe Chamber/Sitting Chamber and the *Mussaman (Mutthaman) Burj* or the Octagonal Tower.[26] The screen carved with the scales of justice, part of the emperor's insignia, formed a transparent vertical boundary between the two central arcaded verandahs on the north and south faces. The Nahr-i-Bahist channel flowing below the screen bisected the open width of the Khas Mahal. This space, cooled by the water channel, seems to have been a favourite spot of the later emperors, who are often depicted in court paintings profiled against the screen of justice, amidst the hint of a breeze and a prospect of marble pavilions.

Projecting out of the Khas Mahal's east face, the Mussaman Burj was once roofed by a dome encased in gilded copper. The dome surmounted a balcony from where the emperor watched spectacles staged on the river bank. It was also from here that he displayed himself to his subjects every morning for the ceremony of *darshan*, the term for an auspicious sight especially of gods and kings. Below the chamber with its viewing balcony was an archway that gave private entrance into the Fort from the river bank. This archway led up into a courtyard immediately adjacent to the emperor's private apartments. It was from here that Shah Jahan, after travelling from Agra on the river Yamuna, entered the Fort in 1648 on its formal inauguration.

The stairs leading down to this entrance still exist, but lie unused on the west face of the Khas Mahal. Scarcely recognisable as an imperial entrance, they descend to a locked arched gateway, held together by stained and flaking sandstone walls. The visitor paths running along the base of the terrace go past the edge of the staircase and the railings, continuing on to a pavilion open on all sides. This pavilion, alternatively reached from the marble court to the north of the Khas Mahal, consists of a rectangular pillared hall, supported on a double row of square columns. The columns rise in a regular rhythm of arches that defer to a central chamber with a marble seat.

This is the Diwan-i-Khas: 'a more wonderful building does not exist in the world.'[27] The facade was originally composed of a unique and elaborate scheme of external decoration executed in colour. Inside the pavilion, cornelians, corals and other precious stones were shaped and inlaid as delicate flowers and foliage. Some of them still remain, having escaped marauders and vandals down the centuries. However, compared even with photographs of the Fort taken in the nineteenth century, these are in a much-reduced form. The descriptions of Diwan-i-Khas by most writers convey a picture of a delicately lavish interior containing painted gold decoration, finely carved marble screens, glass-infill in arched windows, and a ceiling reputedly of pure silver. It is understandable that Shah Jahan chose to have the following words inscribed on its southern arcades: '*Agar firdaus bad zamin ast, hamin ast, hamin ast, hamin ast*!'—if there is paradise on earth, it is this, it is this, it is this![28]

The Diwan-i-Khas pavilion positioned between the Khas Mahal and Imperial Hammam (Photo: S. Mukherjee, 2012)

Khas Mahal, west face, 1997 (Photo: Author)

The Nahr-i-Bahist canal flowed through the Diwan-i-Khas and ran under the floor in the central bays of the pavilion, where the famous Peacock Throne is recorded to have been usually kept.

> It is in this place that the King, seated in a chair, his Omrahs standing around him, grants more private audience to his officers, receives

Mussaman Burj, east face with riverside entrance, 1950s (Photo: 587/97, ASI PL)

> their reports, and deliberates on important affairs of the state. Every Omrah incurs the same pecuniary penalty for omitting to attend this assembly in the evening as for failing to be present at the Am-Kas in the morning.[29]

Today, the pavilion looks out on a lawn bordered by paths. Beyond them can be seen the back wall of the Diwan-i-Am and the trees planted in line with it. The British barracks loom up behind the trees. The original view west from the Diwan-i-Khas was very different from this present conglomeration of nineteenth-century British barracks and later garden plantation.

The Diwan-i-Am was not originally visible from the Diwan-i-Khas. Two courtyards, bounded by continuous walls, separated these pavilions from each other. The actual forecourt to the Diwan-i-Khas was an enclosed paved space, entered through gateways at fixed points and with a central fountain with a marble screen called the *Chaukhandi-i-Diwan-i-*

Khas Mahal, interior (Photo: Author, 1997)

The Emperor's Seat, Diwan-i-Khas (Photo: Author, 1997)

Khas. The focus of the forecourt was the emperor's throne in the Diwan-i-Khas, with which it was centrally oriented. Soldiers of the guard came up to this paved court through an intervening rectangular walled court entered from the Diwan-i-Am forecourt. They presented arms here and paraded before their emperor. The southern boundary of this forecourt was connected through a colonnade with the emperor's private entrance-court and the Rang Mahal garden beyond. The forecourt's northern edge, variously defined by the imperial Hammams, the *Moti Masjid* (the Pearl Mosque) and the intervening arcades, led through a gateway into the *Hayat Baksh* or the life-bestowing gardens.[30]

The imperial Hammam still remains and so does the Moti Masjid, though without their connecting arcades. The Hammam, now a series of enclosed opaque rooms, straddles the east terrace beyond the Diwan-i-Khas, and part of it steps down to the level of the ground outside. From the terrace, the Hammam's facade presents a view of a central verandah bounded by two rooms. The doors into the two rooms and the inner

Diwan-i-Khas, west face, c.1820 (Add.Or. 549, OIOC, BL)

Diwan-i-Khas, west face, 1858 (Photo: Tytler, 53/18, OIOC, BL)

wall of the verandah entrance are all locked, as is another door, entered through steps leading up from the pathways. The only indication of the richness and delicacy of the interior chambers is through partial views afforded by a few windows. These views reveal quietly majestic marble seats, marble tanks, shallow channels inlaid with colours of white, yellow ochre, black and green, and swirling patterns on curved walls rising into domes lit at the top.

The Hammam, as designed, consisted of a series of chambers with tanks equipped with provisions for hot and cold bathing. Doors opened out from the Hammam into the terrace to connect with the emperor's apartments and also directly onto the Diwan-i-Khas forecourt. The Nahr-i-Bahist flowed through the Hammam. If the emperor entered from the terrace, he probably dipped his feet into the Nahr-i-Bahist before continuing in for his bathing routine. The two rooms on either side of the verandah in front of the actual Hammam were, according to popular tradition, meant for the royal children. The other apartments in the Hammam contained tanks that could be filled with hot or cold water and marble seats from which the Hayat Baksh gardens could be viewed.

The chambers in which the fountains and tanks were placed are extant, and the inlay work is in a more complete state than that in the other pavilions. However, the water that once flowed here, reflecting the flowers made of precious stones inlaid in the floors and dadoes to create an indoor garden, is now absent. And the outdoor garden beyond the windows is, today, a shadow of its former self. To reach this garden, one has to descend to the ground level outside the Hammam and continue through a passage between its western facade and a single-storey wall with a delicately

Hammam, south face towards Diwan-i-Khas (Photo: Author, 1997)

patterned bronze door. Behind this door, swelling domes rise up against the sky.

The domes as well as the enclosing wall with its metal door are the only visible parts of a small mosque, appropriately titled *Moti Masjid* or the Pearl Mosque. This mosque, clad in white marble, was originally surmounted by three domes of gilded copper. It provided a private place of worship for the emperor. In the mid-eighteenth-century, the British Resident's daughter, Emily Metcalfe, declared it to be, 'one of the most beautiful buildings in the palace, indeed in all India ... a small white marble mosque erected for, and used by the ladies of the King's household'.[31]

Hammam, inlay decoration (Photo: S. Mukherjee, 1997)

The entrance door to the mosque leads on to a small covered passage, and from there to the actual door of Moti Masjid's courtyard as well as to the steps going up to the parapet. A little water tank, probably for ablutions, stands in the centre of the courtyard. The mosque itself is a two-aisled covered structure on the western end of the courtyard. Its scale is both intimate and comforting, and its detail and richness evoke its imperial function.

The north wall of the courtyard has large screens in it from where the Hayat Baksh garden may be viewed. This garden was originally walled

Moti Masjid (Photo: Author, 1996)

on all sides, and built as a day-time private area for the emperor. Its enclosing walls and terraces are recorded to have contained 'fruitful trees of various kinds ... interlaced with each other in such a way that the sky is not anywhere visible beneath them'.[32]

Old maps and drawings indicate that Hayat Baksh was entered from the Diwan-i-Khas forecourt through a gateway between the Hammam and Moti Masjid.[33] On the east towards the river, Hayat Baksh was bounded by a raised terrace with screens and marble pavilions positioned on it. Another terrace, edged by a wall on its north end, provided visual and spatial privacy from the Fort's peripheral area used by the princes and the military. On its western boundary wall, a central arched gateway opened into another garden, *Mehtab Bagh* or the Garden of the Moon.

A variety of sources suggest that these gardens were for the exclusive use of the emperor and his family members. Water was the predominant motif and formed a vital component. It reflected and flowed in shallow stone channels, rippled down from decorated marble chaddars and rose in slender columns of fountains. In contrast to the paved courts of the Diwan-i-Am, the Diwan-i-Khas and the Naqqar Khana, the trees, flowers

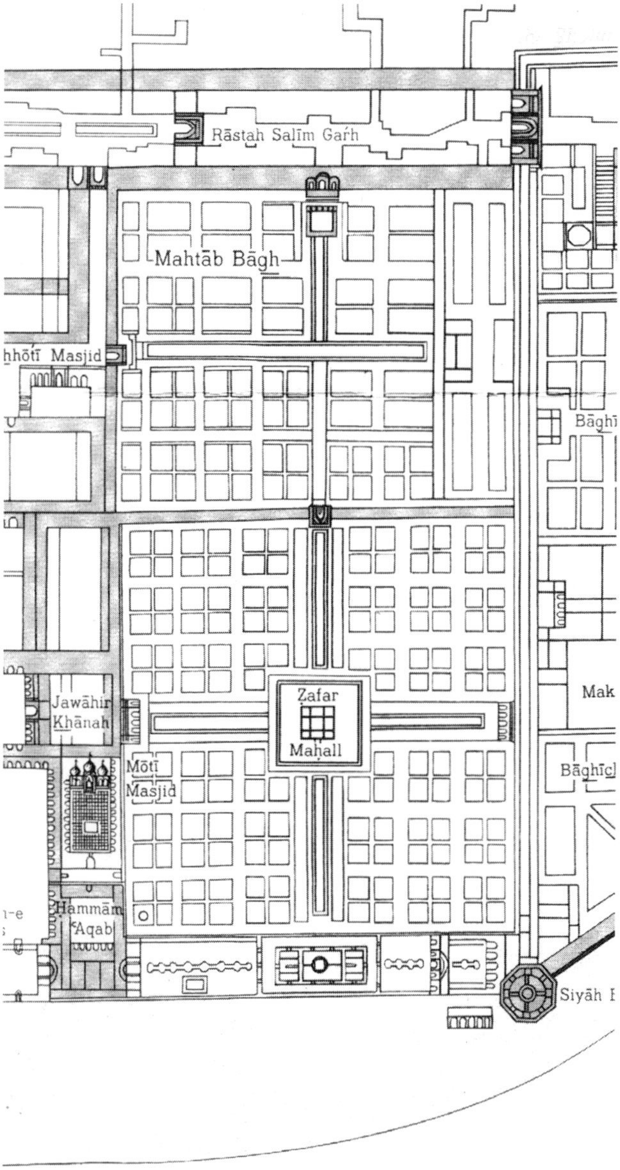

Imperial gardens, Red Fort, 1846-7 (X/1659, OIOC, BL)

and tanks within these imperial gardens would have afforded a cool green retreat both during the night and the day.

Pavilions for informal living were carefully positioned at the ends of the gardens. Paths laid out along geometrical subdivisions led to the

Bhadon pavilion (Photo: Author, 2000)

Sawan pavilion (Photo: Author, 2000)

pavilions and went past sunken flower beds filled with flowers in myriad colours as depicted in miniature paintings. Presenting a sight almost like richly embroidered Persian and Mughal carpets, the flower beds and the pathways would have been cooled by fine sprays from fountains within canals along the central axes of the gardens. White marble pavilions terminated the garden's central north-south axis, celebrating the coolness, texture and movement of water not only in their architectural detail and form but also in their names—*Sawan* and *Bhadon*.

The *Chaumasa* or the four monsoon months are *Asarh, Sawan, Bhadon* and *Asoj*. Plentiful rain was prayed for in the Chaumasa, especially Bhadon. Popular sayings record these expectations. One of these likens the showers of Sawan to those of pearls. Another extols moderation, but clarifies that some exceptions are desirable. Thus,

> Talk as a rule is good, but not too much;
> Silence is good, but not too much.
> Rain is good, but not too much;
> Sunshine is good but not too much.
> But the more we get the better of, rain in Bhadon,
> Or sun in *Jeth*, or talk in our storytellers, or silence in our wives.[34]

The water features in the Sawan and Bhadon pavilions were designed to represent the quality of the rain in the months of Sawan and Bhadon, respectively. While the pavilions mirror each other externally, the internal arrangements for the provision of water features within them vary. The variety of visual and sensory effects that the water would have produced—a unique aspect of Mughal gardens—is evident from this description of these pavilions in Shah Jahan's time.

> [T]hrough the two waterways of the tanks which are made in the centre of these buildings, the water is always issuing gracefully and from the edge of their platforms, which have a height of one and a half *gaz* from the ground, it falls into the tank below, in the form of a cascade ... in the niches, flower vases of gold and silver, full of golden flowers are placed during the day, and at night white wax candles which appear like the stars in the thin clouds are lighted inside the veil of water.[35]

On the eastern end of Hayat Baksh, another marble pavilion called *Moti Mahal* or the Pearl Palace (no longer extant) formed a climax to the garden's central east-west axis. On the northeastern edge, a three-storeyed octagonal tower with a single-storeyed pavilion ended the Hayat Baksh garden. This tower, known as *Shah Burj* or the King's Tower, also marked the northern end of the east face of the Fort.

Today, the oasis-like quality of the original gardens is lost since most of the areas around the pavilions have been re-designed. In Hayat Baksh itself, the fragrant flowers and ordered trees characteristic of a Mughal garden have been replaced, for the most part, by stretches of lawn and an uncoordinated plantation of trees and shrubs interspersed with red sandstone and sand-filled paths. The only structures in the garden dating from Shah Jahan's time are the Sawan and Bhadon pavilions and the Shah Burj.

The red sandstone *Zafar Mahal,* or the palace of Zafar, within the central tank of Hayat Baksh was a later addition by the last Mughal ruler, Bahadur Shah II. Just beyond these pavilions, the garden abruptly ends in a line of trees behind which loom the tall grey buildings of the British barracks. These barracks stand within Mehtab Bagh and what was originally the other half of Hayat Baksh.

Mehtab Bagh is no longer extant, and the original enclosing wall of Hayat Baksh is also absent. With no spatial and visual edges, Hayat Baksh is sporadically glimpsed through gaps between its disconnected boundary. On the east end of Hayat Baksh is the raised marble terrace which contains one small pavilion dating from Bahadur Shah's time in addition to the remnants of the Shah Burj and its attached marble pavilion. Shah Burj, originally a three-storeyed structure, was built during Shah Jahan's reign. It contained luxuriously decorated marble interiors with seats, ornamented tanks, channels and chutes on its lower levels, and was surmounted by a marble domed pavilion at its topmost level. Only two storeys of Shah Burj remain today, but all three stories exist of its counterpoint, the *Asad Burj* or the Lion Tower.

Asad Burj lies on the southern end of the Fort's east face. To reach it, one has to traverse lawns and pathways back towards Rang Mahal and beyond. On the way, a solitary white plastered building is encountered, similar in overall proportions and profile to the other pavilions, but with

Hayat Baksh garden (Photo: Author, 2000)

all its arches closed. This building, the *Mumtaz Mahal*, was used for a time as a museum containing information and artefacts related to the Mughals. Just beyond Mumtaz Mahal, the system of paths, terrace and lawns breaks down into an uneven, neglected stretch of ground.

Mumtaz Mahal was the apartment of one of the royal princesses—probably Shah Jahan's eldest daughter, the *Begum Sahiba*, Jahanara.[36] It formed a part of the royal seraglio, which occupied the space between the Asad Burj and Rang Mahal and contained, 'all the apartments devoted to the King of Delhi's Harem, exquisite buildings of white marble, many of them inlaid with beautiful mosaics of different coloured stones, in the style of the Taj'.[37]

Shah Jahan's grandchildren may also have stayed here, rather than travelling with their fathers' entourages, which were often out on political campaigns. Court accounts of the Mughal emperors indicate that this was a matter of tradition as well as convenience. Young princes were close to their grandfathers since the most influential years of their lives—childhood and adolescence—were spent in their court. Such was the case with Shah Jahan (named Khurram or 'the joyous one' by his grandfather, EmperorAkbar) and his brother Khusrau, who were brought up in Akbar's court. Akbar is believed to have publicly favoured Khusrau as his successor. In the seraglio, thus, there was an inherent danger of sibling rivalries for the throne, to potentially transform into physical harm to the rivals' offspring.

Shah Burj, c.1820 (Add.Or. 540, OIOC, BL)

An incident that exhibits the lethal consequences of such rivalry is recorded in Shah Jahan's court history, Abdul Hamid Lahori's *Badshah Nama*.[38] The incident dates from just before the time Shah Jahan ascended to the throne following his father, Emperor Jahangir's death at the age of fifty-eight years. One of the rival factions in the court at that time consisted of Jahangir's enormously powerful chief queen, the Empress Nur Jahan, and her son-in-law, Prince Sharyar. They were ranged against Asaf Khan (Nur Jahan's brother and the prime minister) and his son-in-law, the then Prince Shah Jahan. Both Sharyar and Shah Jahan were away on campaigns at that time, and the fact that Shah Jahan's sons, Princes Dara Shikoh, Shah Shuja and Aurangzeb were vulnerable since they were in the female apartments with Nur Jahan, implied that Asaf Khan could not openly express opposition against his sister.

A devious scheme of lulling Nur Jahan by temporarily placing Bulaki, a grandson of Jahangir's (through his first-born son, Khusrau) on the throne was devised, and then Shah Jahan's young sons were taken away from Nur Jahan's charge. It was only then that active attempts were made by Shah Jahan's faction, led by Asaf Khan, to capture the throne. This also included the imprisonment within the Lahore Fort and the subsequent deaths of the unfortunate Bulaki and Sharyar.[39]

Shah Burj, 1982 (1627/82, ASI)

Though these developments took place in the seraglio at the Lahore Fort, it seems evident that the imperial seraglio at the Red Fort would also have participated in a substantial way in both the personal and political affairs of the rulers. In fact, the large complex of the seraglio with its pavilions, gardens, fountains, screens, hammams and courts became the scene of intrigue almost as soon as it was founded. It appears to have played a significant role in the war of succession between Shah Jahan's sons. Shah Jahan's daughters Jahanara and Roshanara supported their brothers Dara Shikoh and Aurangzeb, respectively. Each of these princesses had her own quarters in the seraglio, with her own circle of trusted maids and servants from whom she obtained information and passed it on to her favoured brother. Thus, it was that Roshanara managed to discover and convey vital political developments in the court to Aurangzeb, helping him take relevant action to succeed to the throne. The influence of the seraglio was again evident later in the eighteenth century when Qudsia Begum, one of the chief queens, used her special position to control appointments of officials in the court.

The lavishly detailed seraglio pavilions occupied by these powerful inmates contained many of the distinguishing features of the emperor's own quarters such as the Nahr-i-Bahist, which continued through these

Asad Burj (Photo: Author, 1997)

pavilions positioned on the terrace. The Nahr then fell into a *baoli* (stepped well) in the Asad Burj to rejoin the Yamuna through a water gate located near an adjoining triangular tank and barbican, which are believed to have been added on after Shah Jahan's reign.

The space occupied by these buildings that witnessed so many momentous incidents is now open land covered with scrub and weeds, and marked by scattered trees and some insignificant modern-day structures. The forlorn Mumtaz Mahal, practically the only part remaining of the imperial seraglio, is unrecognisable as a once luxurious pavilion.

Beyond Mumtaz Mahal, the octagonal sandstone Asad Burj tower sits alone, terminating the south corner of the Fort's east face and the mournful remains of the imperial terrace. The Burj still retains its silhouette and some part of its detail, although its barred and barbed arched openings reveal only glimpses of dark and shadowed chambers. One of the tall open archways in the high wall that it joins in the south steps down to the baoli and its sealed water gate. Another archway walks into a space cradled by steep ramps. Small central steps punched in the ramps climb up to the Fort's battlements. The continuous terraces reached by the steps look back and forth at the erstwhile seraglio area; at Asad Burj crowning the central axis of the walls, visible at this level as merely a single-storey

Asad Burj, detail (Photo: Author, 1997)

pavilion; at the green, still water in the baoli; at the tumultuous trees pressed against the outer face of the Fort's red walls.

These scarred remnants of the Fort, though individually beautiful, make it difficult to visualise the wealth, variety and pace of life of the Mughals. It is even more difficult to understand the design of this Fort, crowned with the epithet of 'the most magnificent palace in the east' even some 200 years after its founding. To comprehend the reasons for such a description, it is necessary to investigate the circumstances of the Red Fort's founding, and its original planning and design, now so greatly altered. It is equally necessary to understand the manner and reasons for the Fort's transformation to its present form. No less important is the need to be acquainted with its lineage: the formation and transformation of Shahjahanabad, of which the palace was such an integral part, and the Mughal Forts and cities that preceded it.

3

LINEAGE

'Dehli, then, is an entirely new city.'

Francois Bernier, *Travels in the Mughal Empire 1656–68*

The 'Dehli' that the French traveller Francois Bernier refers to is Shahjahanabad—the city of Shah Jahan. Bernier arrived in India approximately at the same time as the war of succession between Shah Jahan's sons. This was barely a decade after the establishment of Shahjahanabad and its palace complex on the banks of the Yamuna. At that time, Shahjahanabad, now termed Old Delhi, was still a city in the making. The daunting construction of this new city and its Fort had been started simultaneously in 1639 CE. Nine years later, when Shah Jahan formally inaugurated the Red Fort, many of the major functioning elements of the manifestly new city had already been laid out, though parts of it continued to be constructed much after this date. Shahjahanabad's title of 'New Delhi' persisted for another 250 years after its founding, even till the early 1900s[1] when another new city of Delhi was established—this time by the British.

However, the name as well as the strategically important larger area of Delhi was neither entirely new nor politically or architecturally insignificant. Therefore, it may be worthwhile to investigate briefly the reasons for the suitability of this area for successive human settlements.

This narrow strip of land with 'a greatest length of 76 miles and an average width of 18 miles',[2] lying between the right bank of the Yamuna on one side and the Aravalli hill range on the other, dates from the earth's earliest geological formation. About 1,500 million years ago, in what is termed the Pre-Cambrian era, this area existed more or less in the same geographical configuration that it is now.

The Aravalli hills, which today run 700 kilometres southwest to northeast from Gujarat to Delhi, used to form part of the continent of Gondwanaland about 250 million years ago—when India, Malagasy, South Africa, South America, Australia and Antarctica formed one land mass. Later in the Quartenary period, the detached hills of Delhi and its neighbourhood, overlain with alluvium and sand, formed the hunting grounds of the newly evolved Homo Erectus.[3] Tools and hand-axes have been discovered in this region, largely in the southern hills and ridges close to water reservoirs. This was the time when the rivers Ganga, Yamuna and Saraswati are believed to have flowed past Delhi. Archaeological investigations show evidence of Delhi's continued popularity for inhabitation in different stages of human evolution in the lower, middle and upper Paleolithic, Chalcolithic and early Iron ages.[4] The locations of these very first human settlements were based on similar reasons as the later, more permanent cities that lent their name to the Delhi area—safe and easy access to the river and to the high ground of the ridge.

This ridge was a few yards wide at its northern end, while its broadest width was at Anangpur towards the south—a probable reason why some of the earliest habitations arose in the southern part of Delhi. The pre- and proto-historic habitants also altered the relative positions of their settlements according to the shifting courses of the Yamuna, which moved substantially, generally eastwards, at least six times during its early life. The early courses, the paleochannels, now exist as thickly cultivated gentle depressions of high moisture content.[5] The present widespread historical remnants in Delhi that represent its earlier urban centres kept moving back and forth across the larger canvas of the area according to the changing course of the river and their political compulsions. These habitats, nearly all of which were located further south from Shahjahanabad, were more than ordinary urban conglomerations. They were built at various times

The relative positions of different cities in the area of Delhi
(Survey of India Map, 1907)

to function as the capital cities of important kingdoms.[6] Though there are no traceable direct precedents to the comprehensive urban design of Shahjahanabad, these earlier cities of Delhi seem to have influenced it to some extent.

Within the Red Fort, the influence of the architecture of the preceding Mughals and the earlier construction in this region may be read in the use of marble for imperial buildings, the predominance of the pavilion as a building typology, the theme of walled gardens used in its open spaces and the combination of stucco, paint, inlay and carving for decoration. These were, however, just one of a compound of influences that Shah Jahan's new Fort and city drew upon—their architectural form, space and decoration as well as modes of construction inspired by a variety of sources, characteristic of the Mughal emperors' eclectic tastes.

These sources included contemporary architectural developments in different parts of the Mughal empire and in parts of the world with which the Mughals came into contact, as well as earlier Indic architecture perfected over hundreds of years, with its skilled work forces and established canons. Babur, Shah Jahan's great-great-grandfather who himself came from a region rich in a tradition of formal architecture and its practitioners, was sufficiently struck by their skills to make a record in his memoirs. Babur specifically noted:

> … the unlimited numbers of craftsmen and practitioners of every trade. For every labour and every product there is an established group who have been practising their craft or professing their trade for generations … in Agra alone there were 680 Agra stonemasons at work on my building everyday.[7]

Babur's ready recognition and employment of the Indian stonemasons' skills in his buildings and Shah Jahan's later experimentation with the Chatta Bazaar roof-form in the Red Fort (said to be modelled after a covered octagonal bazaar in Peshawar),[8] as well as perhaps the influence of European decorative systems in the Fort,[9] are evident instances of the Mughal rulers' eagerness to learn from ideas from other regions and civilisations.

However, these ideas served largely to enrich an existing theme of spatial, constructional and decorative uses in consonance with the climatic, aesthetic and living systems of the region that the Mughals chose to settle in, rather than effect any dramatic changes to the theme itself. The interpretation of all these influences in the Mughal idiom resulted in an architecture that was always inventive, and never literal, in its inspirations. Thus, many modes of construction and decoration were married together in Mughal architecture so that it was difficult to separate them into their constituent original styles.

Additionally, the architecture of Shahjahanabad was also a response to contemporary political events, as well as to the constraints and opportunities experienced by Shah Jahan—self-imposed, or thrust by social, religious, economic and geographical conditions. An understanding of these is a necessary prelude to the specific analysis of the design of the Red Fort as an architectural solution to the demands and aspirations of its ruler and his time. The sequence of these influences is discussed in the following pages in terms of overall chronological development, though references are also made to events or spaces irrespective of their chronological history to explain a particular point as necessary.

Large-scale architecture in the region of Delhi perhaps dates back to Indraprastha, the capital of the five Pandava brothers. This city, mentioned in the great epic Mahabharata,[10] is popularly believed to have existed next to the Yamuna's older course, at the site of the *Purana Qila (Qila-u-Kuhna)*, a sixteenth-century citadel extant in modern-day Delhi. Excavations at this site have revealed evidence of continuous occupation from the third century BCE to the sixteenth century CE, that is, from the Mauryan to the early Mughal period.[11] Scattered relics of painted grey ware, interpreted by some scholars to be characteristic of the time of the Mahabharata, have also been excavated. This evidence suggests that the antiquity of the site may go back to at least 1000 BCE.[12]

As far as architectural remnants are concerned, the earliest city in the Delhi area appears to be Yoginipura or Dhilliikapuri—the capital of the Rajput kingdoms of the Tomar and Chauhan dynasties, who established themselves in this area between the ninth and twelfth centuries respectively.[13] The Tomars may have inhabited Delhi even before this date; there is no unanimity about the exact time of their rule in this area. They are believed to have founded a city in the eighth century, next to the celebrated stepped water tank of Surajkund. Some archaeological fragments of this city were revealed during the late 1800s, when investigations uncovered part of a fort and a dam. Recent excavations here have also unearthed fort walls and redware pottery tentatively dated as early medieval.

Other remnants from this time include the remains of a temple, 8 kilometres west of the Qutub area. This area is now occupied by the earliest extant royal sepulchre in Delhi—Sultan Ghari's thirteenth-century tomb.

Surajkund (Photo: Estate of Anjali Chanda)

Fragments of highly sculptured sandstone lintels and mortised railing pillars[14] reused in this tomb, give an indication of materials and crafts used in the construction of the earlier temple at this site. While such elements have not been found near the fort of the Tomars, the evidence of their foundations indicates that they were both strong and large. Their excavated remains include a 300-metre wall with traces of twenty-one semi-circular stone bastions. Outlines of chambers and streets on the western and some structures on the eastern side point to a fairly widespread settlement within the fort. The orientation of the excavated structures and the gradual slope of the northern and eastern sides, contrasted with the steeper slope on the southern and western sides, indicates that the rest of the town existed towards the valley on the north and east.

These features of the archaeological fragments are consistent with traditional town-planning texts, which specify the desired direction of a hill fort as facing east or north. Coupled with the discovery of Rajput coins, they seem to reinforce the belief that this fort belonged to the Tomar dynasty. The later (relatively more complete) forts of the Tomars and Chauhans were termed *Lal Kot* and *Qila Rai Pithora* respectively, and were located further north from Surajkund. They formed part of what is generally regarded as the first city of Delhi. This area was part of a ridge close to the Yamuna. It contained a temple complex and was called *Yoginipura*—a name retained in the present temple of *Yogmaya/Jogmaya* in the same area.

The inscription on the celebrated iron pillar that still stands in Mehrauli ascribes the pillar to this period, or even earlier.[15] This also seems to be the time that the present-day name of 'Dilli', or Delhi, first made its appearance. Chand, the court poet of King Prithviraj Chauhan (the third Chauhan ruler of Delhi), recounts the following tale in his celebrated work *Prithviraj Raso*, which is still retained in popular tradition as the origin of the word Dilli.[16] This tale, the *Killi Dhilli Katha*, the story of the loose nail or pillar, is of undeniable narrative interest and links the name of Delhi to the early Tomars.

> Anangpal Tomar was a Rajput King, who ruled over the area of Delhi in the eighth century CE. A sage once told the King that the *killi* (the iron pillar at Qutub) rested on the head of Vasuki, the king of the serpents, and that his kingdom would remain undisturbed as long as the pillar remained so. The King, sceptical and curious, ordered the pillar to be dislodged, which it was—after much effort. To everyone's surprise, unmistakable traces of blood were found at its base. The King, shaken out of his scepticism, immediately ordered the pillar to be reinstalled — but it was too late. The sage's prediction came true. The pillar could not be lodged firmly back into the ground. It remained loose and Anangpal's rule met a similar fate.

Other legends claim that the name of Delhi arose in the reign of Raja Dilu, who reigned here in the first century BCE, or another ruler by the name of King Dilipa, the fifth descendant of the Pandavas. The Mahabharata as well as Patanjali's *Mahabhashya* are believed to mention *Bodhi/Bodha* as one of the *Nigams* or districts of Indraprastha.[17] This seems to be a reference to a celebrated pilgrim centre, interpreted to be the same as the present *Nigambodh Ghat* located on the banks of the Yamuna near the Red Fort. Recent excavations in the area support its inhabitation in the early first millennium BCE.

The name of Dhillipura or Yoginipura, attributed to the area of Lal Kot and its surrounding city near Mehrauli, was definitely in use by 1274 CE, as an inscription near *Palam Baoli* reveals. However, very little of the spatial and architectural features of these cities and their royal dwellings remain, since they were, to a large extent, destroyed by Islamic conquerors.

So far, no palace site has been identified accurately in Lal Kot, though remains of part of the citadel have been found. The extant parts of this citadel consist of about a 6.5 kilometres circuit of outlying stone walls. They display features that persist in many of the later forts—thick widths, semi-circular stone bastions, a series of gateways and the provision of a protective moat.

The surviving stone construction from this period generally consists of blocks dressed to fit into each other with no cementing material. Some details of their architectural form and ornamentation may be gleaned from literary sources. These indicate that the ornamentation mainly consisted of statues, carvings and bas-reliefs modelled on complex patterns derived from nature. They also record the construction of royal palaces in wood and refer to the prevalence of groves and gardens for outdoor recreation, as a response to the climate and the necessity of flowers for indigenous customs and worship. Some of the recorded court rituals of this time seem to have been precursors of those followed by the succeeding Islamic dynasties. One such ritual was ringing a bell for justice, which was initiated by Anangpal Tomar as mentioned by Amir Khusrau—the fourteenth-century (1252–1325) Sufi mystic, writer, musician and court-poet of many rulers of Delhi—in his book *Nuh Siphir* or Nine Heavens.[18]

The Chauhan dynasty that succeeded the Tomars was defeated in the beginning of the twelfth century by the Afghan invader, Mohammed-bin Sam of Ghor. This Islamic conquest of Delhi and the destruction of some parts of it did not change its status of a capital city. Though various Islamic dynasties supplanted each other in quick succession and the boundaries of their successive capitals changed, they tended to cluster in the same general area as the earlier cities. The palaces of the first dynasty of the Mamluks were built almost on top of Lal Kot and Qila Rai Pithora, obliterating the earlier dwellings. The settlements, renamed after their new Islamic ruler, Qutubudin Aibak, reused many elements of the earlier indigenous buildings.

Tughlakabad Fort, interior (Photo: Estate of Anjali Chanda)

From the Qutub area around Lal Kot and the Kilokhari area (near Humayun's Tomb) inhabited by the Mamluks, the Khiljis in the early fourteenth century shifted the urban emphasis to their new city of Siri, located near the present-day Hauz Khas area. Excavations in their citadel and the city of Siri reveal that the Fort wall was built of undressed rubble laid in lime mortar and plastered in lime, with foundations in mud mortar. The existing architecture from this period reveals that extensive use was made of arched and domed construction systems with fairly rich ornamentation. Progressively larger cities and forts were constructed in the fourteenth and fifteenth centuries by the succeeding dynasty of the Tughlaks. They first moved south to Tughlakabad, and then north to Jahanpanah. When the traveller Ibn Battuta arrived in Delhi, he saw 'a vast and magnificent city, uniting beauty with strength ... the largest city in the entire Muslim Orient ... made up now of four neighbouring and contiguous towns.'[19] These towns included the areas of Qutub, Siri, Tuglakabad and Jahanpanah. The Tughlaks finally established another capital complex further north at Firoz Shah Kotla along the river. The next dynasty after them, the Sayyids, moved the city centre a little way more south.

As rulers of different dynasties expanded the city or moved away, older settlements continued to exist but with a decreased range of activities. However, as an inscription at Sarban in Raisina dating from 1327 in Muhammad Bin Tughlak's reign reveals, the centre of power did not shift from the Lal Kot area for some time. This inscription terms Dhilli or Dhillika of the Tomars a city and Indraprastha as a *pratigana* (*pargana*) or sub-division. Even the Khiljis and the Tughlaks, despite their new capitals, continued to repair older structures and build newer ones in the Lal Kot area.

The establishment of Islamic rule in Delhi was also accompanied by the coming of Muslim religious teachers. Thus, religion and political power—the major impetus behind monumental architecture in different civilisations of the world—were adequately represented. The zeal of the Islamic rulers manifested itself in a shunning of figurative art and in a reliance on calligraphy for decoration. While it is reasonable to assume that architecture under the early Islamic dynasties in Delhi would have been a reflection of these ideals, the religious orientation of the rulers seems to have been tempered by their dependence on local craftsmen. These rulers also adopted earlier secular rituals such as the use of a bell of justice. Such a bell, hung on iron chains around the necks of two lions at the palace gates of the Mamluk king, Iltutmish, could reputedly be rung for justice day or night.[20]

Today, most of the extant structures belonging to these early cities stand in fragments—isolated fort or city walls, tombs, commemorative towers, shrines and mosques. While these offer some general insights into the construction and decoration of buildings, there is little to show the use and form of royal dwellings in Delhi till the fourteenth century. The towering Tughlakabad fort dates from this time. The form of the citadel, which occupied the higher area and its city, seem to have been dictated by the contours of the land, rather than any formal geometry. Excavations in and around the fort indicate that the citadel and city were enclosed between common walls that covered a circuit of about 6 kilometres, with fairly dense habitation. Even till the late nineteenth century, the fort complex is recorded as containing seven tanks for water and three baolis, apart from underground apartments at depths ranging from 9 to 26 metres.[21]

The extant buildings of the Tughlaks—mainly tombs and mosques—are generally spartan in appearance with decoration limited to accents of coloured tiles, stone or stucco on the local grey quartzite stone that they were constructed in. Some features of their imperial palaces, recorded to have been constructed in wood, seem to bear a resemblance to important spatial elements in the later Mughal forts. One of these was the *Hazar Ustun* or 1000-pillared audience hall, which appears later as the many-pillared Mughal Diwan-i-Am or the Hall of Public Audience. Another feature was the sequence of arrival into Muhammed Tughlak's palace through three successive gates, with flute players and trumpeters reportedly announcing the entrance of notable visitors. A similar sequence of gates culminating in the ceremonial Naubat Khana was a consistent feature of nearly all the Mughal forts.

The palace of the last ruler of the Tughlak dynasty, Firoz Shah Tughlak, was constructed at his new capital of Firoz Shah Kotla on the banks of the Yamuna. This palace is believed to have contained activities similar in range and arrangement to those in the succeeding Mughal ones. Different areas were planned within it to house multifarious functions including gardens, water tanks, baths, mosques, audience halls, royal chambers and seraglio quarters. The location of this palace complex along the banks of the river, just a little way south of Shah Jahan's future Red Fort and the positioning of its more important areas along its river-face, make these similarities in layout even more striking.

The title of capital city was usurped from Delhi by Agra and Lahore under the later dynasties of the Lodhis, Surs and Mughals. Sikandar Lodhi initiated the move of the capital to Agra some 200 kilometres southwest of Delhi in order to deal more easily with constant turmoil and revolt in that region, especially in Gwalior and Bayana. During this time, the area of Delhi, though displaced from its status, continued to be an important urban centre. The Lodhis were succeeded by Babur, a Chaghtai Turk who became the first ruler of the Mughal dynasty in India. After defeating Ibrahim Lodhi, Babur based his brief rule of four years (1526–30) at Agra, even while reiterating the symbolic status of Delhi. In his memoirs, Babur writes that on entering Agra, he camped in Sultan Ibrahim's quarters, followed almost immediately by the observation that

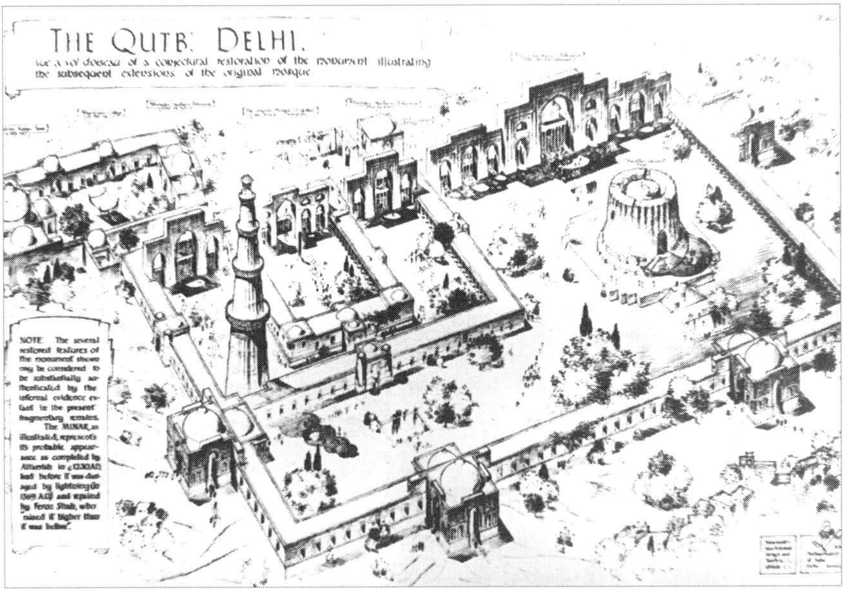

Reconstructed view of Qutub Complex, (Vol. 11, 1929-30, Central ASI PL)

Reconstructed view of Firoz Shah Kotla (ASI Monograph, Firoz Shah Kotla)

'Hindustan is a vast and populous kingdom and a productive realm ... The capital of all Hindustan is Delhi'.[22]

With neither the time nor the inclination for large building projects, Babur concentrated most of his efforts on laying out gardens in the form of charbaghs. Characterised by geometry and symmetry, they were inspired by the paradise gardens of Khorasan, Samarqand and Bukhara that he had visited in his youth and the gardens he had established in Kabul, such as *Bagh-i-Wafa*, the Garden of Fidelity and *Bagh-i-Chinar*, the Garden of the Plane Trees. These gardens had their origins in the traditions of the desert dwellers of west Asia. They were spaces enclosed from a hostile environment, meant for seclusion and informal outdoor living that symbolically and physically celebrated water as the source of life. Architectural decoration in them consisted of flat, almost two-dimensional patterns, and painted and carved stylised figures reflecting their use of languorous recreation. The memoirs of Ibn Battuta, who travelled through Persia at least 2,000 years after the very first gardens were established here, mention the continuation of such uses.

> We then entered the territories of the King of Iraq ... We went on to the town of Birgi where we had been told there was a distinguished professor called Moyi ad-Din ... I found him in a reception hall in his garden, which had a stream of water flowing through a white marble basin with a rim of enamelled tiles. He was occupying a raised seat covered with embroidered cloths.[23]

In the generic charbagh, water channels represent the four rivers of life and intersect at the centre of the garden, dividing it into four quarters. These water channels, raised above the surrounding ground, form a system of irrigating the trees and flowers within the four quarters. On either side of the channels, planted lines of trees accentuate the divisions, sometimes extending beyond the garden to form a wooded park. In most cases, a wall is constructed all around the garden for protection and privacy and pavilions are built inside. Brilliant colours and motifs derived from flowers and calligraphy decorate the built structures because of figurative art being largely unacceptable after Islamic ascendancy.

Though the theme of the four rivers of life that the charbagh employs is common to many ancient cultures, including that of Vedic India, its geometry and layout is especially suited to Islamic thought. The verses of the Quran provide apt justification for the charbaghs, compounded from abstract principles of order, mathematics and a belief in the unity of God.

> So God has guarded them from the evil of
> that day, and has procured them radiancy,
> and gladness,
> and recompensed them for their patience
> with a Garden, and Silk …

And further,

> Whosoever believes in
> God, and does righteousness, He will
> admit him to gardens
> underneath which rivers flow.[24]

The charbaghs that Babur is reputed to have laid out in India would probably have adhered to such principles of design. After his death, his son Humayun was crowned his successor in Agra but returned to Delhi—founding an association with the city that was kept up in some degree by all the Mughal emperors after him. He established a citadel, *Din-panah,* at the ancient site of Indraprastha on the banks of the Yamuna, located further north from most of the other cities of Delhi. The land that the citadel occupied was in the nature of a high mound, part of the disassociated Aravalli outcrops and the shifting course of the Yamuna. This citadel, now called the Purana Qila, is physically and historically one of the closest to Shahjahanabad.

After ten years of his rule, Humayun was displaced from India by Sher Shah Suri, the founder of the short-lived but influential Afghan Sur dynasty. Sher Shah is believed to have pulled down (and perhaps also added to) the buildings of his predecessor at Delhi, and built a new fort and city adjoining it. A piece of architectural construction of this dynasty, which is of special interest with reference to the Mughals in general and Shah Jahan in particular, is the Salimgarh citadel. This fort was located on a strategic outcrop on an island close to the Yamuna's banks.[25] Archaeological investigations in this site have yielded redware,

Baoli, Red Fort (Photo: Author, 1997)

greyware and painted greyware, indications of its attractiveness for human occupation right from the first millennium BCE.

Ironically, the construction of Salimgarh was begun by Sher Shah's son, Salim Shah (also known as Islam Shah) in 1546, as a defence against Humayun, Shah Jahan's great-grandfather. It was never fully completed, owing to Salim Shah's death in 1552. The enclosing walls of Salimgarh still exist, but there is little evidence of much historical architecture within it, though there are some structures in the vicinity dating from the late Afghan period. An octagonal baoli[26] just across the walls of Salimgarh, and a mosque[27] further west indicate that the area may have been in use for some time by Salim Shah before his death paved the way for Humayun's re-entry into Delhi. The citadel was used by Humayun as a base to commence his reconquest of Delhi, and is also believed to have been used sporadically as a pleasure retreat in the shifting political scene of this time.[28]

Architectural works during this period largely consisted of individual building projects—mainly mosques, pavilions and tombs. These were generally concentrated in and around the palace-citadel of Din-panah. Din-panah was no longer used as the emperor's palace when Humayun's

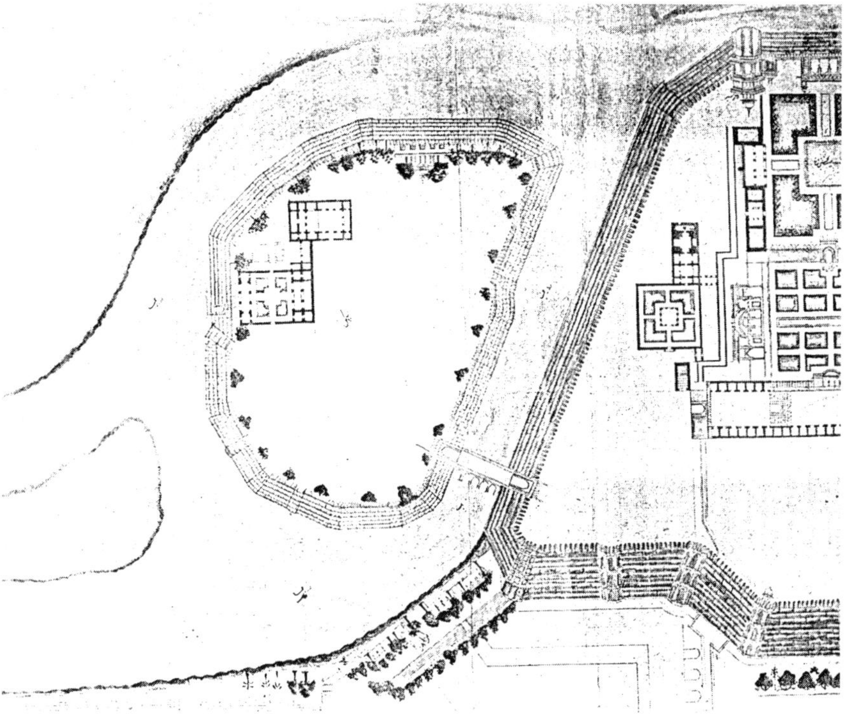

Salimgarh, Plan (3635, Agra, Vol. 1, 1914-15, ASI PL)

son, Akbar, after inhabiting it intermittently for four years, shifted his capital (in about 1560 CE) from Delhi to Agra, and then later to Fatehpur Sikri and Lahore. Akbar's decision to move the capital away signalled the diminishing strategic and political status of Delhi in the rapidly expanding Mughal empire, which now included, or aimed to include, Malwa, Gujarat, Bihar, Bengal, Kabul, Kashmir and parts of the Deccan. The energy and enthusiasm that followed the heady taste of victory in the youthful Akbar's rapidly expanding empire accompanied a growing religious tolerance, and a search for philosophical truth through discussions and debates spearheaded by the emperor. The reign of Akbar was also marked by one of the climaxes of Mughal architecture. Akbar's wide-ranging interests combined with a stable political climate and consequent economic prosperity, led to prodigious building activity, especially in the larger cities. As his court historian Abul Fazl explained, 'People that are attached to the world will collect in towns, without which there would be no progress. Hence His Majesty plans splendid edifices, and dresses the work of his mind and heart in the garment of stone and clay.'[29]

This remarkable period of architectural patronage did not leave Delhi untouched. Improvements in existing facilities continued to be carried out around Indraprastha where most of the population was concentrated. A canal built during the reign of Firoz Shah Tughlak was reactivated in 1561 CE (969 AH) by Shihab-al-din Ahmad Khan, the Governor of Delhi,[30] who extended it to his own estate. In the rest of the city, varied construction activity included mausoleums, mosques and gardens patronised by the emperor and by influential noblemen, especially in the vicinity of Din-panah and Nizamuddin. The architecture of most of these buildings displayed influences in deference to Akbar's ancestry as well as Humayun's sojourn in the Persian court when in exile. Many local traditions were also retained and there was healthy experimentation in forms and finishes derived from varied sources.[31]

This experimentation was visible not only in architecture but also in the choice of building sites, as, for example, in the new palace and capital at Fatehpur Sikri near Agra. Construction materials were also richer than those in previous reigns, reflecting the increased prosperity under Akbar. Perhaps they were also an expression of a resolve to prevent the ruinous condition of the otherwise 'lofty buildings of stone and brick [which] delight the eye and gladden the heart'.[32] The erstwhile Mughal architectural vocabulary, with its white plaster and selective sandstone cladding, was expanded to include a greater use of carved stone decoration in addition to tile work, inlay, coloured stucco and paint. One such example is found in the red and white stone-facing of the monumental eastern gate of the Khair-al-Manzil mosque and its *madrassa*, established in 1561 by Maham Anaga, Akbar's wet nurse.

In 1562, one of Akbar's noblemen got the tomb of the Sufi saint, Nizamuddin Auliya, rebuilt and embellished with an ornamental marble screen on intricately carved pillars. Four years later, the tomb of Atgah Khan, the prime minister, displayed a red sandstone exterior inlaid with white marble and multi-coloured stones. In some buildings, the octagonal, almost exclusively stucco-covered style of the earlier Afghan tombs was followed, as in the tomb of Adham Khan at Mehrauli. Adham Khan was a minister in Akbar's court and the son of one of Akbar's principal wet nurses, whose role in the murder of the emperor's tutor later earned him royal displeasure and death. The architectural style of his tomb may have

Humayun's Tomb (Photo: S. Mukherjee, 1980)

been a deliberate reversion to that of Akbar's father's rivals to deliver a political message to other courtiers.[33]

The culmination of all this construction activity in Delhi was a tomb built in Humayun's memory—the first of the grand dynastic tombs of the Mughals within a walled paradise garden. Designed to occupy the centre of a charbagh, the tomb is an irregular octagon in its plan, and sits atop a high platform punctured by a series of arches. On ascending the platform, soaring entrances lead into chambers within. The surfaces are decorated with inlaid and carved bold geometric patterns in stone and intricate plaster work. The feeling of space and lightness within Humayun's Tomb, and the grand formal external space that it formed part of, is a marked contrast with the darker, more stolid tombs of the Afghan rulers, though these too were often built on an octagonal plan. The balance between the conflicting claims of a humanely scaled internal space and imposing external proportions was achieved by the use of the double dome, reportedly constructed for the first time in India. The prolific use of red sandstone and marble, so evident here, soon became the favoured combination of materials patronised by the Mughals. Akbar took a personal interest in Humayun's Tomb and its surroundings. He

Figurative carving, Gwalior Museum
(Photo: Author, 2000)

visited it on its completion and, shortly after, gave orders for the repair of the mosque at Dargah Nizamuddin located in its vicinity.

In his other favoured cities of Agra, Allahabad and Lahore, Akbar's interventions, though generally limited to the replacement of buildings within and around the forts in these cities, were extensive. His early acts of patronage in the Agra Fort alone are believed to comprise more than 500 buildings,[34] most of which were clad with carved or inlaid sandstone and marble. In 1571, almost concurrently with Humayun's Tomb, Akbar commenced the construction of a new capital city and its palace complex at a hitherto untried site: Fatehpur Sikri near Agra.[35] Sikri, the abode of the Sufi saint, Salim Chisti, was not the most natural location for an imperial settlement. It was founded by Akbar on the strength of religious faith and political impulse. Unlike Agra, which had a very old occupational history dating from the third century BCE—located as it was on the banks of the Yamuna—Sikri was barren.

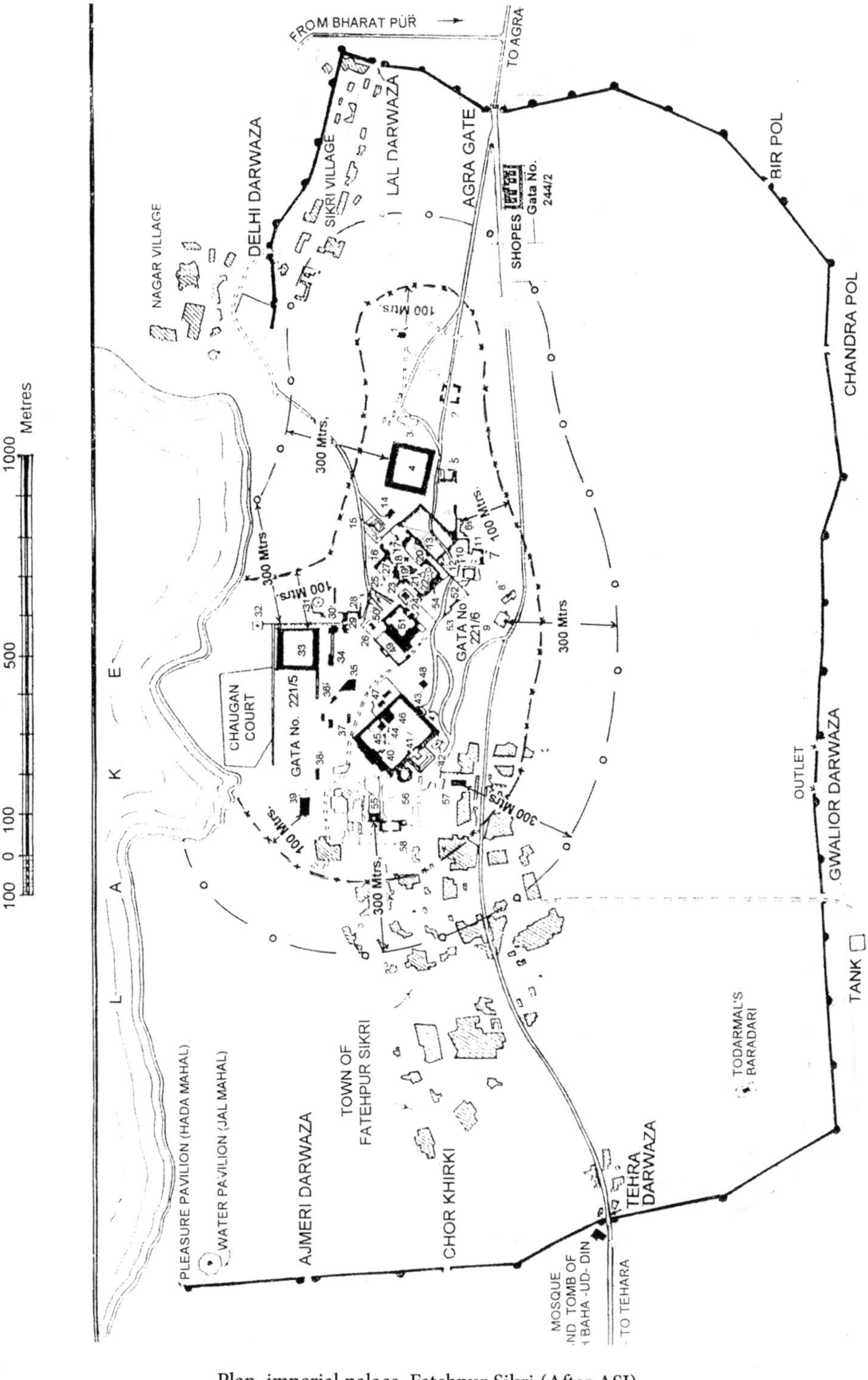

Plan, imperial palace, Fatehpur Sikri (After ASI)

The palace here is the only one of Akbar's built ventures implemented in a complete form on a virgin site. However, fourteen years after its construction was begun, Akbar moved to Lahore and set about re-building it as an imperial city to consolidate his power in northwest India. Fatehpur Sikri was never re-occupied again as part of a capital. Not wholly forgotten by subsequent emperors, and visited for brief sojourns during administrative and hunting expeditions or political campaigns, it exists today—apart from the ravages of weather and time—almost as originally designed.

The palace complex, which dates from a mature phase in design experimentation, has fluid visual and spatial connections often formed by asymmetrical defining axes and an extensive use of courtyards. Ringed by single-, double- and multi-storeyed pavilions, these courtyards form external living spaces for formal as well as personal activities, in a continuation of the indigenous tradition. In fact, classical Indian building codes lay down the appropriate size, proportions and even the number of courtyards for a range of contexts, including those for the palaces of different types of rulers, listing seven courts as the desirable number for *Chakravartin* or world-conquering kings. The extensive presence of water bodies and stepped wells in the palace at Sikri, especially in the area close to the lake, is also reminiscent of the Indic tradition of religious bathing tanks. Conversely, gardens in the formal Persian style appear to be limited to the two that have been identified in the seraglio and in the area west of the Diwan-i-Am.[36] Viaducts running over courtyard walls or colonnades and storage tanks at various levels provided water to these tanks and gardens.

In later architectural interventions initiated by Jahangir and Shah Jahan in Agra, Lahore and Delhi, many palace structures and spaces are derivations of some of the design principles used in Fatehpur Sikri. Among these are the use of shifting axes, indigenous motifs and representational art; delineation of external spaces as an integral part of built architecture; and the development in efficient construction systems.

Akbar's other palace complexes in Allahabad,[37] Lahore, and Agra underwent extensive remodelling by the emperors who succeeded him, and later, some amount of destruction by the British. Although these detract from the original layout of Akbar's vision of imperial space, they

Diwan-i-Am, Fatehpur Sikri (Photo: D.N. Chaudhuri, 1960)

Panch Mahal, Fatehpur Sikri (Photo: D.N. Chaudhuri, 1960)

Diwan-i-Khas, Fatehpur Sikri (Photo: D.N. Chaudhuri, 1960)

are useful in illustrating the evolution of architecture during the reign of his successors. Allahabad, a favoured seat of Akbar, contained built and open structures comparable in breadth and imagination to his other forts. Its occupation by the British has left very few extant examples, but a great hall still exists, evocative of, in its scale and form, the audience halls at Agra, Lahore and Delhi.

In these palace complexes, the proliferation of gardens intermingled with colonnaded buildings was the development of the indigenous social use of groves and gardens, overlaid with formal ideas of design derived from a variety of sources.[38] The establishment of Mughal capitals at different locations in the hot Indian plains, the continued dependence on local craftsmen and regional building materials, and the dilution of Islamic orthodoxy led to the development of Mughal architecture in ways that were both individual and unusual with contextual garden and built forms.[39] The main construction material came to be stone, plentifully available in the Indian plains and eminently suitable for decorative carving, a craft of which the Indian masons were acknowledged masters. Thus, the palace at Sikri, built almost entirely in red sandstone obtained from the extensive stone quarries that surrounded it, incorporated architectural

The hall now called Rang Mahal, Allahabad Fort (Photo: VCOAS Sectt., 2000)

elements characteristic of earlier Indic buildings—rich figurative carving, fretted balconies, muscular columns, carved lintels, chattris, brackets and squinches.

Symbolic motifs from earlier times, despite their deeply religious association, were used extensively as decorative motifs. Some of these, such as the *swastika* (a mystic auspicious symbol), *chakra* (discus of Vishnu), *ghata palava* (vase and foliage) and the lotus motif, later became an intrinsic part of Mughal architecture. In another departure from earlier Islamic monuments, Mughal architecture made only selective decorative use of calligraphy. Following Akbar's conquest of Gujarat in 1573, and his exposure to the use of delicately carved marble in its local religious architecture, white marble was introduced into the Mughal architectural vocabulary. This material had an enormous impact on Shah Jahan who came to employ it consistently in his important buildings. All these variations implanted an organic quality to Mughal architecture that was very different from the strict geometric formality of Persian and Timurid buildings, which extensively used polychromatic tile as embellishment for brick.

Indigenous Indian influences also began to permeate Islamic philosophy and knowledge systems, a synthesis spearheaded by the emperor who made determined efforts to foster a universal faith, *Din-*

i-ilahi, based on inclusion and dialogue. His leading court historian and court poet were sons of a prominent Sufi leader, who openly defied religious orthodoxy and had a preference for the Sufi outlook of life.[40] Akbar's conquest of Kashmir, in turn, broadened the knowledge and use of horticulture. This was reflected in the layout as well as the plantation of imperial gardens which is believed to have included both indigenous plants and those from further parts of the empire. Since the gardens in the hot plains of the sub-continent were positioned near rivers because of the greater need for water, it led to a change in the conventional elements of Persian gardens eulogised by Babur. Thus, wide canals and large tanks were now incorporated within the gardens which, though designed to be self-contained and inward-looking, also framed special views across the river.

The design of imperial palace gardens had to additionally cater for both ritual court ceremonies as well as informal private activities and the seclusion of the seraglio. The garden-form here was consequently complex in planning and designed to provide actual and perceived maximum freedom of movement through the use of running water, cool breezes, carefully framed views and intricacy in spaces. Within the gardens, the theme of a pavilion set within water and shielded by awnings, began to replace the extensive earlier use of underground rooms in this region to escape the heat.

These experiments in formal planning, decorative features and structural systems spearheaded by Akbar were greatly influential in the architectural development of this region and the overall direction of Mughal architecture. And of all the Mughal emperors, Akbar seems to have had the greatest influence on Shah Jahan, especially in terms of his monumental building activity, his military prowess and his incredible self-confidence.

Akbar's immediate successor was Jahangir—Shah Jahan's father. Jahangir tried to seize power in 1600 and when that failed, declared himself emperor at Allahabad in 1602.[41] After his formal ascension in 1605, he based himself at Agra and Lahore instead of Delhi. He spent most of his reign in Lahore and commissioned many buildings and gardens there, investing the city with much more importance than Agra. He got replaced most of Akbar's structures in the private part of the Lahore Fort, especially between the Diwan-i-Am courtyard and the river front.

Thus, the extant pavilions in the Lahore Fort date largely from Jahangir's reign. They consist of narrow structures dispersed within and around courts, and are built in a combination of local brick architecture and the trabeate sandstone tradition used so extensively in Akbar's palace at Fatehpur Sikri. Jahangir's personal inclination, as well as the fact that his greatest patronage was in northwest India where the materials available were essentially brick and wood, led him to combine the heavier Akbari style with elements of Persian aesthetics.

Jahangir also patronised the construction of buildings with richer materials. He introduced an extensive use of white marble and a predominance of inlay decoration in conjunction with the carved decoration preferred by Akbar. Jahangir's passion for gardens, adorned with pavilions set within extensive water systems, led him to encourage the development of the pavilion as an ideal royal residence. On macro and micro scales, symmetrical architectural arrangements were used, usually decorated in a mix of plastered, painted and carved surfaces often featuring elephants, felines and peacocks.

Such figurative art was not confined to carved elements but also painted (as in the vault of the *Kala Burj* at the Lahore Fort) and represented on tile work (as in the Lahore Fort's outer walls on the riverside and western fronts). After his marriage to Nur Jahan, whose Persian parentage was reflected in her aesthetic inclinations, Jahangir's experimentation with formal elements of the charbagh and his interest in the decorative use of mosaic, painting and fine inlay were given further impetus. Similar decorative themes were later incorporated in the Red Fort, most visible in an extensive use of carved and inlaid bird and flower motifs.

Jahangir extended a practice incorporated by Akbar which, though not directly related to architectural form, proved to be influential in the planning of subsequent Mughal forts. Akbar had re-invented the Indian tradition of the ceremony of darshan, wherein the emperor, likened both to father and god, showed himself to his people each morning in a viewing balcony of the palace. Architecturally and spatially, this meant that the emperor's private chambers needed to overlook a stretch of open ground where people could collect for this ceremony.

Chausath Khamba (111/1902-03, ASI PL)

> The object of the institution of this mode of audience, which originated with the late Emperor Akbar, was to enable His Majesty's subjects to witness the simultaneous appearance of the sky-adorning sun and the world-conquering Emperor, and thereby receive without any obstacle or hindrance the blessing of both these luminaries. By their presence in this space, which is large like the mind and hand of the generous, the harassed and oppressed of the population may fully represent their wants and desires.[42]

Jahangir, during his reign, ordered that a bell be suspended from the viewing balcony, to be rung by anyone craving justice—a revival of the ritual followed by some of the very first rulers of Delhi. Ostensibly a reaffirmation of the relationship between the emperor and his subjects, this ceremony was also important for reasons of court intrigue and a ruling system where primogeniture was not a guarantee for succession to the throne. There were many claimants to the royal line—the offspring of the large number of Mughal wives and concubines. Thus, the ceremony of darshan was equally a forum for justice and a symbol of reassurance of the emperor's control at a time when power equations shifted almost constantly.

The bridge connecting Salimgarh to the mainland (J. Luard, Private Collection)

During Jahangir's reign, architectural patronage in Delhi was extended more emphatically to the Salimgarh citadel, beyond the Nizamuddin area traditionally favoured by the Mughals. Jahangir commissioned a five-arched stone bridge that connected the mainland to Salimgarh, renamed Nurgarh, as well as structures within the citadel for his own use when passing through Delhi.[43]

Jahangir's reign also saw the construction of a single-storey pavilion in Delhi made entirely of white marble—the tomb of Mirza Aziz Koka Khan-i-Azam. Such marble chambers are recorded to have been established by Jahangir within the Agra Fort as well. This form of an imperial pavilion was later widely patronised by Shah Jahan, both in the buildings he replaced in older Mughal forts and the ones that he built in his new fort at Delhi.

Despite this patronage of newer forms, the Timurid style continued, as manifested in the tomb of Khan-i-Khanan near Nizamuddin, regarded as the model for the Taj Mahal.

The importance of Delhi was partly due to its emotional attraction for Jahangir 'as former capital and birthplace of emperors',[44] and the place where many saints of the Islamic faith lived, preached and died. It was considered by travellers to be one of the chief cities of India and Jahangir ensured that the city was kept in good repair. Additionally, since Delhi fell on the route to Kabul, Lahore, and Kashmir from Agra, it served as an important halting place for the emperor, who frequently travelled to these places, especially in the summers to escape the heat. Thus, the halts at Delhi combined pilgrimage (visits to Humayun's Tomb and the adjacent Dargah Nizamuddin), pleasure (hunting in the environs of Palam) and politics (overseeing of administrative matters in the area). This tradition was maintained by Shah Jahan.

That plentiful game was found in this region even 200 years after Jahangir, is borne out by the nineteenth-century *Gazetteer of the Delhi District*. It records the presence of foxes and hares on the west bank of the Yamuna; pigs, black and grey partridges all along the bank; blackbuck 'everywhere'; *chikara* (deer) in the hill ranges; leopards in outlying villages close to Tughlakabad; *muggurs* (crocodiles) and *ghariyals* (alligators) in the river, especially around the Old Fort and Okhla.[45]

Shah Jahan finally culminated this association by deciding to found his new imperial capital in Delhi in the eleventh year of his reign. The reasons were several. The construction of a new city afforded the opportunity of appropriately scaled spaces to rectify the overcrowding in existing Mughal cities. The absence of a coordinated design between Mughal forts and their cities had, in the past, caused a number of problems. One of these, as recorded by Jahangir in his memoirs, was the great mass of people in the lanes and bazaars that made movement of the imperial entourage difficult. Even small-scale hunting trips and visits to garden retreats or to the mosque required all able-bodied omrahs on guard for the day to accompany the emperor, who would be seated on a *takht-pawan* (a special couch) or a *palki* (palanquin) or an elephant. That these constituted a fairly substantial procession and required appropriate space is evident from a later description of Aurangzeb's entourage to the mosque every Friday: 'Before he goes out of the Fortress, the streets he is to pass are constantly watered because of the heat and dust. Two or three hundred musketeers form an avenue from the gate of the fortress'.[46]

The widely-held expectation in these times was that powerful kings would mark acquisition and conquest both through acts of aggression and construction. Therefore, '[e]veryone tries as far as possible, to erect a new building of his own, and establish his own reputation alongside that of his ancestors'.[47] Jahangir and Akbar, who preceded Shah Jahan as emperors, exemplified this belief. The prodigious construction ventures and architecture of their dynasty have been termed 'the most universal, the most successful and the most widely influential'[48] of the Islamic dynasties of India.

Shah Jahan's reign was characterised by full coffers and relative political peace. This allowed him to indulge his love for architecture, which was in evidence even before his ascension to the throne. These early experiments encapsulated Shah Jahan's future interests and inclinations. By the age of sixteen, he had already had quarters built inside Babur's Kabul Fort and some buildings redesigned inside the Agra Fort. Later, still as a prince, he established the Shah Bagh in Ahmedabad, and organised the construction of imperial buildings in Udaipur. The layout of the Shalimar Bagh in Kashmir was commenced in 1619[49] and shortly before his coronation in 1628, he ordered the construction of the white marble Jami Mosque within the Chisti Dargah at Ajmer.[50]

He also got added some trabeated pavilions to Jahangir's gardens along Ana Sagar Lake, continuing the concept of pavilions as imperial living quarters. One of these extant Ana Sagar pavilions is divided into two distinct concentric spaces in the tradition of the buildings that Akbar is said to have used. Such an organisation of space—a configuration of a pillared hall within a pillared hall—can be seen in the later Diwan-i-Khas pavilion at the Red Fort. Shah Jahan, however, in a departure from Akbar's favoured red sandstone, inclined towards white marble, a material widely patronised by Jahangir.

After he ascended the throne, Shah Jahan spent the first few years of his reign on military campaigns to quell political turbulence in the south and east of his empire. Those in the Deccan were against the Bundella chief and other rebellious governors. In the east, they were directed against the

Additions to the Agra Fort initiated by Shah Jahan (I 314/1919-20, ASI PL)

Portuguese in Hooghly, given the increasing piracy and brigandage under the weak Mughal governors there.

Even when engaged in these generally successful political campaigns, Shah Jahan found time for architecture. His patronage of palace architecture as emperor began with the reconstruction of a part of the Agra Fort, originally built by Akbar and Jahangir. This consisted of a complex of three courts and their buildings—the east wing of the courtyard of the Diwan-i-Am and the two imperial private courts of *Anguri Bagh* and *Macchi Bhawan*. The form and decoration of most of these structures display compositions of bilateral symmetry on a central axis. The thematic preponderance of symmetry is also seen in Shah Jahan's replacement of many of Jahangir's interventions in the Lahore Fort. This theme also appears to have been used to some degree in the planning of the Red Fort—in its location with respect to the city, in the disposition of its main functions on a central axis, and in the organisation of many of its buildings and pavilions.

In fact, Shah Jahan used the concept of pavilions as palaces more extensively than any other Mughal ruler. The structures that he got rebuilt—a large number of them in the existing forts at Agra and Lahore—were mainly single-storeyed pavilions made in marble. Shah Jahan also patronised the development of imperial mosques as single-storey pavilions, consisting of an additive system of bays constructed

Screens in the imperial pavilions, Shish Mahal, Lahore Fort (Photo: 219, 1902-03, ASI PL)

in the translucent and austerely beautiful Makrana marble. Such an arrangement can be seen in the Nagina Masjid at the Agra Fort and in the later Moti Masjid at the Red Fort. Decoration with *ayina kari*, or mirror inset in plaster used within the Lahore Shah Burj, was later further refined in the Rang Mahal and the Khas Mahal of the Red Fort.

Among the structures added by Shah Jahan in the Lahore Fort is the forty-pillared Diwan-i-Am hall and the Shah Burj (whose foundation was laid in Jahangir's reign) with its marble pavilion and a doubly curved *bangla* roof. This roof-form was later used so prolifically in the buildings of the emperor that it came to be associated solely with the imperial presence. It can be seen in the jharoka (the raised marble-throned-balcony) of the Agra Fort from where the emperor gave audience, in the roof of the throne within the Red Fort's Diwan-i-Am, in the emperor's personal mosques in the Agra Fort and the Red Fort, and in his designated quarters at the Mussaman and the Shah Burj in the Red Fort. The bangla-roof originating in the vernacular bamboo huts and indigenous terracotta temples of Bengal travelled widely after its extensive acceptance by Shah Jahan. It was adopted in the palace architecture of the Rajput and Sikh kings, as well as in the religious architecture of the Sikhs.

The founding of Shahjahanabad, the city of Shah Jahan, was the natural culmination of this architectural patronage. At the time that Shahjahanabad and the Red Fort were established, most of the country was under the Mughals. The emperor had begun to depute his now adult sons on military and provincial administrative matters and could concentrate on overall administration and his passion for architecture. Though fresh territories for conquest were on the agenda—Garhwal and Kumaun in the north, Qandahar and Balkh in the northwest and parts of Khandesh and Bijapur in the Deccan—the defence of the empire was not an overwhelming priority.

In 1638, Qandahar came under Mughal dominance with the complicity of the Persian governor, Ali Mardan Khan, who also had the reputation of a skilled engineer. The defection of Ali Mardan was thus useful for more reasons than the inclusion of Qandahar in the empire, which was recaptured by the Persians in 1648, the same year that the Red Fort was completed. Ali Mardan Khan is believed to have initiated the building of a canal in Lahore, and part of the final supervision of the Red Fort's construction was deputed to his assistant.[51]

The location of Delhi, its land profile, and its proximity to the river Yamuna influenced both its choice as the site for Shah Jahan's new city, and the form and design of that city and its Fort. The official histories of Shah Jahan's reign cite the improved climate of Delhi over Agra as

The Jama Masjid and the Red Fort, Shahjahanabad (Photo: Author, 2000)

the reason for the choice of the new capital.[52] However, though Delhi's climate is marginally cooler than Agra in the summer season, it,

> as might be anticipated from its position … between the plains of the Punjab and those of the more tropical parts of Bengal, has cold weather much like the Punjab with a bleak north-west wind that makes the temperature seem lower than it is and hot weather that makes tents unpleasant after April, and continues upto June.[53]

Geographically, too, there do not appear to be any great advantages of Delhi over Agra. In fact, with the southward and eastward extent of the empire, Agra, at 200 kilometres southeast of Delhi, was more centrally positioned within the Mughal empire. Delhi's re-ascendent position perhaps owed itself to the strong emotional appeal derived from its imperial history. It was referred to as a capital city along with Lahore, even when Shah Jahan was based at Agra. And even if it was not very much better than Agra with regard to overt strategic attraction, it was certainly not worse. It was a desirable distance away from the volatile northwest—sufficiently far away to prevent direct attacks on the emperor and close enough to react fairly quickly to an imminent threat from that direction. At a micro level, the high but virtually flat land-form bounded by the almost continuous Aravalli ridge across its northwest acted as a natural defence against cyclical attacks of invading armies. At the same time, Delhi retained an important feature of Agra, in that it was disposed on the banks of the Yamuna at the mouth of the fertile alluvial belt and the rich revenue source of the Gangetic plain. In brief, it appears that Shah Jahan was eager to establish a new city and, for the reasons outlined above, Delhi seemed to be the best choice.

The layout of his new city was influenced by Shah Jahan's social and religious preoccupations at this time. He had replaced Akbar's universal

Bangla roof, Moti Masjid (Photo: Author, 2000)

Lotus and padmakosh crowning the dome of Moti Masjid (Photo: Author, 2000)

Din-i-ilahi religion with specific Sunni ascendency in religious and secular activities. He demonstrated this shift in a number of ways. One of these was the destruction of newly constructed temples, as well as those built by his political foes. The predominance of Islam as one of the motivating forces in the functioning of the Mughal empire also seems to be latent in this description of Shah Jahan according justice in the Hall of Public Audience: 'If his Majesty orders punishment, He does so in perfect accordance with Islamic Law.'[54]

Notwithstanding his publicly professed inclination for Islam and its symbols, the use of motifs of earlier Indic religions is seen not just in secular but also in religious architecture of this period. So, the *kalash* (pot) and *padmakosh* crown not just the Taj Mahal, the most famous example of Shah Jahan's patronage, but also many congregational and private mosques, and chattris continued to be used to mark out important imperial buildings. However, the choice and form of architecture generally patronised by Shah Jahan during this time indicated his move towards an increasingly orthodox point of view in personal and political affairs.

This orthodoxy was accompanied by a greater formalisation and detailing of court rituals that reflected the supremacy of the court and court religion. Their overwhelming predominance is evident in the layout of Shahjahanabad, and in the deliberate location of the Red Fort and the principal congregational mosque on the two most important geographical features—the Fort next to the river and the mosque on an elevated rock outcrop. Thus, as the empire settled into a pattern of greater refinement in the arts, religion and lifestyle, it began to show signs of greater rigidity.

The expansion of Shah Jahan's empire, its increase in wealth and its access to greater natural and human resources were reflected in an accompanying increase in architectural opulence. This can be gauged from the other ambitious building projects that Shah Jahan initiated almost concurrently with his new Fort and city. The Taj Mahal, begun in 1627, was half-built when construction on the Red Fort started; the Shalimar Bagh in Lahore were completed in 1637, just two years before the commencement of the Red Fort and the creation of the fabled Peacock Throne was also set into motion in this year. It was finished seven years later—when the Red Fort was five years in the making. For the Peacock Throne, it was decreed that

> in addition to the jewels in the Imperial jewel house, rubies, garnets, rich pearls and emeralds, to the value of 200 lacs of rupees should be brought for the inspection of the Emperor, and that they, with some exquisite jewels of great weight … worth eighty-six lacs of rupees … should be handed over to … the superintendent of the goldsmiths' department. There was also to be given to him one lac of *tolas* of pure gold.[55]

Such opulence, also visible in the inauguration ceremonies of the Red Fort, was, along with the form of the built spaces within Shahjahanabad, geared to impress upon both the populace and the visitors Shah Jahan's pre-eminence as a ruler and a builder. The Fort, extolled as the Qila Mubarak, especially needed to be a step ahead of the building activities of Shah Jahan's illustrious predecessors as well as his contemporaries—not just within the empire but also outside it. Just as Shah Abbas, the contemporary ruler of Persia, may have wished to rival the achievements of the Mughals with his city of Isfahan as a challenge to Agra and Istanbul, similarly, one of the unstated objectives of Shah Jahan may have been to rival both Isfahan and previous Mughal capitals. Later descriptions by Mughal chroniclers use Isfahan as a gauge for extolling the virtues of Shah Jahan's new city: they acknowledge Isfahan's beauty but consider it inferior to Shahjahanabad.

A substantial amount of planning, money and manpower was spent to make such a claim credible and render this new city more beautiful than the earlier cities that it sought to overshadow. Shahjahanabad's coordinated design was linked by a system of grand streets and avenues that, while being appropriate for court ceremonies, was also adapted to accommodate geographical features and connections to previous cities of Delhi. A definite improvement on Agra's crowded and narrow streets, the urban design of Shahjahanabad skilfully incorporated mosques, wells and graves dating from earlier times on the site and retained existing road systems as well as buildings such as *Kali (Kalan) Masjid,*[56] Turkman Gate[57] and *Bhojila Pahari Masjid.*

The Red Fort was the focus and climax of these grand urban axes. This positioning appears to be derived, at least in part, from the system of regulated and symmetrical planning used in a traditional Indian city. The capital city in ancient India occupied a special sanctified place as the abode of the king and the site of Brahmanic ritual. It was planned on the basis of an underlying symbolism derived from cosmographic concepts. These concepts were embodied in the *mandala.*[58] The word 'mandala' is from Sanskrit and is a graphic mystic symbol of the universe—typically in the form of a circle enclosing a square.

Within this system, the palace-fortress at the centre of the capital city, with the throne of the king, was regarded as the centre of the universe. Thus, Banaras, the holiest of Hindu cities, was held to be the centre of the world. This system of planning and the belief that powered it persisted even till later times, as in Jaipur founded in 1728 by Maharaja Sawai Jai Singh. A similar attribution of divine status, though naturally within an Islamic frame of reference, is evident in the descriptions of Shahjahanabad as the centre of the circle of Islam, the seat of the empire and the foundation of the eighth heaven.[59]

Significant in this context is a semi-elliptical design called *karmuka* or bow for a site fronting a river or seashore, as mentioned in the Mansara, a *vastushastra* dating from about 400 CE. This has been pointed out by Stephen Blake in his analysis of Shahjahanabad and by Prabhakar Begde in his work on Indian forts.[60] Blake makes valid deductions regarding the layout of the main streets as well as the similarity in the location of the Red Fort in Shahjahanabad with that of the Vishnu or Shiva temple in the karmuka plan—at the most auspicious spot of the junction of the two main streets.

However, it cannot be stated with certainty whether this similarity is derived from the application of the karmuka, or is the result of a logical site-response. While the shape of the karmuka is undoubtedly similar to the location and overall layout of Shahjahanabad, an examination of the *Mansara* shows that it does not list the karmuka in its detailed categorisation of different typologies for capital cities. And even though it states that the difference between a village and a town is primarily one of size and ascribes some common attributes to both village and town plans, it specifically applies the karmuka configuration to a village for the residence of the *vaishyas* or the merchant class.[61]

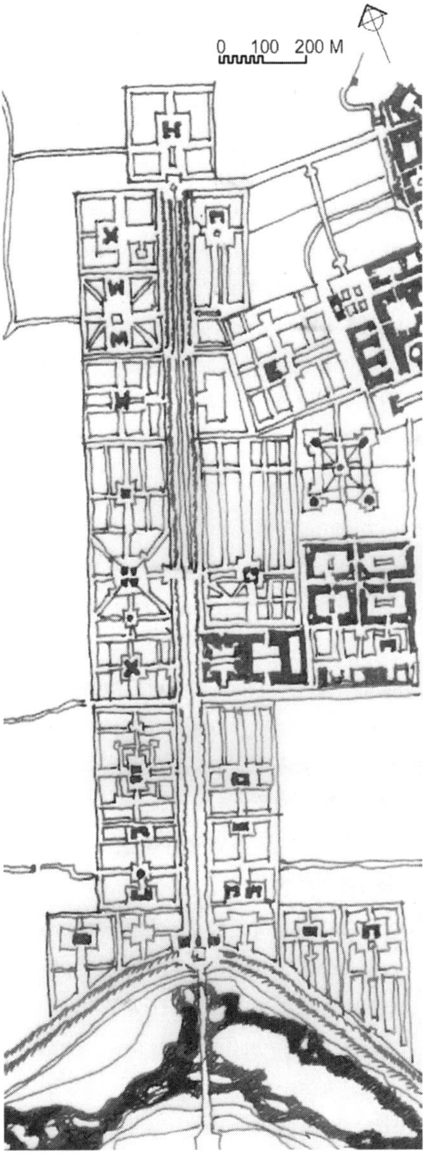

Configuration of the main urban axis, public gardens, and royal palace in Isfahan (Drawing by Author, based on N. Ardalen, and L. Bakhtiar, *The Sense of Unity*)

Notwithstanding this debate, the location of the Red Fort at the junction of the two principal axes of Shahjahanabad seems consistent with ancient town-planning texts. Amongst the criteria that the *Mansara* lists for a *Rajdhani* (capital city or metropolis) are that it should preferably be laid out on the banks of a river, with a Vishnu temple at the city's entrance or its centre, the royal palace in the centre, and a chowk or square at the meeting point of two main axes. As marked by Milindpanah, '[the] king's palace, or rather the palace wall and gatehouse, would seem to have faced onto the central city square, its exit facing down one of the main streets towards one of the city gates'.[62] The overall description of planned early Indian cities, 'fine and regular, measured out into quarters, with excavated moats and ramparts about squares, with cleanly and evenly main roads, with regular lines of open shops, well-provided with parks, gardens, lakes, lotus ponds, and wells, adorned with many kinds of temples of the gods'[63]—is also reasonably valid for Shahjahanabad with the exception that the mosques replaced the provision for temples.

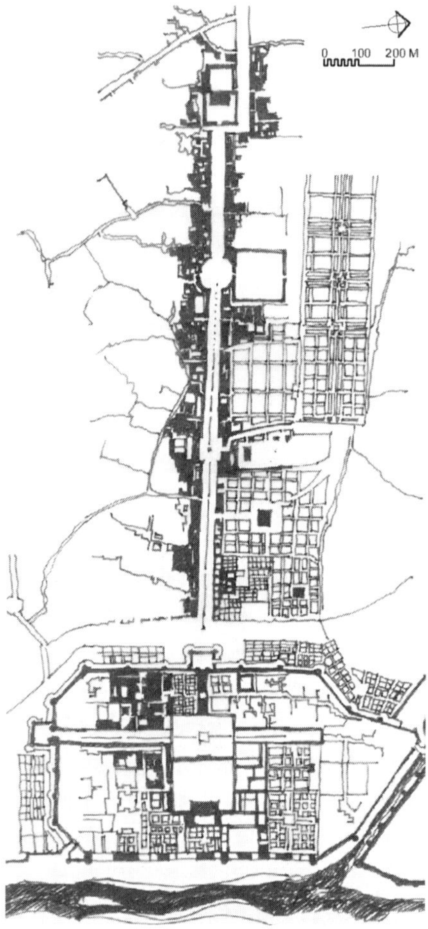

Configuration of the main urban axis, public gardens, and royal palace in Shahjahanabad (Drawing by Author, based on trans. map X/1659, OIOC, BL)

The influence of this tradition of city building was inevitable, given the background and religion of a large proportion of the citizens, the architectural traditions manifest in their built and literary records, the mixed parentage of the Mughals after Akbar, and the eclecticism of the rulers and the ruled. Shah Jahan, with his exacting aesthetic sensibilities and born of a Hindu mother from a Rajput royal family, could not have been exempt from this influence.[64]

Despite this, the main structure of Shahjahanabad seems to have followed the typical Islamic pattern of infill and harmonic order, rather than geometrical order.[65] Geometric order is described as the repetition and elaboration of a chosen form to achieve a unity while harmonic order is the maximum use of an architectonic vocabulary to reach unity. Though earlier architecture in Persia and elsewhere appear derived from geometric order, later developments lay more stress on harmonic order. The influence of Persian art and architecture on the Mughals, acknowledged by scholars at various times, was especially evident after Humayun's return from exile in Persia. Apart from the influx of Persian artists, noblemen, travellers and traders in the Mughal court, the almost contemporary Safavid capital of Isfahan exercised an important influence on Shahjahanabad.

The Safavid emperor, Shah Abbas (1528–1629 CE), built avenues, gardens, palaces and mosques at his new capital in Isfahan about a decade before Shah Jahan began his new city. The defining features of the two cities of Isfahan and Shahjahanabad were the river and the response to the river. The configuration of the main commercial axis of each city with respect to its river, and the disposition of public gardens with respect to this main axis, are remarkably similar. Similarities are also visible in the range of functions in their palaces, in the links between the palaces and urban commercial activities, and in the basic character of these cities being derived from structures built by the emperor and his nobles. In addition, both Delhi and Isfahan shared a corresponding historical development as important urban centres, resettled time and again as capital cities.

Isfahan's main urban avenue was the 1870.2-metre-long and 48-metre-wide tree-lined Chahar Bagh perpendicular to the Zaiunday river.[66] Gardens and forecourts bordered the Chahar Bagh and led to the palace, situated northeast of this axis. Gardens also formed the climax of the avenue on both ends, with the river as an additional backdrop on the south. Ten years later, Shah Jahan decided on an almost identical configuration for his new capital, locating the 1389.8-metre-long and 36.57-metre-wide Chandni Chowk axis, with its central line of canals and trees, located perpendicular to the Yamuna.

Despite this commonality in orientation, there are important differences in the volume and culmination of the urban axes in Isfahan and Delhi. In place of the open view of the river that terminated Chahar Bagh, it is the Red Fort that formed the climax to Chandni Chowk. In front of and around the Fort were a series of gardens. Shops and porticoes defined the Chandni Chowk's length, even though the most magnificent garden of Shahjahanabad, the Begum Bagh, was also sited immediately north of this axis.

In another departure from Isfahan's layout, Shah Jahan included a second commercial axis, the 960.12-metre-long and 27.4-metre-wide Faiz Bazar perpendicular to Chandni Chowk that met it in front of the Red Fort. Thus, while the theme of gardens leading to the palace remains the same in Isfahan and Delhi, the relative positions of the gardens and the palace seem to have been interchanged in the two cities. In the palace complexes too, despite some general commonalities, there are differences in the progression of spaces, materials of construction and proportions of buildings. Though some of the royal buildings in Isfahan were on a grander scale, the progression from public to private royal space appears to have been more coherent in Shahjahanabad.

Nonetheless, both Isfahan and Delhi were capitals of what is termed as a patrimonial-bureaucratic rule[67] where the emperor was represented as a benevolent father who had the welfare of his subjects at heart, who personally oversaw even routine matters in the administrative and political affairs of the empire and who set both the trends and standards of social behaviour as well as artistic patronage.[68] The palaces of both cities include a similar range of functions and display a comparable relationship between built and open space. The palace of the Safavids occupied a circumference of a little more than 5.5 kilometres. It contained gardens, pavilions and mansions, and was larger than the almost 2.5 kilometres of Shah Jahan's Fort that in turn contained imperial pavilions, workshops, kitchens, administrative offices, gardens and residences of military commanders and soldiers.

The reasons for this stemmed from a variety of constraints, one of which may have been the climate of Delhi with its high temperatures for most of the year. In Shah Jahan's new Fort and city, the scale and type of architecture was designed to be of a volume that could be shaded by built or natural elements. For this reason, gardens and palaces or markets and residences were closely integrated, and public open spaces similar to the large Maidan of Isfahan were limited. As depicted in various maps of the city, open spaces were in the form of gardens and courts, mostly located along the Yamuna where the micro-climate was regulated by cool breezes as well as along the central commercial axis with its fountains and trees and in the shade of the Fort's ramparts.

A fair amount of plantation would have been necessary to render the streets and gardens pleasant, since the indigenous flora was not very dense and essentially consisted of *kikar* (*Acacia Arabica*), *jaal* (*Salvadora oleoides*), *pipal* (*Ficus religiosa*), *ber* (*Zizyphus jujuba*), *dhak* (*Butea monosperma*), *jamun* (*Syzigium cumini*) and bushes of *karil* (*Capparis decidua*). The Mughal emperors, who were greatly interested in trees and plants, may have initiated plantation of the varieties of orange, peach, plum, prune, pomegranate and fig trees that find mention as existing in the Delhi area during the early twentieth century.[69]

The cooling effect of the river was also used to maximum advantage, especially in the location of the Red Fort and other influential buildings right on its banks. At an individual-dwelling scale in the city and the Fort, the architectural response to the climatic conditions was a continuation of the use of *sardkhanas* or underground rooms to spend the hot summer afternoons. This typology was supported by the extensive use of water for cooling by architectural features such as double roofs, screens and by a high proportion of gardens. Shah Jahan's vision of an ideal city and palace, through which he envisioned flowing streams of water, overrode defensive aspects—in any case, not a priority in his relatively peaceful reign. Despite this predominance of aesthetics over defence issues, Shahjahanabad also skilfully utilised the presence of both the main natural features of the region. The new city straddled the point where the Aravalli ridge dipped down, and its boundaries stretched from the Yamuna on one side all the way to the ridge on the other, thus gaining not one but two natural defences.

With a substantial area readily accessible by river and road, the site was also at a desirable distance from the older cities of Delhi to allow the realisation of a large, well-designed imperial city; yet, it was near enough to the population in the older capitals for the provision of the necessary infrastructure for workers and movement of goods. The rocky nature of much of this site was an additional advantage since there was less danger of it eroding away, unlike Agra, where the shifting course of the river had eaten away the relatively soft soil and caused many structures to collapse. The essentially flat land profile, except for an outcrop on the southwest and the ridge on the western boundary, simplified building activity. For the imperial Fort, after 'a long search, a piece of ground outside of the city of Delhi lying between the most distant suburbs and Nurgarh commonly called Salimgarh, was selected'.[70]

The selection—fortuitously close to the strong and strategically placed Salimgarh citadel, and furthest away from the northwestern dip in the ridge and, therefore, from the traditional direction of invading armies—was logical. This decision is said to have been aided by advice from Shah Jahan's astrologers who, in 1639 CE, specified the day, time and location of laying the cornerstone to formally mark the construction of the Fort.

Security reasons do not seem to have been of overwhelming consideration in the design of the Fort since even though it was sited next to the river, a large bank of open ground was retained between the Yamuna and its eastern walls. Nor was there any specific defensive plan in its layout or in the placement of interior functions. These, in fact, seem to have been the very antithesis of a secure fortification. The most private and vulnerable parts were located next to the large sandy bank without a moat for defence, on a wall only 60 feet high and at the very edge of the city. The principal gates into the Fort did not use the time-honoured principle of staggered entry in order to thwart forcible entry of its gates with battering rams. The emperor's throne was in direct line from the principal entrance. The imperial quarters, instead of being built at higher levels for safety, were in single-storeyed pavilions.

The decision to keep a distance between the Fort and the river may have been influenced by the fact that for some months each year, the river swelled in volume and overflowed its banks. Since the flood waters lapped the city walls during the monsoons, locating the Fort any nearer to the river may have caused structural and functional problems to the imperial pavilions in it. At these times, the river did serve a defensive function for the Fort, as a British soldier noted two centuries later: 'The Eastern face of the City rests on the Jumna, and during the rainy season of the year, the stream may be described as washing the base of the walls. All access to a besieger on the river-front is therefore, impracticable.'[71]

The river's flooding posed a severe problem even some 200 years after the founding of the Fort, when it was recorded to swell to several miles with a maximum depth of 25 feet. It was also infested with crocodiles. Concerns over the frequent flooding of the Yamuna may, thus, have seemed a more pressing danger to the Fort than attacks on the city at a time when the Mughal empire was reasonably secure. When the river was not in full spate, the imperial pavilions were accessible from the banks and susceptible to potential danger from an invading force. The Fort's later history is a testimony to this danger.

The other reason for siting the Fort on the riverbank was to extract maximum climatic benefit from cool river breezes. Such a positioning also allowed the emperor and his family uninterrupted views over relatively uninhabited fields across the river, and assured him privacy from the city. Apart from such practical benefits, Shah Jahan's decision to emphasise both his presence and that of his religion was dictated by the multi-religious population that he reigned over. The palace and the mosque—symbolic of temporal and divine power—were deliberately highlighted in the choice of their location within the city and in their form of architecture. The Fort's siting along the river ascertained that any visitors would be confronted with its grandeur, whether they entered through any of the main road axes, or whether they came by river. From the city, this positioning guaranteed the predominance of the Fort as the climax of built form—there was no possibility of any grand structure rearing up behind it.

This was especially relevant in the context of the elegant single-storeyed palace architecture of the Fort. This emphasis on single-storeyed buildings was very different from the vertical eclecticism of Akbar, and from the established forms of vertically dominating palaces. Though pavilions formed an important component of traditional Indian palaces and were extensively used—designated for varied functions such as residences, places for dancing and musical performances, wedding ceremonies,

External facade, Gwalior Fort (Photo: Author, 2000)

Outer facade, Raja Mahal, Orchha (Photo: Author, 2000)

bathing chambers, sacrificial chambers and for putting on the sacred thread[72]—these generally probably formed part of a larger unit, rather than individual buildings. Their descriptions clarify that the 'pasada has one, or more often many stories … The palace consisted of two clearly distinguishable parts—the ... lower floors and the ... upper floors'.[73]

Inner courtyards, Raja Mahal, Orchha (Photo: Author, 2000)

Court scene with Akbar watching Chagtai dancers, c.1565 (MS Douce. Or.b.1, F.12 b, Bodleian Library, University of Oxford)

Shah Jahan receiving Ali Mardan, c.1640 (MS Ousley, Add.173, no .13, Bodleian Library, University of Oxford)

River front imperial pavilions, Agra Fort (Add.Or. 929, OIOC, BL)

Earlier palace buildings of the Mughals generally followed such a pattern. The many-storeyed Jahangiri Mahal, one of Akbar's few extant buildings in the Agra Fort, is said to be influenced in layout and motifs by Man Singh Tomar's Palace at Gwalior, admired by Mughal emperors from Babur to Shah Jahan. Akbar also used single- and double-storeyed pavilions in Sikri—such as the Diwan-i-Khas and Birbals' palace—in combination with buildings of imposing heights, such as the Panch Mahal.

The royal architecture of the respective periods of these Mughal emperors reflected their personal attributes as well as the political and social conditions of their time. Shah Jahan, the inheritor of a vast empire encompassing a total area almost half the size of Europe, chose to come back to a tried and tested site with a multitude of practical benefits but no overwhelming geographical landforms. In contrast, Akbar established his new city at the relatively obscure Fatehpur Sikri. In the Agra Fort, he made use of a complex visual interplay with buildings opening out at different levels. In Shah Jahan's new Fort, most buildings were arranged symmetrically in separate spaces defined through courts, laid out on a flat site with a less challenging contour profile. Though shifting axes were used in connections between two spaces, within the space itself the generating order was symmetry.

Notwithstanding these differences, the influence of the earlier Mughal palace complexes at Agra, Lahore and Fatehpur Sikri is evident

in the planning and functioning of the Red Fort. One of the important similarities in all the palace-complexes was the concept of the 'city in miniature', in which the density and complexity of activities associated with urban Mughal settlements were reflected within the palace. Administrative, ceremonial, commercial and manufacturing functions were carried out alongside private residential functions in the Mughal palaces. Abul Fazl, Akbar's court historian, makes detailed references to activities like the royal *karakhanas* (workshops), mint, libraries, offices and markets within Akbar's palace. In accordance with this system, the Red Fort at Shahjahanabad displayed a multitude of functions, unlike the modern conception of a palace as being merely the residence of the ruling power.

The range of activities, the form and the urban emphasis of these palace-complexes, were ordered by the structure of the Mughal empire. The social, political and economic system existed as an integrated whole personified by the emperor. He was the centre of political power and supreme judicial authority. As the head of state, he owned the fortunes of the kingdom. Even estates gifted to noblemen reverted to the emperor on their death. He participated in all activities: he inspected architectural models and construction work, commissioned and composed poetry and paintings, perused court histories before giving royal approval and participated in musical soirees

River front imperial pavilions, Red Fort, Shahjahanabad
(Photo: 3635, Agra, Vol. 1 1914-15, ASI PL)

Shah Jahan's reign was prosperous, yet the spectre of an uncertain future may have existed in the minds of the rich and poor, used as they were to changing economic and political fortunes. In such a climate, permanent allegiance could be owed only to the emperor, whose palace had to convey a reassuring permanence. In keeping with this tradition, Shah Jahan played an indispensable role in public and private life. However, as compared to previous reigns, there was a shift in both the participation and the perception of the emperor. Thus, miniature paintings of Akbar represent him as having a personal interest in the affairs of his kingdom and engaging in ordinary activities such as inspecting construction sites, fetching water from a well after returning from a chase as a young boy and sitting on the ground with the singer Baiju Bawra and with Swami Harnam Das.[74] In contrast, representations of Shah Jahan show him engaged mainly in lordly pursuits such as hunting, seated in court, astride a horse, or standing in a formal pose with a flower in hand. Unlike Akbar's full-face portrait, Shah Jahan is generally depicted in his more flattering profile, his eyes remote and never looking directly into the eyes of the viewers.[75]

His later portraits show an increased association with divinity and the sun, a tradition started by Akbar, amongst whose titles were 'shining forehead of the morning of guidance,—focus of the sun of holiness—sublime concentration of humanity—heir apparent of the sun'.[76] In an obvious derivation of his grandfather's claims, the portraits painted

during his time depict Shah Jahan and his other ancestors with haloes around their heads. This image of the emperor as a deified and remote though a benign figure finds a parallel in architecture.

The Red Fort as his residence, occupied the most dominant location in the city with the view of the river. Within the Fort, the routes from the two main gates—centrally oriented in axis with the gates—met at an administrative forecourt before leading onto the Diwan-i-Am court. This marked out spatially the levels of hierarchy, with the entrance to the Diwan-i-Am being made a more formal act. All these were a reflection of Shah Jahan's rule in which court etiquette and customs became strictly formal as opposed to the more open system of Akbar's time.

The orthodoxy characterising the later years of Shah Jahan's reign also saw the restoration of Persian formality in the planning of gardens and in the two-dimensional use of surface decoration, accompanied by the inclusion of the carved white marble of the Indian tradition. Thus, the Red Fort is far more formal in its plan as compared to the forts at Agra, Sikri and Lahore. It, however, displays a general similarity with them not just in the range but also the location of functions. The system of entrances and the position of the imperial Mughal forts in Lahore, Agra and Shahjahanabad with respect to the rivers in their cities follows a recognisable sequence. The principal entrances in the Shahjahanabad Fort are on its western and southern faces, an arrangement resembling that in Agra but slightly different from the eastern and western entrances in the

River front, Shahjahanabad (Map X/1659, OIOC, BL)

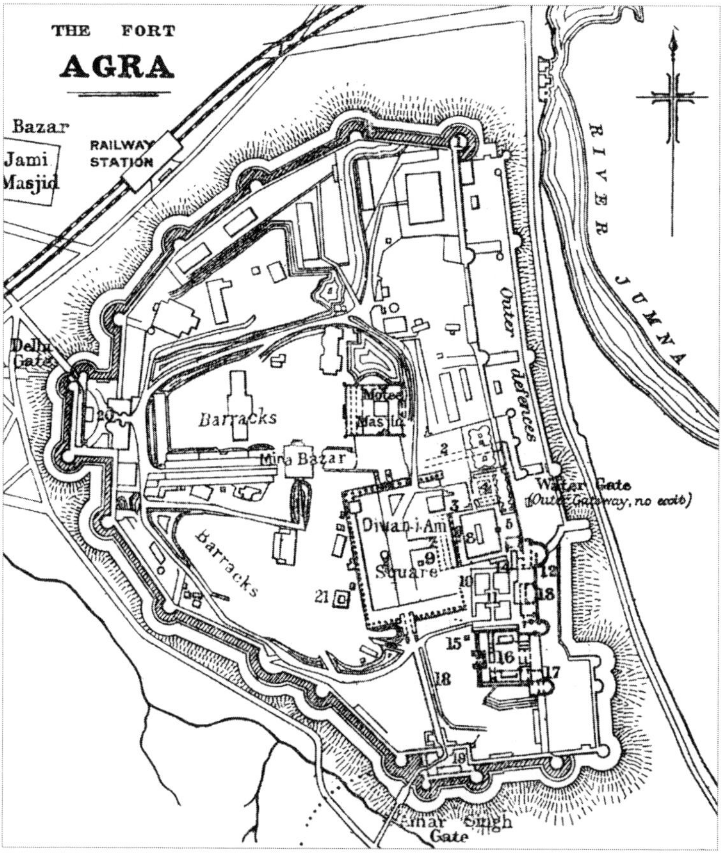

Plan, Agra Fort (ASI Drawing)

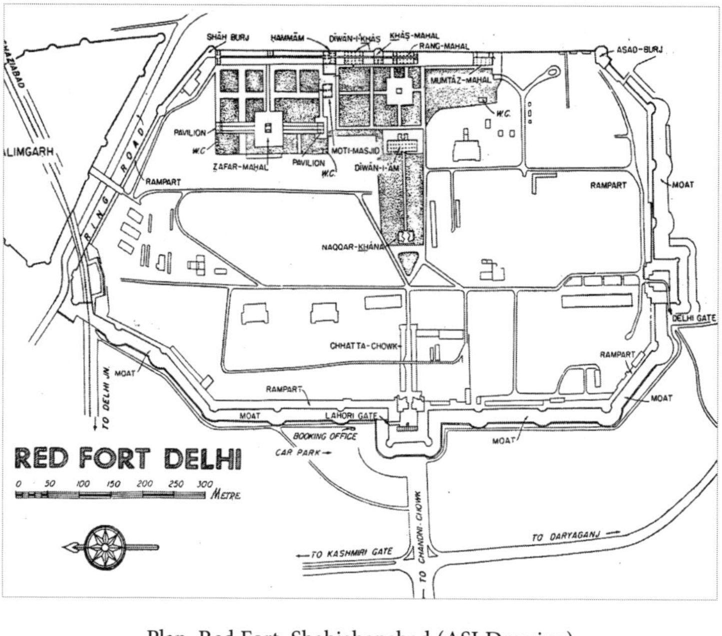

Plan, Red Fort, Shahjahanabad (ASI Drawing)

Diwan-i-Am, Agra Fort (Photo: I 313/1919-20, ASI PL)

Diwan-i-Am, Red Fort, Shahjahanabad (Photo: Author, 1997)

Lahore Fort. The sequence of the Diwan-i-Am, imperial private chambers, and seraglio forecourts is especially similar in the Shahjahanabad and Agra Forts. However, the progression in space, scale and detail is more complex in the Shahjahanabad Fort with an additional administrative court—the Naqqar Khana Forecourt—marking the junction of the entrance routes, which is not present in the preceding Fort complexes.

The imperial quarters and seraglio buildings were sited on the river-front in all the Forts—at Agra, Lahore and Delhi. Consider Francois Pelsaert's description of Agra 'Everyone has tried to be close to the river bank, and consequently the water-front is occupied by the costly palaces of all the famous lords, which makes it appear very gay and magnificent.'[77] Similarly, in Shahjahanabad, the river-front had a concentration of high-profile areas which included the Fort, noblemen's mansions, public and private gardens and sacred bathing ghats—*Rajghat*, *Ghat Kela*, *Nigambodh Ghat*. The river and its bank that formed such an important component of urban fabric at Agra, Lahore and Shahjahanabad did not exist at Fatehpur Sikri.

The other principal differences between the palace at Sikri and the Forts in the above-mentioned three Mughal cities were the absence of a widespread urban environment as well as enclosing fort walls immediately around the palace complex. Within the palace at Sikri, there is a reduced emphasis on the symmetry that characterises the general arrangement in the other three Mughal forts under discussion. In another important difference, the presence of water in the palace at Sikri is limited to the forecourts close to the emperor's quarters, unlike the channels, basins and fountains that traverse almost the entire area of the later Red Fort.

However, with reference to individual building structures, Sikri is an undoubted inspiration for the Red Fort as well as the later structures in the Agra and Lahore Forts. The development in the pavilion form—the most favoured type of residential Mughal buildings—is especially evident in the Diwan-i-Am and its ancillary space, and shows a progression from Sikri to Agra, Lahore and finally Delhi. In Sikri, the Diwan-i-Am is essentially in the nature of a closed room ending in a verandah where the emperor would sit to face his audience in an open courtyard edged by colonnades. The Diwan-i-Ams in Agra, Lahore and Shahjahanabad are an improvement of this concept, since the emperor's throne in them was further defined by a raised plinth. Court paintings depict a spatial arrangement in which the emperor sits in a jharoka centrally aligned within a larger chamber. The imperial doorway is set in axis behind the jharoka, on a wall decorated with inlaid mosaics.[78]

Shah Jahan introduced the concept of enclosing the already existing jharokas at Agra and Lahore within a large hall, so that part of the assembled audience in the forecourt was included within the Diwan-i-Am. These halls were separated from their forecourts by a plinth and a railing. They were much larger with their nine bays and three aisles, in comparison with the Diwan-i-Am at Sikri which consisted of five bays and three aisles. The description by Inayat Khan enumerates the development in the Diwan-i-Am by Shah Jahan at Agra.

> The public assembly of the world monarch was always held in front of the royal balcony (jharoka) of the Hall of Public Audience in the Akbarabad Fort. However, during the reigns of the late Emperors Akbar and Jahangir, no coverings had existed over the area reserved for those standing in the royal presence; and accordingly many had to bear the hardship of rain in the monsoon, and heat in the summer. To alleviate this, His Majesty ordered a spacious forty-pillared Hall (Chihil-Sutun) to be built; and it was completed ... in 1628 ... Orders were issued that a similar hall should be built in front of the balcony at the Lahore capital.[79]

The basic form of the jharokas within these halls may have originated as far back as the third century BCE, as seen in the bas-reliefs at Sanchi Stupa. The word itself may have derived from the Sanskrit word *jali-gavaksha* (latticed window) and its royal or divine implications seem to predate the Mughals. The refinement of the jharoka form under the Mughals can be understood by comparing those at Agra and Lahore with that of Shahjahanabad. The extant jharoka in the Diwan-i-Am at Lahore (which probably dates from Jahangir's reign) consists of a single bay within a chattri projecting out on brackets. In Agra, the jharoka initially consisted of a three-bayed raised niche in the wall, around which Shah Jahan got incorporated a hall in a skilful way that makes the jharoka appear like an internal pierced facade. Unlike Agra and Lahore, the jharoka in the Red Fort is a separate structure that sits on a high plinth within the hall. Its design, thus, retains the jharoka's inaccessibility to the general audience and ensures its distinct identity and, at the same time, incorporates a visual fluidity in the hall.

At a larger level, the complex arrangement of pavilions connected by colonnades and courtyards devised in Fatehpur Sikri influenced the layout within the Red Fort too. However, the combination of lower- and higher-storeyed pavilions with intervening courts used here differed in their relative number and proportions from the palace at Sikri. In the inner palace of the Red Fort, the only areas containing higher-storeyed buildings are the termination points to the two ends of the eastern face (the Asad and Shah Burj). Such a layout, with its majority of single-storeyed imperial structures, called for an impressive progression on the horizontal axis to compensate for the feelings of awe that were normally generated by vertical dominance.

Thus, it was important that the Diwan-i-Am, the Emperor's Hall of Public Audience at the Red Fort should be visible on a seemingly infinite horizontal axis, and access to it be gained by successive entry through a series of increasingly magnificent spaces—progressively grander courts and gateways. In the Diwan-i-Am itself, a rhythm of single and paired columns marked both the desired direction of movement as well as introduced a spatial cadence uplifting it above a mere hall.

The jharoka as the focus of the Diwan-i-Am was constructed in marble, in deference to Shah Jahan's preference for this material. The choice of white Makrana marble, which has a smoothly luminous quality, unlike the opaque perfection of the Greek marbles or the veined richness of Italian marbles, underlined a symbolic association with the colour white prevalent in Islamic religious philosophy: 'White is the integration of all colours ... light symbolically viewed as white descends from the sun and symbolises unity.'[80] This association would have gained even more importance from the latter part of Akbar's rule when the emperor began to project himself as an emanator of light. In fact, starting the day by giving darshan to their subjects congregated on the banks was a manifestation of the Mughal emperors' identification with light.

There was also a tradition of using the riverbanks for ceremonial and celebratory events in which the entire city would participate. These frequently functioned as a showcase for imperial festivities, as descriptions from the *Shah Jahan Nama of Inayat Khan* show. One such occasion was

Agra Fort, river front facade (Photo: I 308/1919-20, ASI PL)

Dara Shikoh's wedding, when the imperial family in the Agra Fort viewed the scene on the riverbanks literally from balcony seats.

> At the close of day, numerous fireworks set up by the future bride's relatives were ignited along the banks of the Jumna, causing great delight to the spectators ... not to be outdone, by His Majesty's command, the gardens beneath the royal chambers and the grounds below the audience balconies, as well as the boats upon the Jumna were illuminated with lamps, and fireworks, which had been provided at his private expense, were displayed on the banks of the Jumna.[81]

Spectacles like elephant fights were also staged here on a fairly regular basis.

> In this very space, there pass before the most holy royal eye, the furious wild man-killing elephants, which it is quite unsafe to bring into the Hall of Public Audience. It is also in this large plain that there are arranged the elephant fights which are peculiar to the Kings of India and worthy of the amusement of exalted sovereigns.
>
> No doubt, without such a large space, the combat of such a pair of demon-countenanced and mountain-shaped beasts cannot take place, for during their fights and pursuits, a world is trodden under the feet of

> the four-pillared Bisutuns … In this very space, the mountain-shaped and wind-footed elephants are caused to run after horses so that the former may become accustomed to attacking brave horsemen in battles. In the same large area, His Majesty reviews horses of the victorious armies and the contingent troops retained by the nobles.[82]

Similar events such as these were hosted on the banks of the Yamuna below the Red Fort in Shahjahanabad, as on the wedding of Shah Jahan's grandson, Sulaiman Shikoh.[83] It was also from here that Shah Jahan entered into the Fort in state, celebrating the return of the imperial court to Delhi.[84] Thus, the role of the Yamuna was not limited to just being the main catalyst for the establishment of pre- and proto-historic settlements as well as all the historic cities of Delhi, including Shahjahanabad. As seen above, its role extended to important urban functions such as those of public recreational spaces, a visual climax, and a means of transport, bearing out the truth of an old Indian saying citing the three necessities of a city as the *darya* (river), *badal* (cloud) and *badshah* (the king). As will be seen, the river and its banks were also vital in the successful implementation of the complex activities that the Red Fort—virtually a city within—encompassed inside its walls.

4

THE CITY WITHIN

[Shah Jahan] … having boarded a boat at the landing ghat of Khwaja Khizr where his camp was pitched, started off in joy and gladness for the new metropolis … and proceeded to make his ceremonious entry into the splendid palaces of the fort … After inspecting the various buildings and edifices, he took his seat on the Jewelled Throne in the Hall of Public Audience, where he held a public levee, whilst the loud beating of the royal drums made the glad sounds of rejoicing peal through the universe'.

The Shah Jahan Nama of Inayat Khan,
Eng. trans. A.R. Fuller, eds. W. E. Begley and Z. A. Desai.

In the tenth year of his reign,[1] Shah Jahan changed the practice of counting regnal years from the *Nauroz*—the first day of the Persian solar year—to the Islamic lunar calendar. In the eleventh year, he ordered the construction of his new city and fort. Actively involved in this huge venture,[2] he employed an array of master designers and masons skilled in architecture, landscape, carpentry, sculpture, inlay, carving and painting, and reportedly spent a 100 lakhs (ten million) on the construction process. Finally, in April of the twenty-first lunar year of his reign, Shah Jahan led the celebrations at the inauguration of this Fort.[3]

Sounds of rejoicing were therefore justifiable. Shah Jahan had, in less than ten years, managed the successful completion of an ambitious enterprise with the aid of his master builders Ustad Hamid and Ustad

Ahmed. This design, that evoked such joy and gladness then, might appear to have some perplexing aspects today. Instances that may excite particular curiosity are the location of some of the most private areas in the Fort (such as the Rang Mahal) on the ceremonial public axis and the displacement of semi-public and ceremonial areas (such as the Diwan-i-Khas) from this axis. The positioning of intensely private activities like the imperial bathing chambers adjacent to semi-public areas and the vulnerability of the Fort, seemingly enhanced by the provision of many entrance gates, are some other features that awaken curiosity.

The key to comprehending the reasons for these and other features of the Red Fort lies in first understanding that its planning, appearance and use was an outcome of the manner in which the Fort—virtually a city in itself—worked with the larger city of Shahjahanabad. The planning of the Fort was also based on the way of life prevalent in the time period and monarchical system of the Mughals. An understanding of the manner in which spaces within the Fort were once demarcated and the rationale behind such a demarcation may be gained through glimpses of the emperor's life and the possible routine of the other inmates. This way of life was, in many aspects, very different from today. So much so that even if all the Red Fort's original structures and spaces were extant, their manner of use might still remain mystifying. Thus, before moving on to scrutinise the design of individual structures in the Fort, an understanding of the larger picture of that time is necessary. This includes the relationship between the Fort and the city, as well as the Fort's appearance, both to a visitor and an inhabitant of the city.

The Red Fort, like most imperial Mughal forts, was the site of a variety of functions—residential, ceremonial, administrative, manufacturing and military—all of which required well-thought-out organisation and use of space. The design of the Red Fort, free of any constraints of previously existing Fort boundaries, formally utilised the opportunity to plan for all these different functions and improve the apparent deficiencies in the earlier Mughal forts. Additionally, the design of the Fort also catered to its links with the larger city of Shahjahanabad. These links were necessary for the realisation of the patrimonial-bureaucratic ideal of the Mughals. The Fort where the emperor stayed not only needed to personify his involvement in all aspects of public life but also to provide an economic mainstay for the city both as an employment centre as well as a market. Such a relationship called for a far greater interaction between the emperor and his subjects than that normally seen between most subjects and their rulers.

The layout of the city and Fort was therefore planned to highlight the symbolism of this relationship and enable the smooth functioning of its practical aspects. To reflect the emperor's dominant presence in all walks of life, the Fort in its sheer size (with a total length of 3,000 feet, a breadth of 1,800 feet, a height of 60 feet on the riverside and 75 feet on the other sides) was built with a view to dominate the cityscape.[4] Additionally, the presence of a 35-feet-deep moat around most of the Fort further enhanced the perception of its actual height. In a recognition of the fact that both the road and river were important modes of transport into the city, the eastern and western faces of the Fort were treated as impressive front facades. There was effectively no rear facade. At the level of overall city-planning, the links between the Fort and the city were present as impressive visual and spatial axes on which the formally designed public structures and spaces of the city—large mosques and important commercial and recreational areas—were positioned.

A progression of designed chowks of different sizes and functions were provided on these axes, both between the Fort and city as well as within the Fort. The two main designed axes of the city were the east-west Chandni Chowk and the north-south Faiz Bazaar. The former connected the western (or Lahori) gates of the Fort and the city, and the latter linked the southern (or Delhi) gates of the Fort and the city. The location of the Fort's principal gates on its western and southern walls is significant. These directions had direct links with two strategic routes. One of these was the Grand Trunk Road that connected Delhi to the traditional land invasion route in the northwest and the other was the road to Agra which led to the Gangetic plains, a rich source of agriculture and revenue.

These directions also had a symbolic importance. To the northwest was the Mughal capital of Lahore as well as the summer court of Kashmir, with the forts and gardens established by Akbar and Jahangir. To the west were the traditional overland routes to the dynasty's ancestral origins in Central Asia; Persia where Humayun had sought and found refuge and finally, Mecca, the home of the Islamic faith of the Mughals. The southern

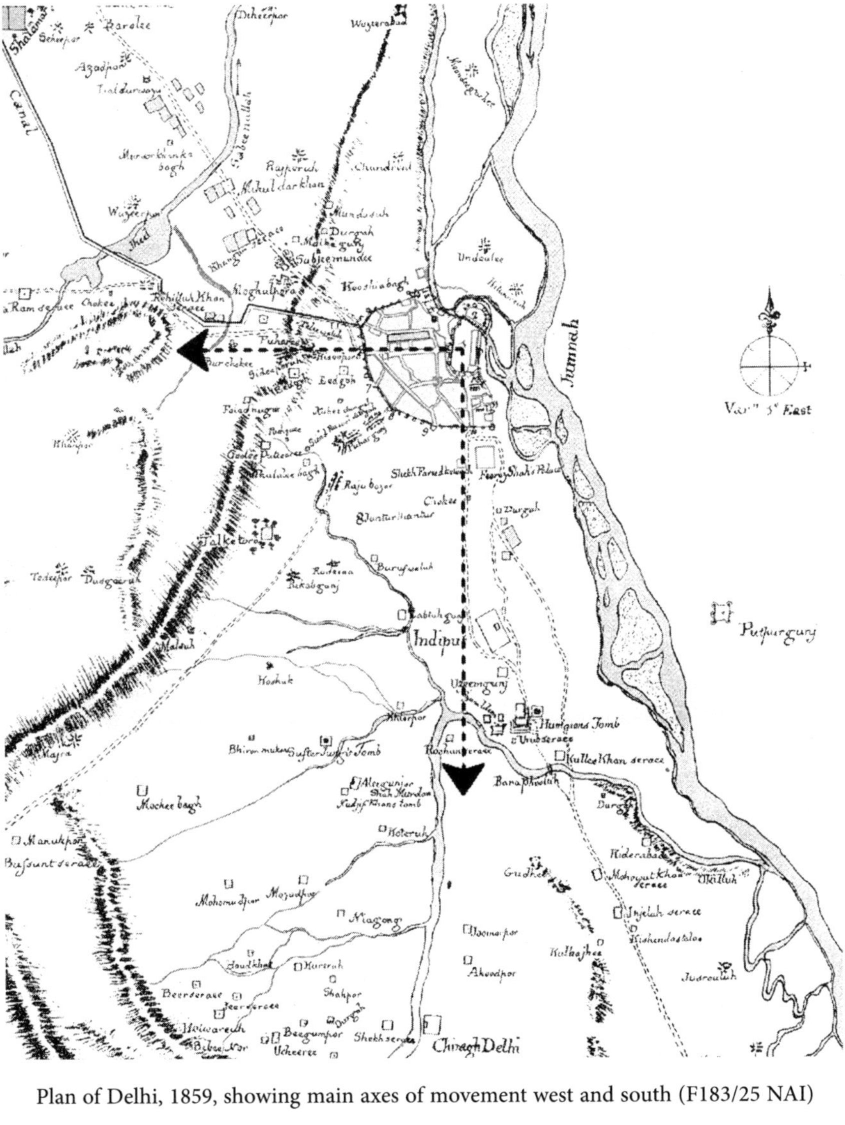

Plan of Delhi, 1859, showing main axes of movement west and south (F183/25 NAI)

direction in its turn led to the earlier cities of Delhi in which Akbar and Humayun had ruled; where Humayun was entombed and many Sufi saints enshrined. Further south was the erstwhile Mughal capital of Agra or Akbarabad, accredited as being 'the headquarters of the banners of glory',[5] where Babur had first established the Mughal standard and where later, Akbar had built a great city.

Apart from such symbolic implications, there were practical reasons for locating the main gates to the Fort on the western and southern sides. After bending towards the northeast, the Yamuna flowed virtually north-south in a straight line some distance to the east of the Aravallis. If the Fort and the city were to be located close to the western banks of the Yamuna (in the tradition of the earlier cities of Delhi), it meant that the eastern and northern sides across the Yamuna were excluded from any large urban development. Thus, the city could develop only on the southern and western edges of the Fort.

The series of chowks located on the south and west axes between the Fort and the city had their own hierarchy. They became progressively larger towards the Fort, finally terminating in the great royal squares at the junction of the Fort's Lahori and Delhi Gates with these axes. These royal squares were followed both in size and significance by the square, rectangular and octagonal chowks in front of (or around) the major mosques, such as those of the Jama Masjid, the Fatehpuri Masjid and the Akbarbadi Masjid.

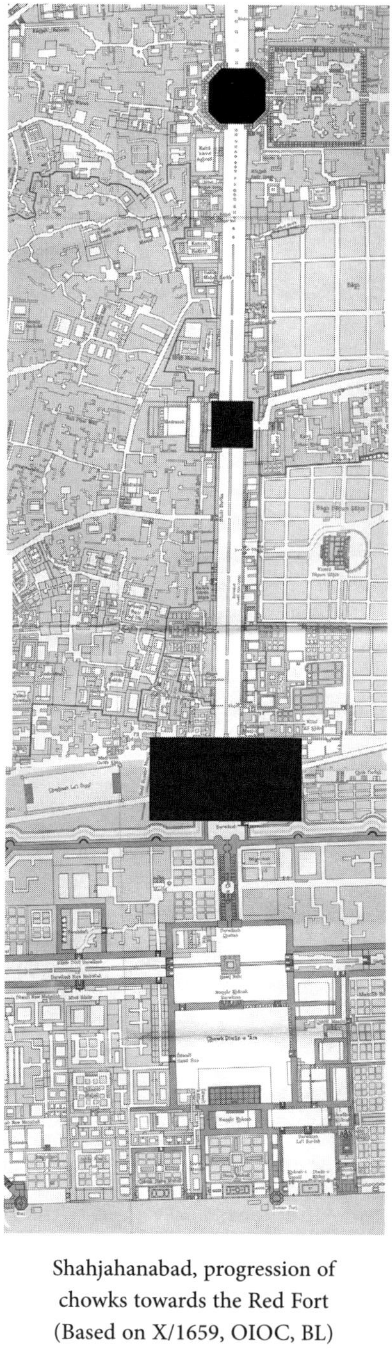

Shahjahanabad, progression of chowks towards the Red Fort (Based on X/1659, OIOC, BL)

Next in the hierarchy were the subsidiary courts positioned at important junctions in the main public streets, such as the chowks that punctuated the length of Lahori Bazar and Faiz Bazar, as well as the chowk midway in the street leading to Jama Masjid. Finally, there were the courts inside semi-public and semi-private areas, such as those within the Red Fort. Shah Jahan had already experimented with the provision of chowks as buffer spaces and appropriate preludes to the Fort at Agra in 1637. The motivation for these chowks is explained by the following passage from the *Shah Jahan Nama of Inayat Khan.*[6]

> Formerly, at Akbarabad, the area just in front of the fort was congested with various public buildings, offices and private dwellings, leaving no open space for a Forecourt (*jilau-khana*). As a result every morning and evening, when the nobles and all the officers of the state came to pay their respects, great inconvenience was caused to the public by the concourse of men and horses, especially on the days of 'Id and Nauroz, royal birthdays and other festivals, and during the occasions of a royal procession. In fact, due to the immense crowds that thronged together, the people's lives were constantly endangered.
>
> Therefore, at this time, on the return of the imperial standards from Daulatabad, His Majesty ordered that a spacious plaza which the natives of Hind call a *chauk,* be constructed in front of the fort gate, with a large bazar laid out in octagonal Baghdadi style, along each longer side of which there were to be cells and apartments, with several shops on each shorter side. Having laid the foundations at an auspicious moment, it was further commanded that on one side of the plaza, which would form a place of assembly for all the denizens of the world, a stately metropolitan mosque should be built at His Majesty's private expense.

In Shahjahanabad, Shah Jahan further improved upon this arrangement devised in Agra, by separating the courts of the Red Fort and Jama Masjid (which generated its own crowds as the principal mosque). In this, he was aided by having virtually a virgin site. Jama Masjid, thus, was positioned on a high rock outcrop, effectively utilising the opportunity afforded by this imposing site feature, which overrode any overwhelming preoccupation with symmetry. The requirements of religion and symmetrical aesthetics were addressed by locating the important Fatehpuri Masjid on the principal axis aligned with the centre of the Red Fort's western face.

Boundary walls, outer face
(Photo: Author, 1997)

Boundary walls, inner face
(Photo: Author, 1997)

Shah Jahan also instituted another important change in Shahjahanabad with reference to the architectural relationship established in Agra between the Fort and the Mosque. The distance between the Red Fort and the Fatehpuri Masjid was increased, turning it into the primary urban avenue. The plaza of the mosque, the bazaar, and the royal forecourts were, thus, separated.

The royal forecourts in front of the Fort were used by the rajahs and other vassals of the emperor to camp in during their weekly guard duty. Bernier observed that at break of day, the royal horses otherwise housed in a spacious stable were exercised here and the horses of those who had been newly received into the service were reviewed by the muster-master.[7] Important public and private structures and spaces surrounded these forecourts even in the later Mughal period, such as the house of *Malik Sabira*, the mosque of *Qazi Katire*, the rose garden, the royal stables and the vineyard.[8] The Lahori and Delhi Gates served as backdrops to these forecourts. These gates, and the bridges that led to them over the 70-feet-wide external moat, formally marked the beginning of the processional journey into the presence of the emperor. Such architectural elements

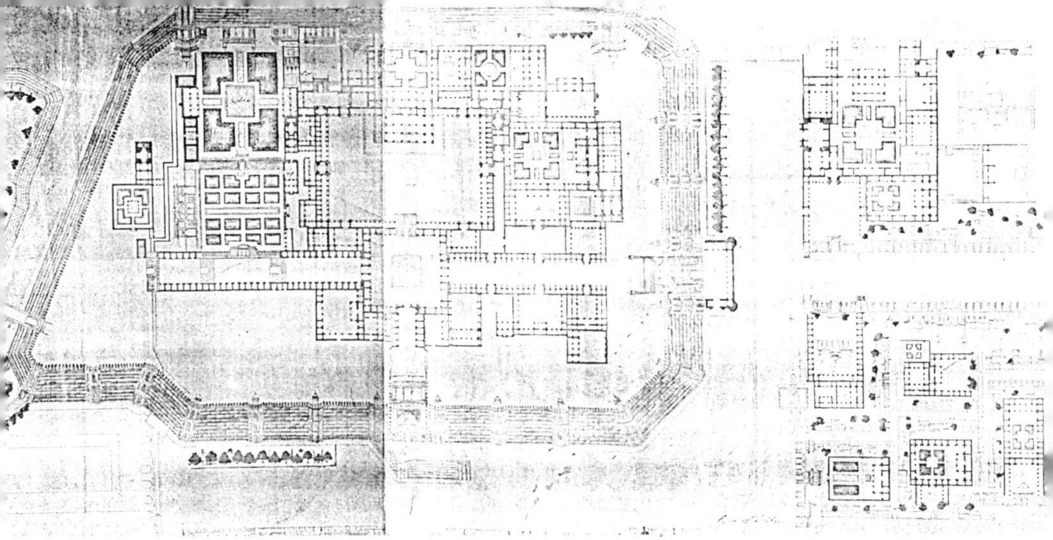

Plan: Red Fort, undated (3635, Agra, Vol. I/1914-15, ASI PL)

had both a spatial and symbolic importance in the Islamic religion, as is evident from the following extract by Laleh Bakhtiyar.

> Through initiation, one enters a gateway and sets out across a bridge. The gateway, in architecture, expresses movement through defined space. The implied sense of passage that the gateway brings is a necessary first step of the journey.
>
> The bridge symbolises the human being as mediator between heaven and earth, as container of both human and divine nature; and it relates to the role of mankind as the vice-regent of God on earth, responsible for preserving nature, and as the servant of God, acting at His will.[9]

The walls of the Fort functioned as high impenetrable barriers, punctured only by small apertures. From the inside of the Fort, the walls housed soldiers› quarters as well as continuous terraces for patrolling. The two public gates that punctuated these walls on the west and south were used by the imperial family on state visits to the city on festive occasions, or to places such as Jama Masjid, Humayun's Tomb, Dargah Nizamuddin, Fatehpuri Masjid, as well as for passage to and from the Fort by noblemen, craftsmen, soldiers, minor officials, visitors, merchants and courtiers. Such a large volume and variety of movement required some sort of system for it to function efficiently. Therefore, different weightage was given to the two gates—in their architecture as well as in their use.

Lahori Gate was planned as the ceremonial entrance for dignitaries and ambassadors. This gate faced west directly towards the Fatehpuri Masjid.

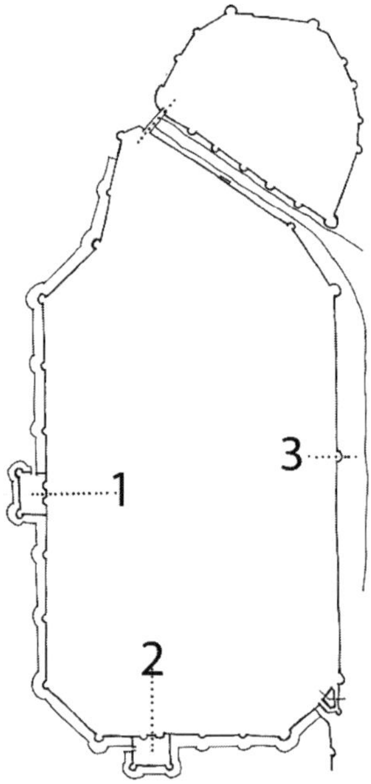

Position of the public gateways (1, 2) and the emperor's private entrance (3)
(Source: Author)

The axis of Shahjahanabad's principal avenue, the Lahori Bazaar (now known as Chandni Chowk), passed through Lahori Gate into the covered Chatta Bazaar, continuing through the Naqqar Khana to culminate in the Hall of Public Audience. The entrance route of Lahori Gate was, thus, designed to offer a direct view between the emperor's throne in the Hall of Public Audience and the city. Delhi Gate, facing southwards towards the city gate of the same name, was invested with a reduced ceremonial role in comparison. The axis of Faiz Bazaar, the second principal avenue of the city, continued into the Fort through this Gate and was mainly used by soldiers, attendants and craftspeople working in the Fort.

Though there were other gates into the Fort—the emperor's private entrance, the gate into Salimgarh, the wicket gate under the Rang Mahal, the water gate, the postern gate between Shah Burj and the Salimgarh bridge (probably used by the military)—they were meant for specific, sometimes secret, functions. Norms were laid down for their use, as for different parts of the Fort, some of which were designated solely for pedestrian use. Horse- or elephant-mounted visitors were allowed in till the Naqqar Khana forecourt. In other parts, entrance was reserved for imperial mounts. One day of each week was set aside for anyone to enter the Diwan-i-Am forecourt for redressal of their problems.[10]

The range of public spaces within the Fort was almost urban, but their relationship to each other was somewhat different from that in the city. In Shahjahanabad, certain areas were dominated by high-profile functionaries, but there was no real segregation between the rich and the poor. The houses of princes and noblemen and their dependants were located in virtually all parts of the city as well as in the suburbs. However, within the houses, the configuration of space and social relationships reproduced in miniature the relationship between the emperor's palace and the rest of the Fort. The houses of an entourage of dependants, including servants, artists and writers, were clustered around the house of their patron, whose name often came to designate the name of that locality. Francois Bernier, who wrote about the architecture and social practices of Aurangzeb's court, himself lived under the guardianship of one such nobleman, and though not a member of his household, had access to his presence and influence.

Conversely, the organisation within the Fort followed a system wherein its western and southern parts (those closer to the city) contained the more public functions and acted as a buffer zone between the city and the private areas of the Fort located in its eastern and northern parts. In keeping with the complex range of functions, there were gradations even within its public western and southern parts. At an overall level, a system of axes and geometrical proportions dictated the positions as well as sizes of the built and open spaces within the Fort. This becomes apparent if one undertakes a geometrical study of the Red Fort. Taking the Lahori Gate axis as the centre of the western face, the Fort's profile resolves itself into an unequal octagon or a *Mussaman (mutthaman) baghdadi* with its two long sides on the eastern and western sides and six small ones along the north and south. As shown by Ebba Koch in her drawing of the generating grids of the Fort, this octagon is derived from a rectangle with the proportions 10:6 (or 1.67:1), assuming each grid to be 82 metres, a multiple of the unit of the Shah Jahani *gaz* or *zira*,

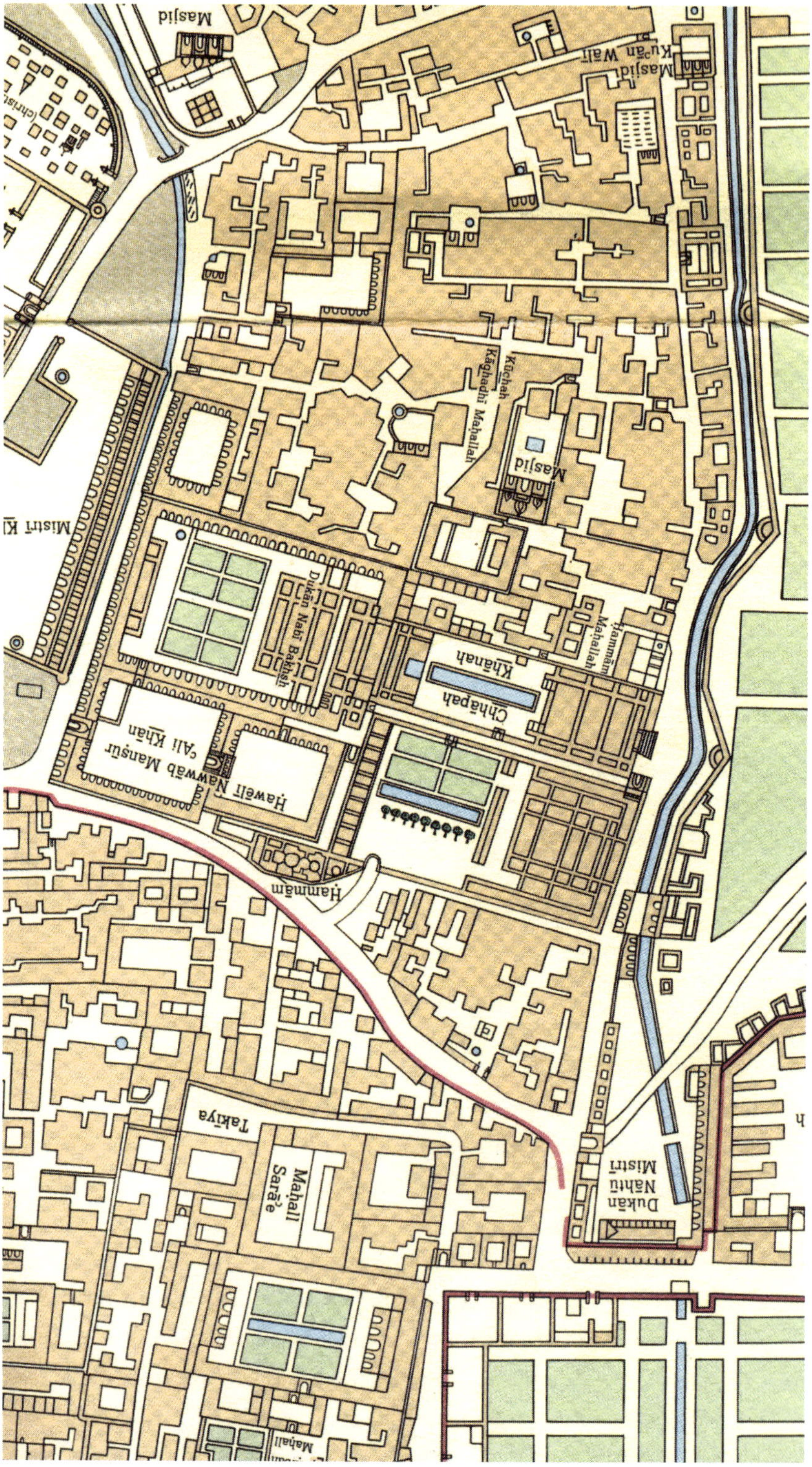

Shahjahanabad, spatial relationship between the houses of noblemen and their dependants (X/1659, OIOC, BL, trans: E. Ehlers. J. Malik, T. Krafft)

ascribed to be equivalent to .81–.82 metres. However, the equal division of the Fort based on its actual proportions, yields a measurement of 83.35 metres—an exact multiple of the value of the zira (.8335 metres) deduced by Irfan Habib.[11]

The idealised mussaman baghdadi underwent a deviation on site because of existing features—the Yamuna, the Salimgarh citadel and the disposition of the land. As discussed in the preceding sections, the riverbank had been chosen as the site of the Red Fort for climatic, aesthetic and city-planning reasons. The exact location of the Fort on this riverbank may well have been decided on the basis of proximity to Salimgarh. The strategic importance of Salimgarh, not generally considered by historians,[12] must certainly have been recognised by the Mughal emperors, who were great pragmatists despite their aesthetic and romantic inclinations. One can infer this from the sustained use of Salimgarh by successive Mughal emperors right from Humayun to Shah Jahan.

This inference is strengthened by studying the influence of Salimgarh on the plan-form of and the positioning of functions within the Red Fort, as well as by the subsequent use of the citadel by Shah Jahan. The walls of the Red Fort follow the profile of the mussaman baghdadi on the eastern side towards the river, and on the southern and western sides towards Shahjahanabad. However, a wedge of land is further added to the mussaman baghdadi towards the north, making the Fort walls parallel to Salimgarh. This was probably done to reduce vulnerable space between the two forts and provide a strategic defensive and offensive zone. That the area within the Fort adjacent to Salimgarh appears to have been inhabited by the resident Mughal military (as indicated in court histories and the presence of extant stables here), supports such a reasoning. The location of the military force would have controlled access into Salimgarh, which functioned as a restricted area with provision of entrances only from the river and the Red Fort. Salimgarh also functioned as a prison for important political rivals. It was here that Aurangzeb imprisoned Murad Baksh, his brother, and Sulaiman Shikoh, his nephew, before sending them on to the Gwalior Fort for permanent incarceration.[13]

Though Shah Jahan's passion for symmetry did not override a sensibility to site requirements, it is interesting to note that within the

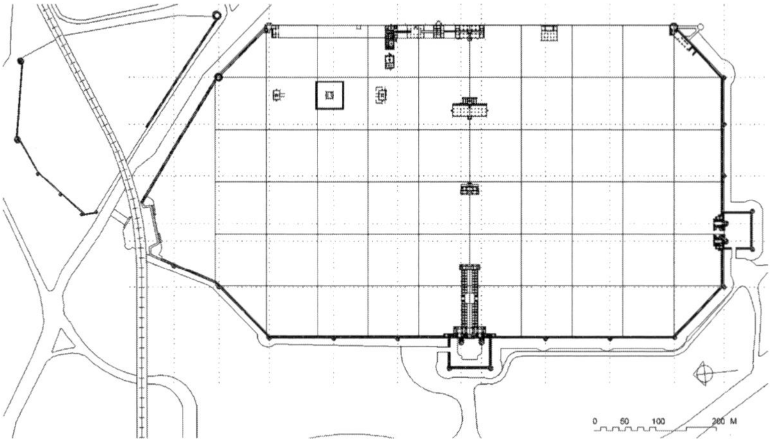

Planning grids: Each 100 imperial gaz (about 83.35 m)
(Drawing: N. Joshi, Author)

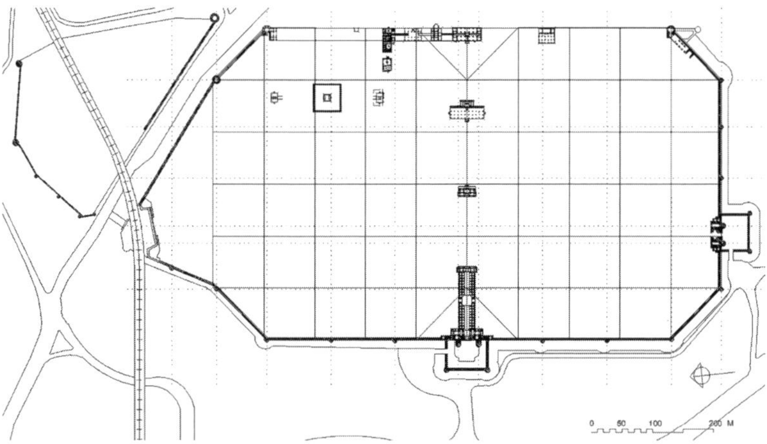

Planning grids: Subdivision into two equal octagons generating position of important buildings (Drawing: N. Joshi, Author)

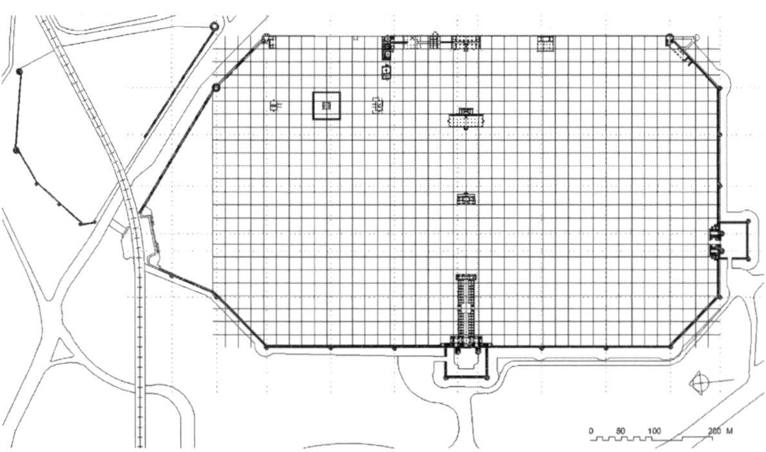

Planning grids: Further subdivision into grids generating dimensions of important buildings (Drawing: N. Joshi, Author)

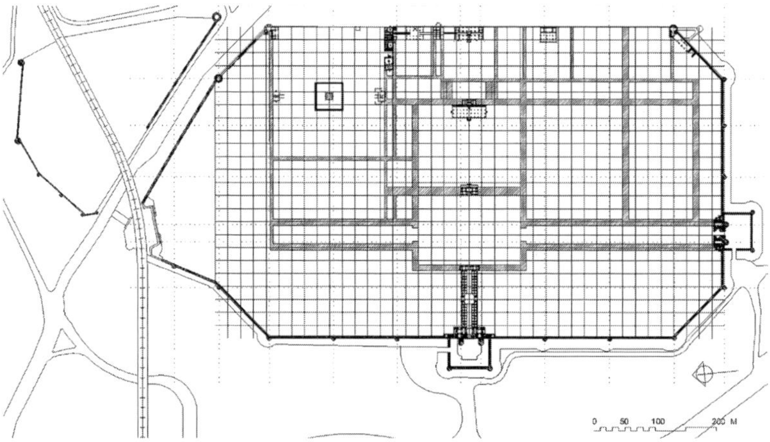

Derived locations and dimensions of original colonnades and courts (Drawing: N. Joshi, Author)

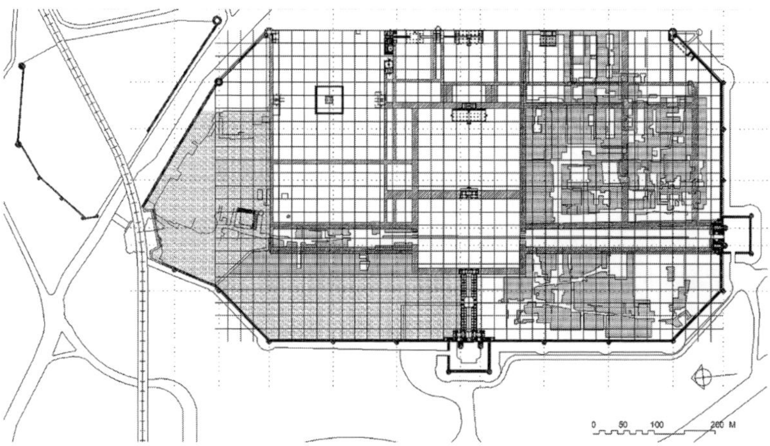

Built fabric of the Fort (mid-nineteenth century) superimposed on colonnades and generating grids (Drawing: N. Joshi, Author)

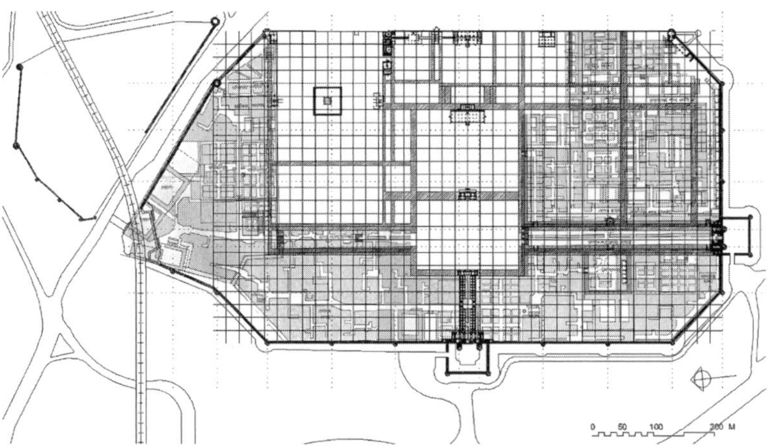

Built fabric of the Fort (late-nineteenth century) superimposed on colonnades and generating grids (Drawing: N. Joshi, Author)

Fort, the imperial private and public quarters were restricted within the boundaries of the generating rectangle for the mussaman baghdadi. On the northern end of this rectangle, to underline the limit of the imperial presence, a high wall separated the emperor's private gardens from the area beyond. This ingenious compromise ensured that the area of Shah Jahan's perception fitted within the symmetrical part of the Fort in keeping with the aesthetic and symbolic implications of that time, while also responding appropriately to existing built and natural features.

A geometrical exploration of the positions and dimensions of the extant parts of the Fort based on an analysis of aerial photographs together with older maps and plans was undertaken to investigate the relationship between the generating grids of the Fort, the bastions and important buildings within its mussaman baghdadi. This study revealed that the generating grids do not coincide with these buildings and bastions. Instead, there exists another system of axes—based on subdivisions of the generating grids—that lays out the positions of the bastions and links them back to the formal buildings, gardens and courts within the Fort. The proportions, locations and dimensions of built and open spaces that are no longer extant have been derived through this geometrical and spatial exploration, which naturally need to be further confirmed by archaeological investigations.

Visual and written depictions from the seventeenth and eighteenth centuries show that the west and south entrance-axes were part of the formal organisation of the Fort. They were clearly in the public domain. The areas immediately bordering them appear to have contained public utilities such as community gardens, mosques and workshop spaces. On moving away from the entrance-axes, these changed to semi-public and semi-private functions—living quarters, religious buildings and recreational spaces of the common people, soldiers and other dependants who resided in the southern and northern ends of the Fort's western sector.[14] The eastern part of the Fort was its most private area and was almost entirely occupied by the residences of the emperor and his family. The public entrance routes did not penetrate here. This location of the imperial pavilions, sited furthest from the city on the Fort's eastern face and closest to the cooling effects of the river, appears to be a logical response to the demands of privacy, climate and urban design.

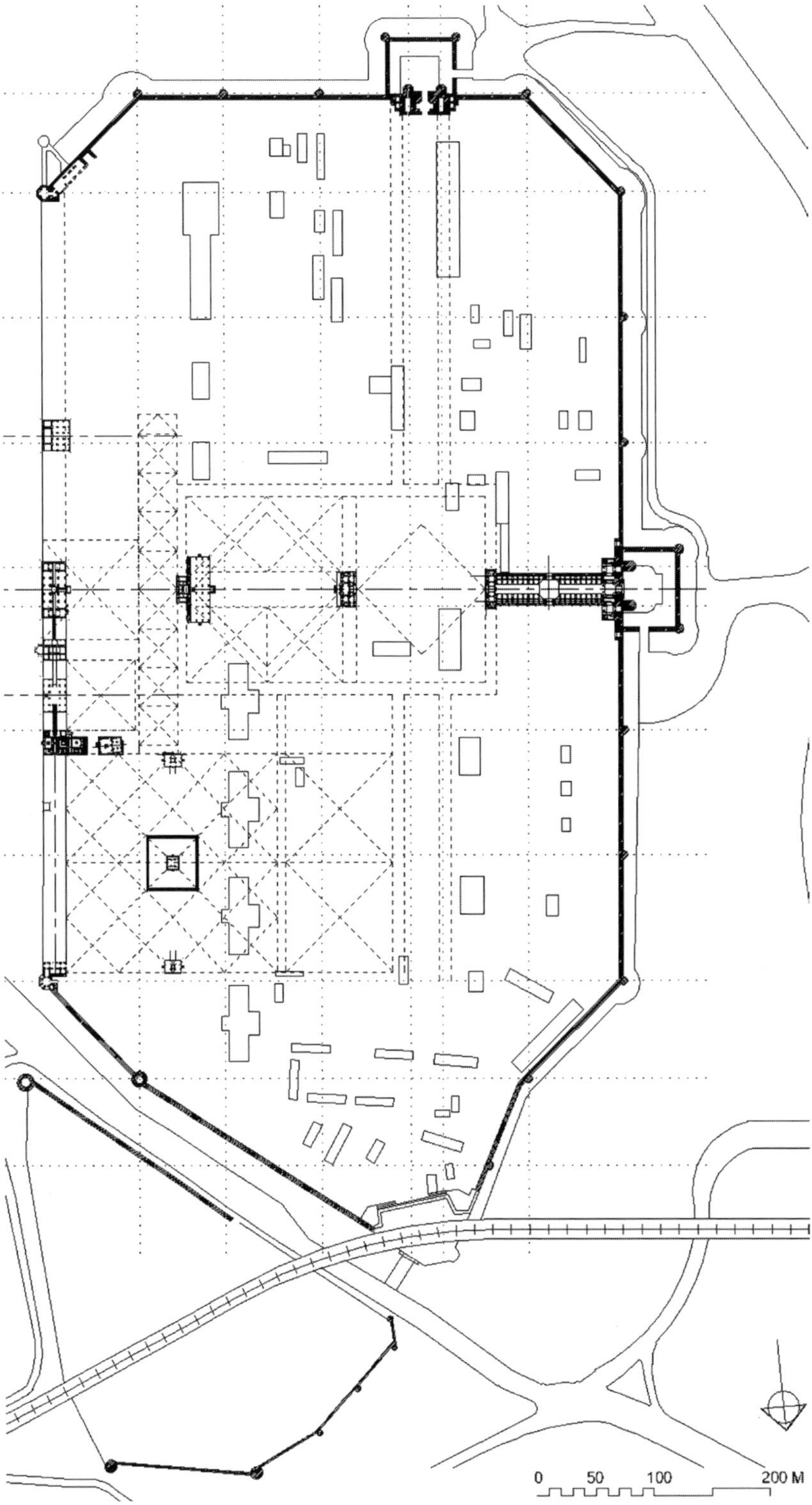

Geometrical exploration of the spaces within the Fort
(Drawing: N. Joshi, Author)

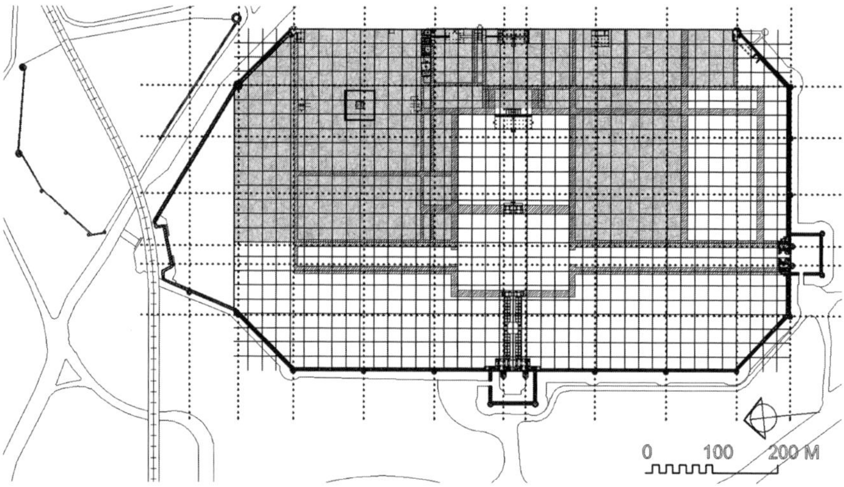

Private Imperial Domain (Drawing: N. Joshi, Author)

However, as discussed earlier, the proximity of these pavilions to the riverbank without a protective layer of peripheral walls increased their vulnerability. Additionally, the private gate below the Mussaman Burj, which offered a direct route into the Fort from the riverbank, was a weak point in the Fort's defences. The gate, which must undoubtedly have been well-guarded, gave access through a staircase to a long court next to the emperor's pavilions, from where further admittance was only possible through a system of sub-courts with just a few entrances that were further guarded. Despite such security measures, it is evident that the inner palace, though designed with many gradations of privacy and use, could have still been vulnerable to infiltration.

The extreme southern end of the inner palace was linked by a direct circulation route with Delhi Gate. The presence of a semi-public circulation-route indicates that the quarters in this part housed the less important members of the imperial household. The emperor's own quarters and those of his family were in the central section of the inner palace. They were connected to walled gardens towards the north, while the area beyond is believed to have been later occupied by some of the royal princes.

In Shah Jahan's reign, young princes were brought up in the seraglio while adult princes maintained independent establishments. This may be inferred from references in the court histories. The *Badshah Nama* of

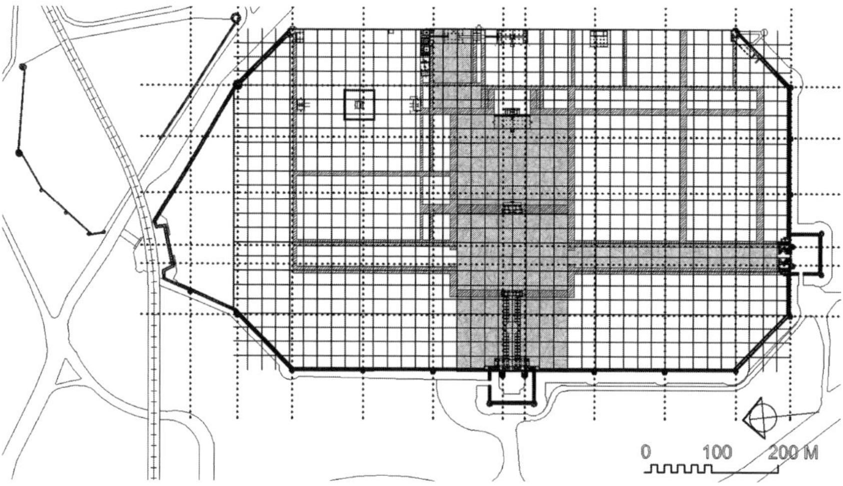

Public Imperial Domain (Drawing: N. Joshi, Author)

Lahori describes the wedding celebrations of Shah Jahan's sons (who were already married by the time the capital was shifted to Shahjahanabad) including the ritual of bringing them to the Agra Fort from their respective mansions.[15] Frequent references are also made to Dara Shikoh's mansion in Agra, which is recorded to have been inhabited by Shah Jahan for a few days in 1656 while the Agra Fort was being cleaned and readied for his stay. There is also a mention of Shah Jahan himself occupying a mansion in Agra on the banks of the Yamuna when he was a prince, which he later presented to Aurangzeb. In continuation of this precedence, it is likely that the adult princes would have stayed in mansions in Shahjahanabad. In fact, Dara Shikoh is recorded to have built himself a lavish mansion just outside the Red Fort along the river.[16]

On the basis of the foregoing analysis, the various spaces within the Fort may be broadly categorised as Public Imperial, Private Imperial, Public Common and Private Common domains. The layout and form of these domains, which overlapped in certain areas, appear to have been activated by different considerations. The basis for the Public Imperial domains was strict symmetry to reflect the might, order and perfection of the Mughal empire and increase the association with divinity. They were designed to be of a substantial size to accommodate the necessities of court ceremonies. On the other hand, the Private Imperial domains

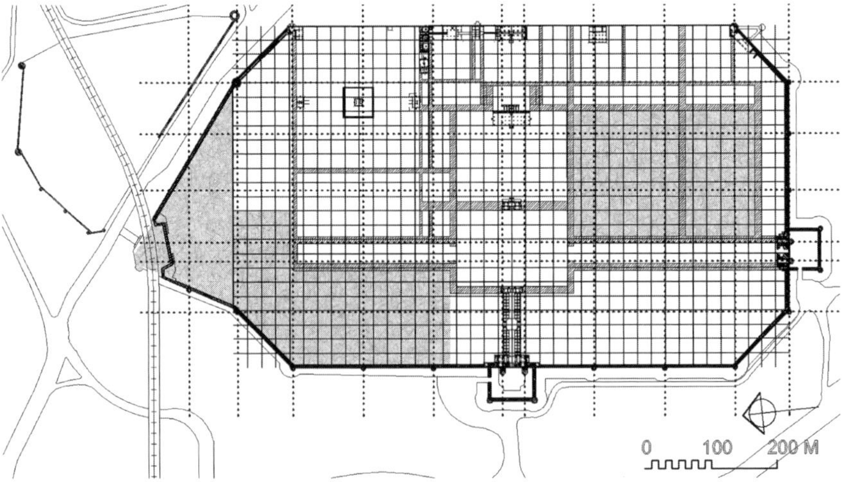

Private Common Domain (Drawing: N. Joshi, Author)

of the Fort were conceived and constructed to maximise privacy and the perception of free movement of its occupants, as well as to convey a formal opulence. To create a sense of balance between the Public and the Private Imperial domains, architectural devices such as scale, symmetry and shifting axes were used at their interface.

The built spaces in both the Public and Private Imperial domains consisted of pavilions, colonnades, cells, arcades, gateways, screens and walls. They were embellished by the use of rich construction materials and they enclosed and connected a succession of open spaces. These built structures also highlighted the geometry of courts and gardens and defined movement routes. In special cases, they were roofed by gold-plated copper domes and chattris to mark the areas specific to the emperor.

The open spaces, consisting of a series of courts, gardens and streets, connected and separated buildings from each other besides providing axes of movement and formal settings for the buildings. They also bestowed privacy on neighbouring activities. Water parterres, tanks, canals and channels bisected the length and breadth of these built and open spaces in both the Public Imperial as well as the Private domains. In some cases, as in the raised eastern terrace in the Private Imperial domain, the central Nahr-i-Bahist water channel provided an active link between built and open spaces.

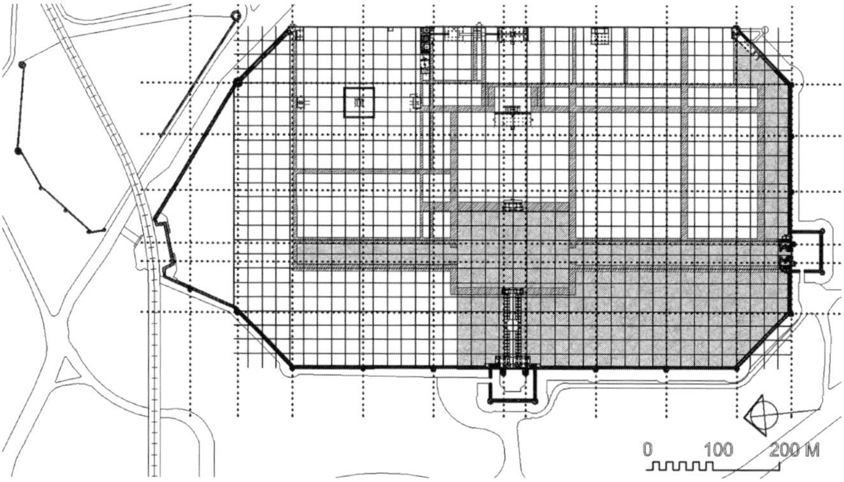

Public Common Domain (Drawing: N. Joshi, Author)

A major component in the appearance and use of the Fort—especially in the imperial domains—were the gardens that occupied more than half the area. These gardens were further refinements of the indigenous adaptations of the original Persian model. Tanks, channels, cascades and fountains within them employed water extensively for the purpose of cooling and rendered the pavilions liveable even in the extreme climate of Delhi. They were frequently eulogised, as in this description of Hayat Baksh, the imperial garden, where its relationship to the built structures is regarded 'as the soul is to the body, and the lamp to an assembly'.[17]

The Public and Private Common domains were less formal and contained some planned areas of commerce and recreation for the support sector of the Fort. Assumptions made on the basis of the representation of this area in maps, along with a study of the comparable built fabric in Shahjahanabad and the functioning of other imperial Mughal forts, suggest that the Public Common domain occupied the southern half of the Red Fort between the western walls, Bazaar Dihli Darwaza and Chatta Bazaar.

A large proportion of gardens appear to have existed south of Chatta Bazaar. This area is depicted with a predominantly open-built typology, and public and community facilities such as a *baradari*, artisans' workshops, artists' studios and a *Rath Khana* (the place housing the royal carriages).

Configuration of space in the Imperial Domain
(Panorama by Mazhar Ali Khan, Add.Or.4126, OIOC, BL)

Configuration of space in the Common Domain
(Panorama by Mazhar Ali Khan, Add.Or.4126, OIOC, BL)

The area north of Chatta Bazaar bordered by Rastah Salimgarh seems to have been the Private Common domain, where the resident soldiers and dependants in the Fort lived. This is borne out by written references as well as by the less formal built typology of this area, consisting of traditional narrow open streets bordered by a continuous built fabric.[18]

These Public and Private Common domains had their boundaries delineated in keeping with the larger plan of the Fort, with their basic circulation systems inserted. For the rest, they were allowed to develop organically. This part of the Fort most resembled the urban fabric of areas of Shahjahanabad inhabited by the common people. It consisted of a high density of built-up area interspersed with narrow, winding streets. The buildings in the Private Common domain of the Fort were constructed in masonry with ordinary plaster, as in the soldiers' quarters running behind the Fort walls or in the residences of the servants, while the buildings in the Public Common domain were generally faced in red sandstone.

These different territorial domains within the Fort were divided from each other through circulation routes. These routes consisted of several independent movement patterns used by the different inmates of the Fort. Based on the division of the Imperial and Common domains, there were strict norms for limiting the use of certain parts of the Fort to certain groups of people.[19] Thus, Bernier's accounts make no reference to Hayat Baksh or the emperor's living quarters and though he mentions the seraglio, he is unable to furnish descriptions based on his own experience.

Although conceptually, the emperor was lord of the entire Fort as indeed of the entire empire, the Public and Private Common domains of the Fort were almost invisible to him and the imperial family. Hence, they developed in ways not normally associated with palaces, and displayed a built structure thematically consistent with the city, even without much enforced control. The segregation of movement patterns and the consequent variety in living spaces was a reflection of the social order at that time—a combination of control and freedom. This combination was effective in balancing the disciplined ceremonial needs of public space and the freedom essential for personalising individual space.

The part of the Red Fort that the emperor used consisted of an area circumscribed by the sequence of his daily movements. An idea of his daily routine is obtained in the following description from Abdul Hamid

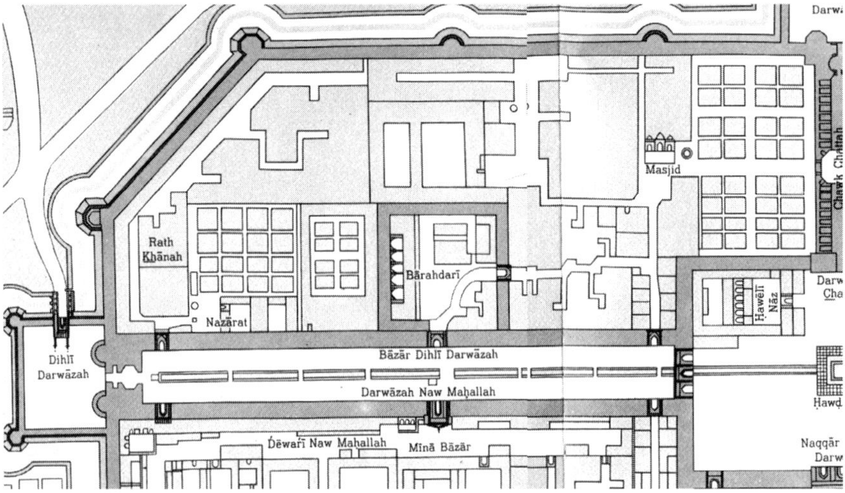

Bazaar Dihli Darwaza and adjacencies (X/1659, OIOC, BL, trans: E. Ehlers. J. Malik, T. Krafft)

Lahori's *Badshah Nama*.[20] Though an account of the emperor's activities at Agra, this schedule, with some minor differences, could well apply to the Fort at Shahjahanabad.

> About four *gharis* (two hours) before daybreak, while the stars are still visible in the night sky, His Majesty awakes from sleep and occupies himself in performing his ablutions and reciting the supererogatory prayers. With the advent of dawn, the prescribed morning prayers (*Fajr*) are accomplished ... whereupon His Majesty begins his regular daily schedule of activities.
>
> About two to three gharis after sunrise, the mercy-crowned monarch appears at the palace window which is called ... the *Jharoka-i-Darshan* ... His Majesty sits here often for two gharis, and sometimes more or less than this, according to the pressure of state affairs and the disposition of his temperament.
>
> From this noble place ... His Majesty goes to take his seat in the *Jharoka* balcony of the Hall of Public Audience (*Daulat-Khana-i-Khass-o-'Amm*) ... After four and sometimes five *gharis* according to the scarcity or quantity of requests and affairs of the high officers of the realm, His Majesty goes from this place to the Hall of Private Audience (*Daulat-Khana-i-Khass*) ... Four or five *gharis* of the day sometimes pass in these transactions ... After finishing

the transactions in the Hall of Private Audience, His Majesty goes to the Royal Tower (Shah Burj) … In this exalted abode of fortune His Majesty sits for two or three *gharis* and sometimes more in case of pressure of work.

… About midday His Majesty makes the auspicious seraglio the envy of Paradise by his august advent. As soon as the time of afternoon prayers (*Zuhr*) approaches, he performs these and other devotions, and takes his food … and sleeps a little at noon according to the sublime habit of the holy Prophet … Even in the sacred seraglio, His Majesty … devotes himself to granting requests of the poor … Everyday in this most sacred palace, a considerable amount of money and ornaments are expended for this charitable purpose.

After the evening prayers (*'Asr*), His Majesty sometimes returns to the *Jharoka* of the Hall of Public Audience, where the … public affairs are transacted according to the time available, and the mounting guards … then take charge of the arsenal. At this time, His Majesty then incurs the good fortune of saying his sunset prayers (*Maghrib*) in the Hall of Private Audience along with those dignitaries assembled here. After these prayers he is busy for about four or five *gharis* in the management of state affairs …. In this pleasant building, His Majesty sometimes listens to various melodies of minstrels and musicians …

After … these … His Majesty says his night prayers (*Isha*) and returns to the Royal Tower. If there is any work which has not been done in the Hall of Private Audience he summons the Prime Minister (*Diwan-i-A'la*) and the Lord Chancellor (*Mir Bakshi*) and disposes of it … and then retires to the auspicious seraglio for the night. There he amuses his mind for two or three *gharis* with hearing some delightful music, after which … he puts his wisdom-fostering head on the pillow of sleep.

So that His Majesty may fall into a sweet sleep, the eloquent members of the assembly read behind the veil works on biography and history, containing accounts of prophets and saints as well as events of the reigns of former kings and emperors … The whole time of his pious sleep is only about two watches (*pahar*).

Based on this record of the activities at Agra, the conjectural daily sequence of the emperor's movements in the Red Fort would probably have begun from his private apartments to the hammams for ablutions, passing by Diwan-i-Khas, silent and uninhabited at this time of the morning. His morning prayers would have been attended to in his private rooms, perhaps followed by a visit to Hayat Baksh.[21] The daily morning darshan ceremony from Mussaman Burj about an hour after sunrise was an important part of the day's events and there are records of it being strictly followed in the Red Fort. After this (according to Bernier, at noon, but according to Lahori, in the early morning), the emperor would proceed to the Diwan-i-Am for the daily assembly and matters of administration. After finishing his work here, he could, by way of continuous colonnades or through open courts and gardens, reach the Rang Mahal and Khas Mahal for rest and recreation or Diwan-i-Khas for discussions of matters of state and the framing of orders for implementation.

The use of the Shah Burj to discuss secret affairs after the Diwan-i-Khas visit appears unlikely in the case of the Red Fort. It is difficult to imagine the emperor's entourage of ministers going to Shah Burj beyond his hammam and gardens. The provision of private gardens would have been defeated if they were to be traversed daily by courtiers, however important they might have been. Courtiers such as Shah Jahan's father-in-law, Asaf Khan, titled Yaman-al-daulah or Right-hand of the State and appointed *Wakil* or First Lord of the Realm, were eminently trusted. But Asaf Khan, affectionately termed *ammu* or uncle, had died by the time that Shah Jahan moved into the Red Fort, and such a close familial relationship did not exist with the other officers. On the other hand, it may be that the Shah Burj, precisely because it was located in a private area away from the rest of the imperial pavilions, was particularly suitable for secret confabulations between Shah Jahan and his state advisers.

In his account of Aurangzeb's court, Bernier omits the morning visit to the Diwan-i-Khas. However, both Bernier and Lahori refer to the late afternoon and evening use of the Diwan-i-Khas for discussions, review of horse-training skills, ceremonial displays of standards and arms, and the occasional reception and entertainment of important guests. The omission by Bernier of the morning episode is understandable since, as a visitor and a foreigner, he would not have been admitted to the inner courts. The exception may have been made for more public and less exclusive functions—such as the afternoon use of the Diwan-i-Khas. Bernier, with his reputation of a skilled physician was allowed to witness

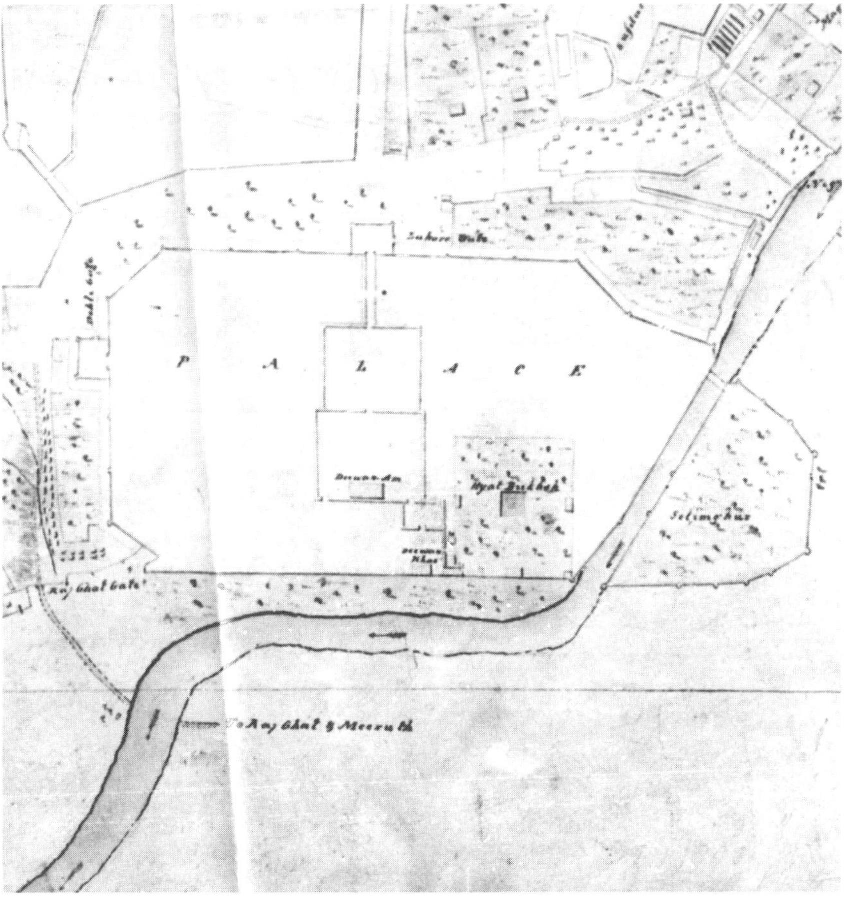

Partial representations of the Fort
(Plan of Delhi by Ensign Peter Lawtie, 1812, F 183/23 NAI)

this, but the majority of visitors would not have had this privilege. Most representations of the Fort illustrate this 'partial perception' that the different domains of the Fort gave rise to, some more obviously than the others.

On special occasions, the sequence of the emperor's activities and movement pattern was altered. Thus, during the Nauroz celebrations on 18 March 1628 CE, the afternoon deliberations in the Diwan-i-Khas at the Agra Fort seem to have been foregone. Though Shah Jahan ascended to the throne on 14 February 1628 CE, the first Nauroz after ascension was traditionally considered as coronation day, and there was a grand festival.

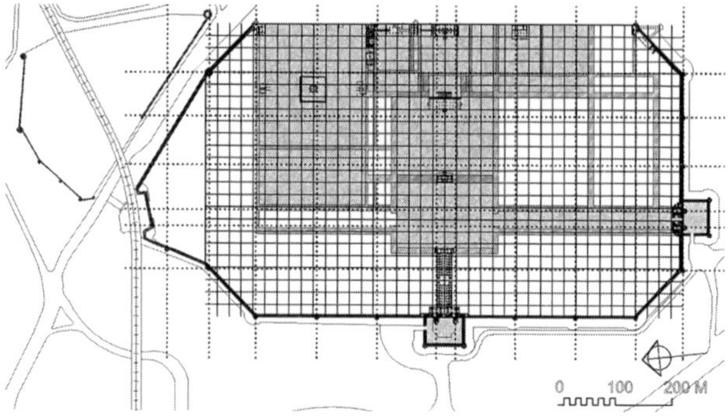

The Fort as it appeared to the emperor (Drawing: N. Joshi, Author)

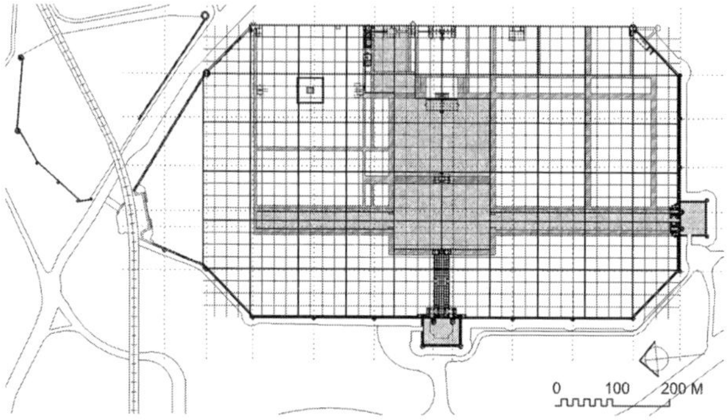

The Fort as it appeared to inmates of the imperial seraglio (Drawing: N. Joshi, Author)

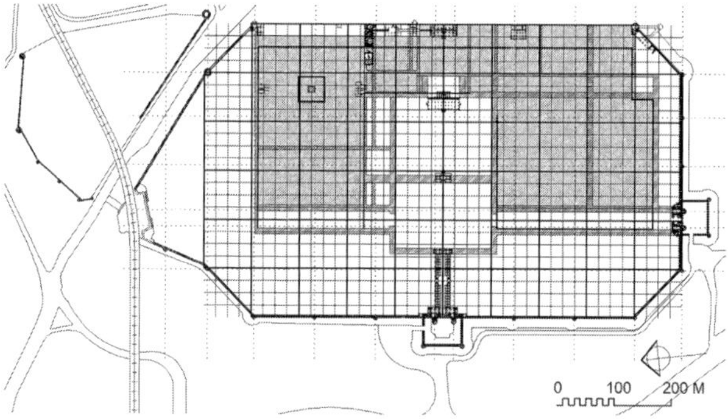

The Fort as it appeared to a nobleman (Drawing: N. Joshi, Author)

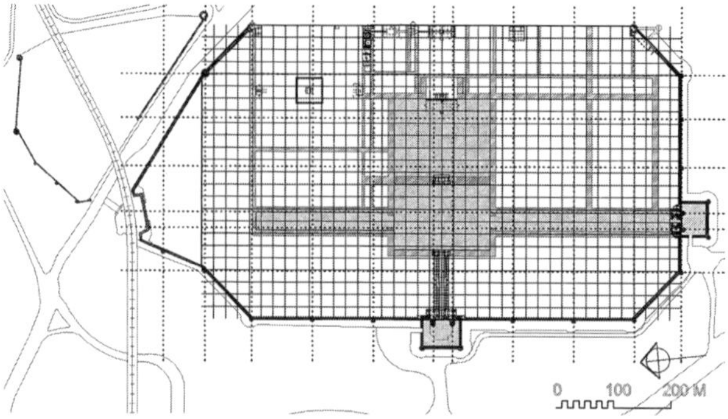

The Fort as it appeared to an inhabitant of the city (Drawing: N. Joshi, Author)

There are references to the emperor proceeding after the conclusion of the public function, straight to the royal seraglio for the mutual presentation of gifts such as gems and ornaments between him and his family.

In the account of the emperor's daily routine, there is generally no mention of the specific use of individual spaces like the Khas Mahal, the imperial gardens, or the many pavilions in the seraglio. It is difficult to ascertain the specific activity in each of these spaces. However, the description of the emperor's schedule leads one to believe that there would have been a flexible use of most courts and pavilions. Though some of these pavilions carried names designating their function, many of their functions were interchangeable. On occasion, the emperor used his sleeping chambers to transact business of a particularly delicate nature, or utilised the chambers designated for the reception of private guests for his personal recreation, or even for ceremonies preceding his sons' wedding festivities.

Just as the private inner palace was used for administrative matters and family celebrations in addition to the daily private activities of the emperor, similarly, the public administrative areas were sometimes used for private celebrations. Thus, the Diwan-i-Am pavilion, apart from its administrative court routine, was used for important public festivals on the emperor's birthday and on Nauroz. At times, the Diwan-i-Khas's function of an official chamber was supplemented by its private use to mark important personal and family events, such as the festivity preceding the marriage of Prince Dara Shikoh with Princess Nadira in the Agra Fort.

> On the first of Sha'ban this year 1042 (11 February 1633), the ceremony of *hina-bandi* was performed in the royal chambers of the Private Audience Hall (*Ghusal Khana*); and from the vast number of candles, torches and lanterns, the surface of the earth rivalled the starry expanse of heaven.[22]

It is probable that the Diwan-i-Khas at the Fort in Delhi would have been used for similar festivities as the one in Agra. Similarly, the Rang Mahal, in addition to its use as private apartments for relaxation, is also recorded to have been utilised for administrative matters concerning the women in the Fort. This multi-pronged use of a space, part of the

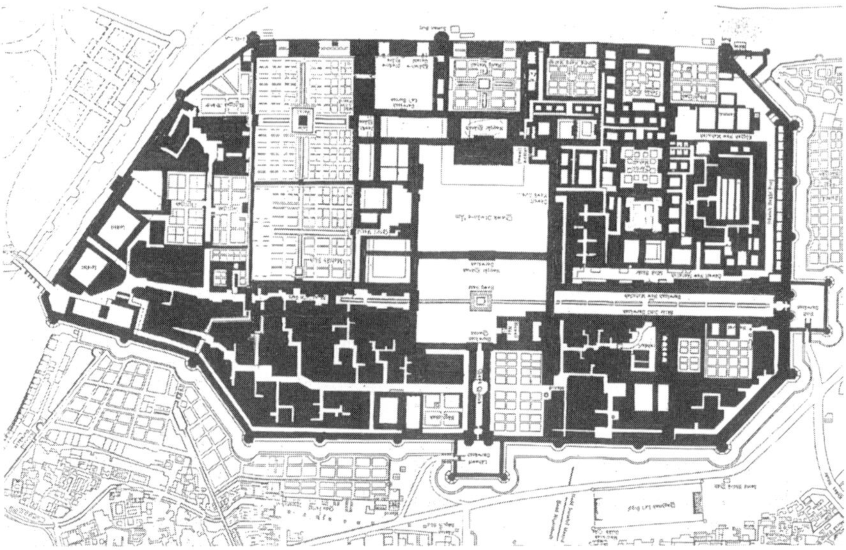

Built and open space configuration: covered areas shaded black
(Drawing: Author)

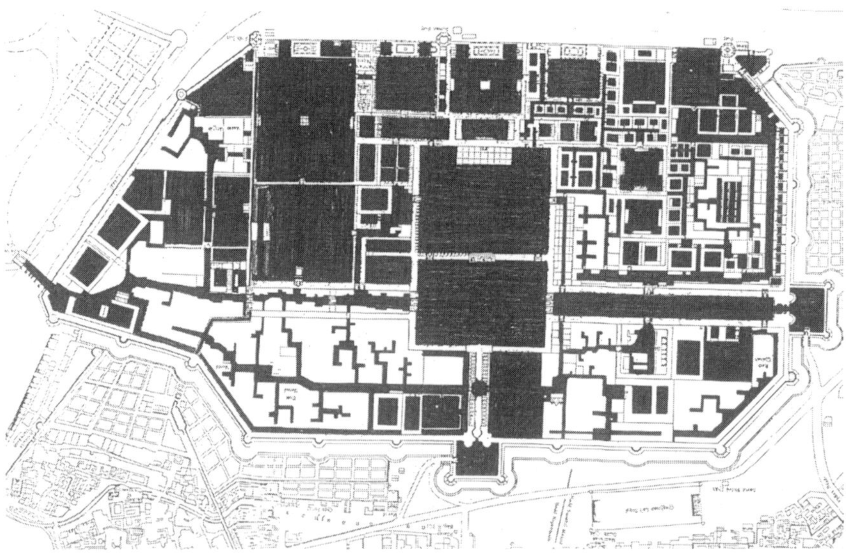

Built and open space configuration: open areas shaded black
(Drawing: Author)

contemporary way of life when the Fort was built, was made possible both by the planning and the design of the Imperial domains. To increase their efficiency and flexible use, built and open spaces were designed with

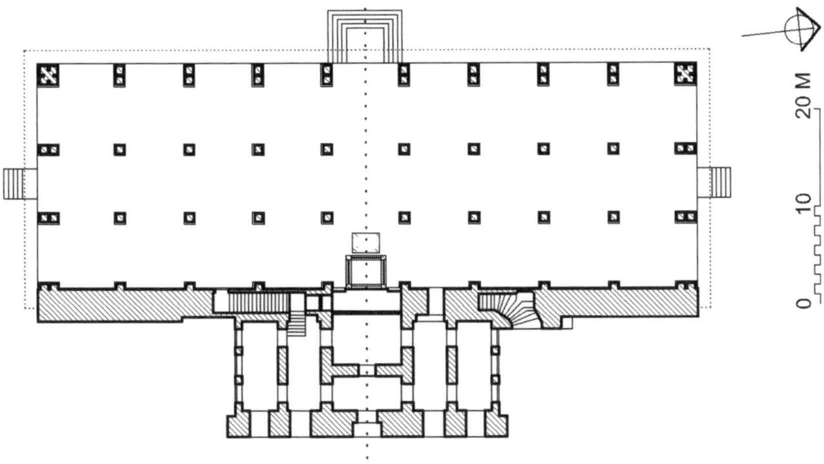

Plan: Diwan-i-Am
(Drawing: N. Joshi, D. Cherian, Author)

minimum extraneous and restricted elements. Instead of separate dining rooms, living rooms, bedrooms or entertainment rooms, most buildings within the Red Fort were designed as pavilions containing screened walls on at least one or more sides. Pavilions were appropriate to the mode of life in the context of the climate of the region, which required living quarters to have a large number of openings for letting in views or fresh breezes.

The current dictionary definitions of pavilion range from 'a large and luxurious tent' to 'a light building for players and spectators of a game' to 'an ornamental and showy building for pleasure purposes'. Despite this range of meanings, the common aspect of a pavilion still seems to be a building of some delicacy of material or detailing, with the principal objective of viewing a natural or man-made event. In the region and time period under discussion, the basic pavilion type was essentially a structure open on all sides, supported on a system of pillars, with an additional symbolic meaning arising from the idea of paradise as a garden in Islamic philosophy. The pavilions in the Fort employed architectural features such as double roofs and screens that were climatically and functionally suitable for informal secluded outdoor living.

The theme of a basic pavilion was extended depending on the function of the building, its location in the Fort, its position relative to the river and the necessary climatic response to the above factors. Each pavilion was preceded by one or more forecourts, with different degrees of privacy. These forecourts functioned as semi-public spaces in the Imperial Private domain, almost like the front gardens of houses in present times. Within the forecourts, areas of greater or lesser privacy depended on the location of movement paths taken by the attendants, and the connections of forecourts to adjoining pavilions. In contrast, the raised courts adjoining the imperial pavilions on the terrace were almost completely private and protected from view through screened walls, awnings and curtains.

These imperial pavilions of the Red Fort were designed as flexible stone tents liberally clothed by awnings and equipped with water channels and fountains. They were generally single-storeyed to maintain an appropriate sense of scale within the space available in the Fort. Most had efficient rectangular proportions in their plan-form, oriented such that their longer sides were aligned along the primary views on the east and west. This orientation had some undesirable climatic implications since it led to a greater surface area being exposed to the sun's rays, and therefore to increased heat intake in the summers. This was sought to be

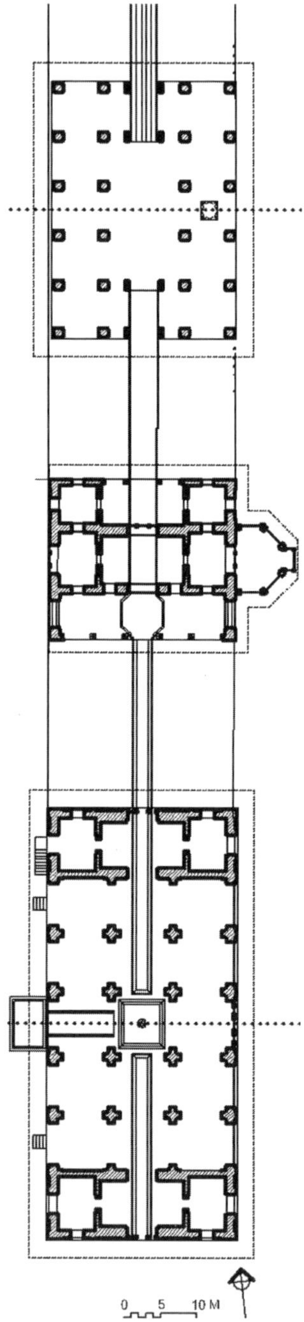

Plan: Rang Mahal, Khas Mahal, Diwan-i-Khas (Drawing: N. Joshi, D. Cherian, Author)

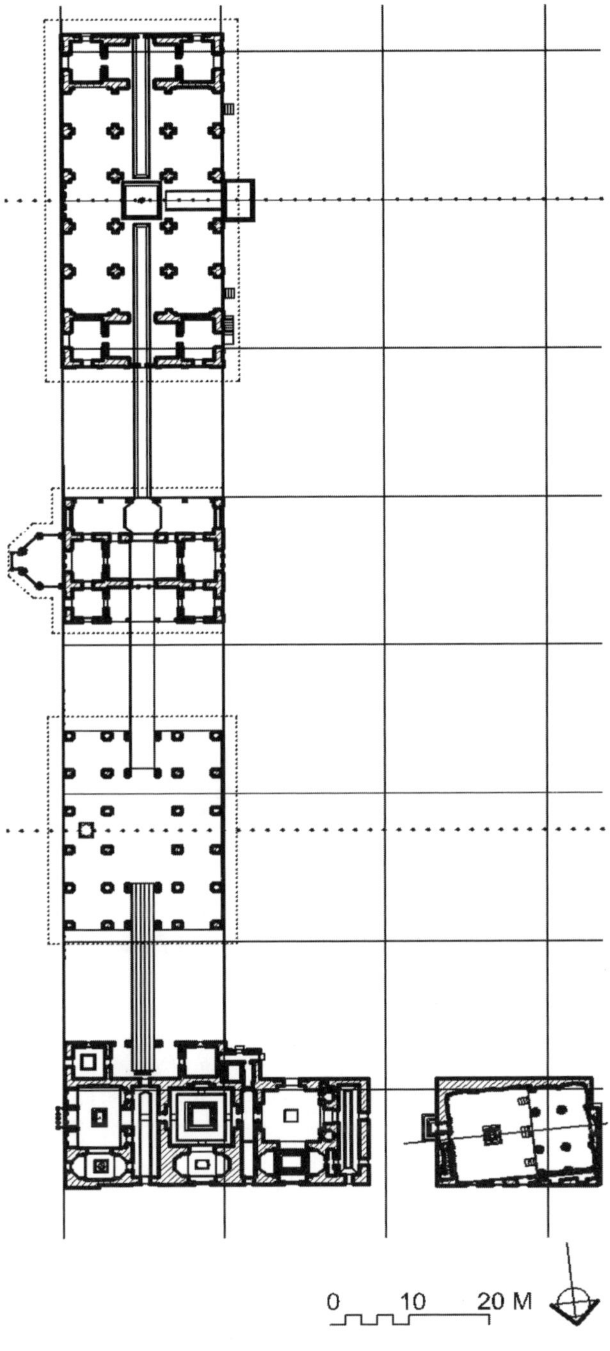

Disposition of imperial pavilions on the Fort's north-south axis
(Drawing: N. Joshi, Author)

Use of awnings to extend the use of space
(Drawing by a Lucknow artist, 1780-90 CE, Add.Or.948, OIOC, BL)

reduced by an extensive use of awnings, screens and water features. In cases where the function of viewing was secondary to privacy—as in the Khas Mahal—the pavilions were oriented with their longer sides on the north and south, and just a few openings on the west face, made opaque in deference to climatic considerations.

Shamianas (tents) and *kanats* (awnings) also performed a spatial function by extending the covered area of the pavilions into courts and

Imperial Hammam, western chamber (Photo: Author, 1997)

Moti Masjid, arcades (Photo: Author, 1997)

Shah Burj, ceiling of inner chamber (Photo: Author, 2000)

gardens to give larger living areas. Extant stone rings under the cornices of many pavilions in the Fort are evidence of this provision for awnings. Poetic metaphors contain many references to these extensions of built space, revealing their importance in the Mughal way of life. For instance, the celebrations on Akbar's birth are recorded thus by Abul Fazl—'They spread the carpet of joy under the canopy of chastity and the curtain of honour.'[23] This extension of space was especially useful on festive occasions, when many more people had to be accommodated. One such occasion was the marriage of Dara Shikoh, when the terrace in front of the Diwan-i-Khas in the Agra Fort was covered by a tented canopy next to the pavilion's awnings. Carpets were hung on screens and railings, incense held aloft by attendants and courtiers and women with *diyas* decorated the terrace and the court below.[24]

There is specific mention in Kambo's court history of an awning that was specially commissioned from the imperial workshops in Ahmedabad for use in the inauguration ceremonies of the Red Fort. Tavernier also describes how awnings of red velvet embroidered with gold were used to cover the public courts of the Red Fort for the festivities marking the birthday of Emperor Aurangzeb.[25]

These pavilions could be subdivided into smaller sections or transformed into more private spaces, by hanging carpets and curtains within and around them. Within the pavilions, the concept of furniture was almost nonexistent. The absence of furniture implied that the intrinsic properties of a space—proportions, detailing and decoration—were the predominant interior design themes. Precious stones were inlaid in delicate designs on the marble floor and dadoes, and walls and ceilings were plastered and painted in ornate motifs such that their individual and overall patterns formed an integrated composition. Light, an essential element in the fashioning and perception of space, was especially important to the aesthetically rigorous Shah Jahan. The concept of light also had additional religious overtones, for the Mughals, whose religion explicitly said,

> God is the Light of the heavens and the earth;
> the likeness of His Light is as a niche
> wherein is a lamp
> (the lamp in a glass,

The Nahr-i-Bahist Channel, Hammam, Red Fort (Photo: Author, 2000)

the glass as it were a glittering star)
Kindled from a Blessed Tree,
an olive that is neither of the east nor of the west
whose oil well nigh would shine, even if no Fire touched it;
Light upon Light;
(God guides to His Light whom He will).[26]

Low cushions and carpets allowed the full appreciation of these compositions and spatial properties of light, volume and proportions, as in the 'Hall of Public Audience, which is of extreme beauty and purity, with carpets on its floor and covered by a portico for protection from the sun, and enclosed on three sides by a balustrade.'[27] This multi-functional use of space is still a feature of traditional Indian houses (though the qualities of proportion and decoration have steadily declined). Archaeological remnants of houses of the Indus-Saraswati civilisation, point to the possibility of such a spatial use even as far back as more than 4,000 years ago.

In the Red Fort, such multiple use was not limited to the imperial pavilions. At an overall level, recreational spaces were designed to have a useful function, even as functional spaces had a decorative aspect. Paved courts were used as assembly spaces or as the setting for court ceremonial, and bazaar avenues were places of both utility and beauty. They contained water bodies such as tanks and canals, as in the Naqqar Khana forecourt and Bazaar Delhi Darwaza. In a similar way, utilitarian gardens, such as those beyond Chatta Bazaar adjacent to the Fort's boundary walls, incorporated a formal decorative function that celebrated aspects of nature.

The primarily decorative gardens, stretching from the north to the south end of the eastern part of the Fort, were of two kinds. The first was where the garden functioned as a forecourt to a residential imperial pavilion. Here, despite a symbiotic relationship, the buildings were predominant both in scale and function to the garden, which formed a prelude to them. The Rang Mahal garden, the Mumtaz Mahal garden and the smaller gardens between the seraglio buildings, were examples of this garden type. The second kind was where the garden was an independent space, inside which the pavilions functioned as ancillary features to highlight the geometry of the garden. Such were the principal gardens of the Fort—the Hayat Baksh and Mehtab Bagh. These occupied a huge area between the eastern terrace, running westwards from Shah Burj and the imperial Hammams until the line of the canal flowing from the Delhi Gate. These gardens also appear to have contained fruit trees. Thus, despite their primary recreational use, they evidently had a more practical function.[28]

Representations of these gardens indicate that trees were planted such that they flanked the central pathways. The small size of the trees and their plantation on sunken beds, combined with the device of raising the pavilions on a plinth, allowed for the provision of shaded walks in the garden without any interruption of views. Such large gardens were also seen beyond the moat outside the Fort. Even in Aurangzeb's reign,

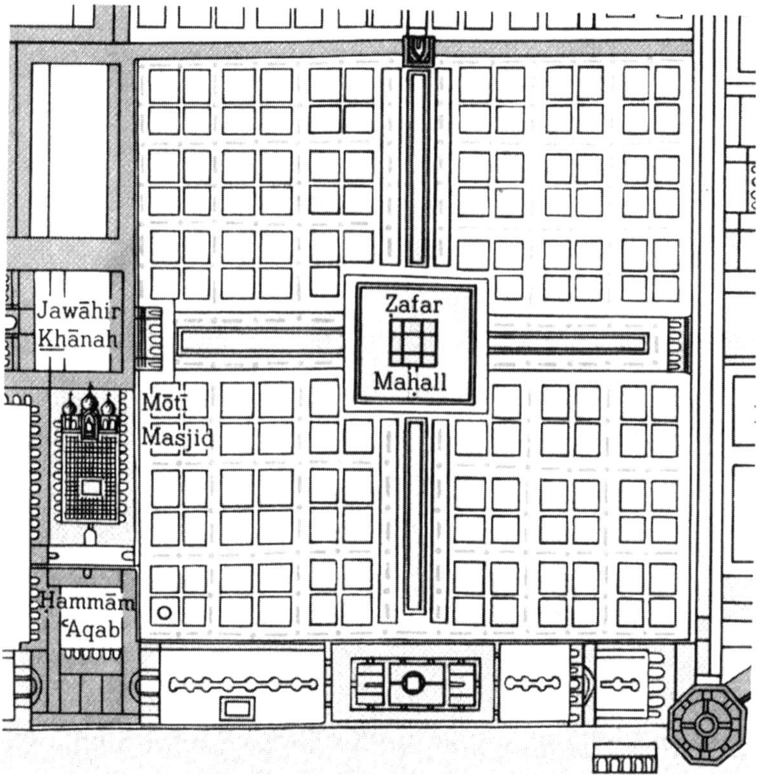

Charbagh as an independent space (detail of X/1659, OIOC, BL, trans. map)

Bernier noted that 'adjoining the ditch is a large garden, filled at all times with flowers and green shrubs, which contrasted with the stupendous red walls, produce a beautiful effect'.[29]

The detailing of the garden divided available space into a series of small definable units such as arched niches on the boundary walls, regular planted bays of flower beds, and arches in multiple planes within the pavilions. This resulted in an increased perception of the overall size of the gardens. These gardens had limited levels and terraces, resulting from the land profile within the Fort, and required well-worked out systems of water irrigation and circulation. It is not entirely clear how the water supply for the vast area of the Fort functioned. That a considerable amount of water was required is clear from attempts by the ASI under the British to revive the cascades and fountains in some channels and tanks within the Fort during the coronation festivities of 1911.[30] It is remarkable that while this effort required continuous pumping for two weeks, more than 250 years before this event, the running of a far greater number of water features distributed across the length and width of the Fort was achieved on a daily basis.

It is possible that the ingenious water system of the Mughals was achieved by effective use of the principle of gravity with perfectly worked-out, almost imperceptible changes of ground levels. This is a refinement of the irrigation method followed even today in many rural areas of India, where raised pathways (*kyaris*) are used to separate planted beds at lower levels. These are bordered by a circuit of channels from which water irrigates one or more groups of kyaris. The source of water is generally a well from which water is drawn out with the help of an oxen or a buffalo, or more commonly today, through mechanised pumps.[31] Thus, the Mughals incorporated a proven efficient system of irrigation and extended it as a decorative feature.

Most of the water sources in the Fort, as seen from older maps and some extant features, seem to be positioned in the northern portion of its eastern and western sectors. The general direction of flow for surface water and groundwater would have, thus, been either southwards in keeping with the flow of the river, or directly east into it. Records of the remains of the *rehant* or water-wheel system within Shah Burj—the northern-most building of the Red Fort's east face—lead to an inference that water from the river was lifted up here. In Mughal forts, generally a system of water circulation was organised such that it was stored in a cistern at the point it entered the fort-complex, and then directed into pipes through levers and other controls to direct its flow. At the Agra Fort, extant structures indicate that water was stored in supply tanks after being lifted up. These, as recorded by R. Nath, were provided with three series of pipe mouths, each with nine inlets.[32] Specific names and uses of separate pipes—for big and small baths, for tanks, canals, and passages—were marked on the tank face from which they flowed outwards.

No traces of these remain at the Red Fort, since the part of Shah Burj where they would have been located does not exist, probably destroyed during the British occupation of the Fort. It is possible that the mechanism for lifting up water here may have been similar to the one used at Jama Masjid. The machinery in the wells of the Masjid included two large Persian wheels supported by heavy beams fixed in the walls of the building which surrounded the well. The records of the officiating executive engineer in 1830 indicate that these helped raise the water of the well to the level of the terrace around the domes of Jama Masjid.[33]

Thus, it seems likely that within the Red Fort, water would have flowed from a storage tank with designated pipe inlets and outlets through copper pipes into the pavilion attached to the Shah Burj, down a decorated chaddar on its south face and further into the Nahr-i-Bahist canal on the terrace. The water in the canal, after rising up as fountains at intervals, would have continued through the pavilions into Hayat Baksh. It would then have entered the Hammams, the emperor's private chambers, and the imperial seraglio, to finally collect in a baoli in the Asad Burj. Here, it was probably used as a watering hole for animals, after which it was allowed to flow back into the river. Since the Yamuna also flowed southwards,[34] the direction of currents would have ensured that this used water would not flow back towards Shah Burj and into the Fort.

The Nahr-i-Bahist also ran through a pavilion termed Moti Mahal which, as shown in old maps, is positioned on the eastern terrace as the climax of one of the central axes of Hayat Baksh. The rest of the terrace that the Nahr-i-Bahist passed through before entering the Hammams appears open to sky. A puzzling aspect of this arrangement is that in such a dusty climate as Delhi's, the water in the Hammams and the private rooms of the emperor was allowed to first flow uncovered. An explanation for this may be that the trees, flowers and plantation both within the gardens and around the Fort produced a micro-climate that ensured reduced levels of dust. It is also probable that at the point at which these channels entered the pavilions or Hammams, a system of filtration removed any adhering particles and purified the water before it was heated and cooled for bathing. Be that as it may, it seems that this water was basically used for cooling and decorating the private chambers of the inner palace, and the emperor's drinking water requirements were met by other means.

Drinking water for imperial use was generally stored in copper or earthen pots and cooled by the use of saltpetre. While Akbar is believed to have only used *Gangajal*, the water of the river Ganga, whether in court or on expedition, Shah Jahan is reputed to have used Yamuna water for drinking.[35] It is said that when he was besieged in the Agra Fort by Aurangzeb during the war of succession, the water supply from the river was cut off. For three days, Shah Jahan and his garrison held out in the height of summer without drinking the water from the wells in the Fort—which had become brackish because of disuse—before surrendering.

In some maps, another channel of water (termed the *Nahr Shutur Gola* in the OIOC map) is shown as entering the Red Fort close to Salimgarh Gate. This was an offshoot from the canal that flowed parallel to the Chandni Chowk axis through the gardens of the city, and was probably used for irrigation or for the common domains in the Fort, since it is unlikely that the emperor would have deigned to use the water that had flowed through a fairly dense area of the city. The Nahr Shutur Gola divided into two parts within the Fort, close to the octagonal baoli. One of these branches ran southwards as a channel in the middle of the streets connecting the Delhi and Salimgarh Gates—*Rastah Salimgarh* and *Rastah Dihli Darwaza*. The other branch ran eastwards on the northern edge of Mehtab Bagh and Hayat Baksh—possibly on the raised boundary wall—and may have been used for their water features and for the water basin in Moti Masjid.

A third source of water in the Fort, an extant octagonal well, appears to be of Afghan origin. This well, located in the northwestern part of the Fort, is depicted in the OIOC map with steps leading down to it on two sides. Its location indicates that it may have been used for watering the gardens. Another well, located in the Hayat Baksh, appears to be a later insertion, since it is recorded to contain an inscription ascribing it to Bahadur Shah Zafar, the last Mughal ruler.[36]

Excavations by the ASI in the beginning of the twentieth century have revealed that the channels and canals in the gardens were generally shallow, with holes in the sides connected to earthen pipes. The overflow from the channels would have percolated back into the earth and was no doubt used for irrigating the flower beds and fruit trees, to finally flow back in the river. In later excavations, the discovery of traces of Mughal drainage systems as in the '[t]renching [which] revealed an underground drain leading to a doorway in the outer wall of the Fort', points to such a possibility.[37] The moat around the Fort is described as being full of fish in clear water. This suggests that the moat was connected to the river in

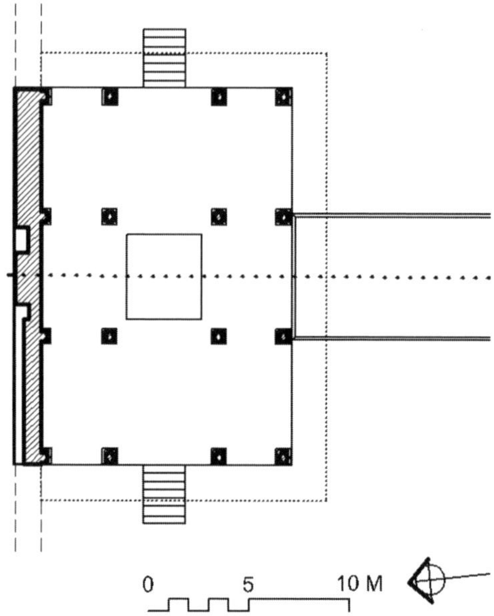

Plan: Sawan
(Drawing: N. Joshi, D. Cherian, Author)

a continuous circulation system, taking in water from the northern end and emitting it at the southern end.

The Fort would also have needed an effective system for the disposal of sewage generated by the many people staying within it. Since large portions of its residential component have been completely destroyed, there is no way of ascertaining these arrangements, apart from further archaeological excavations. Descriptions of houses in the city are also reticent on this subject. The researches of Ebba Koch[38] and R. Nath[39] show that there was a system of cubicles with Indian latrines in the Mughal seraglio. A similar arrangement is seen in contemporary palaces of other dynasties of this period, as in the sixteenth-century Raja Mahal of the Bundella Rajputs in Orchha. Excavations by the ASI at Fatehpur Sikri have also revealed that every large house, particularly those of the nobles, had at least one set of dry latrines segregated for males, females and children. These were linked with a waste water tank and then a soak pit.

It is not clear which part of the imperial pavilions or of the seraglio in the Red Fort would have contained these facilities. Many of the pavilions in the Public and Private Imperial domains do not seem to have had

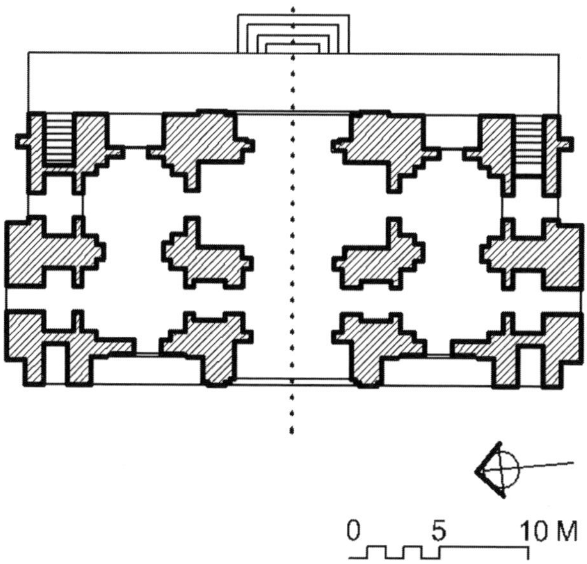

Plan: Naqqar Khana
(Drawing: N. Joshi, D. Cherian, Author)

such a provision. Some of the pavilions catered to functions other than residential ones. Others, even where they functioned as residential apartments, had their service areas often accommodated within adjoining buildings around open courts or gardens.

The thematic variations depending on the exact function of each pavilion were manifested in the internal architectural arrangement as well as in external proportions, though it is interesting that a width varying between 67 to 69 feet was used in many of them. Therefore, though the basic structure of the Diwan-i-Am is of a pillared hall open on three sides, the fourth side is not merely a wall but another layer of rooms, terraces and a stairway. It is not clear from the extant remains if these contained any special services or if they were merely rest-rooms. The Diwan-i-Am housed public imperial activities, private imperial routes and chambers, and additionally functioned as the link between the Public and Private domains of the Fort.

Generally speaking, the degree of complexity of the pavilion increased if it catered to a private function, since the intrinsic form of a pavilion with its high degree of transparency was not conducive to completely private activities. Wherever its function involved a greater need for

Construction Details: Asad Burj Gateway (Photo: Author, 1997)

privacy or embraced more than one kind of activity, the pavilion perforce evolved into a more complex type. Thus, the Rang Mahal has virtually opaque rooms on its two sides while its central pillared hall is open on one side and screened by *jalis* on the opposite side.

The Khas Mahal is the most complex derivation of the pavilion typology in the Red Fort. This is in keeping with its imperial private, semi-private and public ceremonial functions. In principle, the Khas Mahal is a pavilion with two sides open and two closed. However, what renders it different from any other pavilion is an arcaded verandah followed by a layer of screens that prevent direct passage even within the open sides. Though there is a visual connection on the open east-west axis, actual movement conversely is only possible through the more opaque and private chambers on the north-south ends. It is possible that the arcades close to the Khas Mahal were designed to contain private facilities for sewage and waste disposal.

The Diwan-i-Khas is an example of perhaps the purest form of the pavilion typology. It is open on all sides, except for the screened arches on its eastern face that overlook the river. The building takes the form of two concentric spaces, with two sets of supporting pillars. Different bay widths emphasise the important areas within. Of the five bays on the north and south, the central bay is wider to give prominence to the entrance of the hall. Conversely the five bays on the eastern and western faces, chiefly meant for viewing the river and the forecourt, respectively, are of equal width.

The Mumtaz Mahal or Chotta Rang Mahal is another variation of the pavilion. Here, the entire fourth side is occupied by a series of rooms which transforms this into a typology made up of a front verandah and back rooms. The reasons for this were the public responsibilities coupled with the private residential requirements of Jahanara Begum, Shah Jahan's eldest daughter and the chief administrator of the seraglio. The presence of the verandah on the western face of the Mumtaz Mahal shielded her actual living quarters from the strong sun as well as from the passage of attendants in the enclosed forecourt to the Mumtaz Mahal, which was bounded by a further series of cells and courts. The screened walls on the eastern face permitted cool river breezes in the mornings and evenings and a spectacular view at all times.

The simplest pavilion type in the Red Fort was a square or rectangular structure open on three sides, with a wall or a screen on the fourth side—such as the garden pavilions of Sawan and Bhadon in the Hayat Baksh. These pavilions were in the imperial garden, a private area with limited entry to all but the emperor and his favourite family members. Since these pavilions themselves seem to have been primarily used for the purposes of recreation and thus housed a relatively public activity in the private Inner Palace, they could afford to be mostly transparent. Even the Naqqar Khana—essentially a gateway consisting of a central open hall used as a passage on the ground floor—was flanked by two opaque sections used for guard rooms and other facilities. The Naqqar Khana also stretches vertically into an upper level consisting of a central bay bounded by verandahs on its long sides.

These imperial pavilions were made of a basic structure of walls and columns in brick laid with lime mortar. They were spanned by a variety of means—beams, arches, vaults and domes. Despite a conventionally insignificant individual size, they were established as royal buildings through the use of richly carved white marble inlaid in coral, agate, turquoise and cornelian, as well as carved and painted red sandstone. The stone cladding was generally fixed to the brick structure through

Use of double roof in Shah Burj (Photo: Author, 1997)

iron or bronze clamps and bands. *Sisua*—considered the best in beauty and durability out of a range of seventy-two woods identified for use in buildings at the time of Akbar, may have been used in doors, beams and ceilings in the buildings of the Fort. However, it is difficult to state with certainty if such was indeed the case, since the extensive reworking of the few extant buildings in the Fort from Shah Jahan's time has resulted in very little original woodwork remaining.

As extant buildings reveal, the Imperial domains of the Fort appear to have used well-baked bricks of standard sizes laid in lime mortar, though the depictions of the Public and Private Common domains indicate that most construction here used half-baked or sun-dried bricks. It was not uncommon for even buildings of royal patronage to use unbaked bricks—as shown by the reference to the sarai of the garden designated Aizzabad, bestowed by Shah Jahan as a gift to his consort, Akbarbadi Mahal. This is recorded to have been originally constructed of sun-dried bricks. However, it was later rebuilt (during Shah Jahan's lifetime) with baked bricks and mortar.[40] Similarly, the outer walls of Shahjahanabad were initially constructed in stone with mud mortar (perhaps in order to finish the construction quickly), though later, after having developed cracks and breaches under heavy rain, they were rebuilt in special mortar for waterproof construction, called *saruj*.[41]

Construction materials were obtained from different places. While the baked bricks were generally obtained from special kilns, the sandstone and marble used in the Red Fort is believed to have been provided by the noblemen and kings in whose areas it was found, and quarried and brought to Shahjahanabad by road or river.[42] Some specialised materials were brought in from even further away, such as the glass used in Shah Jahan's private buildings reportedly brought from Alleppo (*Halabi*).

Lime, used extensively in mortar, plaster and whitewash, was commonly obtained from gravel (*kankar*) or from special quarries of limestones, or alternatively from fresh water or marine shells, especially near the sea coast of Bengal. A particular kind of lime from Gujarat was reputed to become as hard as marble after being used,[43] though according to Shah Jahan's court historian, Lahori, the best lime (said to be superior to even marble) came from Patiali. Finally, gelatinous, glutinous, resinous and non-resinous agents such as jaggery, reed glue, hemp and pulverised brick were added to the lime for the desired consistency and colour of plaster, mortar or whitewash.

Water was probably obtained at site through the aid of well-diggers and Persian wheels, in a process of construction similar to that in use till fairly recently. Scaffolding, centring and shuttering were done using bamboo or timber. Records indicate that some of the workers were summoned from other parts of the empire to ensure that a sufficient number of the very best masons were available. An illustrative example is a *farman* (imperial decree) from Shah Jahan's reign, at the time of the construction of the Taj Mahal, to Raja Jai Singh asking him not to detain any stone-cutters of the region of Amber and send them to Makrana to expedite work.[44]

It is probable that most of the building components from these materials were made on the construction site itself, where stone-cutters and carvers, brick-layers, carpenters, all worked in unison.[45] Evidence of work organised in this manner may be seen in miniature paintings dating from Akbar's reign, which record the activity at construction sites. However, there is a specific mention in at least one instance that 'a cistern or *hauz* prepared at Makrana and carved out of a single block of marble was brought to Delhi to be installed in the Red Fort'.[46]

Often, arched bays roofed with domes were used next to rooms covered with slabs of stone, depending on which method was most suitable for particular proportions. Flat domes, a constructional feature perfected by the Mughals, were especially valid for the construction of smaller buildings, such as Shah Jahan's imperial pavilions. The system of the double dome, generally used in the large Mughal tombs to achieve monumental outer proportions and appropriately scaled down internal volumes, was not very suitable to the scale of buildings within the Forts. Thus, the innovation of the flat dome, which optimised both usable space as well as building material, was used extensively in the Red Fort, and the curved dome was used only in special instances such as the Mussaman Burj and Moti Masjid. Double roofs were also used selectively to lend prominence to spaces used by Shah Jahan, as in the pavilion attached to the Shah Burj. This type of roof was planned and detailed such that it formed a usable space at terrace-level.

Red sandstone and marble in the various pavilions were used in a variety of ways—as carved elements in plinths, plinth-bands, columns, arch-faces, cornices and mouldings, as slabs used to roof the chambers, as treads and risers in steps and as brackets and projecting elements in chajjas. Apart from identifiable forms imposed by constructional, aesthetic or religious requirements (such as arches, domes, minarets or mihrabs), Shah Jahan did not allow religious preoccupations to overwhelm architectural expression—a mistake his successor Aurangzeb would later commit. Thus, in the Red Fort, both inlay and carved decoration display geometrical and floral patterns, along with figurative representations traditionally banned in Islamic architecture. Carved or inlaid calligraphy as a decorative motif was largely displaced by motifs such as patterns derived from the lotus flower sacred in many Indic religions (adopted by earlier Indian Islamic rulers as well), elaborately carved brackets and column capitals and deep lines of projecting chajjas.

The elements of this eclectic architectural response in the Red Fort generated an architectural vocabulary used without distinctions of religion or even the function and typology of buildings in different parts of the Mughal empire. Sikh buildings, Rajput palaces, residences of different classes and income groups, all absorbed features of this pan-Indian style that Shah Jahani architecture came to epitomise. Thus, many elements of the city within the Red Fort—most particularly those of its imperial domains—came to influence the architecture of many other cities.

5

IMPERIAL DOMAINS

'They are a part of high heaven ... if the residents of the different parts and directions of the world should come to walk round them, as (they walk) round the old house (kaba) it would be allowable.'

Zafar Hasan, *Monuments of Delhi*

The explicit comparisons with heaven, made in the foregoing translation of the inscriptions on the southern and northern arches of the Khwabgah, reflected the admiration that the imperial pavilions evoked from travellers as well as residents of Shahjahanabad. These pavilions were part of the inner palace, reputed to have been built at an enormous cost (recorded variously between 50 to 60 lakhs or 5 to 6 million rupees).[1] As discussed earlier, the inner palace occupied the eastern sector of the Fort and constituted the Private Imperial domain. The ceremonial entrance sequences to this domain began at the appropriately awesome and almost identical Lahori and Delhi Gates. These gates had 24-feet-wide (7.3 metres) entrance arches which towered up to 41.5 feet (12.65 metres),[2] as high as a modern four-storeyed building. From these gates, a progression of spaces unfolded, in which motifs, forms, and materials associated with the imperial presence appeared in a series of built elements. These elements, a compound of several influences, varied from the subtly mystic to the unmistakably direct, and from intricate details to larger forms.

Chattris and domes crowning Lahori Gate (Photo: S. Mukherjee, 2009)

The octagonal geometry that determined the planning of the Fort's imperial domain resurfaced in a slightly different form in the first view of its ceremonial entrances—in the half-octagonal profile of their towers and as flamboyant octagonal pavilions that crowned the width of the gateways. The eclectic coupling of the domed pavilions and the dwarf chattris in the linear screen that linked these pavilions was an unusual reinterpretation of the concentric grouping seen on the roofs of the earlier royal Lodhi and Mughal tombs.

White marble, a material used prolifically and almost exclusively in Shah Jahan's private apartments, marked the surface of these seven miniature domes. The selective use of white marble atop the entrance gates, otherwise clad in the same red sandstone as the rest of the outer Fort walls, achieved a dual purpose. Apart from immediately focusing visual attention on these two gates in a vast continuous circuit of walls and gates, the association with the emperor's trademark building material underlined their function as ceremonial imperial entrances.

Elephant motif, doorway, Khas Mahal (Photo: Author, 1997)

The Delhi Gate entrance arch was additionally flanked by two stone statues of riders on huge elephants. Elephants had, in actual fact as well as symbolically, always occupied a prominent position in the Indian subcontinent. Their attributes of size and majesty naturally singled them out for imperial uses—both functional and decorative—much before the Mughals' rule. The practice of positioning elephant statues at the entrance of Mughal forts, as at the eastern gate of Akbar's Agra Fort and at the gates of Fatehpur Sikri, was begun by Akbar to honour two valiant Rajput warriors who had died while defending the Fort of Chittorgarh against Akbar's army. Elephants had significant associations for the Mughal emperors: they were their favoured mounts both in war and peace, and the watching of elephant fights was deemed by them as a special privilege of kingship. At the Red Fort, the elephant motif was a recurring one and, apart from the statues at the Delhi Gate, is also seen in the decoration of the inner pavilions.

The movement routes from the two public entrance gates, though similar in overall conception, were detailed as completely different spatial experiences. The Lahori Gate route was formulated as a strong longitudinal link, consisting of the vaulted Chatta Bazaar that overwhelmed some visitors as 'the noblest entrance known to belong to any existing palace'.[3] The linearity of this 230-feet-long (70 metres) and 27-feet-wide (8.2 metres) bazaar[4] was accentuated by its enclosed vertical height—a feat of structural engineering—and punctuated by a series of octagonal and half-octagonal spaces. These spaces, in their variation of light, form and volume, emphasised the straight axis with the Diwan-i-Am and served to irresistibly draw a visitor forward. The positioning of the 30-feet-wide (9.14 metre) octagonal open-to-sky court in the middle of the length of this bazaar was both functionally and spatially appropriate. It not only provided sunlight and natural ventilation in a busy populated space, but also functioned as an intriguing magnet in the onward journey.

The bazaar displayed a staggering range of precious goods, set within a regular rhythm of delicate arches. Shah Jahan was perhaps impelled by political reasons to position the Chatta Bazaar at the principal ceremonial entrance. The disposition of this royal bazaar on the sides rather than on the front of the axis allowed the display of the empire's skill and crafted wealth as an almost incidental event in the main activity of movement—a mix of regal disdain and regal munificence. The variety of visual and sensory experience here would have ensured the total engagement of rich noblemen and important visitors who came in to the Fort from this entrance way. As for Shah Jahan and his family, products from the vast imperial atelier of weavers, embroiders, painters and artists were brought for approval in the inner palace itself, as recorded in court histories and paintings.

The products of these craftspeople as well as those from other parts of the empire were used in a variety of ways. Finely woven and embroidered curtains, carpets and awnings decorated the ceremonial parts of the Fort, especially on festivals and celebrations. Jewellery, robes, rich articles of clothing and implements of war were exchanged as gifts

Chatta Bazaar, vaulted roof (Photo: Author, 1997)

between the emperor and his family, as when Dara Shikoh was presented with jewelled daggers and saddles before he embarked upon a military campaign to Kabul and Qandahar. Gifts were bestowed as a mark of favour to noblemen, emissaries and guests. For instance, Ali Mardan, on his appointment as governor of Kashmir, was presented with a robe of honour, a jewelled dagger, gold-embroidered fabrics from Gujarat and Pashmina shawls from Kashmir.

Such articles were used as part of formal presentations to other countries as well, as when the Persian ambassador, Yadgar Beg, was given a special pitcher, cup and salver studded with gems for his emperor, Shah Safi. Other objects were utilised by the imperial family as articles of daily use, such as carved *pandans* (betel leaf holders), inlaid curtain-stops, gold girdles, silver and gold embroidered carpets, cushions and slippers, vessels made of luminous stones and delicate muslins worked in gold.[5]

Similar goods may have been displayed in Chatta Bazaar which would have additionally functioned as a sort of high profile 'shopping mall' and promenade space for visitors of high rank. This bazaar was a refinement of the social and commercial activity as well as the built typology of the

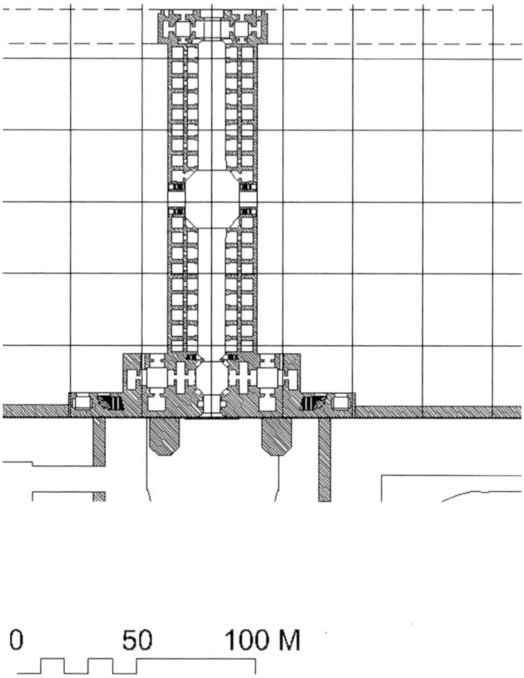

Chatta Bazaar in axis with Lahori Gate (Drawing: N. Joshi, Author)

city's principal axis, Lahori Bazaar (the present-day Chandni Chowk). Thirty-two arcaded cells were positioned on either side of the covered Chatta Bazaar street at the first- and ground-floor levels. The lower cells consisted of two rooms, the front one for the actual display of wares and the one at the back possibly used for storage, manufacture or business transactions. This appears to have been similar to the system in the city's two main streets, which are recorded to have had:

> … arcades on both sides ... generally separated by partitions, in the spaces between which are open shops, where during the day artisans work, bankers sit for the dispatch of their business, and merchants exhibit their wares. Within the arch is a small door, opening into a warehouse, in which these wares are deposited for the night.[6]

Unlike the city's main streets where merchants lived on the floors above the shops, sheltered from public view beyond terraces, the upper part of Chatta Bazaar may perhaps have been used as special shops or associate spaces for official transactions related to its commercial

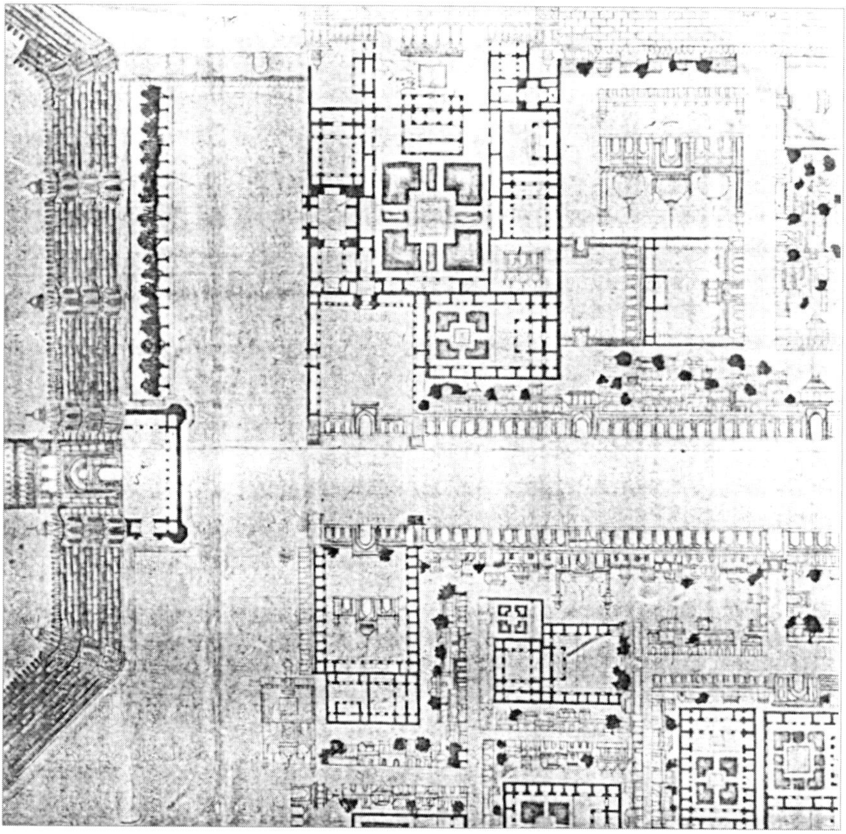

Faiz Bazaar in axis with Delhi Gate: Detail of Red Fort plan
(3635, Agra, Vol. 1/1914-15 ASI PL)

function. Given its ceremonial attribute of ushering in royal visitors and important noblemen to court, neither a completely private nor an active public use at the upper level of this bazaar seems likely. The fact that the arched windows at this level would have been especially visible to elephant-mounted visitors leads one to infer that a private residential activity could not have been accommodated here. Their sole links to the ground floor by staircases limited to the ends of the covered street also appears to rule out active public use at this level.

In contrast to the contained length of Chatta Bazaar, the axis from the Delhi Gate—the Rastah Dilhi Darwaza/Bazaar Dilhi Darwaza—was uncovered, and formed a longer and broader street. Though with a comparatively decreased ceremonial function, it was an important part of the imperial domain, and is described in the *Badshah Nama* as a 40-gaz-wide (approximately 33.5 metres or 110 feet) bazaar. The relationship between Bazaar Dilhi Darwaza and Chatta Bazaar echoed the relationship between the city streets that each of them were linked with. The second principal street of the city, Faiz Bazaar,[7] was connected in axis with the Bazaar Dilhi Darwaza and Delhi Gate. It was shorter and of less commercial or visual importance than the Chandni Chowk connection to Chatta Bazar.

Rastah Dilhi Darwaza was also the street taken by soldiers and officers of the imperial bodyguard when they entered the Fort on horseback, and it was here that they mounted guard at night. A canal bisected the length of the street and emphasised its centre. Raised platforms lined the two sides. Continuous two-storeyed arcades beyond the platforms occasionally rose to form taller entrance gateways, allowing access into semi-private areas. The arcades housed craftsmen as well as officials engaged in administrative and commercial transactions. The linearity of the street was emphasised by the canal on its horizontal axis and the variations in height, light and colour on the two enclosing sides. Despite lacking the dramatic quality of the covered aisle of Chatta Bazar and its beautifully decorated octagonal court, this street must have been a pleasant space, cooled and enlivened by its central canal and shaded by raised arcades on both its sides.

The impetus of the linear axes from the Lahori and Delhi Gates propelled a visitor on through tall gates into the principal forecourt. This large forecourt, defined by arcades and adorned by a central water tank and a canal running along the middle of its length, afforded a much-needed release of space after the controlled linearity of the two axes. The different scales and heights of the central gateways on its four sides, with the Naqqar Khana as the tallest and most ornate, clearly signalled the hierarchy of movement within the forecourt. The resounding sound effects from the Naqqar Khana further emphasised its significance as an imperial entrance.

The uninterrupted crescendo of the ceremonial axis that the Naqqar Khana and its forecourt participated in had both symbolic and spatial meanings. Beginning from the Fatehpuri mosque at one end of the Chandni Chowk street, this axis ran under the towering Lahori Gate and the vaulted Chatta Chowk, and further down the principal forecourt

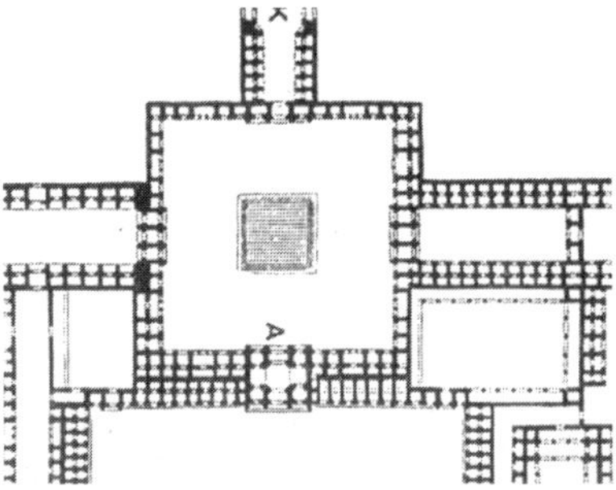

Naqqar Khana forecourt depicted as a square in archival maps (Pl.431, J. Fergusson, *History of Indian and Eastern Architecture*)

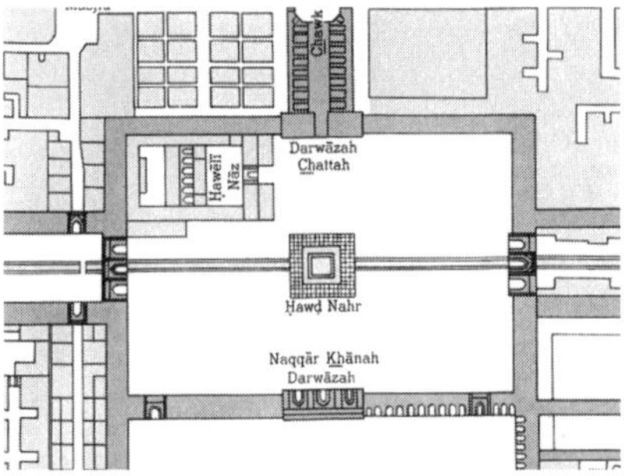

Naqqar Khana forecourt depicted as a rectangle in archival maps (Trans.X/1659, OIOC, BL)

and its Naqqar Khana gate, into a formal court arranged around the Diwan-i-Am. It finally culminated at the emperor's throne—called the *Nashiman-i-Zille-Ilahi,* the seat of the Shadow of God—inside the Diwan-i-Am. Perpendicular to this route was the Rastah Dilhi Darwaza, its axis defined by the forecourt's central canal. This secondary axis led through the fourth gateway on the forecourt's northern edge, into the Rastah Salimgarh and to the Public Common domain inhabited by the resident Mughal military.

It was through this forecourt that noblemen, bearers of imperial regalia, visitors and the public proceeded towards the ceremonial Naqqar Khana while soldiers and guards moved towards their quarters or the Salimgarh citadel. Minor officials sat within the arcaded cells all around the edge, sorting out administrative matters. Thus, the forecourt, as the meeting ground of all these varying human activities, enclosed a public ceremonial area and its periphery contained a semi-public function, reflecting a multi-dimensional use of space.

An analytical study of the extant buildings of the Fort and their drawings was undertaken to ascertain the likely shape of the original forecourt, which is depicted varyingly as a square or a rectangle in old maps and accounts.[8] This geometrical exploration and analysis of the Fort's built and open spaces leads to the inference that the forecourt was rectangular in form, with its sides in the proportion of 1:1.5.[9] A rectangular form is also spatially appropriate, since the stability and the sense of equal importance in all four directions suggested by a square shape is at variance with the

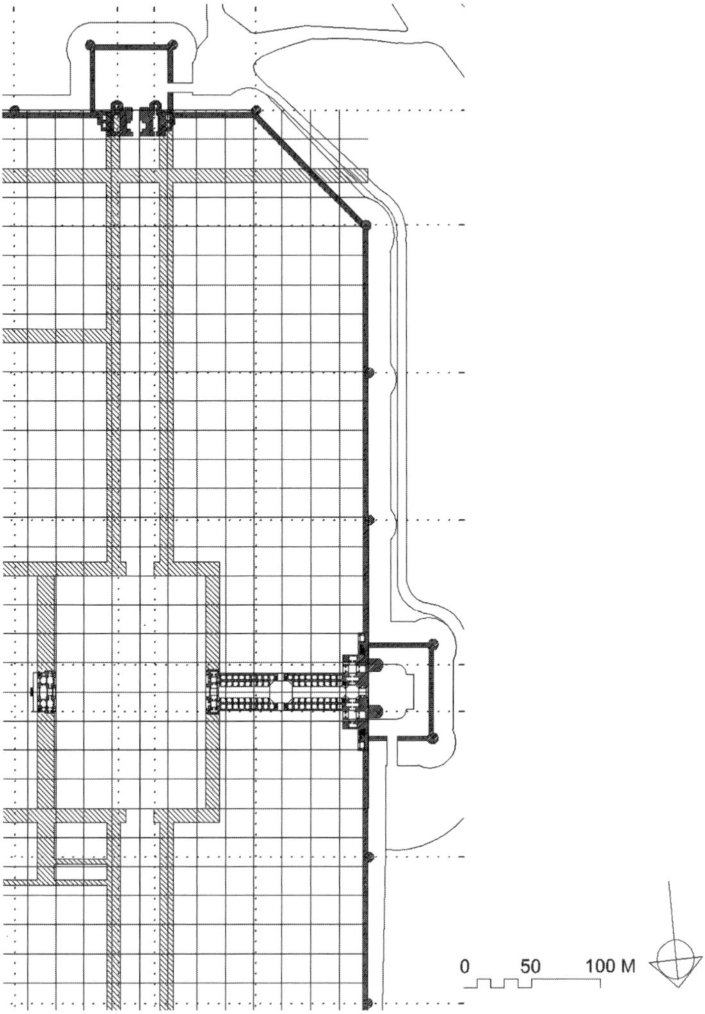

Naqqar Khana forecourt at the junction of the main entrance streets of the Red Fort (Drawing: N. Joshi, Author)

primary function of this forecourt: to indicate clearly the pre-eminence of the axis that led to the Imperial Public domain of the Fort.

Symbolically, this axis was a reflection of the accessibility of the emperor and his justice to his citizens. The direct line of sight from the Diwan-i-Am to the Fatehpuri Mosque at the other end ensured that the emperor, likened with divinity, faced his divine guide when he sat on the throne to administer justice. Spatially, the fact that it was both visible and

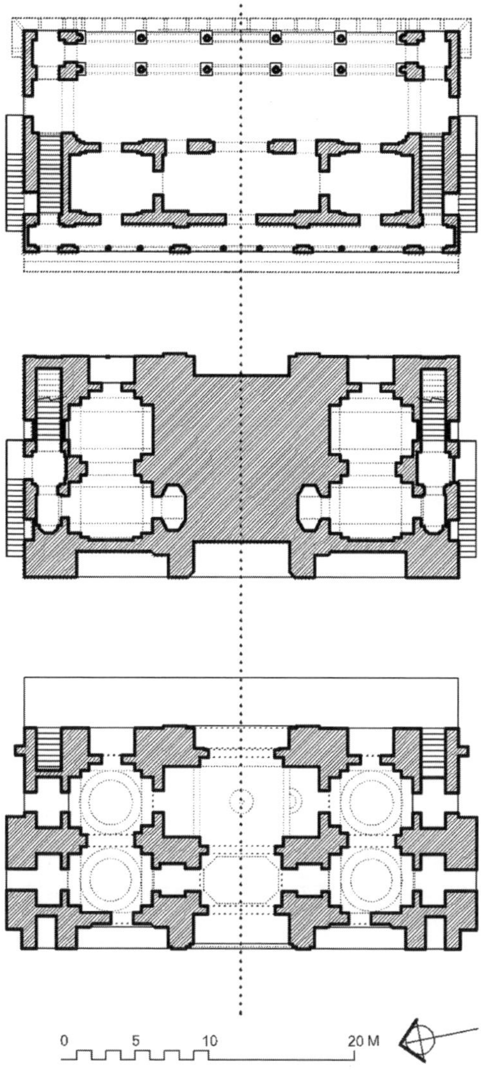

Naqqar Khana: Ground-floor, First-floor and Second-floor Plans
(Drawing: N. Joshi, D. Cherian, Author, based on 584/97, Delhi, ASI PL)

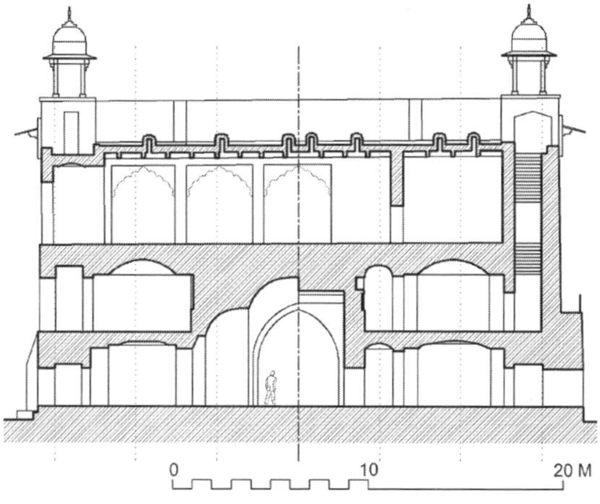

Naqqar Khana, section through the central archway
(Drawing: N. Joshi, Author, based on ASI Drawing)

Naqqar Khana, facade detail (Photo: S. Mukherjee, 2009)

yet distant, reached after many successive passages and courts, meant that when one finally came into the presence of the emperor, one would be appropriately overwhelmed. Space was articulated in the manner of a stage set to achieve a desired emotional and behavioural response. This spatial sequence was also a physical manifestation of the patrimonial-bureaucratic style of governance of the Mughals. It emphasised the benevolent justice of the emperor, both king and father and impelled with the avowed interest of his subjects' welfare, while ensuring that his regal distance as a lofty being on a different plane was maintained.

The Naqqar Khana that formed the final transition into the emperor's presence is recorded in measured drawings made by the ASI as 99 feet (30.175 metres) wide, 68 feet (20.7 metres) deep and 56 feet 6 inches (17.2 metres) high from plinth to roof-top.[10] Clad in delicately carved red sandstone and impressively proportioned, the Naqqar Khana conveyed its status of an imperial gate in deference to which everybody except those of royal blood dismounted. Thus, Muhammad Salih wrote, 'of the three gates of the courtyard, the western gateway is built of red sandstone with splendid carvings'.[11]

The elevational proportions of the Naqqar Khana are very definitely rectangular, its length almost twice as long as its height. The elements that constitute its elevation—its central archway, the upper series of smaller arches banded across its length, the vertical panels of carved niches—all form a logical formal order, with just enough variation to prevent both visual fatigue or disinterest. This elevational composition varied on the east and west faces. The west face was detailed as a two-storeyed building, its tall cusped arches echoing those of the Diwan-i-Am. The east facade, in contrast, announced its internal arrangement of three storeys in the positioning and the number of its arches, whose profiles were similar to those in the other public gateways of the Fort. The facades of the Naqqar Khana were also related by a system of proportions to that of the adjoining arcades. This is evident from an exercise of geometrical analysis of the facades, based on old photographs dating from the mid-nineteenth century.

The Naqqar Khana is spatially organised as a sequence of two central rectangular chambers, preceded by high niched archways. From its forecourt, a 29-feet-high (8.8 metres) and 16-feet-wide (4.87 metres) central entrance arch leads on to these chambers and further on to the Diwan-i-Am forecourt. Each chamber is flanked by and connected to a set of rooms that may have been waiting areas or housed guards to monitor entry. At the further ends of the Naqqar Khana were two corner staircases, accessed from the Diwan-i-Am forecourt. These led to the upper floors from where music by the royal musicians rang out five times a day. The segregation of movement would have allowed the musicians to appear and disappear efficiently from their perch above the gateway,

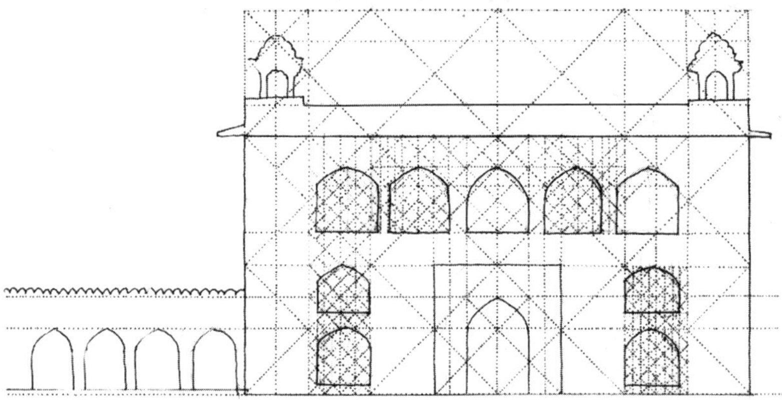

Naqqar Khana, geometrical analysis, east Elevation
(Drawing: Author, on the basis of photograph 52/29, OIOC, BL)

without encountering the stream of visitors—almost like the provision of separate backstage and audience entrances to an auditorium.

The Diwan-i-Am forecourt, like the Naqqar Khana forecourt preceding it, has been described in different terms and with varying proportions and measurements in written accounts and maps.[12] A rectangular shape seems almost certain given its spatial and organisational function, which was even more complex than the Naqqar Khana forecourt. Rectangular forecourts are also observed in the Diwan-i-Ams of the earlier Mughal Forts. A detailed geometrical and spatial exploration of the Diwan-i-Am forecourt in the Red Fort, based on a study of the proportions of the extant Mughal buildings in the Fort together with the mid-nineteenth-century OIOC map of Shahjahanabad and the 1911 ASI map, strengthens the probability of the proportions of this forecourt being rectangular. The results of this exploration point to the dimensions of the forecourt being in the ratio of 1:1.3. Though the depth of the forecourt has been given as 300 feet in the ASI listing, actual site measurements indicate that it was about 425 feet or 1.55 planning grids, close to the measurement of 160 zira (or about 436 feet) recorded in the *Badshah Nama*.

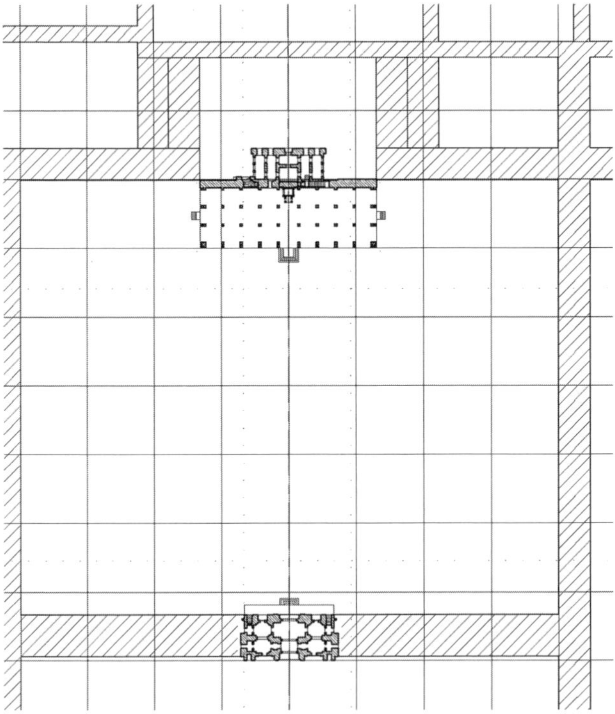

Geometrical exploration, Diwan-i-Am forecourt (Drawing: N. Joshi, Author)

The application of the generating grids additionally reveals a planned relationship between the forecourts and buildings of the Diwan-i-Am and the Naqqar Khana in terms of site planning, locations and dimensions.[13] It appears that the edges of these forecourts were aligned to coincide with two of the planning grids of the Fort. As a multiple of this grid of 83.35 metres or 100 gaz (as mentioned earlier, a Shah Jahani gaz was approximately equal to .83 metres), the widths of the forecourts work out to about 166.7 metres (546.9 feet). This corresponds closely with the width mentioned in the ASI listing of 1911[14] and with the recorded dimensions in the *Badshah Nama*. Further, if the planning grids of each forecourt are subdivided, they are seen to relate directly to the dimensions of the Naqqar Khana and the Diwan-i-Am pavilions. On the basis of this geometrical analysis, the width of the Diwan-i-Am (180 feet or 54.8 m) works out to be almost exactly a third of the width of its forecourt.

The Diwan-i-Am, as the centre of the Imperial Public domain of the Fort, was essentially used for all administrative matters that required public participation. In the daily assembly presided over by the emperor, oral and written requests were presented through emissaries. Envoys, soldiers and princes were granted audience. Deserving religious men and officials were awarded titles, marks of favour and cash, and reminders of orders, finance and accounts were issued. Court writers gathered within hearing distance and recorded everything that the emperor said; musicians and artists offered their respects; officials from distant and near provinces periodically brought news of their areas as well as gifts.

The open part of the forecourt further away from the Hall was the area where nobles assembled and soldiers paraded. Spectacles of animal fights were staged here and imperial ceremonies observed on the occasion of various celebrations. It was also here that horses and elephants were reviewed, the physical prowess of nobles tested and instruments of war examined. Tame leopards, antelopes, Uzbek hunting dogs and birds of prey used in field sport, were paraded before the emperor. Each Wednesday, the routine would differ slightly: 'In order to make an inquiry into the grievances of the broken-hearted and oppressed. On that day of justice, none are admitted but the Ministers of Justice, Muftis, various honest and pious scholars and some nobles who are constant attendants of the court.'[15]

Since this forecourt also functioned as a point of entry to other spaces in the inner palace with differing degrees of privacy, movement patterns from here were strictly controlled through two gateways on its east wall. One of these led northwest to the Diwan-i-Khas, and the other led northeast to the imperial seraglio. Other gateways were positioned centrally along the width of the forecourt. The one on the north boundary wall connected to the imperial state rooms, regalia chambers and kitchens. These could, thus, readily serve both the Diwan-i-Am and Diwan-i-Khas, with additional access on the north-south road from Delhi Gate, in the nature of a service entrance. The other gateway on the forecourt's south boundary wall led through the *Dewari Hawa Sira* to the more public part of the seraglio.

However, these gates and their adjoining arcaded cells were secondary compared to the Diwan-i-Am and its spatial connection to the forecourt of the Diwan-i-Khas. The Diwan-i-Am was the most important building within the forecourt in terms of function, form, craftsmanship and built material. It contained the emperor's jharoka throne within it: the climax of the ceremonial route into the Fort. The surrounding arcades in carved sandstone were repetitive elements, whose presence, though vital in providing a setting for the Diwan-i-Am and its jharoka, merited far less architectural ornamentation in comparison to the Diwan-i-Am These arcades, two cells deep and almost 3.5 feet above the ground, were assigned to the *omrahs* (noblemen) on duty and derived their individuality from the manner in which they decorated them with carpets, curtains and furnishings.

Successive rectangular enclosures emanated from the Diwan-i-Am into the forecourt to emphasise the centre of radiating power. These enclosures were defined by layers of awnings, carpets and railings that increased in magnificence closer to the jharoka. Raised and selectively screened, the jharoka allowed the emperor to be secure despite visual and physical proximity to his assembled nobles and ensured that he was always literally and symbolically higher than those around him. Because of the elevation of the jharokha to a level almost a floor higher than the rest of the pavilion and the system of successive railings around it, everyone—except accompanying guards and trusted kinsmen—was obliged to keep their distance. In fact, it is recorded that when Shah Jahan descended to the pavilion from the safety of the jharoka on one occasion, he barely escaped an assault by a disaffected courtier.[16]

The success of the jharoka design in separating the emperor from the public and, at the same time, visibly allowing him to be a part of the space within the Diwan-i-Am, is also evident from a later attempt by the British to carry out an investiture ceremony here. This ceremony was to be jointly presided over by the viceroy and the king of England's brother. The exact situation of the seat of 'the representative of the Sovereign' was the subject of much discussion. Both the actual jharoka that was once occupied by the 'Great Mughal' and the lower level occupied by his minister, were considered.

> These sentimental considerations, however, had to yield to the fact that the throne platform is so lofty (... and is inaccessible from the front) that a steep flight of steps would have been required for anyone to ascend to it from the body of the hall ... it would have been almost impossible from such an altitude to have conducted the intricate Ceremonies of an Investiture.[17]

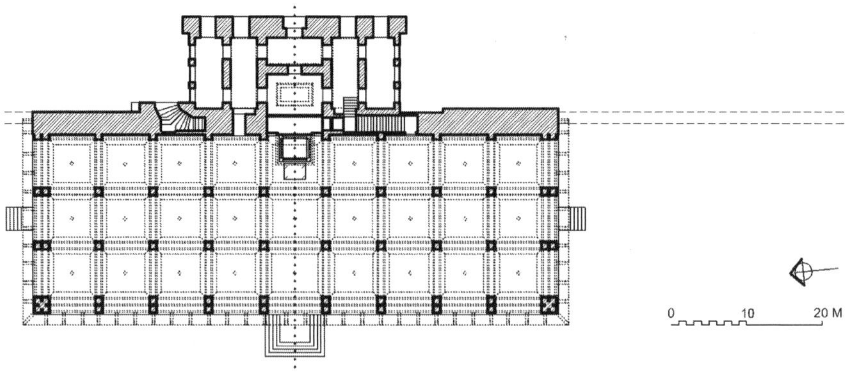

Diwan-i-Am, Plan
(Drawing: N. Joshi, D. Cherian, Author, based on 580/97, Delhi, ASI PL)

During Mughal times, a 40-feet-long and 30-feet-wide railed area around the jharoka was reserved for the highest nobles of the realm while the rest of the hall, its limits marked by another balustrade, was used for the next rank of officials. Around the hall in the forecourt was the *gulal bari,* a rectangular enclosure shaded by a red awning designated for minor officials, and beyond it was the rest of the assembly. These different enclosures ensured that only a few high officials were close to the emperor's throne and the private entrances of the Diwan-i-Khas and the imperial seraglio. The succession of railings and awnings also helped to increase the perceived size of the Diwan-i-Am, with a few observers adding the gulal bari to it.[18] Thus, its dimensions, as recorded in *The Shah Jahan Nama of Inayat Khan,* are 50 yards (41.675 metres) long and 15 yards (12.5 metres) broad—while they are given as 67 gaz (55.8 metres) by 24 gaz (20 metres) in the *Amal-i-Salih* by Muhammad Salih Kambo as well as in the *Badshah Nama* by Muhammad Waris. Reference is also made by Waris to a podium (104 zira long and 60 zira broad) on which this hall is situated.

Structurally, the Diwan-i-Am is divided into a series of arches spanning three aisles. Each aisle is composed of nine parts supported on more arches. The imperial jharoka is framed within the central arched bay of the aisles, which is wider than the four bays flanking it on either side to emphasise its importance. The rhythm of these parallel and transverse arches simultaneously encloses and transmits space through and across the pavilion so that form, structure and space become inseparable.

Such a pavilion form was particularly appropriate for an audience hall, since it embraced the enclosures in the forecourt and afforded the emperor a view on three sides. A balcony was positioned immediately behind the jharoka for the princes and personal attendants of the emperor. The rest of the back wall, solid unlike the other sides and embellished with rich carving and inlay, afforded an arresting backdrop to the emperor. It also worked as a private route from his living quarters to the jharoka in the manner of a stage entrance. A door in the wall led into a square chamber connected with a double row of verandahs looking on to the inner palace and gave covered access to a staircase. Through this door behind the jharoka, to the accompaniment of drums, cymbals and salutations, the emperor would have appeared suddenly and magically at his throne before his waiting audience in the hall.

The uncharacteristic use of red sandstone rather than marble in the Diwan-i-Am, undoubtedly an imperial building, is explained by the fact that originally the red sandstone used in it was not visible at all. Old prints and drawings depict this as a brilliant white pavilion. It is recorded in court histories as having been covered by layers of fine *chunam*—white plaster[19] that rivalled marble in its whiteness and brilliance—which would have stood out in contrast to the red arcades and gateways around its forecourt. Allusions to the marble pavilion of the Diwan-i-Am in references by travellers show that the plaster did indeed simulate marble.[20]

Though a single-storey pavilion, the height of the Diwan-i-Am is actually equivalent in height to a modern three-storey building, with its

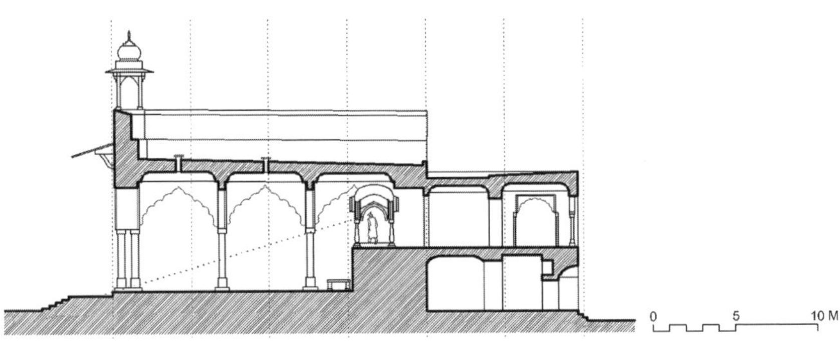

Diwan-i-Am, Section through the Jharoka Throne
(Drawing: N. Joshi, Author, based on ASI Drawing)

plan dimensions recorded as 180 feet wide and 68 feet deep.[21] Its height is less imposing than that of the Naqqar Khana gateway. However, the original decoration and colours of the shimmering white Diwan-i-Am pavilion, enclosed by silver railings, crowned with golden-domed chattris and shaded by rich red velvet awnings within its large forecourt would quite unmistakably have dominated this entire space. The interjection of smaller arcaded apartments between the Naqqar Khana and the Diwan-i-Am, all around the forecourt's edge, would have also helped to prevent any direct comparison of their respective heights.

An increased height was lent to the Diwan-i-Am without reducing the perception of its lightness, by the domed chattris positioned on top of the northwestern and southeastern corners of its roof. These rooftop chattris were dispensed with on the east facade of the Diwan-i-Am towards its smaller private courts. This may have been because these courts did not have the necessary foreground to view the Diwan-i-Am's entire height. Here, the emphasis was on its walls which, as the most keenly observed plane, were articulated and accentuated in a series of niches and doorways. These were rendered white with sang-i-bahtali, the special fine white plaster used in imperial buildings, and adorned with paintings. The eastern face of the Diwan-i-Am also had two storeys internally instead of one, since the need for a large hall and, therefore, a proportionately tall ceiling, was unnecessary on this face.

Contiguous with this facade of the Diwan-i-Am were the two gateways on the eastern wall of its forecourt that led to the inner palace. Of these, the connection to the Diwan-i-Khas, the *Lal Darwaza,* was more important than the one to the seraglio, termed the *Dewari Adalat* in the OIOC map. However, in terms of placement of entrances, they were equally arranged. Given the strict rules that were laid down for admittance to an imperial Mughal seraglio, it seems uncharacteristic to locate an entrance to it from the forecourt to the Hall of Public Audience.

The explanation for this may lie in the fact that the Dewari Adalat actually led to another intervening maze of passages and courts (none of which exist today) and not directly into the seraglio. Passage to the Diwan-i-Khas, too, was gained by way of a series of two courts. A similar organisation of space was followed for the imperial kitchens and the

Diwan-i-Am Jharoka Throne: The climax of the public ceremonial axis into the Fort
(Photo: Author, 1997)

Diwan-i-Am Interior: Note the provision for fixing rails on the columns
(Photo: S. Mukherjee, 2009)

regalia chambers which were entered through their own sub-courts from the northern edge of the Diwan-i-Am forecourt.

The large area of the inner palace was divided into two main parts—the emperor's quarters and the imperial seraglio. The emperor's quarters were in the northern half, while the seraglio was located in the southern half. Within both these areas, as mentioned earlier, were a series of built and open spaces for daily activities, recreation, administration and worship. Nearly all these spaces were accessible in some degree to all the residents within, yet there were areas of restricted entry even for them. The imperial pavilions were entered through separate colonnades, walled gardens and paved courts. At no one time were they visible simultaneously, except in some areas where successive spaces were linked visually. Thus, it was possible for different pavilions to have a system of proportion and geometry that was linked to adjoining spaces, but not necessarily in a predictable symmetric progression.

The few people who were allowed access into the emperor's quarters could only do so at certain specific times. Of the areas meant primarily for the emperor, the important ones were the Khas Mahal, Rang Mahal, Diwan-i-Khas, Shah Burj, imperial Hammams and the gardens of Hayat Baksh and Mehtab Bagh. Though the emperor passed into the seraglio at will, the above areas were specifically his domain. From the Diwan-i-Am, the sequence of the inner palace pavilions commenced with the Rang Mahal. This pavilion, termed Imityaz Mahal in the court histories, is described as the most monumental building here. Its overall dimensions are recorded as 153 feet 6 inches (46.8 metres) by 69 feet 3 inches (21.1 metres). The emperor would have viewed the western face of the Rang Mahal as he came out from the doorway behind his throne. Beyond the Diwan-i-Am, the central axis linking the Lahori Gate and the Diwan-i-Am continued in the symmetrical layout of the Rang Mahal and its forecourt.

However, the Rang Mahal, though reputed to be part of the seraglio, does not appear to have been a residential building. To its north, beyond a paved terrace, was the pavilion consisting of the emperor's personal rooms. To its south was the pavilion of Princess Jahanara. Positioned in an area that was part of the emperor's quarters as well as the seraglio, and with access from both, the Rang Mahal probably functioned as a buffer between the actual residence of the emperor and those of his wives,

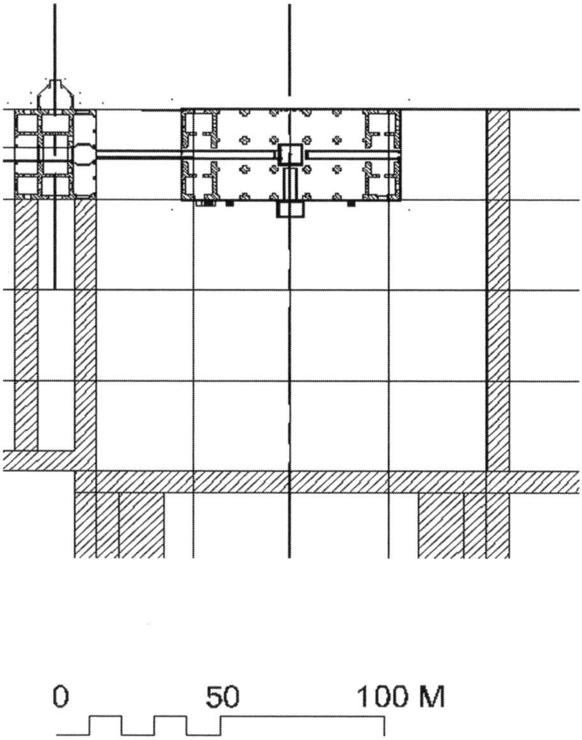

Rang Mahal: Organisation of the pavilion with its forecourt
(Drawing: N. Joshi, D. Cherian, Author)

daughters, concubines, young children and their maids. It was directly connected from the raised eastern terrace to these imperial spaces north and south of it. The emperor could approach the Rang Mahal pavilion from the Khas Mahal, the Diwan-i-Am, or the seraglio. Therefore, all these routes had to be planned with the care befitting a monarch with exacting aesthetic tastes. The spatial connection to the public ceremonial Diwan-i-Am additionally needed to be designed in ways that retained the Rang Mahal's privacy. Thus, a sequence of two intervening courts, bounded by covered colonnades, formed the route from the Diwan-i-Am.[22] A similar arrangement existed in the Lahore Fort, where an intervening rectangular buffer court existed between the Diwan-i-Am and the private quarters of the emperor, the *Burra* Khwabgah.[23] Some historical maps show only one court in front of the Rang Mahal; however, based on the spatial use as well as descriptions in court histories and other depictions, it seems more likely that there did exist two courts in front of it.

The Rang Mahal forecourts could also be serviced by attendants, who would have traversed them in the direction perpendicular to the route taken by the emperor. A fourth entrance to the Rang Mahal from a set of underground chambers is said to have provided a secret exit to the riverbank. The entrances to these chambers are now closed and used as stores by the ASI. They are believed to have been bricked up in the times of the Mughals[24] and thus the existence of the exit cannot be corroborated. However, excavations of this area in the beginning of the twentieth century do not record the discovery of any such exit. It is possible that these underground rooms were essentially for use as sardkhanas, though none of the other extant imperial pavilions appear to have contained underground chambers for living. The *Badshah Nama,* in its list of six entrances into the Fort, refers to two doors towards the river: one within the Shah Mahal for the emperor 'to reach the river front and board the imperial boats', and the other outside the *Daulatkhana-i-mualla* 'for the use and passage of the grandees'.

Of the two courts behind the Diwan-i-Am, the first court is depicted as a rectangle leading on to the actual forecourt of the Rang Mahal. The forecourt is arranged as a charbagh, and would have provided a formal setting for the pavilion as well as a space for outdoor living. The northern and southern boundaries of this charbagh have been worked out through a geometrical exploration.[25] This geometrical exploration indicates that the dimensions of this rectangular forecourt were derived from a square, whose limits include the eastern terrace between the adjoining Khas Mahal and an equivalent distance on the other side of the terrace court. Excavations in the early twentieth century suggest that within this charbagh there was a tank with a small square building in its centre.[26] The *Badshah Nama,* too, makes mention of a central tank, inside a baghicha measuring 177 zira by 115 zira. The tank is recorded to have had twenty-five fountains and to have been connected to a channel on its east and west sides through them. Apart from these, the *Badshah Nama* makes a reference to a walled garden here of fine red sandstone.

Drawings dating from the nineteenth century depict two projecting and separately roofed rooms at the two ends of the Rang Mahal. These

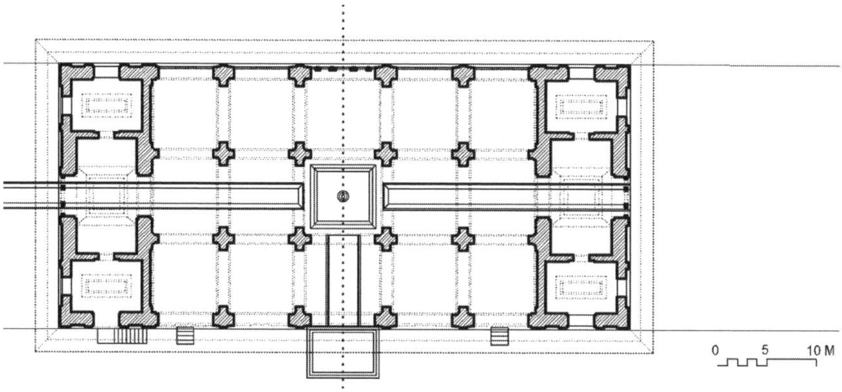

Rang Mahal: Plan
(Drawing: N. Joshi, D. Cherian, Author, based on 582/97, Delhi, ASI PL)

two rooms are no longer extant and it is difficult to ascertain if they are additions by the later Mughals, or are part of the four *chaukhandis* adjacent to its podium, mentioned in the court history of Waris. The literal meaning of Rang is colour, though it is also used poetically to denote sensuous pleasure. The Mughals were enlightened patrons and many of them were themselves skilled exponents of the arts, such as the composition and rendering of poetry or *sher-o-shayari,* vocal and instrumental music, dance and painting. In all these arts, the emphasis was both to build upon existing rigorous classical traditions and to absorb new influences for further innovation. The Rang Mahal—with its delicately patterned columns decorated in gold, its dado of gleaming white plaster ornamented with paintings, its glittering walls inset with tiny mirrors, its gilded ceiling and its extensive and intricate water features—was akin to an expensive stage setting for the presentation of the performing arts and other activities connected with recreation. It had reportedly cost 5.5 lakh (half a million) rupees to build. Centrally aligned with the Diwan-i-Am, and positioned on the eastern wall of the Fort with flanking terraced courts, it overlooked the beautiful riverbanks which were themselves the scene of festive gatherings. It is interesting to note here that there seems to be a precedent for the provision of a *Ranga Mandapa* (a theatre hall or pavilion) in earlier Indian palaces also, as borne out by texts such as the *Mansara*, which specify the location of such a hall within the palace.

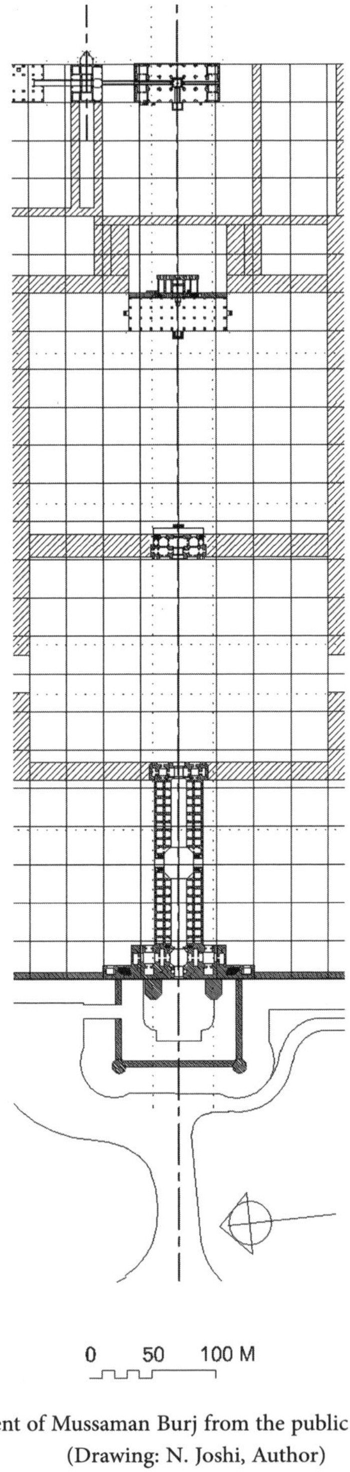

Displacement of Mussaman Burj from the public ceremonial axis
(Drawing: N. Joshi, Author)

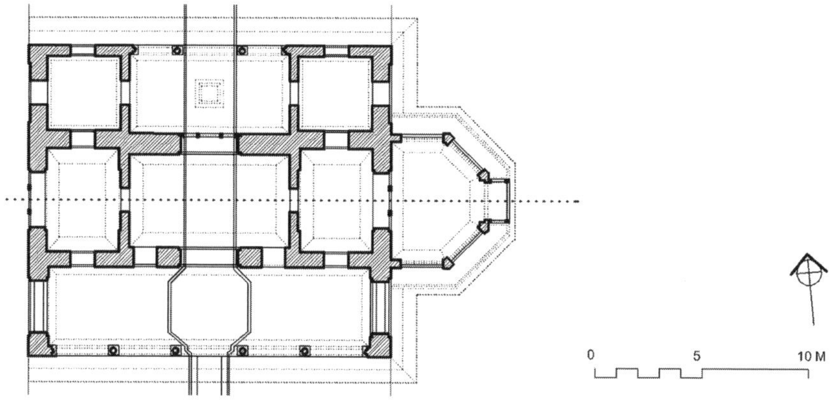

Khas Mahal: Plan
(Drawing: N. Joshi, D. Cherian, Author, based on 577/97, Delhi, ASI PL)

Within the pavilion, there were different domains of privacy. The Rang Mahal has a built configuration of an open fifteen-bay central hall flanked by walled chambers. The hall is divided into 20 feet square bays supported on 6 feet square pillars encased in marble. While the movement route on the central north-south axis and through the open arcaded hall would have been more public, the chambers had greater privacy. The Nahr-i-Bahist in a channel measuring 10 feet 9 inches wide flowed through the length of the hall and branched off in the centre to circulate in an inlaid fountain basin, and from there through a niched marble chaddar into a channel in the charbagh.

The symmetrical organisation of the Rang Mahal gave way to a more complex system of planning on either of its sides, especially in the pavilion to its north. This, the Khas Mahal, consisting of the set of rooms termed the Khwabgah, Tasbih Khana and the Mussaman Burj, made up the emperor's personal chambers. Recorded to have cost 28 lakh (2.8 million) rupees, these were meant for the exclusive use of the emperor. The pavilion is large in area, about 10,000 square feet (930 m^2). The northern and southern sides of the Khas Mahal have a high degree of transparency, with open arcaded verandahs which suggest the direction of movement into the building. The pavilion's western and eastern ends have more solid and shorter walls. The Mussaman Burj tower, which terminates the central part of the Khas Mahal's eastern face, originally had a high gilded dome. It would have, thus, been a point

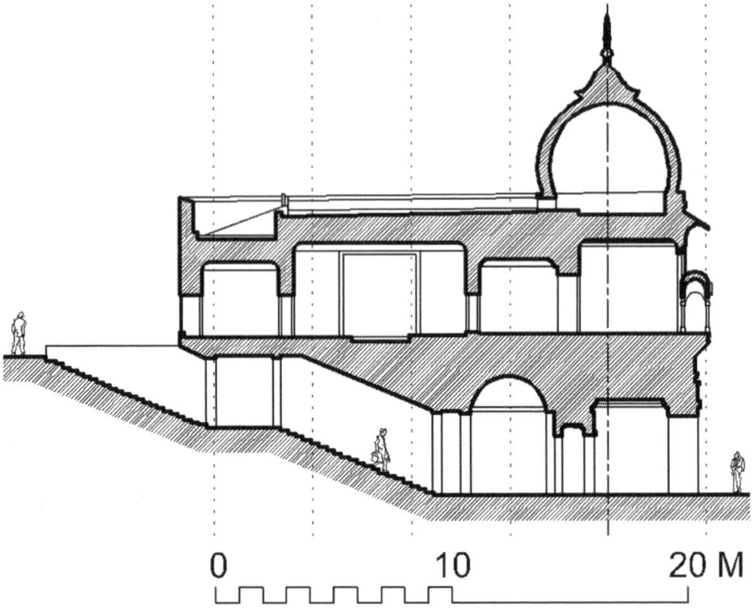

Section through Khas Mahal and Mussaman Burj
(Drawing: N. Joshi, Author, based on ASI Drawing)

of orientation from both inside and outside the Fort, proclaiming the emperor's quarters.

This Burj, from where the emperor displayed himself to his subjects unfailingly every morning, had both spatial and organisational importance to warrant its location on the Fort's public-formal central axis, which was supposed to specifically lead to the emperor. To have displaced the Mussaman Burj balcony and the Khas Mahal to the north of this axis, in favour of the Rang Mahal was an unusual step. The reason for this arrangement was probably due to the overwhelming need for privacy in all parts of the inner palace. This predominant concern would have necessitated at least a visual discontinuance of the emperor's area of private residence from the public-ceremonial central axis. That being the case, positioning the Khas Mahal on this axis would have been reduced to the purely symbolic.

Another reason may have been the height of the Mussaman Burj. As a building that visually signified the emperor's presence, this tower was one of the higher buildings in the Fort and was covered by an

Mussaman Burj on the public central axis of the Fort, as depicted in an archival painting, c.1780-90 (Add.Or. 948, OIOC, BL)

arresting gilded dome. Architecturally, it constituted a counterpoint in the sequence of successive reductions in height as one came closer to the emperor's quarters, though it retained the theme of increasing richness of proportion, material, and ornamentation. It might be that the aesthetically rigorous Shah Jahan did not want the tower of the Mussaman Burj to interfere with the skyline behind the beautifully proportioned pavilion of the Diwan-i-Am. It might also be that he wished to clearly separate the grandeur of public ceremonial space with the personalised scale of his private quarters.

A later artist, who depicted the Red Fort in his sketches showing the Mussaman Burj in axis with the Diwan-i-Am and the Lahori Gate, clearly did not share the emperor's line of thought. Or it may have been that this artist did not have sufficient knowledge about the internal plan of the Fort, and assumed that the Fatehpuri Masjid–Diwan-i-Am axis continued right up to the Mussaman Burj. This would have been the normal expectation, and the size of the Fort would have made it difficult to perceive the shift in axis. It is also possible that Shah Jahan and his architects anticipated that people would not realise the reality of the shifted axis.

The Mussaman Burj and the northern face of the Khas Mahal—the set of three rooms termed the Tosha Khana or Baithak Khana—were the formal part of the emperor's apartments. The southern verandah was part of the Tasbih Khana and led on to the Khwabgah. Both the southern and northern verandahs were connected to the Mussaman Burj as well as to other flanking chambers, and separated from each other through the celebrated Screen of Justice. The Nahr-i-Bahist flowed under the screen and through the verandahs and cooled the entire building. Since the emperor used both verandahs, there was no designated front and back to the screen, or the Khas Mahal. Its northern face looked on to the Diwan-i-Khas; its southern face was visually linked to the Rang Mahal; its eastern face was visible from the river and its bank and the western facade gave onto the forecourts leading to the imperial riverside entrance. All these were distinguished by identifiable symbols of power and aesthetics, both in their overall form and details.

Such an architectural treatment with equal attention given to all facades was also seen in other imperial pavilions, since their western facades were oriented to the public ceremonial domain, and their eastern

Mussaman Burj interior, looking out towards the Yamuna
(Photo: Author, 2000)

facades overlooked the river, which too was in the public realm as a busy travel route in those days. The pavilions' northern and southern facades were selectively open to view for the emperor and his favoured courtiers or family. This system could work efficiently because of the segregation of service areas and living areas. The imperial pavilions did not need to have a rear, non-formal facade containing attached kitchens, baths or other services since these were located in separate spaces bounded by their own courtyards. The emperor would go to these areas when he needed to, such as to the Hammam, and wherever possible, services such as cooked food or products of the imperial workshops were brought to him. This was an extension of the overall layout of the Fort, in which both its river and city faces were in the nature of front facades.

The Diwan-i-Khas was next in sequence after the Khas Mahal, and separated by a 46-feet-wide marble pavement from it. This pavilion, along with the Khas Mahal and Rang Mahal, personified the spirit of refinement that characterised Shah Jahan and his rule. The Diwan-i-Khas was especially celebrated for the beauty of its proportions and the delicacy

Rang Mahal: Ceiling detail (Photo: Author, 1997)

Screen of Justice, Khas Mahal (Photo: S. Mukherjee, 2009)

Diwan-i-Khas: Ceiling detail
(Photo: Author, 2001)

Hammam: Floor detail
(Photo: Author, 1997)

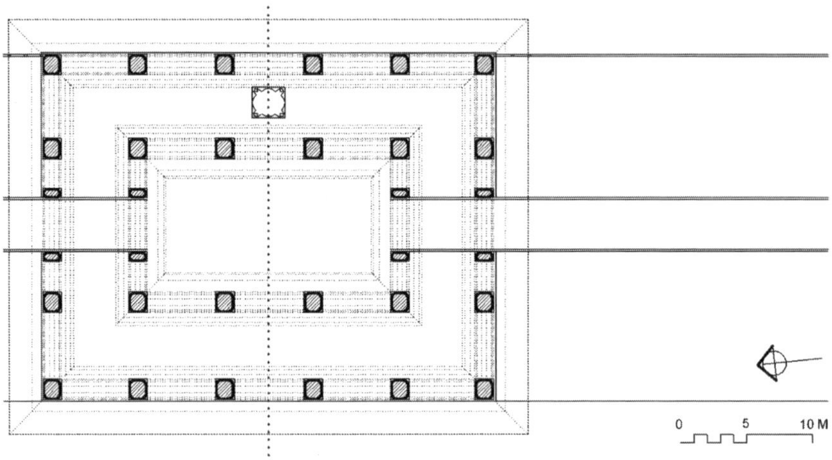

Diwan-i-Khas: Plan
(Drawing: N. Joshi, D. Cherian, Author, based on 583/97, Delhi, ASI PL)

of its ornamentation. Recorded to have been built at a cost of 14 lakhs (1.4 million) inclusive of its silver ceiling and fittings, it measured 34 by 26 yards[27] or 90 feet (27.4 metres) wide and 69 feet (21.03 metres) deep.[28] At least 200 after its founding, Emily Metcalfe, the British Resident's daughter wrote enthusiastically in her diary that 'no picture can give an adequate idea of it, for in design, proportion, material and finish, it was faultless.'[29]

The positioning of the semi-public Diwan-i-Khas between the two very private spaces of the Khas Mahal and the imperial Hammam seems awkward, till one recalls that the location of the pavilions in the inner palace was logically related to their multiple uses and to their sequence. The semi-public function of the Diwan-i-Khas was occasional, and lasted only for some hours each day. Compared to the mid-morning crowded assembly in the Diwan-i-Am, the Diwan-i-Khas was primarily used in the evening for reviews with selected courtiers, or on special occasions for the reception of important guests. A few higher officers also attended the daily noon session here for state discussions, when the emperor, with his attendants, moved between the Diwan-i-Am, Khas Mahal and Diwan-i-Khas.

Thus, in the early morning, afternoon and late evening, when the emperor attended to his personal ablutions or participated in family or recreational activities, the Diwan-i-Khas was virtually a private space. At other times of the day, it additionally functioned in the nature of the emperor's private office and reception area for selected guests. As a semi-private building, it was sometimes accessed by officials for more sombre ceremonies, as on Shah Jahan's death when, at Jahanara's bidding, they entered the Diwan-i-Khas at the Agra Fort in 1666 CE to make the necessary funeral preparations.

However, during the course of normal routine, the official duties of the emperor at the Diwan-i-Khas essentially consisted of administrative decisions made in consultation with high officials and his prime minister. It was here that he revised, sealed and signed orders; instituted grants of land and endowments; decided on daily charity to the needy; responded to petitions from governors of various provinces, issued royal *jagirs* (properties) and stipends of officials. He also examined designs from the imperial workshops—paintings, art objects, weaves, jewels, enamelled work and architectural plans of royal edifices. Arms were paraded in the forecourt every evening; birds and beasts of prey were brought for inspection; horses of different breeds were made to gallop by skilful trainers. On occasion, the pavilion was made 'resplendent owing to the abundance of camphor candles in vases set with precious stones'[30] and the emperor listened to melodies played by minstrels.

The organisation of space within the Diwan-i-Khas at the Red Fort was based on two concentric rectangular enclosures, formed by a series of square columns. The central three bays formed an inner enclosure clearly set out as the focus, with a platform in the centre where the emperor would sit. The dimensions of this are given as 18 gaz (15 metres) in length and 10 gaz (8.335 metres) in breadth. The ring of space around the centre was designated for officials, craftsmen whose work was brought for inspection, minstrels who played for the emperor's pleasure, and for the movement of special attendants.

The longer sides of the pavilion faced east towards the river and west towards the forecourt. The forecourt, recorded to have measured 70 (58.3 metres) by 60 (50 metres) yards,[31] was rectangular in shape. The emphasis of its proportion was directed at the Diwan-i-Khas. The forecourt's eastern and southern edges were connected to the emperor's quarters through gates entered at specific points. The northern and western boundaries of the forecourt were linked to the Hayat Baksh and the Jewel Chamber and to the Diwan-i-Am respectively.

Within the pavilion, the shorter northern- and southern-facing sides were the routes that the emperor took from the Hammam or the Khas Mahal. Of the five bays on these northern and southern facades, the wider central bay gave prominence to the entrance of the hall. The five bays on the east and west appear to have been chiefly meant for the emperor to view the river and the forecourt respectively, and were designed to be of equal width. Accentuating the centrality of the forecourt was the marble fountain in front of the central western arch of the pavilion. The western facade was covered by a layer of double arcades that afforded the emperor shelter from the strong afternoon sun and reinforced the cooling effect of the fountain.

Besides being referred to as the *Shah Mahal* or the emperor's palace, the Diwan-i-Khas was also known as the *Ghusal Khana* or the bathing chamber. There is an interesting story with regard to this, in the *Shah Jahan Nama of Inayat Khan*.[32]

> During the reign of the late Emperor Akbar, between the hall of Public Audience and the royal seraglio, there was a bath chamber (*hammam*) in which the Emperor used to bathe. In this place only the most trusted royal attendants received admittance; and it was here that the Prime Minister (*Wazir* or *Diwan-i-Ala*') and the Lord Chancellor (*Mir Bakhshi*) being honoured by the royal presence, presented to the Emperor their urgent requests. Because of the bath chamber built nearby, this hall came to be called the Ghusal-Khana (or 'Privy Chamber') by both high and low, but now it is referred to as the Hall of Private Audience, as his most holy Majesty Shah Jahan has named it.

Thus, the hammams functioned not just as bathing rooms as we understand today, but also as places for extended repose, where the emperor could relax both body and mind, and intersperse formal work with social interaction. The Red Fort's imperial Hammam, located between the Diwan-i-Khas and the imperial gardens had two entrances: one on the southern face, leading on through the terrace to the Diwan-i-Khas; and the other on its western face, just in front of the doorway to the Moti Masjid, affording a direct connection for prayer after ablutions. Spatially, the Hammam consists of a series of three bays running from east-west with intervening narrow aisles. These contain water tanks and fountains, reportedly meant for hot and cold bathing. One of the aisles also afforded a covered connection to the terrace of the Hayat Baksh. As a prelude to the actual bathing chambers, was a south-facing verandah flanked by two rooms. These perhaps functioned as ancillary dressing rooms or cloak rooms. The Hammam and the Hayat Baksh, are together recorded to have cost Rs 6 lakh (0.6 million).

Since its function required a greater degree of privacy, the Hammam did not follow the typology of a pavilion. It visually and spatially terminated the sequence of the imperial pavilions connected on their raised river-front terrace. Beyond the Hammam, further connection to the terrace was possible only through its covered aisle—or more circuitously by walking into Hayat Baksh through the Diwan-i-Khas forecourt. Looking out on Hayat Baksh through small screened windows in largely opaque wall stretches, the northern face of the Hammam actually formed part of the garden and allowed in a glimpse of flowers and scents.

The location of the Hammam ensured that the emperor was the first to use the water lifted up from the river, which as described in preceding sections, entered the Fort at Shah Burj, fell down an ornamental marble chaddar and traversed the channel on the eastern terrace before flowing into the Hammam. The eastern chambers, externally screened through jalis with glass inserts, allowed views of the river while affording visual privacy and protection from river-breezes when bathing or changing. The apartments here, perhaps used as dressing chambers, are said to have contained three fountains, one of which reputedly sprayed rosewater.[33]

The eastern and central chambers are separated by a marble channel for the Nahr-i-Bahist, which disappears briefly under the floor close to the entrance of the verandah on the terrace. Another passage leading from the Diwan-i-Khas forecourt, lies between the central and western chambers. The central chamber, meant for hot or cold bathing, has a tank positioned in its middle. On its northern end is the *Shah Nashin*, the Emperor's Seat, built of an inlaid and carved block of marble. The western chamber has two rooms—one with a submerged tank looking out on to the Hayat Baksh, and the other with a flat tank with thin grooves to give out vapour for a steam bath.

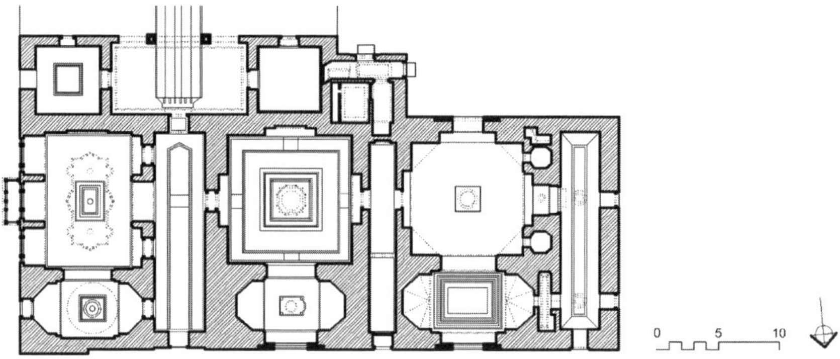

Imperial Hammam: Plan
(Drawing: N. Joshi, D. Cherian, Author, based on 579/97, Delhi, ASI PL)

The niches on the western wall would have originally carried the water-heating apparatus. The hot water operation is recorded by a historian in the reign of the last Mughal emperor to have consumed 125 maunds of wood.[34] Hot water was generally used in the imperial hammams, as borne out by excavations in Akbar's Palace at Fatehpur Sikri. These excavations adjacent to the hammam and its wall have yielded copper as well as clay pipes, iron and copper foils, and in an adjacent trench, pieces of charcoal and ashes.[35]

The Moti Masjid in the Red Fort was designed and constructed in close proximity to the Hammam. As an inscription on it certifies, it was completed in Aurangzeb's reign. He is reputed to have used this mosque for daily worship both in the early morning and late evening. His chroniclers write that 'from his great piety, he passes whole nights in the mosque which is in his palace.'[36] Though the inscription on the mosque establishes the date of its completion, it is possible that the construction of the Moti Masjid was started by Shah Jahan. Since its appearance and plan are very similar to Shah Jahan's Nagina Masjid in the Agra Fort, and quite different from the general style of mosques constructed by Aurangzeb, this appears to be a reasonable assumption.

It must also be remembered that Shah Jahan was one of the most prolific builders of mosques amongst the Mughals,[37] and that he barely stayed for ten years in the Red Fort before being displaced from the throne due to illness and the war of succession between his sons. While much of the Fort was completed by 1648 when Shah Jahan inaugurated it, construction work in Shahjahanabad continued even after this date. Thus,

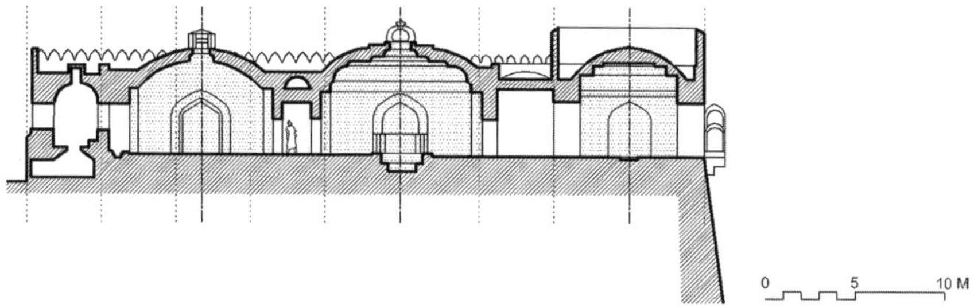

Imperial Hammam: Section
(Drawing: N. Joshi, Author, based on ASI Drawing)

the Idgah just outside the city walls was completed only in September 1655, seven years after the Fort's inauguration. It may have been possible that work on some parts of the Fort was also carried on during this time.

The inference that the Moti Masjid was established by Shah Jahan is strengthened by the fact that, in December 1653, a similar mosque is recorded to have been completed in the Agra Fort. The construction of this mosque in white marble (which Shah Jahan had commissioned when he moved from Agra to the Red Fort) had taken six lunar years. In 1653, Shah Jahan journeyed to Agra expressly to offer prayers in this new mosque. It might well be that its image was fresh in his mind, making him wish for a similar one in the Red Fort at Shahjahanabad.[38] If the time taken for the construction of this new mosque is assumed to be roughly comparable to the one at Agra, then it would have been completed in Aurangzeb's early regnal years and naturally, his titles appear on the records of its completion.

Since Shah Jahan frequently moved between imperial cities in different parts of his empire, new construction work within the forts would have been quite feasible. Additionally, the location of Moti Masjid, with its separate access courts from the Delhi Gate–Salimgarh route, would have ensured that, even when in residence, the emperor's normal entrance routine from the ceremonial Diwan-i-Am and Diwan-i-Khas forecourts would remain undisturbed despite any continuing construction work. It may also be inferred from the design of the Moti Masjid within an independent courtyard with high boundary walls that construction work here need not have intruded upon the activities of the emperor and his family in the adjacent pavilions and courts. The other advantage in

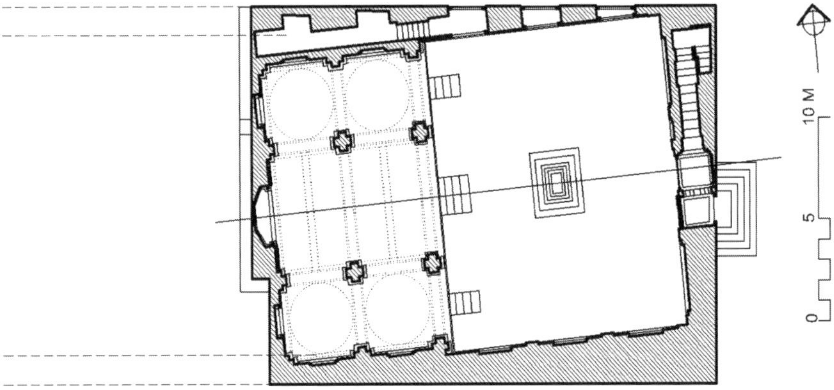

Moti Masjid: Plan
(Drawing: N. Joshi, D. Cherian, Author, based on 576/97, Delhi, ASI PL)

enclosing the mosque within a walled court was that the mosque could be oriented towards Mecca, while allowing its outer walls to be oriented to the geometry of the surrounding imperial pavilions and courtyards of the inner palace.

The boundary walls of the mosque-complex are recorded as 64 feet 2.5 inches (19.5 metres) from east to west, and 50 feet 3 inches (15.3 metres) from north to south. They enclose a court of 33 feet 10 inches (10.2 metres) by 40 feet 4 inches (12.2 metres). The remaining length is occupied by the mosque, which consists of a double-bayed entrance aisle and an inner hall. Three arches lead into the aisle and frame the central *mihrab*, with the central arch appreciably wider than the side ones—13 feet 1 inch (4 metres) versus 7 feet 9 inches (2.35 metres). The mosque facade echoes this arrangement: the central entrance arch is articulated in nine cusps as compared to the seven cusps on its flanking arches, while the central dome is also slightly higher than the side domes. The curved chajjas projecting above the arches follow these curved profiles. Such an organisation of space is similar to the Nagina Masjid in the Agra Fort, though there is a difference in the size of the two mosques.

Moti Masjid—with its roof of triple domes soaring above the walled court, their copper profile gilded and surmounted by lotus petals (padmakosa) supporting golden kalashes—constituted the other vertically arresting feature in the emperor's private domain. Bernier specifically marked their presence:

Moti Masjid: Shift in axis between courtyard walls (Photo: Author, 2000)

Moti Masjid: View from courtyard (Photo: Author, 2000)

> The entire mosque and courtyard and surrounding walls were all of beautiful white marble, highly polished, and the mosque itself had all its arches and interior inlaid with gold tracery, and was crowned with three beautifully shaped domes covered with plates of pure gold.[39]

As evident from this observation, the mosque would have formed a visual landmark, comparable to the similarly gilded Mussaman Burj dome, from within and outside the Fort. The effect of its domes on visitors is evident from many of the later drawings of the Fort both by Indian and British artists. Forbidden entry into the inner palace, with only a distant view of it from where the domes were predominant, they magnified the effect of the domes by often enlarging their proportions or representing the Fort with a virtual forest of domes.

Moti Masjid and its court marked the edge of two open spaces—the Diwan-i-Khas forecourt on one side and the Hayat Baksh garden on the other. This garden and the Mehtab Bagh, meant as they were for imperial use, were filled with flowers, trees and flowing water. Their plantation is not clearly described in court histories or travellers' accounts, though there are references to fresh grass, roses and fruit trees. However, the efficiency of Hayat Baksh's design as a daytime garden for informal living is evident from the reference to 'the fruitful trees of diverse kinds ... interlaced with each other in such a way that the sky is not anywhere visible beneath them'.[40] As Bernier points out, a substantial amount of tree plantation was the norm, 'the grandees having always made it a point to plant trees in the gardens and the courts for the sake of shade'.[41] Later drawings also show this area to be densely planted but without clear details of the type of trees, since the artists were probably not allowed into this part of the Fort. Written descriptions from Bahadur Shah Zafar's reign, however, do list different kinds of trees, shrubs and flowers in Hayat Baksh.

The location of these gardens was within the strict geometrical limits of the rectangle that generated the mussaman baghdadi. Their planned dimensions and well-detailed arrangements were emphasised by clearly defined walls or terraces and the provision of built, planted or water features in geometrical subdivisions. The proportions of Hayat Baksh (depicted as a square in all the available maps of the Fort including two of the more detailed maps)[42] were symbolically consistent with a typical charbagh configuration. Water channels and pathways divided it into four parts, and met in its very centre to form a tank that measured:

> 60 gaz by 60 gaz ... as a sunlike mirror, decorated with 49 silver jets, besides 112 more jets which play around it; in all its four avenues, each of which is made of red sandstone and completed with the breadth of 20 gaz, there is a channel six gaz broad which flows with 30 playing fountains in its centre.[43]

The Zafar Mahal, added within the tank in the reign of the last Mughal emperor, blocks the length and breadth of the Hayat Baksh. It reverses the original principle of situating built structures only at the edges of gardens and courts, which was especially efficient in the relatively constricted space within palace-forts and the consequent limitations on size and access to views, as compared to gardens in the hills or tomb-gardens. Thus, by ensuring that pavilions and other building were planned only on the periphery of such palace-gardens, the perception of available space was increased and the boundaries of the garden utilised for more than one function.

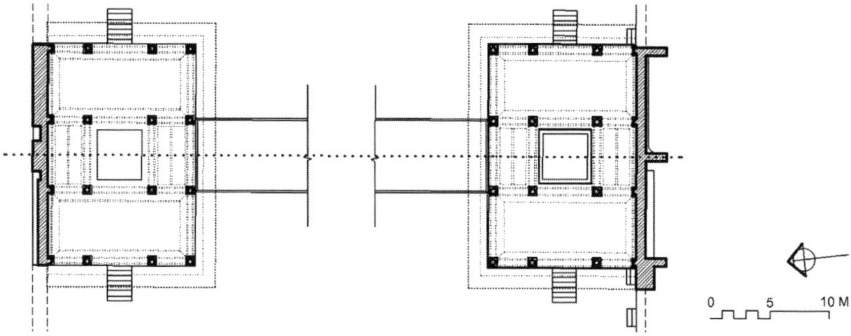

Plan: Sawan and Bhadon
(Drawing: N. Joshi, D. Cherian, Author, based on 579/97, Delhi, ASI PL)

In Hayat Baksh, this multi-functional theme was incorporated within its formal geometry—the centre of each of its four sides was marked by pavilions or gateways. On the northern and southern edges were the Sawan and Bhadon pavilions, and on the eastern and western ends, respectively, were the Moti Mahal pavilion and the connecting gateway to Mehtab Bagh. Moti Mahal, now no longer extant, is represented as a white pavilion in miniature drawings. Written descriptions, however, portray it as a red sandstone building, externally plastered, painted and gilded, with a marble tank in its centre.

The single-storeyed marble pavilions of Sawan and Bhadon are still extant, though without their adjoining walls and colonnades. Mirror images of each other externally, both measuring 48 feet 3 inches (14.7 metres) by 32 feet 10 inches (9.98 metres), they are organised slightly differently inside with differing water features. These are believed to have recreated the sounds and sights of rain in the months that each was named after. Thus, one of the pavilions has a large tank in its centre through which water would have flowed and cascaded abundantly. The other pavilion is designed with a shallow water channel in addition to the central tank, perhaps for added provision of lighter fountain sprays. The niches within both these tanks are recorded to have been decorated with vases holding flowers and candles. This would have heightened the aesthetic effect of flowing water, light and verdant views of the garden. The rectangular proportions of the Sawan and Bhadon pavilions, both in plan and elevation, are also designed to accentuate their spatial relationship with the garden. The triple arches on their longer viewing facades are oriented towards the central tank of the Hayat Baksh. Conversely, their shorter facades towards the boundaries of the garden are provided with a central wider arch in another triple-arched series to indicate their access routes.

The positions of these pavilions at the two ends of the central north-south axis of Hayat Baksh have been used as a basis for determining the limits of one dimension of this garden. The Hayat Baksh has been uniformly depicted as a square in the plans of the Fort. Thus, the confirmation of one of its dimensions in plan helps to obtain its overall size and boundaries. This leads, in turn, to a logical deduction of the position and dimensions of the no longer extant Mehtab Bagh. Mehtab Bagh lay in the northeastern section of the Fort and has been recorded to have existed between Hayat Baksh and Rastah Salimgarh (the arcaded street running west from the Naqqar Khana forecourt). The Bagh was probably connected by lockable entrance gateways from Hayat Baksh, Rastah Salimgarh and from the south wall between it and the Diwan-i-Am forecourt.

Since the Rastah Salimgarh bordering Mehtab Bagh, as discussed earlier, would have been largely used by the resident military and the emperor's guard, this garden would have been quite secure despite its semi-public nature. On its southern side, Mehtab Bagh was connected to the smaller courts of the imperial kitchens that formed a functional buffer between it and the Diwan-i-Am. The older Afghan baoli was also incorporated into the gardens positioned around it in a manner that responded to the octagonal geometry of the stepwell.

Together with the Shah Burj, the imperial gardens of Hayat Baksh and Mehtab Bagh marked the northern end of the mussaman baghdadi. The Shah Burj was a three-storeyed structure built in a combination of sandstone-clad masonry for the tower and middle pavilion, and marble-clad masonry for the pavilions on the ground and upper levels. The enclosed central chamber at its lower level was provided with an opening for a fountain in its floor. It had both a recreational and utilitarian function, with ceilings decorated in glass, channels, tanks and marble seats for viewing the river. A single-storeyed marble pavilion at the Shah Burj's southern end opened out on the east terrace of the Fort. This pavilion whose dimensions are recorded as 69 feet 2 inches (21.1 metres) by 33 feet (10.05 metres),[44] is crowned by the bangla roofs indicative of

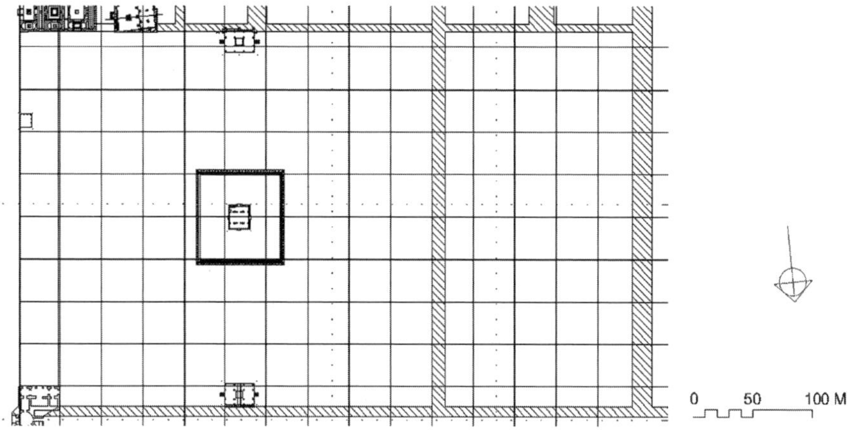

Hayat Baksh and Mehtab Bagh: Spatial organisation
(Drawing: N. Joshi, Author)

the imperial presence. This pavilion also marked the beginning of the Nahr-i-Bahist.

As discussed earlier, Shah Burj may have been designated for meetings between the emperor and a few of the trusted officers of the realm. Decisions made at these meetings had often to be delivered verbally to reach nobles in parts of the empire where it was not prudent to use written documents. The extent of secrecy associated with this use of the Shah Burj in Agra Fort can be gauged from the following description:

> In this exalted abode, none but the Fortunate Princes and a few trusted confidants are admitted without special permission; and so strictly is this adhered to that not even High State Officers (*Khidmatgars*) would come in without orders, but would rather delay the work they are entrusted with.[45]

The Shah Burj tower, which marked the northern end of the Red Fort's eastern face, was not an isolated building. It was spatially linked to continuous battlemented walls which had terraces that were patrolled and had steps connecting them to the rooms below. Conversations in all but the highest pavilion of the tower could be eavesdropped upon. It is likely that it was the pavilion at the highest level—also of use as a look-out space—that was designated for secret discussions.

The visual counterpoint of the Shah Burj was the Asad Burj located at the other end of the mussaman baghdadi. The octagonal profiles of these towers, which symmetrically flank the eastern elevation of the Fort, seem particularly suitable to negotiate the corner of the Fort's larger octagonal boundary. Though Asad Burj is spatially more complex than Shah Burj, their depictions indicate that their overall volume and proportions were similar. The original proportions of Asad Burj are extant, indicating how Shah Burj may have looked if its highest pavilion was still intact.

The function of Asad Burj is difficult to ascertain since there do not appear to be detailed references to it in court histories or other written accounts. It probably did not have a sufficiently important ceremonial function, neither does it seem to have been easily accessible to travellers. Some views of the river-face of the Fort show a single-storeyed white marble pavilion attached to Asad Burj,[46] similar to that of Shah Burj but without the imperial bangla roofs of the Shah Burj pavilion. This was perhaps an indication that the emperor did not frequent this space. The provision of a stepped well under Asad Burj and of steep ramps with central steps also point to its more utilitarian use. Part of the Burj was separated from the inner palace by a semi-public route, Rastah Bakht Burj, which directly led from Delhi Gate to Asad Burj (also called Bakht Burj). As a direct circulation route, it was probably used by guards for watering elephants and for transporting goods and ammunition brought by boats.

Even though Asad Burj was located in the private sector of the Fort and bounded the imperial seraglio, it occupied part of the semi-public domain since it also bordered the city. This is unlike Shah Burj, which looked out onto the sandy banks of the river and Salimgarh. Thus, to increase security, Asad Burj was equipped with a triangular water gate reportedly added to the baoli within it by Aurangzeb.

The imperial seraglio which occupied almost the entire southern sector between Bazaar Dilhi Darwaza and the river-face was, with the exception of two pavilions, razed to the ground in the nineteenth century. Information about this area is derived solely from their plans as depicted in available maps, some references in court histories, and stray accounts by visitors. Since most visitors were not permitted within, there are no pictorial representations and only a few accounts. One rare recorded instance of a male visitor is about the ambassador of Rum (Turkey) paying his respects to Begum Jahanara outside her apartments.[47] This was,

Asad Burj: Upper pavilion (Photo: Author, 1997)

however, an exception. Even Bernier, otherwise allowed access into the private inner palace, including the evening sessions in the Diwan-i-Khas normally reserved for favoured nobles, was debarred from entering here.

He writes in his memoirs that, '[i]t would afford me pleasure to conduct you to the seraglio, as I have introduced you into other parts of the Fortress. But who is the traveller that can describe from ocular observation the interior of that building?'[48] Bernier's search for a traveller

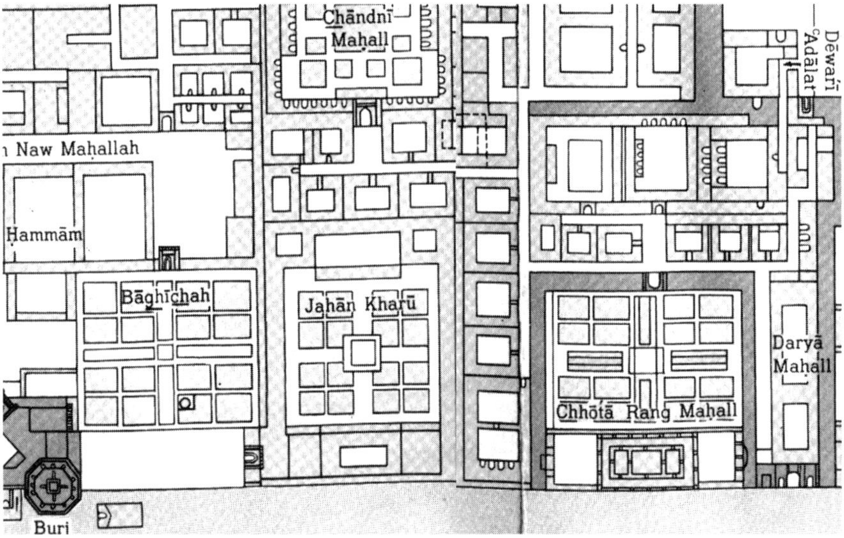

Imperial seraglio
(Trans.X/1659, OIOC, BL)

who could accurately describe for him the splendours of the imperial seraglio remained unfulfilled. On one occasion he did succeed in entering the seraglio in the capacity of a skilled physician, but was led blindfolded through successive courts. Around 200 later, as the power of the Mughals waned, and the strict boundaries between the public and private domains became diluted, some women visitors did manage to enter the seraglio. But their descriptions are brief and lack both the detailed observation of Bernier as well as the knowledge and imagination to fathom the complexity and organisation of the space that lay beneath the outer symbols of decay.

Both the density of built structures as well as the types of buildings in the seraglio were graded according to the status of the occupants. Those in the western part, closer to the public north-south axis, were less luxurious in their construction as well as in the amount of available open space. In the eastern part of the seraglio close to the river, the pattern of built structures was similar to the extant imperial pavilions. They were positioned at the centre or head of courtyards which, in some cases, were designed as courtyard gardens. These gardens were bounded by a colonnade or a series of small cells around individual courts. At least three pavilions with such private gardens are depicted in the more

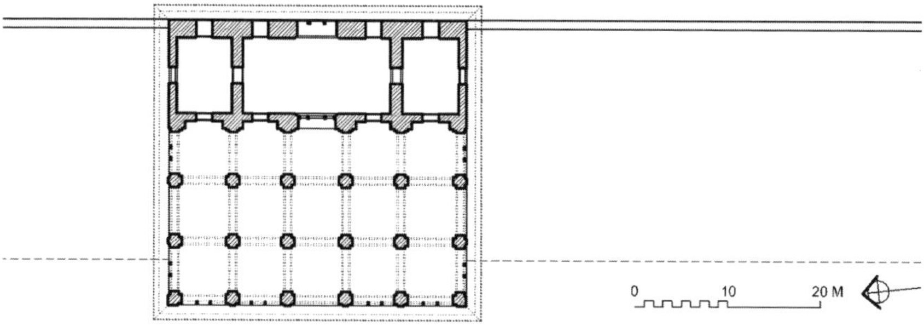

Mumtaz Mahal: Plan
(Drawing: N. Joshi, D. Cherian, Author, based on 581/97, Delhi, ASI PL)

detailed maps of the Fort.[49] These apartments, located in the more secure private part close to the Rang Mahal and the emperor's quarters, were occupied by his immediate family.

By the time the Red Fort was constructed, Shah Jahan's beloved queen, Mumtaz Mahal, in whose memory the Taj Mahal was raised, had been dead for about twenty years. Though Shah Jahan had other wives, his eldest daughter Jahanara came to occupy the role of chief advisor to her father. The private seal of the emperor was entrusted in her charge, and she is reported to have occupied the most important seraglio building. This, the Mumtaz Mahal (also called the *Chotta Rang Mahal* and Khas Mahal by Sir Syed Ahmed, and the mansion of Nawwab Begum Sahib by Muhammad Waris), was located closest to the Rang Mahal.[50]

The Mumtaz Mahal's proportions in plan are almost a square—88 feet 2 inches (26.89 metres) by 82 feet 2 inches (25.06 metres)—and deviate from the decidedly rectangular proportions of the rest of the imperial pavilions. Internally, however, this pavilion may be spatially sub-divided into two rectangular spaces—an outer verandah and an inner apartment of three rooms. The canal of water that ran through the eastern terrace also passed through Jahanara's rooms, and continued into the other terrace pavilions of the seraglio, to finally fall into the Asad Burj baoli.

South of the court of the Mumtaz Mahal were a series of smaller courts bounded by cells, perhaps occupied by Jahanara's personal attendants and companions of noble birth. The theme of an important pavilion surrounded by subsidiary ones may have been a continuation of the practice common in the city, in which each nobleman's dependants clustered around his house. Since the seraglio contained many different queens and princesses, they were effectively like different establishments within a larger common area, united in their confinement within the Fort but susceptible to the rivalries of people living in close proximity.

The seraglio, thus, was not merely a residence. It was also a place for entertainment, recreation and the daily needs of the women and children living within it. As part of the emperor's daily routine, he administered matters here, including requests for help to poor and needy women, grants of land, cash and daily allowances concerning its inmates. The seraglio's secrecy and security also implied that it had other uses. Records of Shah Jahan's daily activities in the Agra Fort observe that letters and orders dictated by him were sealed and signed by the *Sahib-i-Risalat*, or the master of correspondence and the prime minister and thereafter sent to the 'sacred seraglio to be ornamented with the exalted royal seal ... in the keeping of her Majesty, the Queen Mumtaz-al-Zamani'.[51]

Beautiful and varied as it was, prolonged residence in the seraglio for the daughters, mothers and wives of the emperor would certainly have been occasionally tedious and frustrating. There were restrictions on their movement beyond the private domains of the palace, though their companions, slaves and maids had a greater deal of freedom. They could go out into the city to buy supplies and were often entrusted as messengers in personal romances or political intrigues. The queens, however, ventured out of the Red Fort only on special occasions to enjoy the charms of the Begum Bagh in Chandni Chowk or to visit other parts of the city and its environs.

There are records of the constraints on their movements being relaxed on other occasions as well, but these appear to be few and far between. The official court history of Shah Jahan's reign mentions an incident soon after his ascension when his three elder sons Dara, Shah Shuja and Aurangzeb arrived in Agra from Lahore. At this time, their mother, the Queen Mumtaz Mahal, rode out to meet her sons along with her other children, though only after seeking permission from the emperor. Since Mumtaz Mahal was Shah Jahan's favoured queen, she and her children also accompanied the emperor on his formal visits to the house of her father, Yaman-al-daulah,[52] or on political expeditions and pleasure visits to various parts of the empire.

These opportunities to move out were obviously events to look forward to, though, even on these occasions, there was an attempt to maintain the privacy and seclusion of the seraglio. As later descriptions by Bernier and Tavernier reveal, the retinue of Roshanara Begum, Shah Jahan's younger daughter, consisting as it did of a procession of elephants, eunuchs and guards, made certain that no members of the public gazed upon her.[53]

Within the Fort, the degree of security and privacy decreased southwards towards Asad Burj and westwards towards the axis from Delhi Gate. These, the more public part of the seraglio, were for the eunuchs, attendants and maids who served the emperor's private family. Their residential, recreational and commercial buildings and open spaces were located here. Most maps of the Fort depict a street separating the seraglio from the Asad (Bakht) Burj. This street, termed Rastah Bakht Burj in the mid-nineteenth century OIOC map, would have functioned as a buffer between the princesses' pavilions and the soldiers' patrolling area. Gardens and baths (probably for the dependants of the seraglio) and a denser built area (probably maids' quarters) were placed adjacent to the Rastah Bakht Burj.

This part of the seraglio where the maids and servants resided had other entrances into it from the arcaded street that connected Delhi Gate to the Naqqar Khana forecourt. While most maps of the Fort indicate that this southern edge of the seraglio had a linear built-form, the mid-nineteenth-century OIOC map specifically designates this area as the *Mina Bazaar*. The eastern side of Mina Bazaar is represented with a typology of cells around open courts. This side probably functioned as residences or small workshop spaces within the seraglio.

The denser collections of dwellings separated by narrow streets seen here were the opposite of the planned formality of the emperor's precinct. Thus, this part of the seraglio had a similar built-form as seen in the less formal parts of Shahjahanabad. Virtually no visible remains of these areas, which formed such an inseparable link in the Red Fort's functioning as well as its appearance, are extant. Their disappearance, along with other intervening parts of the imperial domains, has almost completely broken the spatial as well as functional links between different parts of the Fort. To rediscover these links, it is important to revisit the assaults—both premeditated and unplanned—on the use and transformation of all these spaces in the Fort.

6

UNPLANNED ASSAULT

'... for, the "shape" is not made by the relation of stone to stone, but by the relation of human being to human being.'

Virginia Woolf, *A Room of One's Own*

The shape of the Red Fort had been fashioned out of a complex alchemy of human relationships. These relationships varied from those between the emperor, and his noblemen, architects, and family, to those between the imperial court and its subjects. They arose from the specific governance systems of the Mughals as well as their unique social, religious and cultural customs. Inevitably, all these personal and political encounters underwent some changes with the passage of time. These changes were hastened by the volatile social and political conditions of those times. The transformation of the Red Fort, almost immediately after Shah Jahan's reign, mirrored these changes.

An important part was played in the Fort's transformation, by shifting power equations over a much larger canvas than its actual boundaries. These power equations, always tenuously balanced, snapped violently in the reigns of Shah Jahan's successors. Political and financial troubles soon followed—perhaps an unavoidable descent from the heights that Mughal rule had consistently risen to for over a century. The damage to the Red Fort's built fabric as a result of these reversals was, thus, inevitable.

The shape and use of the Fort consequently transformed in wide-ranging ways. The nature of these transformations may be gleaned from a study of the official and unofficial court histories as well as from travellers' accounts, maps and drawings of this period. These transformations ranged from a partial neglect of the Fort's original designed spaces and the insertion of newer and less refined buildings, to a weakening of the sanctity of the imperial domains. All these amounted to an unplanned assault, as it were, on the design of the Fort.

More unnatural were the violent transformations enforced on the Red Fort as a result of political invasions. These invasions, abruptly and sometimes fatally, ended passages of its life-story. The first of these was the sacking of Shahjahanabad and the Fort by the Persian Emperor, Nadir Shah. This was followed by attacks from the Afghans and from local invaders such as the Marathas and the Rohillas. Finally, when the British wrested power from the last Mughal ruler, Bahadur Shah II, the Fort was changed completely. The banishment of Bahadur Shah and most of the surviving members of the royal family to Burma caused the complete erasure of the way of life for which the Fort was designed. And the subsequent clearing away of large areas in the Fort and the city removed almost all physical records of that way of life.

The journey of the Red Fort from a vibrant miniature city—graced by the seat of 'the shadow of God'[1]—to a handful of ravaged buildings playing reluctant hosts to an unfamiliar way of life may be said to have commenced during the last years of Shah Jahan's reign. On the sixth of September 1657, Shah Jahan fell ill at the Red Fort. For about a week, he was unable to follow either the administrative routine of the court or the ritual of giving darshan to his subjects.[2] The illness of an emperor was always a signal for intrigue in a political system with no clear system of succession. In this case, the presence of four adult and ambitious princes, who were already governors of vast provinces, led to an all-out race for the throne.

The eldest, Prince Dara Shikoh, had a head start in this race. He was fortuitously present at the imperial court in Shahjahanabad when Shah Jahan fell ill. He also had the benefit of his father's public nomination as heir-apparent. Dara conveyed Shah Jahan to Agra, ostensibly in the hope that the change of climate would facilitate his speedy recovery. Important components such as the treasury, as well as part of the administrative activity were also shifted to the Agra Fort. In earlier times, the emperor's absence from the capital was a regular event necessitated by the Mughal style of governance: constant movement to different parts of the empire was required for reasons of administration, politics or pilgrimage. However, this time, the removal of the ailing Shah Jahan to Agra was ominous. Even without completing the formalities of accession, Dara began to direct events at the imperial court. He also stopped all news regarding his father's health, resulting in rumours of Shah Jahan's death.

The outcome of all this was a war of succession amongst Dara and his brothers, each of whom overtly or covertly asserted their right to the throne. Shah Jahan played almost no part in this war that involved nearly all parts of the empire, remaining at the Agra Fort with his favourite daughter and other members of the seraglio. However, despite his manifest advantages, it was not Dara but Shah Jahan's third son, Prince Aurangzeb, who crowned himself the new emperor in 1658 after defeating his brothers and forcing his father to abdicate. This did not signify the end of war. Dara evaded capture till the following year. The battle with Prince Shah Shuja, the governor of Bengal, continued till 1660.

Prince Murad Baksh was finally beheaded after Aurangzeb had ascended to the throne, in order to prevent further unrest through an uprising of his followers. The continued conflict caused famine conditions in many parts of the empire. Naturally enough, the emphasis during these years was not on building activities, though symbolic supremacy continued to be vested in the Red Fort. It was the Fort that Aurangzeb hastened to, in a bid to formalise his claim to the empire. Later, when the troubles of war were over, he decided to hold a second crowning here. After Aurangzeb's formal ascension, the Red Fort continued to be intermittently occupied as a ceremonial palace for some years. During this time, the Agra Fort also enjoyed an almost equally important status, as is evident from Aurangzeb's decision to transfer the imperial treasury (that he had moved to the Red Fort at Delhi in 1662) back to the Agra Fort in 1666.

However, the pattern of active conquests that Aurangzeb reintroduced soon after his ascension kept him away from the capital city. During this time, many parts of the Mughal empire had begun to assert their independence, especially the Afghans in the northwest, the Rajputs in Ajmer and Chittor in Rajasthan and the Marathas in Burhanpur, Ahmednagar and Aurangabad (Daulatabad) in the Deccan. After 1685, a little more than half his reign, Aurangzeb did not inhabit Shahjahanabad. He was accompanied in camp by a substantial portion of Shahjahanabad's population—many of the officials, courtiers, soldiers, attendants, artisans, recorders and messengers employed at the Mughal court. In their absence, the economic, social and political status of Shahjahanabad declined and the Red Fort became virtually empty. A proportion of dependants continued to reside in the Fort such as wives, daughters, very young sons, personal guards, some ministers, attendants and some artisans of the imperial workshops. Their activities, largely unrecorded in court histories, were probably confined to their own quarters in the Fort. The emperor's private and public domains, forbidden to most courtiers and inmates, would have, thus, largely remained silent and unoccupied.

During the time that Aurangzeb did reside in the Fort, he substantially altered its functioning and appearance. These alterations seem small when examined individually, especially seen in light of the overall transformations that the Fort has been subject to through its history. But they significantly altered some of the basic precepts of the Fort's design. The erosion of its social and cultural institutions soon followed. One of the first of these alterations was the change in the Fort's entrance systems and its urban relationship with Shahjahanabad by the construction of a barbican in front of the Lahori Gate, which blocked its axis with Lahori Bazaar. An additional gateway was introduced at right angles to the Gate's axis. At 40 feet high and 24 feet wide,[3] this gateway is merely the size of the Lahori Gate entrance arch. In an obvious derivation from the Lahori Gate, this gate also had a battlemented parapet that terminated in slender minarets. However, neither its motifs nor its materials bear the distinguishing marks of Shah Jahan's imperial ceremonial entrance.

The gateway's construction was probably motivated by Aurangzeb's predominant concerns of defence over urban design or architecture. These concerns were not limited to the Red Fort. In 1659, Aurangzeb ordered the construction of a fortified wall around the Agra Fort as well. And in 1673, he ordered the building of Alamgiri Gate in the Lahore Fort as well as the completion of Badshahi Mosque at Lahore near the Fort.[4]

Popular versions of the reason for this new indirect entrance into Lahori Gate attribute it to Aurangzeb's thoughtfulness in saving the inhabitants from paying obeisance to the emperor every time they viewed the direct axis of his throne in the Diwan-i-Am. However, such interpretations do not explain the construction of a similar barbican and gateway ordered in front of the Delhi Gate, since this Gate did not afford any direct visual or spatial link with the imperial throne in the Fort.

While the construction of the secondary gateways introduced some measure of defence, it completely negated the impact of the central entrance axes that linked the Red Fort and Shahjahanabad. Shah Jahan, alive and imprisoned in Agra Fort, responded to this by writing to Aurangzeb: 'Dear son, you have made the Fort a bride and put a veil upon her face'.[5] The change in the profile of the Fort's boundaries also affected the symmetry of the gardens aligned on either side of its Gates. Instead of passing straight into the Lahori or Delhi Gates, the court retinue had to follow a circuitous route that ate up a large part of the gardens. Aurangzeb additionally demolished two stone statues of elephants installed at the Delhi Gate, the *Hatiapol*, 'to put down uncanonical innovations'.[6] Thus, the formal architectural relationship between the Red Fort and the city was to a large extent, reduced in Aurangzeb's reign.

There were some changes within the Fort as well. The bereaved mothers, wives, daughters and other female dependants of Aurangzeb's brothers were accommodated in the seraglio, creating additional stress on the services and space available. Though the emperor's private domain would have been assuredly spared from the effects of this population increase, it would have been affected functionally and, to some degree, architecturally. This transformation in the design and use of the Fort was concurrent with the last years of its construction. A mosque for imperial use—Moti Masjid—was completed at this time[7]. Accounts of its date of construction vary between 1659 CE (AH 1070) to 1663 CE (AH 1073). The mosque stands in a private walled court, and its construction would not have interrupted existing activities in the imperial areas. But its position between Hayat Baksh and the Diwan-i-Khas forecourt led to inevitable changes in the boundary and entrances of these areas.

Records of the first ten years of Aurangzeb's reign indicate that his way of life within the Fort's Public and Private Imperial domains continued

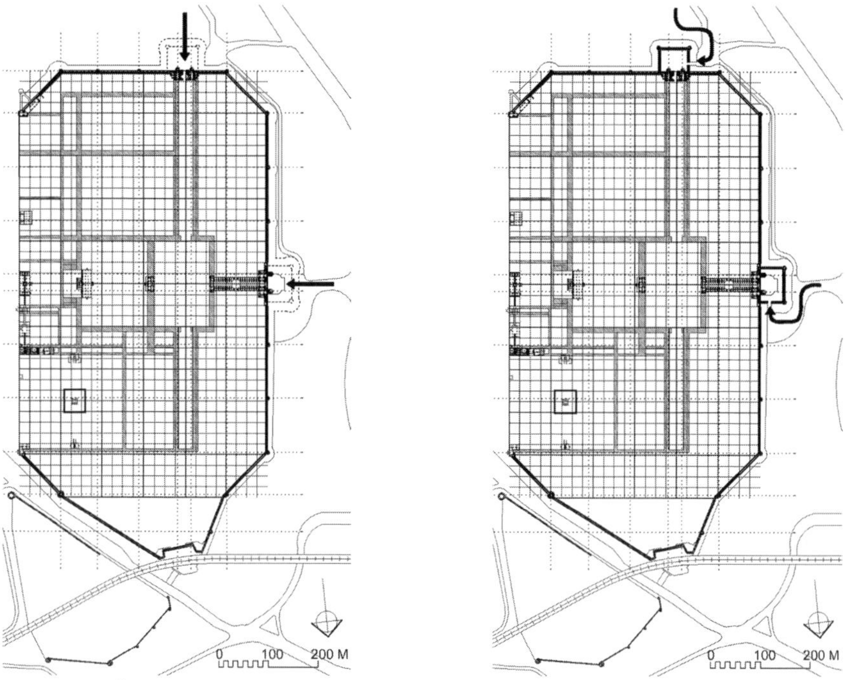

Movement system into the Lahori and Delhi Gates before and after Aurangzeb's intervention (Drawing: N. Joshi, Author)

to be much the same as his father's. He continued to use built and open space in the Mughal tradition. In fact, Aurangzeb had himself crowned at a favourite recreational spot of the imperial family, the Shalimar Bagh, built in Shah Jahan's reign by one of his wives, and situated in the outskirts of Shahjahanabad. He also did not relinquish the dependence on astrologers. The auspicious day for accession being indicated as 21 July, and in the absence of sufficient time to reach the Red Fort and make preparations for the event, these gardens were chosen as the crowning site.[8] As chronicled by Bernier as well as by court historians, the river banks next to the Fort continued to be thronged by citizens each morning, enlivened by regular spectacles of elephant fights and occasional lavish celebrations.

Within the Fort, the appearance of, and flexibility in, the use of space was also much as in Shah Jahan's time. So was the accompanying pomp and ceremony. On the occasions of Aurangzeb's coronation as well as on festivals such as *Id-ul-Fitr*, both the Diwan-i-Am and Khas were decorated for celebrations. Robes, jewels, horses and promotions were given as rewards to noblemen and princes.[9] The daily activity in the Diwan-i-Am, as Francois Bernier observed, was an impressive sight where,

> the monarch everyday, sits upon his throne, with some of his sons at his right and left; while eunuchs standing about the royal person flap away the flies with peacock's tails. Immediately under the throne is an enclosure, surrounded by silver rails, in which are assembled the whole body of Omrahs, the rajahs and the ambassadors.

The rules governing the use of this space were also followed strictly, as the incident of the expelled king of Kashgar discussed in Chapter 2 shows.[11] The emperor's private domain was guarded zealously as before and reserved solely for his use. Occasionally, political affairs of a particularly intimate nature concerning the imperial family were transacted here. One such occasion was when Aurangzeb initiated a reconciliation with his estranged son, Muhammad Sultan, who had rebelled and joined forces with Shah Shuja during the war of succession. The reconciliation was effected in the Khwabgah, where Aurangzeb also gave audience to Sipihir Shikoh, Dara's younger son.[12]

Sipihir Shikoh had been held prisoner of war by Aurangzeb, but spared death. He was granted imperial pardon, and persuaded to become a part of the emperor's family by marrying Princess Zubdatunnisa Begum. Aurangzeb consistently followed this method of healing the breaches brought about by the protracted war. To avoid further contention within the family, he married the surviving children of his brothers to his offspring. Though Mughal princesses in earlier reigns were often not allowed to marry, Aurangzeb married his daughters, Zubdatunnisa and Mihirunnisa, to Sipihir Shikoh and to Murad Baksh's son, respectively. His sons, the Princes Muhammad Sultan, Muhammad Azam and Muhammad Akbar, were in turn married to Murad Baksh's daughter, Dostdarbanu, and Dara Shikoh's daughter, Jahanzebbanu, and granddaughter, Salimabanu.[13] Descriptions from court histories indicate that Aurangzeb's sons lived in relative splendour in mansions within the Fort, though one of them, in the tradition of adult princes residing in independent establishments, is recorded to have stayed in a mansion on the riverbank.

The location of the mansions of some of Aurangzeb's sons may be inferred to be in the immediate north of the imperial gardens—in the quarter between Shah Burj and Salimgarh Gate. This was probably due to a combination of economic and political factors. The protracted war of succession would have resulted in financial losses to the treasury and a consequent decrease in allowances to the princes. The position of the princes' quarters in the Fort between the resident military, the imperial private quarters and the Yamuna, was theoretically under greater surveillance by the emperor. They were also constrained within a comparatively small area, with reduced access to the river and other parts of the city.

Thus, most of the princes would have been unable to live in the opulent style patronised in the times preceding the war of succession—as, for instance, by Dara Shikoh in his grand mansion located outside the Fort on the banks of the Yamuna in Shahjahanabad. In fact, Dara's continued popularity with the citizens of Shahjahanabad could also not be ignored. His humiliation and death at the orders of Aurangzeb generated much public lamentation, as observed by Bernier and other contemporary writers. Though it was unlikely that this distress would manifest itself in any concerted violence, the prudent Aurangzeb may have considered it safer for his sons to live within the Fort. Aurangzeb's disciplined sternness towards his subjects and family, and his increasing discriminatory and rigid policies, especially after the first ten years of his reign, resulted in a decrease in individual freedom as well as in the arts and in social life. There are various recorded instances of the populace seeking to attack him in publicly accessible places such as the Idgah, and nearly all his sons attempted insurrections at one time or another.

Many of Aurangzeb's unpopular decisions were clothed as religious dictats, possibly motivated as much by the need for economic bolstering as for the propitiation of conservative and powerful courtiers. Soon after he ascended the throne, Aurangzeb ordered the demolition of a temple at Agra.[14] In 1669, he caused the demolition of the Vishwanath temple at Kashi,[15] which alienated a great number of his subjects. His decision to impose the *jaziya,* or tax on non-believers in all parts of the empire, caused a further divide in the populace. The repeated protests of a number of Hindu residents around Delhi, who are also recorded to have gathered below the jharoka window of the Fort to express their inability to pay the jaziya, went unheeded.

In 1668, at the celebrations marking his fifty-first solar birthday, Aurangzeb stopped the ceremony of weighing the emperor against silver and gold that was traditionally given to charity. Part of the reason for this was his pious temperament that forbore exuberant display. The other equally valid but unstated reason may have been the decreasing coffers. In this year, he also forbade his official historian from writing the history of his reign.[16] The dependence of the arts on court patronage resulted in the migration of artists, poets and musicians to more sympathetic patrons. The imperial court acquired sombre overtones by degrees.

The next year, on the occasion of the marriage of his son, Aurangzeb countenanced the decoration of the area leading to the prince's seraglio with gold, silver and plain cloth. He himself sat on a throne of gold. But, three days later, he announced that men should not use gold in their garments as this was opposed to the Holy Law. Music, considered an especially frivolous and wasteful pursuit by him, was expressly outlawed. However, ceremonial music was retained till 1670. After this, Aurangzeb ordered a change in the tradition of the naubat playing all day on the emperor's birthday, and declared it was henceforth to be played only after the passing of one *prahar*, as on Sundays.[17] Initially, the chief musician and his retinue were allowed to attend court on the condition that they did not make music. Later, musicians and singers were excluded from the court altogether. All these orders implied a decrease in the ceremonial and celebratory use of the Naqqar Khana, which had hitherto been a pivotal space in the entrance sequence of the Fort.

Gradually, music was forbidden entirely. A popular story records the dramatic fashion in which this dismal event was commemorated by the distraught citizens of Shahjahanabad.[18] They sung a dirge past the Fort and within the emperor's earshot, loudly lamenting the death of music. However, this did not wring any sympathetic response from the impassive emperor, who merely inquired what the commotion was about, and disdainfully expressed the hope that music be buried deep enough for it to not surface ever again.[19] Aurangzeb also declared the practice of darshan idolatrous in his later years, and discontinued it. Consequently, the early morning use of the Mussaman Burj by the emperor for the daily ritual interaction with his subjects and their congregation on the riverbank would also have stopped. Thus, over time, the public use and urban function of the river and its environs decreased substantially with Aurangzeb's gradual relinquishment of all these pursuits.

Aurangzeb's ban on music lasted till his death in 1705 CE, which ended an almost fifty-year reign. His immediate successor was his son, Bahadur Shah, who spent his rule in political campaigns. It is said that Bahadur Shah did not ever enter Delhi as emperor. During this period, though there was reduced cultural and economic activity, some architectural patronage by members of the imperial family did continue in the form of mosques and shrines—in Mehrauli as well as in Shahjahanabad. One of Aurangzeb's daughters, Princess Zinatunnisa, commissioned a mosque, the *Zinat-ul-Masjid*, on the Yamuna banks south of the Fort.

The practice of leaving imperial palaces unoccupied was not new. The Mughals had, in the past, moved frequently between different imperial cities. However, the period of absence was normally not greater than a few years. The Red Fort, in contrast, had not been inhabited by the emperor for almost thirty years. It was only after the death of Bahadur Shah in 1712 and another war of succession, that his son, Jahandar Shah, reigned as the next Mughal emperor from Shahjahanabad. With the return of its imperial court and most of the active population, Shahjahanabad revived almost immediately. So did its arts, including music and poetry. The Red Fort, an empty shell in the absence of the emperor, his retinue, and his routine, would have again resounded with naqqaras and salutations. Its imperial pavilions would have once again been shaded and surrounded by special red awnings and tents that signified the emperor's presence.

However, this revival occurred at a time when the empire's political boundaries and economy had begun to diminish. The result of the long absence of the previous emperors was also manifest in the role of the court ministers entrusted with the responsibility of the Fort and Shahjahanabad. These ministers, with almost independent charge of the capital city, developed pretensions to power. Outwardly, they functioned as representatives of the Mughal emperor—till he remained a powerful figure. When the rulers to the throne began to display signs of political weakness, the ministers sought to wield actual power. The successors of Bahadur Shah gave their ministers this opportunity. Inexperienced and weak, they were puppets in the hands of opposing factions in the court.

Jahandar Shah, his son, after a struggle for ascension, ruled for barely a year before being murdered.

Jahandar Shah's successor was his nephew, Farukhsiyar, who had revolted against him. Farukhsiyar ruled for six years before he too was murdered by his minister. The six years of his rule were not free of strife or persecution. Some of his political decisions had lasting repercussions. It was Farukhsiyar who granted the first special farman to the East India Company, after reportedly being successfully cured of a disease by one of its doctors.[20] During his reign, the Sikhs invaded Shahjahanabad but were defeated, and their leader Banda was executed.

Within the Fort, there appears to have been some decrease in the magnificence of its buildings, as evident from the fact that the silver ceiling of the Imtiyaz Mahal or the Rang Mahal is believed to have been replaced at this time with a copper ceiling to raise money.[21] In such a situation, it is reasonably certain that other parts of the Fort, though not necessarily subjected to this stripping, could not have been furnished or repaired with the splendour of former years. The use of the Naqqar Khana to serve as a prison for Farukhsiyar before he was reportedly killed in this place, is also an indication of the unpleasant transformation in its original function.

After the assassination of Farukhsiyar, two young princes were put forth as contenders for the throne by powerful ministers. They were unable to survive for very long, signalling the decline of the imperial family. The shift in power was reflected in architectural patronage—an activity that consumed a substantial amount of time, money and manpower. Provincial courts, some of them still vassals of the Mughals, such as in Rajasthan, Hyderabad and Lucknow, evolved their own version of architecture based on Mughal precedents, and became the new centres of patronage.

The next Mughal emperor was Muhammad Shah, a great-grandson of Aurangzeb. He ascended the throne in 1719, a year that ominously coincided with an earthquake[22] which caused some damage to the Red Fort. The people of Shahjahanabad, referred to Muhammad Shah who was a connoisseur of the arts and a skilful writer and composer, appropriately, as *Rangila* or the Colourful. Some of his works are still sung today as part of classical music compositions. He continued the tradition of patronage

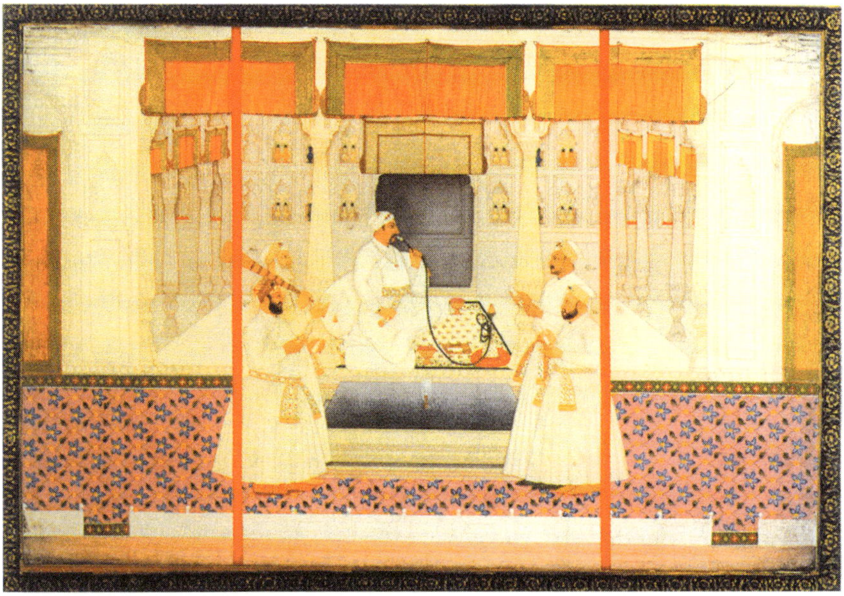

Muhammad Shah Rangila with courtiers, by Bhupal Singh, 1730,
(MS Douce. Or.a.3. f.14, Bodleian Library)

Muhammad Shah Rangila playing Holi c.1738-9
(MS Douce. Or.b.3 no. 22, Bodleian Library)

of the arts including writing, which also ensured that detailed accounts of his reign were recorded in court histories.

Among the important architectural events that took place during his reign (1719–48) was the construction of the *Jantar Mantar* in 1724, a unique observatory with large, immovable masonry instruments. This complex was constructed outside the city walls on the initiative of Maharaja Sawai Jai Singh, the ruler of Amber and a vassal of Mohammed Shah. Other members of the court also made architectural contributions—such as the *Fakhr-al masjid* in Kashmiri Gate and the enclosure walls of *Chiragh Dilhi*. Though policies such as the abolishment of the jaziya and celebrations of the festival of Holi spurred the populace's faith in him, Muhammad Shah also weakened the sanctity and security of the imperial quarters, whose use was strictly regulated right from the time that the Red Fort was founded. He chose to marry a dancing girl and established her as his queen in the Fort, and, more disastrously, her brother as his special advisor.

With no serious interest in administration, Muhammad Shah handed over management of important areas of the Fort which, in earlier reigns, was essentially based on appropriate qualifications to whoever temporarily gained his favour. There are records of him confining his son to the seraglio and a reluctance to train him in any princely pursuits.[23] Such disregard for administrative and political matters was responsible for an accelerated decline in Mughal fortunes, as revealed in an account by a contemporary historian.

> This neglect on the part of the Sovereign was speedily taken advantage of by all the *amirs* and nobles, who usurped possession of *subas* and *parganas*, and appropriated to themselves the revenue of those provinces, which in former days were paid into the Royal treasury ... As the Royal treasury gradually became emptied, the emperor's army was reduced to great straits and was at last, entirely broken up; whilst the nobles of the land ... now amassed large sums of money from their own *jagirs*, and from those Government lands of which they had seized possession.[24]

The reduced imperial finances were further strained by an attack on Shahjahanabad in 1737 CE by the Marathas under Baji Rao Peshwa. Though repulsed, this compounded difficulties in revenue collection and

Burra Imambara, Lucknow (Photo: Author, 1995)

did not make for a climate where architectural patronage was a priority.[25] Such a situation had implications on the use, maintenance and appearance of the Fort. It was also during this period that internal differences grew to the extent that the governor of Hyderabad, a former prime minister, resigned his post and founded an independent kingdom in Hyderabad. The serving prime minister of the emperor, a vassal only in name, functioned independently from Lucknow in Avadh. As a result, when the Persian Emperor Nadir Shah marched to Delhi in 1739 after subjugating Qandahar, Ghazni and Kabul, the Mughal army surrendered after a brief battle. The Red Fort is not recorded to have suffered much damage in the battle and its aftermath. However, its fabled Peacock Throne and other treasures were removed. Nadir Shah was escorted into the Fort as a victor and lodged in the imperial quarters vacated for him by Muhammad Shah, who moved to the Shah Burj pavilion.

This abject invitation to an invader, into the area reserved strictly for the imperial household, signified the emperor's lack of strength. In a Fort where the use of space was based on the demarcation of power zones, such a change marked the levels that the power of the Mughals had diminished to. This breach of court etiquette may be identified as the turning point in the political, architectural and social history of the Fort and city. It was the very reversal of the patrimonial-bureaucratic ideal, portending the actual destruction of the Fort as well as the Mughal empire. When the emperor was unable to protect the dignity of his own person, there was no force in his claim to protect his empire. Indeed, this claim was soon tested and found wanting. Fighting broke out between the Persian soldiers and the inhabitants of Shahjahanabad, ostensibly caused by the rumour that Nadir Shah had been murdered.[26]

The Persian emperor's consequent anger at the assault on his soldiers led him to publicly sanction looting, unchecked destruction and wanton killing—showing his summary contempt for the once mighty House of Timur, despite the verbal assurances of equality sealed by the embrace of one Islamic ruler for the other. Many areas of the city were burnt down and its inhabitants killed; hundreds of craftsmen, animals, materials and fabled treasures removed to Persia as booty.[27] Apart from the bloodshed and carnage, this dealt a severe blow to the physical form and economic resilience of the city, as well as its architectural patronage.

> The Chandni chouk, the fruit market, the Daribah Bazaar, and the buildings around the Masjid-i-Jama were set fire to and reduced to ashes. The inhabitants, one and all were slaughtered ... The Persians laid violent hands on everything and everybody, cloth, jewels, dishes of gold and silver, were acceptable spoil ... The ruin in which its beautiful streets and buildings were now involved was such that the labour of years could alone restore the town to its former state of grandeur.[28]

Apart from this terrible destruction, the image of the emperor suffered indelibly. Nadir Shah's departure after three months left Muhammad Shah on the throne at Red Fort as before. But he was emperor of a ravaged city and Fort. The imperial treasury had been emptied; all the noblemen as well as the citizens of Shahjahanabad compelled to pay a ransom; the all-powerful Mughal reduced to a figure of history.

Nonetheless, after some time, normal life in Shahjahanabad limped back. Court practices resumed. Musical soirees were suspended in the Fort, but the practitioners of varied forms such as khayal, qawwali, tarana and jangla continued to increase. Older styles such as dhrupad flourished: its exponents included the descendants of Tansen, the legendary court musician of Akbar.[29] Delhi was still the favoured residence of mystics and saints. Creative writing in both Persian and Urdu remained undiminished, as did the vigour and delicacy of associated arts like calligraphy, book-binding, illustrations and paintings. Several books on music were also written, as recorded in the memoirs of Dargah Quli Khan, an important official in the autonomous principality of Hyderabad under Nizam Asaf Jah I.

Dargah Quli Khan visited Shahjahanabad with his patron from 1737 to 1741 CE, during Muhammad Shah's rule. His impressions of the city reveal that while religious and cultural patronage continued, there was a change in the patrons. Some of the most famous poets of Urdu lived and wrote in this time. Their satirical compositions depict the effects of the turns in fortunes from one social class to the other.

> Those who once rode elephants now go bare-footed,
> And for want of a pair of shoes wander about disconsolately.
> Those whose wardrobes were packed with costly clothes,
> Go about naked, unable to lay hands on rags.
> Those who yearned for parched grains once,
> Are today owners of property, places, and elephants as marks of rank.
> The jackals have usurped the place of lions,
> And in the garden, crows are cawing in place of the nightingale.[30]

Despite decreased imperial patronage, some of the emperor's courtiers initiated some important construction. A madrassa, tomb, and mosque near Ajmeri Gate was built in the name of Ghazi-u-din, a prime minister. In Faiz Bazaar, another nobleman, Roshan-ud-daulah commissioned the *Sonahari* (golden) Masjid. The use of gardens and pavilions for celebrations continued, as when the grave of a local Afghan nobleman, Mir Musharraf, was adorned by his son on the *Urs* or anniversary of his father. The aromatic garden around the grave, with its canal and trees, was the setting where other noblemen and artists were invited to partake of in the festivities.[31]

The frenetic activity and the range of goods in the main marketplaces of the city belied the recent scale of destruction. The streets and forecourt, from the Chowk Saadullah Khan to the gates of the Fort, are recorded to have been once again occupied by a varied populace—dancers, storytellers,

Route from Agra to Delhi, 1789 (F 12/13, NAI)

fortune-tellers, astrologers, doctors, arms-sellers, dry-fruit sellers and wild bird and beast sellers. Shops selling cloths, rubies, gems, perfumes, essence, wine cups, glass *huqqas* and chinaware interspersed with coffee-houses patronised by poets and their admirers were found in and around Chandni Chowk. However, in the larger context, the weakness of the emperor had been exposed, and local rulers like the Marathas and the Jats waged repeated attacks on the city. These caused some damage to the Red Fort, especially to the pavilions on the exposed river-front.

Muhammad Shah was succeeded by Ahmad Shah in 1748 CE. Though the imperial residence was still the nominal focus of the Mughal empire, a period of lawlessness prevailed till 1788 CE, both in Shahjahanabad and in many other regions. The armies maintained by the imperial court and the nobles now included men from diverse areas in the empire and outside it, and did not present a united front. The reduction in imperial income together with the decrease in administrative control also meant that payments to the soldiers and other court dependants were not handed out in time. In such a situation, the imperial force was easily defeated by the rebellious Rohillas in Awadh, and had to turn for aid to their erstwhile arch rivals, the Marathas.

The entire countryside around Shahjahanabad became increasingly susceptible to attacks; smaller fortifications arose at almost every bend in the river.[32] This unsettled political situation caused ruin and famine in the surrounding farmlands and in the old city or the *Shahr-i-Kuhna*.

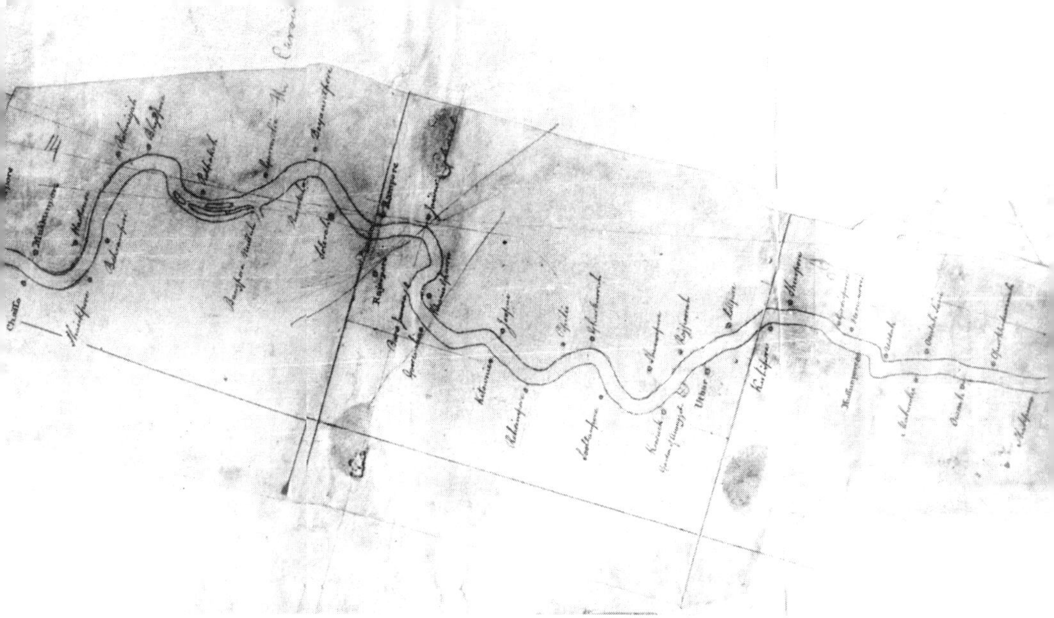

In Shahjahanabad, invasions and intrigue were followed by instances of unprincipled looting both by city thugs and marauding armies. Dissatisfied soldiers of Ahmad Shah are believed to have participated in this as much as the attacking Afghan, Pindari, Sikh, Jat, Gujar and Maratha armies.[33] The Red Fort appears to have been generally spared these indignities of pillage. Though safe from external attacks, occasional cannon balls from battles on the opposite side of the Yamuna did fall within the Fort.

Within the Fort, the boundaries of the imperial domains further weakened. An incident on 20 September 1753 CE, recorded by a resident of the city, notes how some soldiers entered the Fort and created a row over arrears of payment.[34] They reportedly closed the treasury offices and the gates of the Begum's residences. The emperor himself had to come to the Diwan-i-Am to pacify them, a state of affairs that Shah Jahan would have found impossible to believe. In a precarious balance of power, the scales were often in favour of members of the seraglio or imperial household. State decisions were dominated by the emperor's mother and by the head-eunuch, Javed Khan. Javed Khan, in-charge of the seraglio during Muhammad Shah's reign, was now appointed *Darogha Diwan-i-Khas* or superintendent of the Diwan-i-Khas. This was a post of great responsibility, held among others in the past by Saadullah Khan before he became Shah Jahan's prime minister.

During this time, the rivalry of ministers traditionally from the kingdoms of Awadh and Hyderabad began to manifest in active attempts to gain control over the emperor. In the rivalry between Safder Jung (a former prime minister) and Imad-ul-Mulk (the son of a former prime minister, Ghazi-ud-din Khan Asaf Jah), the Jats and Marathas were called in by them to support their respective claims.

However, despite this political volatility, architectural patronage in Shahjahanabad did not cease. Within the Fort, Ahmad Shah got a wooden mosque, the Chobi Masjid, built in a court between the Diwan-i-Am forecourt and the imperial gardens. Such a modification resulted in an increase of density within the imperial domains, and altered its spaces. The construction of the mosque in an area originally reserved for storage and service functions changed both the use as well as the appearance of this part of the Fort. The emperor and his immediate family also commissioned some large architectural complexes, such as the imposing Qudsiya Bagh just outside the city on the banks of the river. The gate of the Bagh and a mosque outside it still exist, but in a much-reduced form.[35]

Powerful noblemen and ministers displayed their growing power by popular acts of patronage, largely in their native areas but some in Shahjahanabad too. Javed Khan ordered the construction of the *Sunehri Masjid,* sufficiently close to the Fort (near its Delhi Gate in the important Faiz Bazaar) to signal his importance in affairs of the state. Safder Jung bought the erstwhile mansion of Prince Dara Shikoh, located in one of the most prestigious quarters of the city, which came to be known as Safderjung's Palace. After Safder Jung's death, a tomb in the vicinity of the Lodhi Tombs was built in 1754 CE on the orders of his son. Of substantial size, and in the Mughal tradition of a charbagh, the tomb must have required considerable expense, effort and skill. Its construction points to a fairly supportive political and cultural climate. However, the dwindling coffers and reduced extent of the empire are evidenced from the story that the sandstone facing of this tomb was not acquired from quarries, but by removing it from an older structure, the Tomb of Khan-i-Khanan.[36]

During the reign of Alamgir II, who succeeded Ahmad Shah in 1754 CE, Shahjahanabad was sacked by Ahmed Shah Durrani. Three years later, it was captured by the Marathas. It is unlikely that any architectural work was commissioned in this time. Alamgir II spent his last years in virtual

Qudsiya Bagh, river-front, Delhi Museum 1911-12, Vol. 1, e422 (ASI CPL)

captivity in the Fort, only to be finally murdered by his minister Imad-ul-Mulk in 1759. Alamgir II's son and successor, Ali Gahar perhaps averted a similar fate, escaping in 1758 with the aid of a rope from Shah Burj on to the Yamuna bank. The residential arrangements of the princes that had been merely restrictive earlier now proved to be a grave threat because of enemies within the Fort. Their living area adjoined Shah Burj and was hemmed in on other sides by high walls. Fortunately for Ali Gahar, the river had moved away in the 100 years since the Fort's founding, and the large stretch of its bank afforded safe escape.

In 1759, the Marathas and Jats took advantage of this shift in the river's course to mount a military offensive, bombarding the Fort from the *raiti* or sandy side with three European guns. Many imperial buildings including the Asad Burj, Mussaman Burj, Diwan-i-Khas, Rang Mahal, Moti Mahal and Shah Burj were damaged. Subsequently, some valuable decorative materials from the Fort as well as the city were plundered, and the canal which brought in water to the city and Fort ceased to function.

Ali Gahar proclaimed himself Emperor Shah Alam after his father's murder, though not in the Red Fort. Till 1771 CE he was emperor in absentia. During his absence of almost thirteen years, various minor princes were put onto the throne at the Fort, which had become the stage for the machinations of rival factions. Meanwhile, some distance away, the Afghans and the Marathas continued to battle at Panipat and Shah Alam attempted to consolidate his claims elsewhere in the empire—in

Safderjung Tomb (Photo: Author, 2001)

Awadh, Bihar and Bengal. His defeat against the British (in 1761 in a battle at Bihar, in 1764 in the Battle of Buxar, and in 1765 in the Battle of Kora) resulted in both the decrease and the redefinition of Mughal authority. Shah Alam retired to Allahabad and signed a treaty which left him Kora and a portion of Allahabad. In exchange, the British East India Company was granted the productive Dewani of Bengal, Bihar and Orissa for a payment of 26 lakh (2.6 million) rupees.[37] In 1774, a Regulating Act further built upon this treaty. It made Warren Hastings the Governor General of Bengal with supervisory powers over Bombay and Madras, and created a Supreme Court of Justice at Calcutta. The focus of political activity shifted away from the fabled Red Fort.

Apart from the decrease in importance due to the growth of Calcutta as a rival city, Shahjahanabad was also subjected to a series of attacks during this time. Its outskirts of Shahdara and Faridabad were frequently looted by the Sikhs, Gujars and Maratha mercenaries in quick succession. Its insecurity grew to the extent that the safety of the population could not be guaranteed unless they remained within the city walls. This triggered the migration of many rich noblemen to Bihar with its more settled political and civic conditions and its similar social, lingual and artistic setup. A large proportion of the wealth that city could have utilised for potential political and artistic initiatives was also lost.[38]

Despite its dwindled and precarious position, Shahjahanabad still held considerable magnetism as the capital of the once great Mughals. In Allahabad, Shah Alam 'sighed in secret for the pleasures of his capital.'[39] Finally, in April 1771, he actively sought to reclaim it from one of Aurangzeb's great-grandsons, who was a pawn in the hands of powerful ministers. After entering into an agreement with the Marathas, and promising them 40 lakh (4 million) rupees as well as the districts of Kora and Allahabad, Shah Alam set out for Delhi. Though he succeeded in obtaining the Red Fort and Shahjahanabad, the Marathas almost immediately conspired with the Jats and took back most of the territory.

The emperor's possessions were now confined mostly to the area of Delhi, a mere 70 purgunnahs.[40] His authority was continually challenged—by the Rohillas, Jats and, in 1788, again by the Marathas under Scindia. The political turmoil was reflected in the appearance and use of the Red Fort. The imperial aura of its original spaces and structures was so reduced by neglect and the absence of their furnishings, that a visitor recorded that:

> [t]he Court has no magnificence at all. The pompous spectacle of the audience of Aurangzeb which Bernier has described for us with so much pleasure and exactness has been replaced by the strictest parsimony which is born of real poverty and not of a weakening of the taste for external pomp ... Finally with the exception of the external respects we

find nothing that conforms to the idea which the former narrative gave us about the riches of the Court of the Great Mughal.[41]

This appearance of parsimony did not completely dispel the general conviction that some part of the legendary riches of the Mughal court still remained. The Rohilla rebel, Ghulam Qadir, impelled by this conviction is reported to have dug up the floors and gardens of the emperor's quarters in search of buried treasure. Angered when his search yielded nothing, he reportedly blinded Shah Alam in the Diwan-i-Khas and thereafter imprisoned him in Salimgarh.[42] The desecration of the emperor's person and of his private domain at the imperial Fort marked one of the lowest moments in the history of the Red Fort. Yet, though reduced to a mere figurehead, the aura of his ancestors proved too strong to dislodge Shah Alam. The Marathas rescued him from the Rohillas and treated him with courtesy. The populace continued to regard him as their rightful ruler despite the physical disability that, according to Mughal rights of succession, should have disqualified him from ruling. However, for all practical purposes, the Marathas took over actual authority.

During the last years of Shah Alam's rule, the British East India Company became increasingly involved in the political affairs of Shahjahanabad. In 1803, their help was enlisted to drive out the Marathas from the city. The ensuing Battle of Delhi at Hindon, in which the British led by Lord Lake were victorious, marked the beginning of a power shift. Lord Lake was admitted into the sacred Diwan-i-Khas, thanked ceremonially, and invested with titles in the manner of a Mughal commander.

Along with material gains, which included a considerable strip of country to the west of the Yamuna in the neighbourhood of Shahjahanabad, the British took over fiscal and administrative responsibilities, including revenue collection in the name of Shah Alam, whose jurisdiction shrank to within the Red Fort. No longer emperor even in name, he was retitled the king of Delhi. The only revenue the king now derived was from a portion of his territories on the Yamuna banks. Assigned in part to maintain himself, his family and their palace, in actual fact, even these lands were under the charge of the British, who established themselves in the city with an official Resident. The monthly expenses given to the royal family were Rs 90,000[43]—the culmination of the decline in Mughal fortunes from the time that Shah Alam bartered away the province of Bengal to the East India Company in 1776.

The decrease in power and income, and the demands on Shah Alam from a large extended family (comprising above 500 women and nearly 70 children, besides grandchildren) resulted in decreased architectural patronage. In contrast to Shah Jahan's sons, who had established independent mansions in the expensive part of the city, and Aurangzeb's sons, who had occupied a designated area in the Fort's northeastern corner, the residences of some of Shah Alam's adult sons were situated within the inner palace. Bereft of economic and political means, and with decreased military engagements, the princes spent almost all their time in and around the Fort. Allocation of funds for the repair, maintenance and decoration of the imperial buildings and gardens became increasingly difficult.

Some of the princes did attempt to make independent careers. In 1784, Shah Alam's eldest son, Jawan Bakht, followed his father's example. Using a ladder of turbans, he descended from the Shah Burj to the banks, eluding the vigilance of his father's minister. For the most part, however, the princes stayed in the Fort, with either a lack of opportunity or the will to leave it. This overpopulation led to a dilution of the strictly controlled domains that had earlier characterised the Fort. This, in turn, led to a change in its built form and reduced its formal elegance with the addition of newer minor buildings patronised by the princes.

In the larger context, howsoever humiliating Shah Alam's personal status was, the new political equation did ensure some return of administrative stability to Shahjahanabad. The area of Delhi became relatively safe to travel in. Contact with other urban centres increased. Shahjahanabad resumed its cultural leadership, even in comparison with British-established cities such as Calcutta, Madras and Bombay. Its economic revival took a little longer. The unsettled political conditions and preoccupation with defensive requirements had resulted in lower agricultural production—one of the mainstays of the Mughal economy—and insufficient revenue collection.

The civic facilities had also fallen into disrepair. The drying up of the canal that brought water into Shahjahanabad, which formed part of a larger system of irrigation,[44] resulted in sole dependence on wells and rainwater for crops, orchards and gardens. This consequently must have affected agricultural and commercial production in the farmlands and suburbs, and a general reduction in the appearance of the gardens that formed such essential decorative features of the city. However, the effectiveness of the original urban design was such that the city was still beautiful and was described by one of the first Residents as allowing one to 'ride for miles as through a highly cultivated garden'.[45]

Shahjahanabad, in the meantime, underwent accelerated change, especially in its northeastern sector near the Yamuna. This part of the city, prominently visible from the Yamuna and its large volume of river traffic, was traditionally inhabited by powerful men of the realm with their magnificent mansions and gardens. The British Resident now established himself here. The house that he occupied and transformed with an envelope of European architecture, had been constructed by Dara Shikoh. Later, influential prime ministers lived in it. With the altered appearance of this prominent mansion and the establishment of English gardens and churches in its vicinity, a perceptible foreign strand entered the urban fabric of Shahjahanabad. A similar strand developed near the southern boundary of the Fort, where the chaplain and the military detachments established themselves.[46]

The succession of Shah Alam's heir, Akbar Shah, 'the champion of the faith, the king of the world, the world-conqueror of the age, and the shadow of God'[47] in 1806 CE, did not stem the trend of this Europeanisation of Shahjahanabad. By 1812, the immediate boundaries of the Red Fort were transformed by the addition of built structures. Though few, they substantially changed the appearance and use of the Fort, and its relationship with Shahjahanabad and the Yamuna.

Due northwest outside the Fort, the front view of the already transformed Dara Shikoh's (also known as Safderjung's) Palace was further altered by the provision of a magazine and powder room just behind the city's Kella Ghat Gate. Battalion lines were constructed near Lal Gate, ahead of a British-style residence adjacent to Safderjung's Palace. West of the Fort, battalion lines with a hospital and bazaar were established in Daryaganj. Later, in 1836, the large St. James's Church was consecrated near Kashmiri Gate. The British, firmly ensconced on the coveted river-front, transformed its once luxurious aspect by such utilitarian buildings. These were often added at the cost of available open spaces and gardens, some of which were as large and important as the Safderjung Palace gardens and the Daryaganj gardens. The sweep and sequence of Mughal gardens and buildings on the river edge, of which the Red Fort formed the most compelling component, thus became fragmented and incoherent.

The partial appropriation of the riverine vistas and views by British construction, the consequent loss of some of the original gardens and the decrease in river traffic from the north combined to lessen the impact of this sequence. The positioning of British residences and battalion lines also reduced the accessibility of the river face for the citizens of Shahjahanabad who had earlier used it extensively to perform ablutions and prayers at the ghats in the morning, for strolls and excursions in the public gardens in the evenings and to view firework displays on festive occasions. In general, there was a change in the traditional use of space and a disuse of some parts of the Fort and Shahjahanabad.

The other view of the Red Fort—from Shahjahanabad—was similarly transformed. The formality of the courts and gardens that led up to it was weakened by ad hoc construction. The space within the great royal square in front of the Fort's Delhi Gate was reduced by the construction of Nawab Bahadur's Mosque on its central movement axis. The gardens bordering this square at the foot of the Fort walls almost completely disappeared. Such transformations occurred at both macro and micro levels, and the Mughal rulers took the lead in participating in many of these changes. Thus, in 1811 CE, Akbar Shah ordered the construction of masonry bridges to replace the wooden drawbridges built in Aurangzeb's reign that led to the Lahore and Delhi Gates from Shahjahanabad.[48] These were replaced with the help of a British engineer, and would have differed in both material and detail from the earlier bridges.

Changes were also apparent in the city's main urban axes. Their original typology consisted of continuous arcades in front of shops on the ground floor, and terraces fronting the homes of the merchants on the floor above. The open terraces on the upper storeys were the first to transform. New structures were built here; most of these emulated European styles, as photographs of this period show. While the main streets now presented a view where western architectural elements sat on original Mughal arches and other architectural details, the majority of the inner residential areas continued to follow a traditional typology. The house of a rich court nobleman and his family in Farrashkhana, next to the Chandni Chowk, was described thus even three decades later.[49]

> The house in which I was born was a double storeyed building, the lower portion of which consisted of a *dhalan* in a *dhalan*, with rooms to the right and left and with a courtyard in front for kitchens, etc. To the left was the entrance gate, and in front of this were small side rooms. The upper storey was a small courtyard with a verandah and side rooms.

Politically also, the British sought to play an increasing role in the administration. An official document of 1815, records their intention of clearing the Shahjahanabad canal—'a work, so dignified, so popular and so beneficial',[50] notwithstanding the willingness of several local people to contract the necessary excavation and clearing. The canal was running by about 1819. Road systems within Shahjahanabad and connecting it to other parts of the country were also repaired. Emily Metcalfe, the daughter of Thomas Metcalfe, Officiating Agent to the Governor General, Delhi Agency, on her return from England as a young woman of eighteen, records that she and her companions travelled unprotected to Shahjahanabad. Despite rough horse carriages, they accomplished the 450 miles (724 km) between Allahabad and Shahjahanabad in a week.

Within the Red Fort, the neglect of existing spatial features from earlier times was combined with the addition of new buildings. Among these is a balcony with a curved bangla roof in front of the Mussaman Burj, constructed on the initiative of Akbar Shah. Older buildings were also repaired, including Asad Burj, which had been demolished by bombardment. In 1828, Akbar Shah also got a two-storeyed pavilion and a well laid-out garden developed inside Salimgarh Fort, which he is believed to have visited often. The relatively undisturbed circuit here would have offered a pleasant contrast to the steadily increasing population inside the Red Fort.

The first places to suffer from neglect were the Fort's open areas—the formal courts and gardens inside it and around its boundary, the sandy banks of the river that it overlooked, the small gardens in front of the emperor's private apartments, the princes' mansions and the seraglio. The forecourt and channels dotted with fountains in front of the Rang Mahal

Pavilions and garden inside Salimgarh (Detail of Add.Or.1790, OIOC, BL)

were crowded with ad-hoc buildings. However, the remains of an orchard within them, recorded to be surrounded by a screen-like railing of red stone decorated with 2,000 finials of gold, were still suggestive of their former splendour.

Bishop Heber visited the Fort in 1826 CE, and wrote that the imperial gardens in the Fort at this time, though 'not large … must have been exceedingly rich and beautiful. They are full of very old orange and other fruit trees, with terraces and parterres, on which many rose bushes are growing, and even now a few jonquils in flower'.[51] The main buildings and pavilions, less vulnerable in contrast to the open areas, retained their imperial presence to a large extent. Bishop Heber refers to the tower and vaulted aisle of Lahori Gate as the noblest gate and vestibule he ever saw, bringing to mind the image of a gothic cathedral.[52] However, he disparagingly describes the Naqqar Khana forecourt as a ruinous and dirty stable yard. Similarly, Fanny Parks, on her visit to the zenana in the Red Fort in 1838, passed through what she terms narrow, dirty and wet passages, to arrive at

Chandni Chowk, transformation in the city structure in the nineteenth century (752/16 (5) OIOC, BL and Delhi, Fort Museum, 767/75, ASI PL)

'a superb hall: formerly fountains had played there; the ceiling was painted and inlaid with gold'.[53] Apart from Heber and Parks, other European travellers visited the court and were allowed in till the Diwan-i-Am and Diwan-i-Khas.

The British made incursions into the Fort, both through their physical presence and through the influence of European additions to existing buildings. A part of the British military also began to reside in the Fort. After the favourite son of Akbar Shah made an attempt on the life of the British Resident, permanent quarters were built for a British commandant of the guard within the Fort. With his establishment, two separate social and cultural life-systems began to function within the Fort. Inevitably, some sort of interaction between the king and the commandant was necessary; but, for the most part, they carried out their lives insulated from each other.

The social network of the British within the Fort was the same as in any cantonment town, replete with afternoon teas and introductory visits. Emily Metcalfe tells of a visit, paid almost on the first day of her arrival in Shahjahanabad, to the two Miss Robertsons who lived with their brother 'over the principal gateway of the King's Palace as he was the Official Assistant to my Father and represented British Authority in the Palace'.[54] Major Robertson as the Assistant Resident was Thomas Metcalfe's immediate subordinate, and even Emily knew that he was stationed to maintain surveillance over the Fort.

The upper rooms above the Lahori Gate were adapted to accommodate him and his family, and the verandah and arcades were closed. The British occupation of the ceremonial entrance in the Public Imperial domain signified their de facto assumption of power. Besides occupying these spaces, they also took over imperial gardens and resorts. Shalimar Bagh, the scene of Aurangzeb's coronation, was converted by General David Ochterlony, an earlier British Resident, into his second residence and used as a summer retreat. Thomas Metcalfe got rooms built in the verandahs and gardens of a tomb in Mehrauli, and remodelled its surroundings around the Qutub ruins. Emily Metcalfe writes in her diary that 'as soon as all the first visits had been paid, my Father took me out to spend a few days at the Kutub, where he had built another house ... it was a delightful residence, and a very quaint one, for it was originally a Mohammedan tomb, surmounted by a big stone dome'.[55]

The appropriation of Mughal pilgrimage centres and pleasure resorts directly affected the use of spaces within the Fort. As the area of recreational and social use outside the Fort steadily decreased, the king and his family were constrained to spend most of their time inside the Fort, with little opportunity for the recuperation of its built fabric or its residents. More indirectly, the British also adopted an almost imperial Mughal way of life along with a semblance of the cultural and architectural patronage, colour, and pageantry that characterised this way of life. This seems to have led to a perception from the British point of view that the rituals of the Mughal king and his court were superfluous.

As the decades progressed, the British, who at first represented themselves almost as ministers of the Mughal court, grew increasingly reluctant to do anything that would increase its life and the Fort that housed it. This reluctance, initially masked in polite bureaucratic delays, later became more pronounced and rankled with the king. Akbar Shah recorded in a letter, dated 1 January 1830, to the Governor General in Fort William, Calcutta, that most Residents and officers of rank in earlier years had maintained a relationship of mutual respect and visited him at least once a fortnight.[56] Now, however, Francis Hawkins, Acting Resident of Delhi, gave up all pretence of respect to the niceties or necessities of court etiquette.

The list of offences recorded against him in this letter are long. The foremost is 'the bold and insolent intrusion'[57] into the palace when the king was away on a customary visit to the shrine of Khwaja Kutubuddin Bakhtiyar Kaki at Mehrauli. Hawkins and his companions, regardless of the sentry at the Naqqar Khana, forced an entry on horseback into the forecourt of the Diwan-i-Am as well as that of the Diwan-i-Khas. While Hawkins was promptly removed from his duties in the palace, which was placed under another officer,[58] his behaviour was a clear indication of the change in relationship between the British and the Mughals. The initial fascination of the British for the fabled oriental imperial court at Delhi had been replaced first by mere tolerance and then contempt.

This change was no doubt brought about by the familiarity of too close a contact, and heightened by an imperfect understanding of the Mughal court's customs. An unrepentant Hawkins made no secret of his anger at what he considered a humiliating ceremony of presenting *nazars* or gifts to the king. He contended that he was in the right when he refused to stand amongst 'black domesticks' when being presented to 'the lady said to be the queen', or when he did not accept the flowers from the royal garden traditionally gifted by the king on his return from the shrine of Nizam-u-ddin Auliya.

In 1832 CE, more complaints were made against Englishmen entering the Jama Masjid and also the Diwan-i-Khas with their shoes on; of seating themselves on the crystal seat reserved solely for the king and of striking the chowkidar when remonstrated.[59] Such behaviour, by no means common to all British officials and visitors in Shahjahanabad, was nonetheless, representative of their growing feeling of superiority. This was reflected as much in policy decisions regarding Mughal possessions as in personal relationships with the Mughal royalty and nobility. Even allowances requested for the repair of the Red Fort were turned down on some pretext or the other.

A letter forwarded from T. Metcalfe on 7 May 1835, addressed to the officiating secretary, political department, Agra,[60] recommends a minimum monthly sum of Rs 5,000 for the repairs and maintenance of the palace wall, Salimgarh, and Diwan-i-Am, on the basis of advice from his superintending engineer. Metcalfe suggests that the funds might be made over for the period of at least a year, at the expiry of which a more accurate judgement could be made of the repairs needed. The reply in response to this assessment, from the foreign department in 1835 to the officiating secretary, political department, concurs with Metcalfe's suggestion but ensures no change in status quo, stating:

> [the] Council is not aware of any objection to setting aside five thousand rupees for the repairs of the Palace ... but these arrangements are not to take effect until a plan for disposing of the entire augmentation shall be determined upon.[61]

A section of British opinion openly favoured the removal of the Mughal king to the Qutub area. However, this did not happen and on Akbar Shah's death, his eldest son, Bahadur Shah II came to the throne in 1837 and continued to reside in the Fort. During Bahadur Shah's rule, cultural and architectural patronage continued, albeit on a reduced scale, and mainly within the Fort. Much of the construction activity took the form of mosques or garden buildings built by the king as well as by the ruling nobility, or the repair of civic facilities. The clearing of the important canal of Shahjahanabad, which had again fallen into disuse a year after Bahadur Shah's ascension, also implies a rejuvenation of at least some of the many gardens of the Fort and city.

Shahjahanabad was still considered the vanguard of culture and, together with Agra and Lucknow, famed for its poetical language. Bahadur Shah was himself an accomplished poet, writing under the name Zafar. Arguably the greatest Urdu poet—Mirza Asadullah Khan Ghalib (1797–1869 CE)—lived in Delhi in this time, as did the famous Muhammad Ibrahim Zauq (1788–1854 CE). A large part of the populace and almost all the noblemen spoke and wrote a version of Urdu famed for its elegance. The son of one of the court nobles wrote of his father's book:

> The original autobiography is in Urdu, and is written in choice language and in a style which would only be attained by a Delhi man, and one who had intimate associations with the Red Fort, where the best and most elegant Urdu was spoken.[62]

Apart from this continuity of the Fort as the leading patron of arts in Shahjahanabad, the urban elements emphasising the relationship between the Fort and its city also remained largely the same. The form of their connecting axes was much as originally designed—a linear sequence punctuated by large squares—though the formality of the squares as well as their function changed with the insertion of newer buildings. Some of these buildings do not seem to have been architecturally remarkable or particularly impressive. For instance, the hereditary mace-bearers of the king, after paying a ground rent to him, constructed their house consisting of one hall and one room in front of the Fort, close to the termination of the urban axes.[63]

The more public spaces in these axes, to a larger extent, retained their form as well as their function. One of these was a chowk of 80 square yards in the middle of the Chandni Chowk axis called the *Kotwali Chabutra*. Situated at a distance of 480 yards from the Fort's Lahori Gate, this was a familiar landmark for the citizens of Shahjahanabad. At a distance of 400 yards from the Kotwali Chabutra was the actual Chandni Chowk,

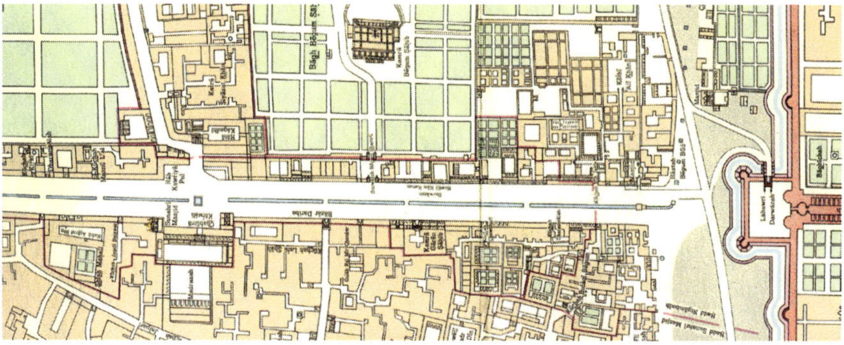

Areas of change in urban built fabric, Shahjahanabad (X 1659, OIOC, BL)

an octagonal chowk of 100 by 100 yards in size.[64] This gave access to the popular *Sahibabad* and Begum Bagh which continued to retain their overall forms, though their ownership and consequently, part of their physical profile changed when a portion of the Bagh was made over to Begum Samroo, who built her house and garden in it.[65] This altered their formal design and further reduced the royal family's stake in the gardens originally established by Princess Jahanara.

The focus of imperial activity shifted away from Chandni Chowk and Lahori Gate, once the main axis of movement, to Faiz Bazaar and Delhi Gate. The Lahori Gate link had become unsafe and infrequently used with repeated invasions from the north and west. Additionally, many parts around this area were now under the control of local chieftains, resulting in a decreased use of the gardens in the western and northern suburbs beyond Lahori Gate by Bahadur Shah and his family. The riverbank along the Fort wall, a favoured recreational space during Shah Jahan's time, began to lose its imperial appearance, though it is recorded to have been used for picnics and festive gatherings by the king and his family. The river-front of the rest of the city was still attractive with bathing ghats and pavilions, and the edges of the Fort towards the city were in a better state of maintenance.

While public gardens continued to exist around Lahori and Delhi Gate, their extent and form now incorporated elements different from the original profile. The construction of new roads around the Fort led to a loss of part of the Gulabi Bagh. Its counterpart, the Anguri Bagh, shrunken in size, continued in its name as well as its function, as the

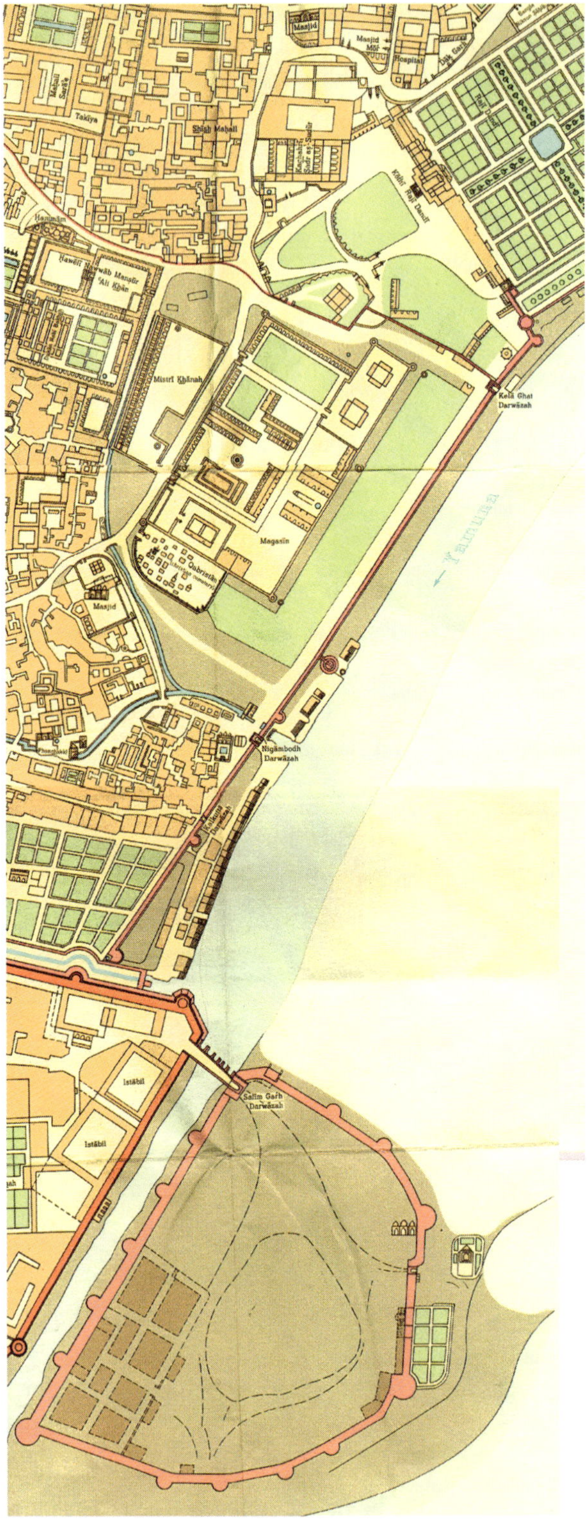

Transformations in the Fort's adjacencies, mid-nineteenth century
(X 1659, OIOC, BL)

events of the morning of 11 May 1857 showed. A crowd of four or five hundred townspeople is recorded to have collected in this garden, shortly after the news of the arrival of the Indian forces reached the city.[66]

Though Bahadur Shah and his sons did establish gardens such as *Buland Bagh Badshah* and *Bagichah Mirza Gawhar* containing mosques, shrines and boarding houses around the Fort walls, these were overlooked by many British buildings. A church and a chaplain's house were sited around the southern edge of the Fort; across the gardens along the western face of the Fort was the Delhi Bank (a European-style building with a pediment) and a large red sandstone tank was made southwest of Lahori Gate. This 500-by-150-feet tank was constructed on the orders of Lord Ellenborough in 1846 CE. It connected to the canal in Chandni Chowk and had practical benefits, but further reduced the visual and spatial formality of the square in front of the Fort. All this signalled the growing British presence, who, apart from strengthening the city walls with bastions at key points, came up to the very gates of the Fort in their physical as well as political interventions. In contrast, the Mughal rulers either limited their patronage to the Red Fort, or to the suburbs south of Shahjahanabad, closer to the older cities of Delhi.

Mehrauli became the favoured retreat of King Bahadur Shah II; its route was well-frequented and well-maintained, and some new structures were commissioned and constructed. These excursions into the older parts of Delhi would undoubtedly have been a welcome relief to the king, who, with his restricted movements and powers, was otherwise largely confined to the area in the vicinity of the Red Fort and the river.

Within the Fort, Bahadur Shah II exercised whatever influence he had in commissioning some repairs and some new construction. Shortly after he ascended the throne, the dilapidated 'gulal bari'—the enclosure of red arcades surrounding the Diwan-i-Am court—were repaired. He is also credited with the construction of a small mosque south of Chatta Bazaar.[67] Later, in 1842, Bahadur Shah II caused two pavilions to be made in the Hayat Baksh. These were the Zafar Mahal and *Hira Mahal*. Hira Mahal, a marble pavilion, was a typical Mughal baradari. It had twelve open arches, three on each face. With its proportions of 22 feet and 5 inches in length and 19 feet and 5 inches in width, it was smaller than the other pavilions in Hayat Baksh. Both the architecture and planning of

River front, Red Fort (J. Murray, 1858, 52/28, OIOC, BL) and
(Delhi, Vol. 4, 1919-21, No. 230, ASI PL)

River front with pavilions and ghats, north of Red Fort (53/30, OIOC, BL)

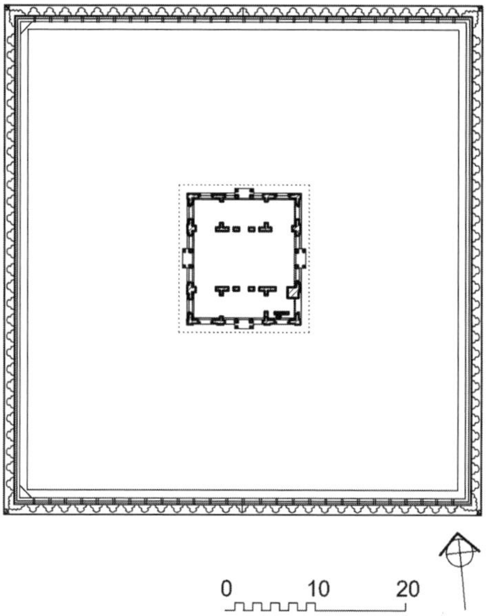

Zafar Mahal within the central tank of Hayat Baksh
(Drawing: N. Joshi, Author, based on ASI drawing)

Hira Mahal displayed a reduction in aesthetic rigour compared to Shah Jahan's patronage. Its position at the head of the subsidiary channels of Hayat Baksh drew attention away from the garden's main central axis. It also caused an asymmetry in the original number of garden pavilions made by Shah Jahan, and reduced the sense of spaciousness in Hayat Baksh.

Zafar Mahal, the other pavilion that Bahadur Shah II built within Hayat Baksh, was located in the very centre of the garden, within its central tank. The tank, an original feature of the garden, was deepened to provide sufficient space for the red sandstone pavilion, which in its conception is ingenious. A double layer of chambers on its northern and southern ends, and arched screens on its eastern and western faces, enclose a central court. The entire pavilion is raised above the water level of the tank on a series of arches. Water flowed under these arches into the central water court. Zafar Mahal, thus, seemingly floated on water and looked out on to water on all sides—through sandstone screens on the outer wall, and through larger arched doors in the private inner walls. However, at an overall level, Zafar Mahal constituted an obstruction

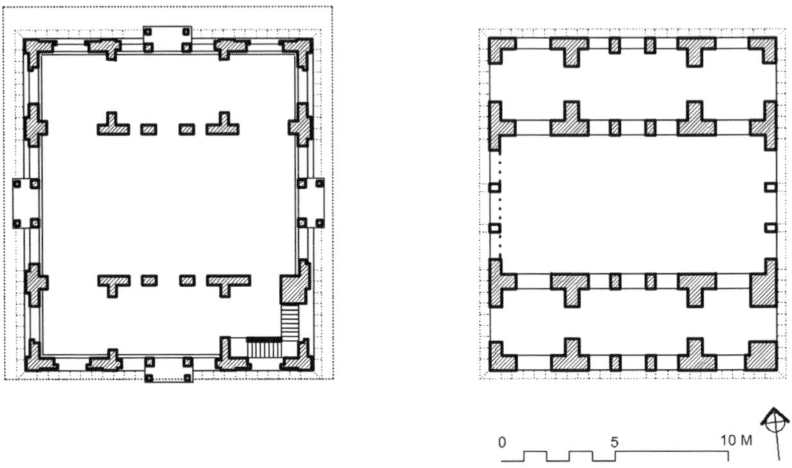

Zafar Mahal: Plan of upper and lower levels
(Drawing: N. Joshi, D. Cherian, Author, based on 574/97 (Delhi, ASI PL)

in the central axis of Hayat Baksh, originally visualised by Shah Jahan and his architects as affording an unbroken view over the shallow mirror-like water in the tank.

Though the celebrated original silver fountains of this tank had been pillaged by this time, Bahadur Shah II did perhaps endeavour to get it filled with water. A well, bearing an inscription that gives its construction date as 1840 CE (AH 1256), was provided in Hayat Baksh to the northeast of Moti Masjid. Mehtab Bagh, the other imperial garden in the Fort, was also not excluded from Bahadur Shah's architectural efforts. He introduced a fountain, of which Sayyid Ahmad, a contemporary historian of that time, wrote:

> In the middle of this garden, a large canal flows very pleasantly. His exalted Majesty, Sirajjuddin Muhammad Babur Shah has now made a 'jhirna' of red sandstone near the canal towards the west like that of the Qutb sahib, and the garden has been much improved by this.[68]

The plantation in Hayat Baksh during this time is recorded to have contained fragrant and colourful flower beds and fruit trees of many kinds: mangoes of different varieties, guava, pomegranate, grapefruit, jackfruit, mulberry, Indian blackberry, lemon, fig, plum, along with flowers such as marigold, sunflower, motiya, chameli, jui, raibel, gulaab,

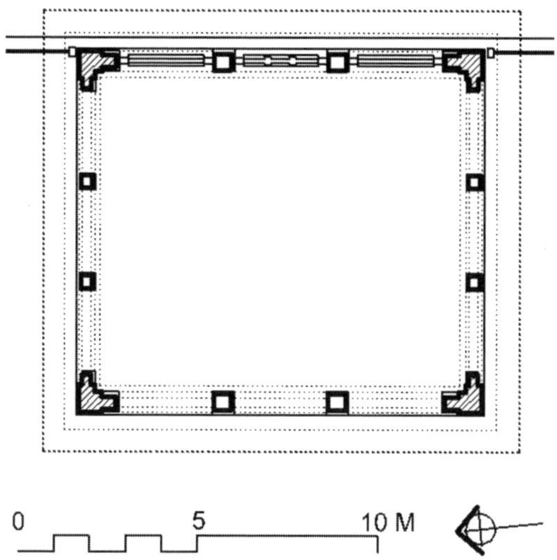

Hira Mahal: Plan
(Drawing: N. Joshi, D. Cherian, Author, based on 578/97 Delhi, ASI PL)

sewati, madmaalti, maulsree and many others. On special occasions, tents were also erected here and stalls set up for the king and for the queens, princesses, women and children of the seraglio.

The other additions and alterations in the Fort, for the most part, deprived it of its original beauty. The designed formality of many of Shah Jahan's original buildings, open spaces, and gardens was transforming inexorably, their neglected state compounded by piecemeal additions. Within the principal forecourt of the Fort—the Naqqar Khana forecourt—a large building was constructed (as depicted in the OIOC map) on the southwestern corner. This building projected out beyond the measured symmetry of the arcades of the forecourt. The Diwan-i-Am forecourt and its surrounding arcade were bare, and recorded to have been used as stables or lumber rooms. The degradation of this forecourt moved Thomas Metcalfe to pronounce, 'Shame to the ruling power, whether it be the King as immediate, or the British Government as Lord Paramount.'[69]

The reduction in Mughal authority was accompanied by the mushrooming of structures within the Fort, in a debased mixture of European and Indian styles fashionable at this time. These buildings, primarily by the princes, were constructed even within the imperial domains. The houses of the heir-apparent loomed up behind the important

Diwan-i-Am, intruding on its meticulous proportions. To the south of Rang Mahal, the Choti Baithak reputed to be an extremely beautiful building, was recorded to have lost much of its charm due to alterations by one of the princes, Mirza Jahangir Bahadur.[70] The *Darya Mahal* was constructed on the eastern terrace within the measured sequence of the imperial pavilions facing the river-front.

These examples of adult princes actively inhabiting Bahadur Shah II's personal area, signify the growing weakness in aesthetic tastes as well as in the imperial domains of power. The mingling of architectural domains was representative of the sharing of power between Bahadur Shah II and his sons. This was a long journey from the separate establishments of royal sons outside the Fort in Shah Jahan's time, and even their separately accessed and bounded mansions within the Fort during Aurangzeb's rule. The chief princes, apart from indulging in architectural whims in the imperial private part of the Fort, also appropriated important parts of the ceremonial public realm for residential purposes, such as the area bordering the Naqqar Khana forecourt, and the entrance axis from the Delhi Gate.[71]

The usurping of the main public entrance spaces of the Fort by the British and the king's sons, respectively, may be read as an interesting recurrence of the motif of the Fort's spatial use portending actual power equations. Everyone who entered the Fort was first subject to the scrutiny of either the British commandant of the guards, or the sons of Bahadur Shah II. Thus, control over who did or did not enter the Fort was vested in them rather than with the king. Though the court ritual still celebrated the Mughal king and revolved around his wishes and his routine, the virtual cornering of Bahadur Shah II into the private imperial parts of the Fort signified his retreat from active political influence. At the same time, the percolation of the princes' architectural authority into the sanctity of the architectural spaces of the Private Imperial domain foretold their disregard of the king's wishes in the acute administrative and military crisis that soon followed in 1857.

The siting of the princes' residences around the main circulation nodes of the Red Fort ensured that key decisions that triggered future events took place here, even before the king was made aware of, or could react to these decisions. The shrinking power domain of the king within the Fort reflected a microcosm of his shrinking power in the city. Just as he receded into the innermost areas of his palace, similarly, the influence of the court retreated to the immediate vicinity of the Red Fort. Thus, the image of the Fort as a city within a city still functioned, though actual control had shrunk from the entire country to the physical boundary of the walls of the Fort.

The perception of the Red Fort by both its occupants and its visitors changed. Outwardly, many of its rituals continued with the British commissioner replaying the role of the wazirs of the earlier emperors. The handing of petitions to, or the presentation of gifts, on behalf of the king seated on his exquisite marble throne in the Diwan-i-Am, did not cease even if they did recede in splendour. Nor did celebrations marking important events such as the anniversary of the king's coronation, or festivities on various occasions such as Nauroz, Muharram, Eid, Dusshera, Diwali or Holi. On the other hand, the surroundings in which these rituals and festivities took place were shorn of much of their earlier magnificence. Despite this, the power of the original spatial sequence and planning of the Fort and its city still succeeded in impressing visitors.

> The palace itself covered an enormous space of ground, in fact it was quite a form in itself, thronged with thousands of natives, hangers-on of an oriental court … It was open to the river all along one side of it, where sublimely beautiful buildings were erected, intermixed with gardens.

And,

> … Delhi was really a most beautiful city …[72\]

7

ASSAULT

'Inside the palace of the Mogal Emperors the traveller will now search in vain for the celebrated buildings of Shah Jahan, which have been the admiration of the world for upwards of two centuries.'

Major General Cunningham, a memorandum regarding the old Muhammadan buildings of Delhi, 24 May 1865, File Misc/19, R. R. Delhi Archives

The buildings of Shah Jahan, admired by travellers even two centuries after their establishment, suffered an indelible assault by the British from the year 1857 onwards. One of the important events in the long sequence of incidents leading up to this assault was the dissolution of Awadh, the kingdom of the erstwhile prime ministers of the Mughal emperors, by the directors of the British East India Company in London. The addition of Awadh to the already large list of areas annexed by the British evinced trepidation amongst many Indians. At the same time, British policies alienated even segments of the population trained to serve their interests—namely, the Indian soldiers in the military system commanded by British officers. The most controversial of these policies, perceived as sacrilegious by both Hindu and Muslim soldiers, was the one that reportedly made compulsory the use of pig and cow fat for greasing rifle cartridges.

These incidents were part of a sustained cultural and social imposition on the Indian way of life. Karl Marx, who at this time and the years preceding it, was following the political events connected with India, described the situation with some insight. Commenting on the vacuum thus created, he observed that the 'loss of his old world, with no gain of a new one, imparts a particular kind of melancholy'.[1] This particular kind of melancholy soon transformed into growing restlessness and unease, and came to a head in the summer of 1857. It finally resulted in what has been variously termed as the Indian Mutiny, the Great Rebellion, the *ghadar* and the First War of Independence.

The focus of the war was Shahjahanabad, though the reasons for it as well as its range were spread over many parts of India, including Luckhnow, Kanpur, Meerut, Gwalior and Jhansi.[2] Its immediate beginnings may be traced to an attempt by Mangal Pandey, a soldier of the 34th Bengal Light Infantry, against British domination. This incident occurred in the month of March at Barrackpore in the Bengal Presidency, though the first signs of unrest in this year had started in the 19th Bengal Light Infantry at Behrampore, some distance away from Barrackpore. The retribution meted out for daring to assault a British officer was swift and Mangal Pandey as well as another soldier were hanged shortly after the incident.

However, the act of hanging did not stem the tide of unrest, and only served to justify Mangal Pandey's contention. Many other soldiers, covertly and overtly, began to look to their Indian rulers for leadership. The 'immediate cause for the mutiny' according to a British army officer writing in the beginning of the twentieth century, was the fact that on 9 May 1857, eighty-five troops of the 3rd Regular Bengal Light Infantry stationed at Meerut were court-martialled and 'sentenced to considerable terms of imprisonment, owing to their refusal to handle cartridges which for years they had used without the slightest protest'.[3] The sentence and the public humiliation of the soldiers was to have momentous consequences. Their comrades, angered and provoked by such a degrading and severe punishment, resolved to set them free. They violently rebelled against the British officers, killing who they could. They then made for Shahjahanabad.

Other Indian soldiers and leaders also congregated from across the country to the Red Fort to swear allegiance to the Mughal king, in whose

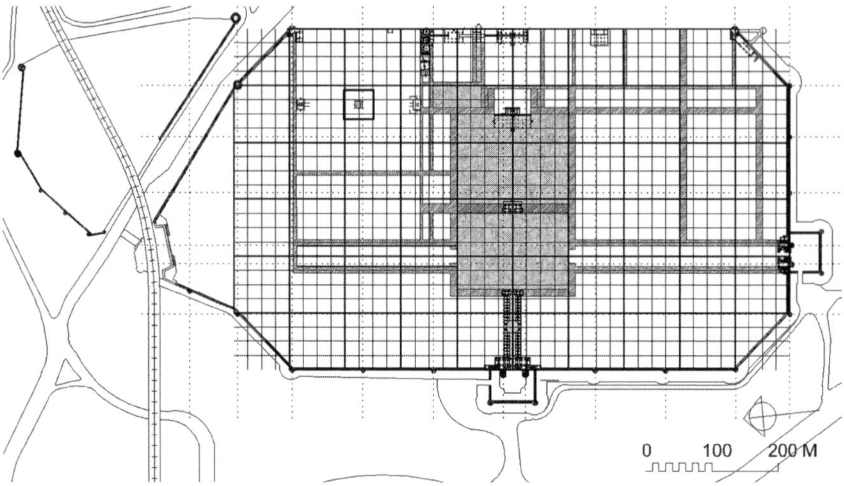

Areas of incursion into Public and Private Imperial domains by British officials (Drawing: N. Joshi, Author)

name the British had been ruling for over a hundred years. The first batch of soldiers rode in from Meerut on the morning of 11 May. They were initially refused admission by the British-controlled administration in Shahjahanabad, who locked the city gates at the sight of the soldiers' approach across the river. There are conflicting accounts of where and how the soldiers first succeeded in entering the city. They are believed to have attempted an entrance through the river gates to the immediate north and south of the Red Fort. According to some records, they first made an appearance on the riverbank below the jharoka balcony of the Red Fort's Mussaman Burj.

The imperial pavilions faced the river, and would have been easy to access in the height of summer with the consequent receding of the river. However, the initial response of King Bahadur Shah II, on being informed of the soldiers' presence, was to call for Captain Douglas, the British Commandant of the Guards residing in the Fort. The captain is believed to have commanded the soldiers to leave, speaking to them from the king's private balcony. Douglas is then reported to have returned to his quarters above the Lahori Gate, taking the passage next to the Khas Mahal[4] rather than through the more usual public route from the Diwan-i-Khas forecourt. Such familiarity with the various passages into the Private Imperial domain underlines the fact that their use was now no longer strictly limited to the king and his family. The dependence on Douglas for counsel also demonstrates the ascendancy of the British over the affairs of the Fort and the city.

The soldiers finally succeeded in entering Shahjahanabad through the Rajghat, Calcutta and Zinat-al-masjid Gates. Almost immediately, their leaders sought an audience with the king—reportedly gaining admittance to the Fort through a gateway of the Salimgarh citadel[5] and through Lahori Gate, the moat around which was dry.[6] After successfully convincing Bahadur Shah of their objective, the soldiers made a formal claim to the city on his behalf. The claim was put into action by targeting British administrative and judicial institutions, residences and cantonments. Though some of these were outside the city walls, British presence had percolated close to the Fort as well—particularly in Daryaganj, Kashmiri Gate and Chandni Chowk. These places were attacked. The *kotwal* was challenged; the joint magistrate, Sir Theophilus Metcalfe, was driven out of the city. Captain Douglas was killed. So was the commissioner, Simon Fraser.

Many British and European residents moved out from the proximity of the Fort, where most of the soldiers had assembled, to the Flagstaff Tower on the northern ridge or to houses near the city gates. Some of them then travelled out of the Delhi region altogether. Almost immediately, the regiments stationed in the Delhi cantonment outside the city walls joined forces against the British and marched into Shahjahanabad. The road to the Fort was barred by groups of soldiers who took up positions at the chowk in front of it. The soldiers and by extension, the king, now controlled both the Fort and the city.

This overthrowing of existing administrative and military norms created confusion, anarchy and conflicting notions of loyalty. A large number of the civilian population closed their shops and hid in their houses, while some took advantage of the events to plunder and loot. Contrary to present perceptions of the defined roles played by the Indians and Europeans at this time, European mercenaries also joined hands with the soldiers against the British. Reportedly, one of the most active members of the Indian camp was a European, a discharged soldier of the 17th Regiment.[7]

As is more well-known, many Indian soldiers also comprised part of the British force. 'It was a force of British and loyal native troops, drawn from the Punjab at great peril to the security of that province, which without the aid of a single soldier from England, recovered Delhi, broke the back of the rebellion and lent their aid to Lucknow,'[8] as British army officers later recorded. The inhabitants of Shahjahanabad initially reacted with fear, but soon grew accustomed to the situation. One of them, a young boy, later recollected:

> I well remember that when the Indians entered the city it was morning time. I was going with my servant, *Rahim Buksh*, to my maternal uncle's house in the *Bulaki Begum* Street, and when we reached the "Dhareeba," we saw people running in all directions in fright. Rahim Buksh, a well-made, strong man, at once lifted me on his back and bolted. When we reached our aunt's, the gate was being closed, but Rahim Buksh struck at the gate and entered it with such force, that, inside, we both fell prone and hurt ourselves badly.
>
> After a day or two, however, we became used to the new conditions, and I returned to my own house ... It was hot weather at that time, and every night we used to see the glare of the cannon-balls passing overhead; and we considered them pyrotechnics. One day a cannon-ball tore through the roof of the upper storey and fell on to the verandah, where we were having our meal. My uncle at once ran towards it and threw a lot of water over it.[9]

In the city, it may have been possible to ignore some of these events, but it was not possible to do so in the Fort, the centre of all activity. Of the initial six regiments of infantry and cavalry and the artillery battery allied to Bahadur Shah II, apart from some regiments positioned at the Lahori, Ajmeri and Delhi Gates of the city, the rest remained in the Fort. The infantry encamped near Salimgarh Gate and Lahori Gate, the artillery battery in the Diwan-i-Am and the cavalry inside Mehtab Bagh.

This ingress of armed soldiers into the private part of the Fort without permission was an unheard of transgression in court etiquette and domains of use. It was countenanced because the Fort required protection from the riverside. Since there were insufficient personal guards, it was not possible to dispense with the services of the soldiers. In a shadow of the earlier relationship between the emperor and the subjects, the king assured the soldiers that they would be treated like his children, but was unable to command from them sufficient or sustained respect.[10]

The British-trained soldiers, who had come to the Red Fort from different parts of the country, looked up to the king as the emotional and symbolic figurehead around whom they rallied. However, they were neither versed in the traditional Mughal military system nor in the necessary rules of etiquette when interacting with the king in person. At the same time, Bahadur Shah II, while wishing to break free of British control, was unfamiliar with the methods of dealing with these soldiers, trained as they were by British officers in a variation of the British military system. Though he acted quickly and decisively initially—issuing orders prohibiting any unlawful acts by the troops or citizens, announcing that those engaged in plunder would be severely punished, publicly pulling up lax officials and soldiers, stressing discipline amongst the regiments, ensuring the city's regular administration and himself coming out in ceremonial procession to restore the confidence of his people—he later forbore to deal with these issues directly. Instead, he directed his sons through his minister and physician, Hakim Ahsanullah, to assume command of the regiments. Meanwhile, more troops arrived in the Fort from Ferozepur, Mathura, Gwalior, Nasirabad, Nimach, Jalandhar and Bareilly. Zealous and sometimes recalcitrant, the men who formed these troops were generally without sufficient weapons and money. Their swelling numbers heightened the pressure on the Mughal court.

As their insistence on being admitted into the king's presence to apprise him of their loyalty and present their demands became more raucous, they often entered parts of the inner palace without permission, even riding into the Diwan-i-Khas forecourt reserved for royalty or for its trusted servants. Though the powers of the Mughals had denuded considerably from the time of the Fort's establishment, the norms of the use of the imperial pavilions had been generally observed, apart from a few isolated instances. Now, these norms were overrun by the soldiers with impunity, who even walked into the Diwan-i-Khas with their shoes on. Their protracted stay in the Private Imperial domain of the Fort, especially in the imperial gardens, caused injury to these as well as inconvenience to 'the Royal cortege [which] frequently condescends to go in that direction'.[11]

Forcible entry into the Private Imperial Domain was a circumstance that the king did not accept. He ordered all the regiments to encamp outside the city gates—with the exception of one inside the Fort and another on the Yamuna banks. He also expressly forbade the oppression of his people by the troops. However, he continued to issue these commands through the medium of the princes, who often did not follow his instructions. Though he frequently reminded the princes that '[t]he government of a nation and the control of an army are not to be treated with the same levity as child's play',[12] Bahadur Shah did not succeed in establishing absolute authority over either them or over the soldiers. The soldiers obeyed his wishes only partially and replaced many of his hereditary attendants with their own men.

Inside the Fort, the boundaries between different domains—the Private Imperial, the Public Imperial and the Public Common—became increasingly blurred. Threatened nobles were afforded protection in the king's own quarters; the soldiers were accommodated in the imperial gardens; magazine stores were kept in the Diwan-i-Am; the princes and the king disagreed even in public; council meetings with different members of the court were sometimes held within the Khas Mahal. Ironically, in the midst of this disorganised occupation, some of the original practices that the Fort had been designed for, and which had all but relapsed into perfunctory rituals, were revived.

While the inhabitants were reassured by the sight of royal processions headed by the king mounted on an elephant, daily audience was held at the Diwan-i-Am—often at the insistence of the soldiers to ensure a hearing. *Nazars* were presented on behalf of the different rulers professing loyalty to the king, who himself inspected arrangements for the Fort's defence. Council meetings took place in the Diwan-i-Khas to discuss how best to defend the city, establish contact with other parts of the country and generate funds and military support. Id was regally celebrated, with the king and princes attending prayers at the Jama Masjid.

During this time, assaults and skirmishes took place regularly. Initially, these were confined to the northern and western areas outside the city. British reinforcements arrived from this direction, mainly from Punjab, and pitched camp on the higher ground at the ridge. One of the first battles, between the soldiers loyal to the king and the

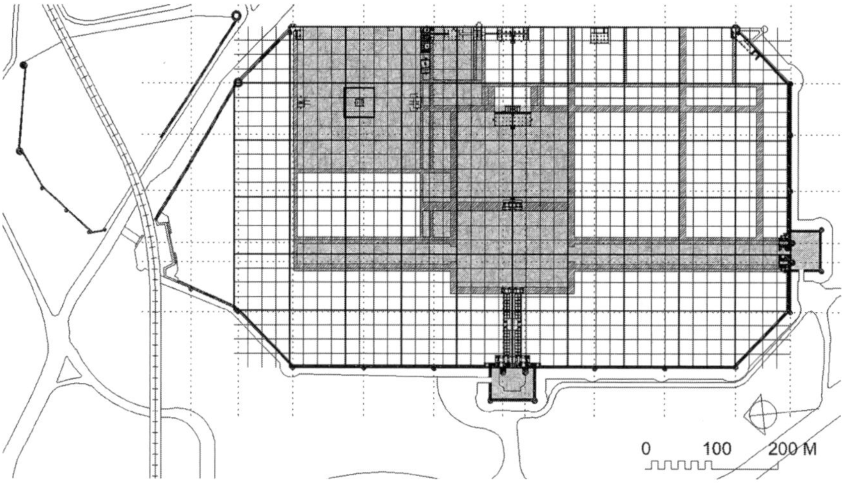

Areas of incursion into Public and Private Imperial domains by Indian soldiers (Drawing: N. Joshi, Author)

British, took place at the end of May near the Hindon river. The Indian soldiers had to retreat into Shahjahanabad. The effect of a large military force inside the city with restricted passage outside soon produced a situation of siege where grain and funds needed to be extracted from wealthy citizens.[13] Meanwhile, more British reinforcements arrived, including those under Brigadier John Nicholson. In the month of June, they engaged with and defeated the Indian troops at Najafgarh, 15 miles southwest of Delhi.[14]

Reinforcements to the troops for the aid of the king arrived mainly from the east. The onset of the monsoon, coupled with the collapse of the bridge across the river, made their passage into the city increasingly difficult. While the bridge was being repaired, they had to be ferried across. This proved a setback to the defence of the city. There were also stray incidents of treason in the Fort. Guns on the Salimgarh bastion that commanded a wide circuit for firing on British positions outside the city walls were, on more than one occasion, found to be filled with stones, gravel and string.[15]

In the middle of June, cannonballs fell into the Fort. Recriminations followed, with Ahsanullah Khan and even the chief queen suspected of treachery. In an atmosphere of mutual suspicion, courtiers entrusted with important commissions were suddenly removed from favour or put under guard.[16] Such an atmosphere was neither conducive to cohesive action nor to firm decisions, and the results of divisions between the king and his advisors soon became apparent in the battle for the city.

Though in the initial days the king had issued forth repeatedly into the city, much of the normal interaction between the Fort and the city ceased as he remained closeted inside his palace. Faced with only a partial compliance of his orders, he was unaware or unwilling to intercede actively in the troubles of Shahjahanabad. Innocent people were killed. Parts of the city were subjected to extortion by different bands of soldiers. The actual and symbolic distance between the Fort and the city increased during this time.

Since the British forces were positioned near the northern ridge, they tried to enter the city through Kashmiri Gate. Their efforts took effect in early September after the arrival of more men and ammunition. Heavy batteries were erected, and two practicable breaches made near the Kashmiri and Water Bastions on 14 September. The British force moved along these breaches in the direction of Mori and Kabul Gates, and from here towards Lahori Gate, Begum Bagh and Chandni Chowk. However, their progress was not easy and they were beaten back to Kabul Gate. The area of Qudsia Gardens, Idgah, Kashmiri Gate, Kabul Gate and Lahori Gate was damaged, plundered or destroyed in this conflict. Thus, in the battle for control over Shahjahanabad, the western and northern parts of the city suffered the most.

From here, the focus of the struggle shifted to the main entrance routes to Shahjahanabad from the northern and western sides, and then to the entire boundary of the city. Soldiers loyal to the Indian and British cause, occupied by turns the Subzi Mandi gardens, Begum Sumroo's house, Begum Bagh, Kishenganj quarter, Ajmeri Gate, Daryaganj and Jama Masjid. The Delhi Bank house facing Chandni Chowk and two houses just below the palace, known as those of Major Abbot and Khan Mohammed,[17] fell into the hands of the British. On 19 September, a letter sent by the British from Delhi stated: 'Our Mortar batteries continued to fire during the night towards the south of the palace and in the direction of Durriaganj. We have now turned in the direction of Jumma Masjid'.[18]

They then trained their guns towards the main entrance to the Fort and the stronghold of Salimgarh[19] from where cannons had been mounted to respond to British guns. The river-front walls and buildings were the most vulnerable in this exchange of fire, and the pavilion atop Shah Burj is believed to have been destroyed in this attack. As the fighting increased in intensity, so did the soldiers' demands for pay. The king had to distribute money from the treasury and sell precious silver goods of the royal family. Finally, the guns of the Indian defenders were captured by the British. They followed this by blowing an opening in the Fort's Lahori Gate on 20 September. The very next day, Delhi was declared a dependency of the British Crown, and the headquarters of General Wilson were established in the Diwan-i-Khas.

Thus, after four months of punctuated defence and siege, the battle in Shahjahanabad finally ended with the British being victorious. This did not imply that the War of Independence was over since opposition to them in other parts of the country had not been curtailed. However, their victory in the battle for Delhi had great symbolic value, due to the continuing importance of the Red Fort as the centre of the Mughal dynasty's rule and the rallying point for this war.

During the last few days of this battle, as the situation within the Fort worsened and its effectiveness both as a refuge and a stronghold decreased, the king with his sons escaped 'secretly under the palace window'[20] through the private route to the riverbank, to finally shelter in Humayun's Tomb. Soon after the takeover of the palace, they were enjoined to surrender on promises of safekeeping by British soldiers under Captain Hodson—promises which were barely kept.

As in the takeover of Shahjahanabad by the Indian soldiers, many innocent people were unintentionally and intentionally killed, so it was in the British capture. The British shot dead or hanged most of Bahadur Shah's sons and the soldiers who fell into their hands. They indiscriminately[21] killed all men inside the Fort and compelled the inhabitants of the city to leave it. They annexed the states in the vicinity of Delhi that had supported Bahadur Shah and hanged their rulers.

Bahadur Shah was imprisoned in a small house inside the southern part of the Fort, in the area flanking the erstwhile public ceremonial street connecting Delhi Gate to the Naqqar Khana forecourt. A photograph of this area, taken some months after 1857, serves to illustrate the urban character of this part of the Fort even in its captured state. Though many of the buildings display European architectural features on their first floors akin to those in the Chandni Chowk, it is evident that the larger spatial organisation of the street was unaltered at this time.

Meanwhile, the British freely moved within all parts of the city, including the hitherto forbidden inner palace of the Fort. Their disdain and contempt for the Mughal king, who they referred to as an 'imbecile puppet', did not blind them to the beauty of the 'gorgeous domes and minarets'[22] of his city and Fort. A soldier recorded his first impression of the Red Fort thus: 'Passing on, we wandered through the courts, wondering at the vast size of this castellated palace, with its towering embattled walls.'[23] The unimpeded access into the Fort, faded as its beauties were, seemed to afford a vicarious satisfaction to the conquering British army. They revelled in the fact that special thanksgiving services were held in the beautiful Diwan-i-Khas, associated so unquestionably with the Mughal kings.

Bahadur Shah II was tried by order of Major General Penny, the divisional commander, in the very same Diwan-i-Khas. Presided over by and comprising British army officers, the group conducting the trial was grandly titled the European Military Commission. On the basis of the arguments of Major Harriot, prosecutor and deputy-judge advocate general, Bahadur Shah was found guilty of treason, rebellion and murder. He was banished to Rangoon (Yangon), along with his chief wife, Begum Zeenat Mahal. His favourite son and his wife, whose lives had been spared as a condition of surrender, accompanied him, as did some other members of his immediate family and some old attendants.

While the British officers and soldiers were sealing their victory with such formalities, they were also simultaneously looting a large quantity of valuables from the Fort and city. Later, this was carried out in an official manner with the appointment of prize agents from the British army who systematically assessed and removed valuables from different parts of the city.[24] Since the population of Shahjahanabad was debarred from the city for over a year, this plunder continued undisturbed.

As one of the participants in the battle, later an assistant to an officer with a permit to search for plunder, frankly admitted, '[i]t would

Area around Jama Masjid (Alkazi Collection)

have been contrary to human nature, and utterly at variance with the predatory instinct had the soldiers failed to take advantage of the facilities for plunder that surrounded them on every side".[25] This predatory instinct decimated the city. Walls, floors and staircases of houses were knocked down in search of hidden treasure. Places of worship were also not spared. A recollection of the treasures concealed in the Hindu idol at the famed Somnath temple broken open by Sultan Mahmud Ghazni in the twelfth century, propelled the marauding members of the British army to do the same.

The first to suffer from this assault was an idol in a small temple in Chandni Chowk. It was demolished in true iconoclastic style with hammers, and the brilliant cache of jewels and gold within it was transferred to the pockets of the plunderers. After systematically stripping the city of all its remarkable wealth, the unsatiated British further augmented their riches by selling its different streets and houses back to the inhabitants from whom they had appropriated them.[26] The same soldier, who had succumbed so readily to human nature and the facilities for plunder, arriving a little late to other parts of the city, wrote that:

> We entered several of the large houses belonging to the wealthier class of natives, and found every one in the same condition, turned inside

The house in which Bahadur Shah Zafar was imprisoned, Note the gateway to the Naqqar Khana forecourt in the distance (F. Beato, 1858, 765/75, ASI PL)

> out, their ornaments torn to pieces, costly articles too heavy to remove, battered into fragments, and a general air of desolation pervading each building ... Not a single house or building remained intact, and the damage done must have amounted to thousands of pounds.
>
> When quiet returned and the inhabitants of the city began to flock back to their former homes, whole streets, in which no doubt treasure had been concealed and had escaped the search of the prize agents, were sold to the people for sums ranging from 5000, to 50,000 rupees.[27]

With the removal of the Mughal king from the throne and from the country, all authority vested in the British, who declared Calcutta as the capital of their Indian empire. On 1 November 1858, the government of India was directly assumed by the British Crown.[28] This displacement of the Mughals as rulers reduced Shahjahanabad to a provincial town. It no longer bore the distinction of a capital, neither did the Red Fort remain a royal palace. Removal of imperial status was followed by a calculated destruction of the famed Mughal city and Fort.

This destruction was not confined to the Red Fort and Shahjahanabad, or indeed to this time. Imperial property in other Mughal cities—Agra,

A Jain temple, Shahjahanabad (F. Beato, 1858, 768/75, ASI PL)

Lahore, Allahabad—had been destroyed earlier by the British. The tomb of Shah Jahan's mother had been blown up in 1832. In 1857, the eastern gateway and facade of Jami Masjid in Agra was dismantled.[29] However, after 1857, the scale of destruction in Delhi, a symbol of the erstwhile imperial seat, was at its most ruthless with a great portion of Shahjahanabad—its walls, gates, buildings—demolished.[30] In October that year, the officer commanding Delhi passed the following orders: 'You will blow up or otherwise destroy all fortifications and you will so far destroy the walls and gates of the city as to make them useless for defences'.[31]

Not only were the walls and fortifications destroyed, but also the streets and roads as well as secular and religious buildings. The rationale

Naqqar Khana forecourt after the British takeover of the Fort
(F. Beato, 1858, 766/75, ASI PL)

for some of these actions appears inexplicable, as the covering over by a footpath of the central aqueduct, a decorative and cooling feature in Chandni Chowk.[32] A similar canal that ran in the centre of Faiz Bazaar was also filled up. In other cases, the reasons for the destruction appear more straightforward. Public symbols and structures associated with Mughal power were demolished, including important mosques, sarais and mansions. Royal gardens and retreats were confiscated. Fatehpuri Masjid, which performed an important urban and religious focus for the city—and was one of the climaxes of the Chandni Chowk axis—was annexed and auctioned off along with other parts of the city. It was restored for religious purposes only in 1878. Zinat-ul Masjid, that had been founded on the initiative of the Princess Zinatunnisa, was run as a bakery[33] and later as a European hospital.[34] Shalimar Bagh, where Aurangzeb had been crowned, was given over for cultivation. The large Akbarabadi Masjid in Faiz Bazar (endowed by Shah Jahan's wife, Akbari Begum) and Jahanara's Sarai in Chandni Chowk, (where the most favoured of noblemen and the richest merchants had once vied for accommodation) were two of the more famous symbols of the city that were razed to the ground.

Chandni Chowk canal covered over after the British takeover of Shahjahanabad (Bourne (?) 1860s, 752/16/5, OIOC, BL)

Clock tower, Chandni Chowk (Delhi Museum, Vol. 3, 1911-12, p. 45, ASI PL)

Such destruction of urban space and architecture was followed by another assertion of power—the remodelling of Shahjahanabad. Structures symbolic of British civilisation were grafted on top of destroyed buildings, such as a town hall on the site of Jahanara's Sarai in Chandni Chowk. A clock tower was installed opposite the town hall. That these interventions sat uncomfortably within Shahjahanabad's urban form is evident from an observation during the Coronation Durbar in 1903, when the 'tall pinnacle of the gothic clock tower, halfway down the street, was the centre of a scheme of decorative festoons, and thereby lost its usual air of being entirely out of place in an Indian City'.[35] Begum Bagh was re-christened and reinterpreted as the 'Queen's gardens', with elements of British notions of landscape imposed on it. C.M. Villiers-Stuart, who visited the sites of many imperial gardens in her extensive travels in India during the early twentieth century, recognised the impact of such spatial elements, observing that:

> ... it is the new roads more than anything else which have ruined the old pleasance of the Princess Roshanara, or the Queen's gardens in Delhi City; the winding drives which give a sense of restlessness and exposure as they cut up the garden with their broad bare gravel sweeps.[36]

But the large majority of British residents in Delhi appreciated this re-invention. Thus, H.G. Keene, in a handbook on Delhi written at the turn of the century, writes: '[t]he visitor should by no means fail to drive around the Queen's gardens, which are very tastefully laid out in the English style'.[37] The buildings of the city that were allowed to remain were also appropriated and, when not actively misused, allowed to decay. A letter to the Commissioner of the Delhi Division, written by Carr Stephen in 1872, records that:

> The destruction of historical and other remarkable buildings in this city and its environs since the mutiny has been unprecedented. From 1851 when the Court of Directors sanctioned the repair of the Jama Musjid down to '56 these architectural memorials were tolerably well preserved; but since 1857 the interest in them has been either slack or spasmodic.[38]

The other visual climax of Chandni Chowk, the Red Fort, as the seat of the king and all its associations of Mughal rule, was almost completely destroyed. The palace demolition order was carried out in 1863. Five hundred yards around the Fort were ordered to be cleared completely of gardens, pavilions and mosques—with injunctions to leave some of the temples intact.[39] The rationale for these clearances is attributed to reasons of military security. However, that this was not really the case is borne out by a letter from the executive engineer, Delhi Division to the Commissioner of Delhi, proposing the way forward to ensure demolition.

> It is simply this, that the extent of clearance, should no longer, as a general question, be discussed on Political grounds but on Military ones & that instead of deciding that this or that street … shall be the Boundary—a Committee composed of Engineer and Artillery Officers of High Rank and standing shall be assembled to decide what is the least distance from the Walls of the Fort at which native houses can be allowed to remain standing & this decision to be final & everything within the distance settled by them to be swept away without exception of Building or person.
>
> This limit once fixed Political grounds might be allowed to modify it to a certain extent so far as to spare for the present, detached temples, an important street and so on, but we should have something tangible to go upon & the Political arguments could be duly considered and weighed against the Military ones. Should this proposition meet with your approval, I will submit it to the Brigadier and should he also approve (& I have no doubt that he will) I will at once send it on to Department Head for submission in due course.[40]

Within the enclosing walls of the Fort, the British reduced the meticulously planned complex of Shah Jahan's builders and craftsmen into unrecognisable rubble. Later, the British officials involved in the conservation of the Fort highlighted its ruinous condition before the destruction by the British, in order 'to dispel the idea, held by so many, that its spoilation was wholly the result of the English occupation after the Mutiny'. Nonetheless, they admitted that:

> … [w]ith the exception of the more important buildings on the East front of the Fort, and the Diwan-i-'Amm and the Naubat Khana, a clean

Area cleared around the Fort after 1857 (Alkazi Collection)

Area around the Fort in 1870 (Photo 2/3, 76, OIOC, BL)

> sweep was made of the rest of the palace buildings, so as to give the accommodation and space necessary to a garrison.[41]

Thus, the fact remains that, stripped of many of its decorative components as the Fort had become by 1857, the typology and extent of

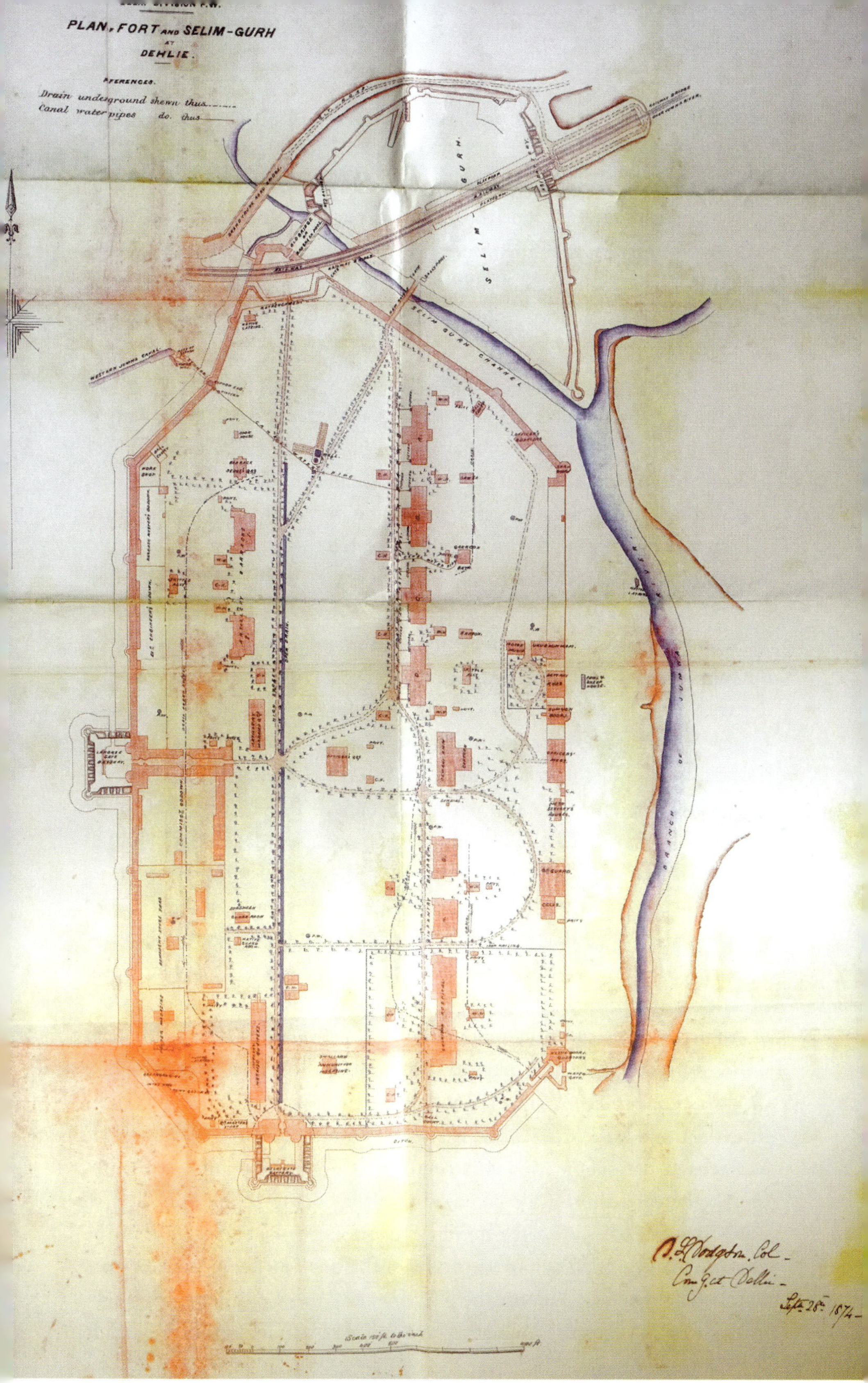

Artillery and Infantry Barracks in the Red Fort, 1869 (F 178/12, NAI)

its built spaces had remained largely intact. It was only after its takeover by the British military that the imperial gardens and colonnades; the formal paved courtyards and streets with their arcades, central canals and fountains; the seraglio with its baths, pavilions and courts; the karakhanas and royal kitchens and the entire public and private common sector were razed to the ground.

The original sequence of movement and planning in the Fort, along with the open spaces and ground levels that characterised this sequence, was thus also obliterated. The plantation, paths, tanks, fountains, flower beds of the celebrated Hayat Baksh and Mehtab Bagh were swept away. The Fort's decaying but still coherent facade of marble screens, pavilions and balustrades was picked apart into isolated, forlorn structures bereft of the colonnades and courts that defined their edges and marked their climax.

Scattered portions of the Public Imperial and Private Imperial domain were left standing, with a handful of pavilions that had escaped destruction—the Diwan-i-Khas, Rang Mahal, Mumtaz Mahal, Asad Burj, Imperial Hammam, Diwan-i-Am, Shah Burj and Moti Masjid. Some of the pavilions in the imperial gardens, such as the Hira Mahal, Zafar Mahal, Sawan and Bhadon, were also partially retained. The main gates into the Fort, Lahori Gate with its covered Chatta Bazaar and Delhi Gate, though spared from destruction, were deprived of their connecting colonnades, arcades, screens and courts. The battlements of the barbicans in front of the Lahori and Delhi Gates (retitled the Victoria and Alexandra Gates)[42] were removed and the tops of the walls covered with earth for purposes of defence.

That the destruction of most of the built structures in the Fort was unnecessary, as far as the practical function of the British force residing in it was concerned, is clear from the use of other Mughal forts at this time. In these forts, the British destroyed comparatively less built fabric and reused the extant Mughal structures to a greater extent. A plan of the Citadel of Lahore (not dated) shows that many of the buildings in the Fort were taken over for military functions. The arcades around the Diwan-i-Am in this Fort are depicted in this map as being used as store rooms. The map also records the placement of a row of military barracks in front of some of these arcades and the accommodation of magazine

River Face, Red Fort: after destruction and takeover of Shahjahanabad by the British (Delhi, Vol. 12, 1931-32, No. 5914, ASI PL)

store rooms around the Burra-Khwabgah Court. In this drawing, the lodgings of the Indian officers are shown in rooms below the Fort wall, and those of British officers in rooms around the Hazuri Bagh.[43]

In the Red Fort, the pavilions that did escape demolition did not escape ravishment. Valuable effects and decorative features of the imperial quarters were looted. The celebrated inlaid black marble panels behind the Diwan-i-Am throne as well as the inlaid panel of Orpheus before the throne, 'the sole examples in India of this particular form of technique',[44] along with other decorated panels, were appropriated by Colonel (later Sir) John Jones. He sold them for 500 pounds to the British government, who deposited them in the South Kensington Museum.[45]

The inlaid precious stones in the Diwan-i-Khas were picked apart, the culprits perhaps divided between the Indian soldiers who entered it during 1857 and the British soldiers who gained access to it after their victory. The gilded copper domes of the Mussaman Burj and Moti Masjid, as well as the sheets of copper from the chattris on top of the Diwan-i-Khas roof, were stripped and auctioned as moveable assets by a prize agent.[46] Even

Shah Burj pavilion, southern face
(Delhi, 91/1902-03, ASI PL)

the British dead were made recipients in this stripping of the Fort. For instance, the gravestone of Brigadier-General John Nicholson was made of a large stone slab taken from the Red Fort.[47] In the space of less than eight years, the shape of the more than 200-year-old Fort was drastically changed.

Such an assault continued, almost unchecked, in the subsequent occupation of the Fort by the British. Gun batteries replaced pavilions. A parade ground was made over Mehtab Bagh and the royal store rooms, kitchens and regalia chambers.[48] The general principle of coexistence, with different kinds of people accommodated within the Fort by the Mughal kings, was altered. Instead of it being the site of a complex range of activities, only one uniform use was now made of the Fort—that of a cantonment. The British military resided within it, in large barracks constructed hastily, or in Mughal buildings altered unrecognisably for their use. They had little or no contact with the city or its inhabitants, segregated even from the Indian soldiers in their regiments who were moved out in the adjoining Daryaganj area.

The dense conglomeration of streets, gardens, houses and mosques within the Private Common domain north of Chatta Chowk was removed

Hayat Baksh with central tank filled up, Zafar Mahal bricked up, and barracks constructed by the British (Delhi, 103/1902-3, ASI PL)

entirely. It was replaced by construction completely unsympathetic in scale, material and detail—a series of married officers' quarters, barracks, wash houses and cook houses. Roads displaced the geometrically organised paved paths and flower beds, while desolate open ground stretched over the graceful forecourts enclosed by arcades and decorated with fountains and canals. The inner edge of the Fort wall where Mughal soldiers once used to patrol now housed workshops and godowns of the executive engineer and barrack master, and the military works departments used many of the remaining palace buildings as barracks or stores.

Lahori Gate, formerly part of the grand vibrant entrance into the Fort, was transformed by inappropriate additions, and the colourful Chatta Bazaar parodied into a regimental bazaar selling supplies for European soldiers. The Naqqar Khana, the gateway to the Mughal ruler's presence, was made to serve as the staff sergeants' quarters.[49] The Diwan-i-Am was converted into an open lounge for officers. The emperor's private entrance route to it was used as a canteen and as refreshment rooms. Such imposed reuse was also visible in other Mughal forts: for instance, the Lahore Fort where the Diwan-i-Am was used as a soldiers' dormitory, and the Chhoti Khwabgah as a church.[50]

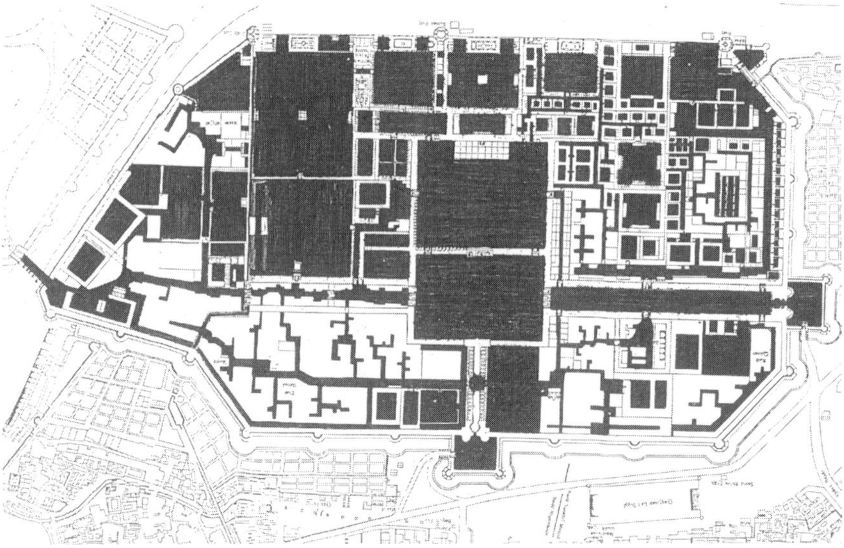

Original built and open space configuration: open areas shaded black (Drawing: Author)

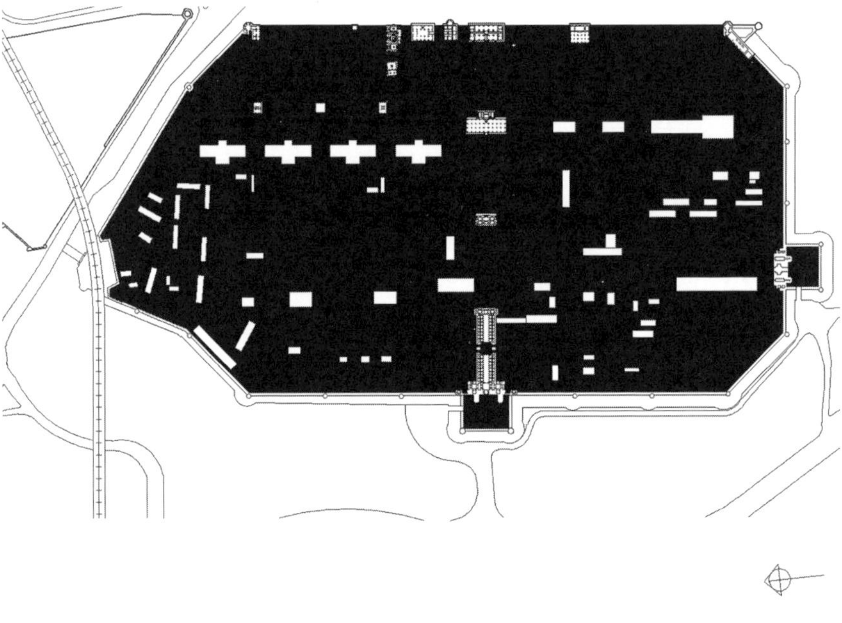

Transformed built and open space configuration post 1857: open spaces shaded black (Drawing: Author)

The British isolated the Fort into an island, and deliberately housed activities in it sacrilegious to the delicate beauty of its buildings. An 'unhappy little garden'[52] was planted in front of the Diwan-i-Khas, while wash houses and urinals were positioned in front of the Hayat Baksh's Sawan and Bhadon pavilions. Of the imperial pavilions allowed to remain, Rang Mahal was converted into a temporary mess lounge for officers, while Mumtaz Mahal was used as a military prison and then as a sergeant's mess, its marble walls defaced by prisoners' incisions. Photographs of the river-face of the Fort, from the period between 1858 to 1860 CE, clearly show evidence of British occupation. The Mughal railings and screens, visible even in photographs just before 1857, have been replaced by barrack-style unplastered brick-walls inserted with rectangular windows. Even Mussaman Burj, devoid of its gilded dome and with its riverside entrance appropriated by the British, appears as just another barrack.[51]

The pavilions of the Shah Burj, the Emperor's Tower, are seen to follow a similar pattern of use with their cusped marble arches roughly bricked up to provide a temporary military office. The chamber behind it, with its ingenious provision to lift water from the river, is recorded to have been converted into an armoury shop and the *Jul Mahal* (Zafar Mahal) into a swimming pool for the British officers. Not all British residents approved of such brutal interventions and their dramatic result on the majestic Fort. In his 'Memorandum regarding the old Muhammadan buildings of Delhi', dated 24 May 1865, Major General Cunningham wrote:

> The Diwan-i-Khas, or Private Audience Hall of the Mogal Emperors, which was seen and described by Bernier, Thevenot, and Tavernier, is still in good order inside, but the outside view of its marble pillars is utterly spoiled by a thatched Verandah, the ugly remains of its former occupation as a Barrack. This building is now used as a Museum, but I would strongly recommend that … the Diwan-i-Khas be restored to its original state of an open audience Hall.[53]

A later report also regrets the changes made in the Diwan-i-Am. It records:

> As for the Hall of Public Audience, the great pillared Diwan-i-Am, with its fine marble mosaic canopy and throne, is used as a canteen, and

Shah Burj pavilion (P 270/89, 1902-03, ASI PL)

> on the right of the throne is a bar for serving liquor! To the left of the throne is an enclosure of bamboo screen work, in which Nubee Bux keeps a soldiers' coffee shop![54]

The inhabitants of Shahjahanabad, traditionally allowed regular access to this Diwan-i-Am, were debarred from even entering the Fort. The banks of the Yamuna adjacent to the Fort were now forbidden to the public. The gardens and pavilions around the Fort were replaced by a stretch of unfriendly open land—embodying the physical and symbolic barrier between the British in the Fort and the Indians in the city. The Fort and the city which had earlier been functionally, spatially and visually integrated so closely, now had all these connections severed. The social and religious community celebrations in which the Mughal kings had prayed with their people in the Jama Masjid and Idgah, or had set forth at the head of flower processions celebrating communal amity (*phulwallon ki sair)*, came to an abrupt end. So did the cultural rituals involving the darshan of the king from his balcony, and the poetry and music sessions that had been held frequently within the Fort. All these activities, like the king himself, vanished in the overwhelming assault of 1857 and its aftermath. Thus, the attributes, the perception and the uses of space within and around the Red Fort changed almost completely.

8

A RETURN IN PARTS

'Histories have always been contested territories, and the power to define the past is an index of domination.'

Eileen Hooper-Greenhill, *Museums and their Visitors*

In the beginning of the twentieth century, the oft-contested territory of Delhi was dotted with a number of monuments, reminders of its long and tumultuous history. These rendered Delhi, 'the Rome of Asia', and made it, with its 'ruins spreading over a length of ten miles by a breadth averaging little less than six ... more interesting than Agra, if less beautiful'[1]. Some of these ruins had been added on during and after 1857. In the meantime, the British had also remodelled the city in their bid to emphasise their authority as sole rulers. This practice of redefining the past—a familiar assertion of most conquerors—transformed Shahjahanabad into a shadow of its Mughal origins, interrupted by British buildings, institutions and spaces. The Red Fort, from being an imperial Mughal Fort, was changed into an exotic British cantonment.

The British influence exerted itself, not merely in the architectural but also in educational, cultural and economic spheres. Missions, places of Christian worship, Christian schools and colleges came up in different parts of the city. The famous traditional handicrafts of Shahjahanabad—ivory miniatures, works of jewellery, carvings in metal, blue pottery, engravings, gold and silver embroidery—declined for some time, though, as records by travellers show, they did revive within a few years.[2] Shahjahanabad also did not expand much physically. Its banks, hospitals, churches, and main shops were concentrated in and around Chandni Chowk. The British civil station lay beyond the city's northern wall, but fifty years after its large-scale destruction in 1857, Delhi was still contained within the walls of Shahjahanabad[3] with a population of merely 1,73,393.[4] That Shahjahanabad was perceived as synonymous with Delhi is apparent from a record in 1903, which noted that the Nizam of Hyderabad, 'visited all the Muhammaden shrines in and around the city, and even took the ladies of his zenana so far as the Kutub Minar, some eleven miles distant from Delhi.'[5]

During this time, the Red Fort continued to be occupied, reshaped and misused by the British military. As has been mentioned in preceding sections, two of the most arresting features within it and the inspiration for many fanciful images in British drawings of the Fort—the gilded domes of Mussaman Burj and Moti Masjid—were removed after 1857. The dome of Mussaman Burj was then re-erected in staid masonry and plaster which did not follow the curvature of the original Mughal dome. The domes of Moti Masjid, rebuilt in marble by the British, are recorded to have been 'wholly disproportionate particularly in respect to the size of the mosque'.[6] The sheets of copper from the chattris of the Diwan-i-Khas

Red Fort, view of the inner palace (Photo: Author, 2000)

and the celebrated inlaid plaques behind the jharoka in the Diwan-i-Am had also been looted.[7] Even the sweep of the Fort's famous red walls was not spared. The views of its Lahori and Delhi Gates from the two main axes of the city were altered. The battlements of their barbicans were removed and the moat around them filled up.

Another major intervention in the city by the British authorities was the introduction of the East India Railway in 1864–65. The railway route was made to enter the city from the east through Salimgarh, and the station was planned to be located just behind the Queen's gardens. To accommodate the railway route and station, a large portion of Shahjahanabad as well as part of the Red Fort were destroyed. In Shahjahanabad, the Calcutta Gate and the areas immediately north of the public gardens of Chandni Chowk were completely removed. Even till the 1850s, as records show, this quarter had contained large havelis of important noblemen—including that of Nawab Wazir and buildings such as the *Shish Mahal, Sahib Mahal, Zinat Mahal*—as well as gardens such as the *Baghicha Munna Baghban* and a dense built fabric of houses and streets.[8]

Closer to the river, the railway route was taken through the northwestern end of the Fort, and through Salimgarh. Consequently, the bridge commissioned by Emperor Jahangir in 1621, close to Salimgarh Gate, was demolished. So were the Fort walls in the vicinity. The railway route was later expanded, leading to more changes in this part of the city and adjacent areas. As a communication from the Deputy Commissioner of the Delhi Division 1895 records:

> The advent of the A.D.C. railway round by the west wall of the town & the construction (now in progress) of its "Delhi Sadr" station on this side of the City, has very much altered the aspect of condition on this side, where a very large station yard, locomotive yard and enclosure for staff quarters is now to stand in between the city proper & the Sadr Bazar & Paharganj, the Sadr Bazar being linked with the City proper by a couple of bridges over the permanent way of this Railway and the RMR goods siding at this point ... (This siding having been constructed after 1873).[9]

The cycle of destruction and misuse was finally stemmed by a recognition of the unique attributes of the 'most magnificent palace in the East', and its city. By the end of the nineteenth century, there was a partial reassessment of the alterations imposed on it. Some British officials, while intensely proud of the part their countrymen had played in 1857, publicly rued the transformation of the Fort. For instance, H.C. Fanshawe, the Chief Commissioner of Delhi Division, writes that the 'effect of the extremely beautiful walls of the Fort ... is sadly spoilt by the glacis that was made in front of them after 1857, and is needlessly obstructed by the trees that have grown up at the foot of this'.[10] The re-evaluation of the state of the Fort, though too late to remedy most of its destruction, did result in a reconstruction of some parts of its spaces. It also coincided with a growing interest in monuments all over India. Such an interest soon crystallised into the formation of an organisation for their conservation—the ASI.

The ASI was an extension of the Department of Archaeology founded in 1862. The annual records of the ASI, especially from 1903 to 1913, are an important source of information on the state of the Fort in these times, which marked another significant change in its perception and use. The annual report of 1911-12 is of special interest since it encapsulates the work done on the Fort in the first decade of its active conservation. This report forms the basis for the discussion outlined in the following pages as it records, for the first time, a concise description of the complete conservation scheme implemented by the ASI since 1902. Hitherto, this was still being worked out and, thus, only part of the conservation effort is recorded in the previous annual reports.[11]

The Department of Archaeology that preceded the formation of the ASI had concentrated most of its early efforts on recording excavations, and on the preservation of ancient statues and monuments. This concentrated emphasis, ironically enough, often resulted in seemingly contradictory activities. Thus, in 1863, concurrently with the destruction in the Red Fort and the removal of its decorative elements, 125 fragments were recovered of the original elephant statues at its Delhi Gate.[12] These were reconstituted into an elephant statue and set up in the Queen's Gardens opposite the railway station, almost at the same time as the gilding on the Mussaman Burj and Moti Masjid

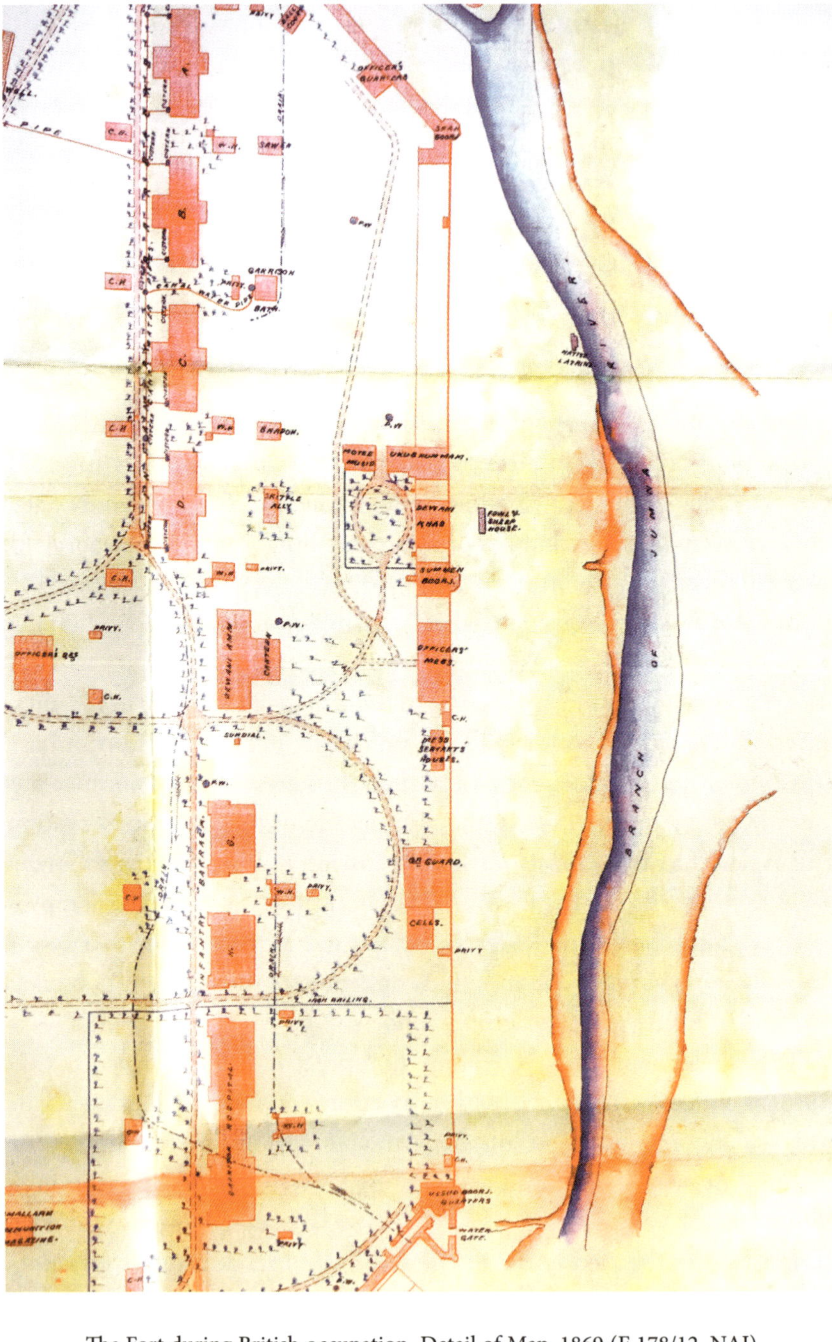

The Fort during British occupation, Detail of Map, 1869 (F 178/12, NAI)

domes was being stripped, and the buildings in the Red Fort were being demolished!

The Department of Archaeology later extended its scope to include the protection and sympathetic reuse of secular historical buildings and sites of interest that were likely to be less controversial than religious buildings. Though the Red Fort was among these, its decreased status in the eyes of the British may be interpreted from its description in the *Delhi Gazetteer* of this time, as 'the Mughal palace, now the Fort'.[13] An additional political catalyst for the Red Fort's conservation, apart from its manifest historical and architectural value, was the palpable interest that Delhi held for the British as the erstwhile capital of the famed Mughals. The Red Fort and Shahjahanabad were symbols of the Mughal dynasty that the British had ousted. It became natural for British travellers, especially for the royal and other dignitaries visiting India, to include the Fort in their itinerary. The visit of Edward VII, Prince of Wales, to Delhi in 1876, was one such important occasion.

To welcome him, the ancient Indian royal custom of durbar was re-enacted by the British on the first day of the new year in 1877. Summoned by the Viceroy, Lord Lytton, the durbar was held about 5.5 kilometres from Kashmiri Gate. At this durbar, in the Bawari plain across the drainage canal north of the Grand Trunk Road, Queen Victoria was proclaimed Empress of India. During this visit, a ball was held in the Diwan-i-Khas of the Red Fort in honour of the Prince of Wales. In the bid to decorate the Diwan-i-Khas for this occasion, it is reported to have been 'disgracefully treated'.[14] The designs of the carved wooden ceiling in it commissioned by the later Mughal kings, were reinterpreted and painted in black, red and gold instead of the original white and gold. Many of the coloured and gilded patterns on the pillars are also recorded to have been painted over in modern and inferior colours.

King Edward VIII succeeded to the throne of England on the death of his mother on 26 January 1901, a year before the establishment of the ASI. Another durbar was planned in Delhi to commemorate his coronation. The king's brother, the Duke of Connaught, and his wife were deputed as the royal representatives at this durbar, which was held on 1 January 1903 at the same site as the 1877 assemblage. By this time, the condition of the Fort had according to some reports, 'improved considerably since the

British barracks constructed on the erstwhile Bazaar and Rastah Dilli Darwaza (Photo: Author, 1997)

Diwan-i-Khas was used as a Museum and the Diwan-i-Am as a canteen'.[15] However, 'the red walls of Shah Jahan's palace fortress, [were] still scarred with memories of a momentous siege.'[16]

Within the Fort, the Rang Mahal continued to be used as a mess house and the Naqqar Khana and Mumtaz Mahal were still occupied by the British military. Though funds had begun to be allocated for the repairs of the buildings in the Fort shortly after 1883-1884, these had been carried out in accordance with the military works handbook. This handbook had probably been devised for the military buildings constructed in India by British engineers, which followed a very different mode of construction and style of architecture from that of Mughal buildings. The appropriateness of these repairs, thus, seems questionable. In fact, the floor of the Diwan-i-Khas is recorded as having been restored badly; its piers reportedly disfigured and its roof tawdry. In 1882, there had been some attempts to restore the celebrated mosaics of the Diwan-i-Am. This restoration, overseen by Major Cole, had used an inferior quality of materials in the work. Instead of the original jet-black marble, a greyish-black marble is reported to have been used, and ASI records also state that many of the destroyed marble panels inset with precious stones were now filled in with plaster.[18]

However, by the time of the second durbar—the 1903 coronation durbar—John Marshall, the director general of archaeology, had already made recommendations concerning the conservation of the Red Fort to

Mumtaz Mahal, northwest view showing its closed arches (PD 1729/1908-09, ASI PL)

the Government of India. These recommendations, put forward in 1902, were based on the Fort's erstwhile political and architectural importance and the problems brought about by its widespread destruction, and transformation into unrecognisable, isolated military buildings.

The stated scope of the recommendations made by John Marshall was the acquisition of as much of the inner palace of the Red Fort from the military as possible, and the separate enclosure of this area to afford it protection from further molestation and damage. It included the thorough conservation of the buildings within this area, and the removal of roads made by the military to enable the restoration of the older ground levels. It also visualised the laying out of pleasant lawns in the archaeological area.[19] Thus, for the second durbar, in keeping with the stated intention of conservation, the use and the additions to the Mughal buildings within the Fort were done in a more thoughtful manner than in 1876. Alterations made to the pavilions in the Fort for the events associated with the durbar were generally of a reversible nature and were removed after the festivities.

The occasion of the coronation durbar provided an additional stimulus for the conservation of the Mughal buildings in the Fort. Since there was no space or structure in Delhi specifically designed for hosting

The transformed appearance of the Diwan-i-Am for ceremonial use (ASI PL)

ceremonial functions, a substantial amount of planning and construction had to be done before each such function. For this durbar, as for the first one, some temporary structures such as amphitheatres, exhibition halls, stages and tents were erected. At the same time, it was doubtless felt necessary to provide some permanent local flavour to the ceremonial venues. The Mughal buildings within the Red Fort, universally recognised as a pinnacle of imperial taste and opulence, and used in the previous durbar, were deemed to be more than suited to fulfil this void. Thus, the conservation of the Fort was propelled by the need to use it on such ceremonial occasions, for which it was necessary to redeem at least some of the abuse it had suffered.

H.C. Fanshawe voiced the sentiment that the protection of historic buildings around Delhi would be given a boost, 'in view of the special interest which is certain to be taken in these memorials of ancientry by the large numbers who will be gathered at Delhi for the Coronation Durbar'.[20] In fact, the Fort and its surroundings formed the hub of many of the festivities held to commemorate the durbar. A grand display of fireworks is recorded to have been held between the Fort and Jama Masjid, in the Champ de Mars next to the Elgin Road. The British names of these streets seem rather incongruous in their setting between the Mughal profiles of the Fort and the principal congregational mosque. This area was also called the Khas Maidan and had earlier housed the grape and rose gardens around the Fort and the royal forecourts.[21]

The festivities in the Fort were equally alien, especially the investiture ceremony with 2,000 guests, and a dance with 1,000 bedecked participants promenading amongst palm trees, lights and flowers in the Diwan-i-Am. For the ceremonies of the Chapter of the Indian Orders and the state ball, the Diwan-i-Am was temporarily enlarged to thrice its size by two replicas made in continuation of it.[22] In the Viceroy's mind, the bestowing of honours, amidst the magnificence of the Mughal palace, enhanced their value. The investiture ceremony and ball-dance were followed by a supper in the Diwan-i-Khas. Shah Jahan's 'paradise on earth', even with its original decorative detail diminished, was described by the chroniclers of the event as one of the most beautiful buildings in the world, echoing Emily Metcalfe's sentiments voiced almost three-quarters of a century earlier.

The direction of the conservation efforts at this time was based on the perceived requirement for such functions, as well as on the constraints resulting from the large-scale destruction and alteration of the Fort. Records of its former appearance were not easily available. The original planting of its gardens had by this time either succumbed to the vagaries of time or been deliberately destroyed. All of this meant that it would be a herculean task to restore the destroyed Mughal pavilions, courts and gardens in order to reveal the original form of the Fort.

Thus, the Fort's display and projected use as a reception centre for visiting British royalty and officials not only affected the decision to conserve it, but also the manner and method in which it was conserved. Conservation attention largely focused on the extant buildings and their surroundings. At this time, the philosophy deemed appropriate for conserving ancient buildings, as Sir John Marshall stated later in a conservation pamphlet brought out in 1907, was that since 'historical value is gone when their authenticity is destroyed ... our first duty is not to renew them but to preserve them.'[23] Thus, repair was to be attempted only in cases where its advisability was undoubted. Exceptions could be made, as in specific instances where the reproduction of geometrical designs was admissible, particularly in living monuments of the Islamic period.

However, despite the Fort not being a living monument in the sense of a continuing historical use, and despite its large area as well as the absence of detailed records, it was decided to follow a policy of renewal

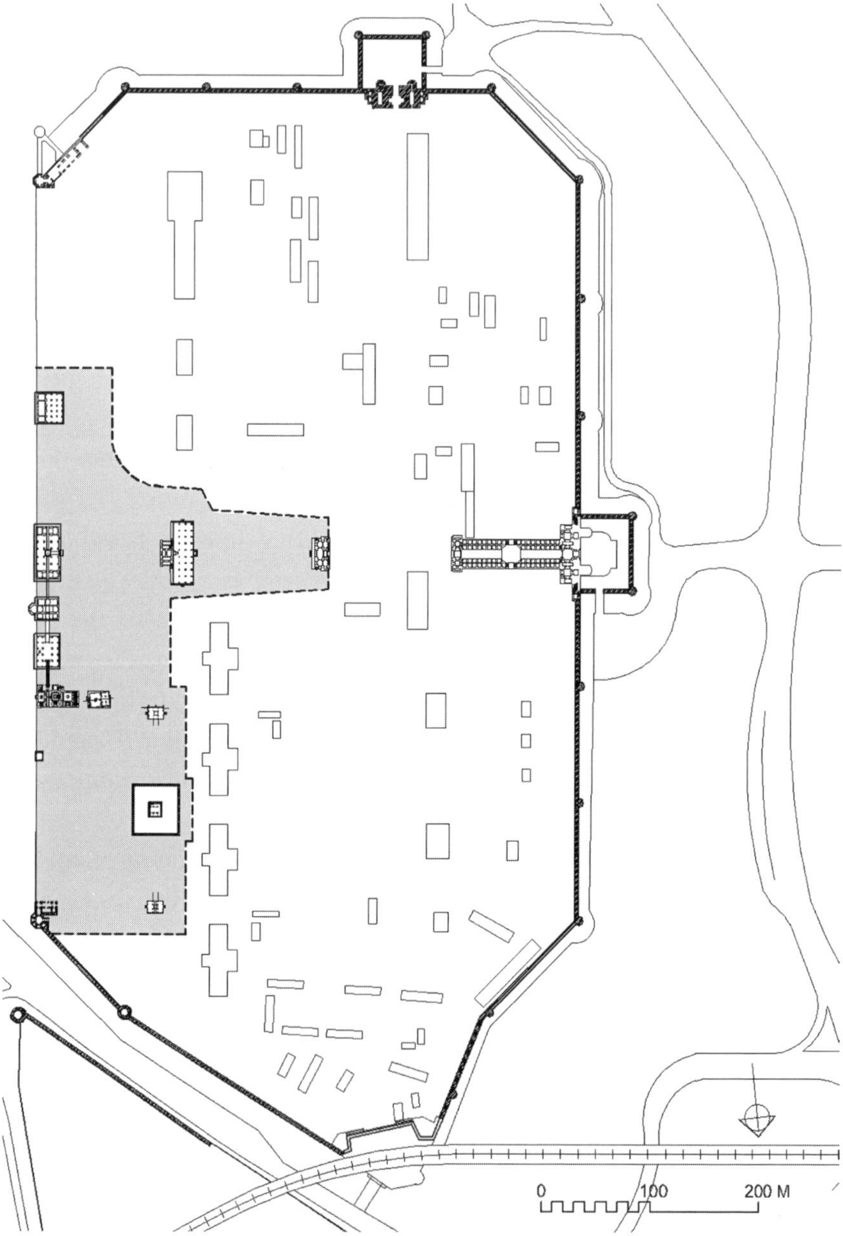

Delineation of the archaeological area in the Fort, early twentieth century
(Drawing: Author, N. Joshi, based on 586/97 ASI PL)

Zafar Mahal, soon after being vacated by the British military (ASI PL)

and restoration, professedly in order 'to make it worthy of its former glories'.[24] A more active conservation effort was put into place rather than simply a policy of preservation. A proportion of the original architectural and decorative attributes were recovered or restored. It seemed apparent to the officials involved in the conservation of the Fort that 'restoration of this kind would not have been undertaken, had not the Diwan-i-Amm, with its throne, been a building which would be used for the highest functions of state by the King or the Viceroy.'[25]

Actuated by these relatively benign motives, the Fort underwent another cycle of transformations. Its reduced and ravaged form was partially redefined into an imperial Mughal Fort. Extant pavilions were restored into a semblance of their former appearance, luxury and refinement. The evidence of craftsmanship lost during the British occupation was reconstructed with the help of a living tradition embodied in skilled Indian craftsmen. However, these efforts were limited to only a very small part of the Fort, and even within this reduced scope of conservation work, attention and funds were confined primarily to just a few buildings.

An additional dilemma in the conservation was that many of the original features of the Red Fort had been removed from their positions and transported elsewhere. As stated earlier, the inlaid mosaic panels of the Diwan-i-Am were in the Victoria and Albert Museum at London, then called the South Kensington Museum, while the elephant statue of Delhi Gate had been erected in front of the Queen's Gardens. It was moved to Chandni Chowk in 1892, and then ten years later to the Delhi Institute in Shahjahanabad.[26] A tank, recorded in Shah Jahan's court history as being carved out of a single piece of Makrana marble, had also been moved from the Rang Mahal forecourt to the Queen's Gardens. Attempts to reinstall some of these within the Fort were partially successful. In 1902, the highest political authority in India, Lord Curzon, interceded to reclaim the inlaid panels of the Diwan-i-Am from the South Kensington Museum, and 'sought their restoration from the government with a view to replacing them in their original site before the Delhi ceremonials ... Though they did not reach on time for the Durbar, they were reinstated the next year.[27]

These were restored to their original location by an Italian craftsman, and the missing stones replaced by new ones on the basis of old drawings. The beginning of the Fort's conservation may be said to date from this time, based on the initiative to restore some of its original decorative features. Records of the expenditure on it by the ASI are also indicative of a growing interest in its well-being. Thus, the listed amount of money spent on it between 1900 and 1913 works out to be equivalent to seven and half times of the amount recorded to have been spent from 1883 to 1899.

Apart from restoring the decorative aspects of the pavilions, work on reforming their surroundings was undertaken. One of the first conservation proposals in the Fort dealt with the reconstruction of Hayat Baksh. The efforts were hampered by the presence of the British military which was reluctant to relinquish its control within the palace. The only parts that it withdrew from were the Diwan-i-Khas and Hammam and some pavilions in Hayat Baksh. These were cordoned off into a separate archaeological area. Systems of entrances and exits were reorganised.[28] However, the military retained the use of some structures within the archaeological area—servants' quarters, gun batteries and roads. The

Naqqar Khana, Mumtaz Mahal, Shah Burj and Rang Mahal continued to be used by the garrison, and barracks continued to stand in half of Hayat Baksh.

Excavations in Hayat Baksh were commenced on a large scale only in 1904-1905. The conservation work of the buildings simultaneously began with a partial assessment of the condition of the imperial pavilions, and an appraisal of the extent of their features obliterated by later interventions. This was followed by a proposal to remove some buildings and roads made by the military. However, this had to be postponed till alternate buildings were constructed in other parts of the Fort to accommodate the military functions. Traces of foundations of some Mughal boundary walls and arcades were uncovered in the excavations, and their positions corroborated by old plans of the Fort in possession of the ASI.

Gordon Sanderson, in charge of the conservation of the Fort at the beginning of the twentieth century, proposed to lay out 'pleasing lawns and shrubbery'[29] to represent the positions of these destroyed Mughal courtyards and colonnades. Acting on these motives, grass lawns were made to represent the twin courtyards in front of the Diwan-i-Khas, as also in the Diwan-i-Am and Mumtaz Mahal, and shrubberies were grown to define the former Mughal colonnades. These were planned to be composed of an encircling closely-trimmed inga hedge, backed by rows of acalypher and duranta, behind which were to stand taller shrubs of murya, havelia, bougainvillea, hibiscus and tecoma.[30]

The lawns and shrubbery around the Mughal pavilions were a definite improvement on the disconnected roads and buildings made by the British military. These proposals aimed to recreate, to some extent, the spatial boundaries of the Mughal courts and gardens. However, the detailing of the proposals was insufficient to communicate the design of the original spaces—their volume, texture and architectural attributes—despite Sanderson's optimistic assertion about the area around the Diwan-i-Am that:

> The vastness of the courtyard, wherein a throng of courtiers daily assembled before the 'Great Mughal' is now suggested by a pleasant stretch of lawn and the gorgeous colonnades decked out in rivalry by the nobles of the realm, by screens of flowering shrubs.[31]

The intricate relationship between the Diwan-i-Am, its forecourt and its arcaded cells, could not be replaced by shrubbery or trees. The plantation could not possibly achieve the effortless spatial integration of the original design, where open space formed the necessary prelude to built structures and built structures provided the focus to, or defined, open space.

The arcades, apart from their function of accommodating the noblemen in attendance on the emperor, additionally imparted a sense of enclosure and scale to the Diwan-i-Am as the most important building in the forecourt. Similarly, the gateways occurred as special accents in the regular heights and arched rhythm of the cells around the boundary, and also marked out the desired paths of movement in the forecourt. The size of the forecourt, divided into a series of rectangular enclosures, was linked to the dimensions of the Diwan-i-Am, while the proportions of the surrounding arcades were related to the dimensions of the forecourt, the Diwan-i-Am and the Naqqar Khana. Thus, the arcaded cells and the forecourt were essential to the original appearance and functioning of the Diwan-i-Am.

When the British chose to remove the surrounding arcades and gateways, they were expressing themselves as conquerors, as well as representing their own cultural and political background. One of their first acts after 1857 had been to convert the imperial Mughal palace into an ordinary British cantonment. In their subsequent decision to conserve the Fort, they only partially restored the original attributes of the Mughal buildings and continued to treat the pavilions as individual buildings within a cantonment.

Since in their spatial and climatic context, the use of courts and arcades for daily living was generally impractical and unnecessary, the vital importance of the courts and colonnades in formulating the original shape and use of the Fort could not be appreciated by the British. Their conservation effort concentrated on restoring the unique decorative aspects of the pavilions, and landscaping the open spaces around them in a manner reminiscent of the buildings set within an English garden as individual 'follies'.[32] The reclamation of open areas in the conservation work was with reference to British, and not Mughal concepts of aesthetic beauty in external space and landscape.

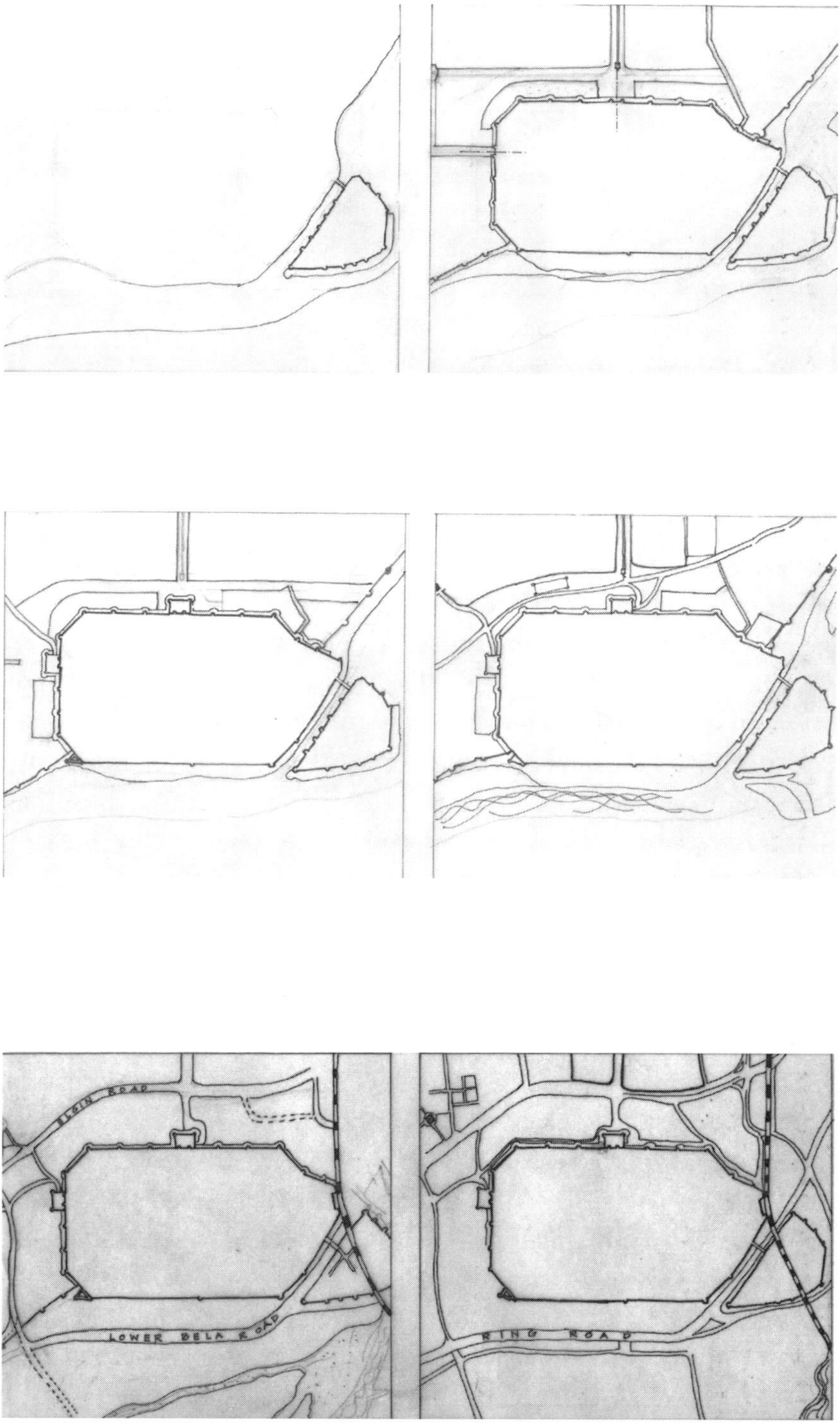

Transformation in the Fort's site boundaries and adjacencies (Drawing: Author)

As a result of such a reinterpretation, the Naqqar Khana stood bereft of its enclosing arcades and announced a point of entrance without any signals about the appropriate direction of movement around the Diwan-i-Am. The Diwan-i-Am itself was made to stand in green lawns instead of a paved courtyard. It could, thus, only be reached through a paved path that cut across the central axis of the lawn. The resultant space was the very reverse of the intended vastness communicated by Shah Jahan's forecourt. Matters were made worse by the military roads and structures that colonised the areas adjacent to the Diwan-i-Am and prevented a true restoration of the boundaries of its original forecourt.

The piecemeal implementation of the conservation work reduced its impetus as well as its impact. Though part of the Naqqar Khana was vacated in 1904-5, it continued to be used as quarters for officers stationed in the Fort well until 1907. The lawns and shrubberies around the Diwan-i-Am were incorrectly aligned because of a military road on the south and barracks on the north.[33] Similarly, the barracks in Hayat Baksh prevented a restoration of nearly half its original area. When its conservation was attempted, the garden lay buried under 3 feet of earth, debris and roads, with almost no trace of its causeway and channels. In fact, its pathways and water tanks could not be excavated in a consolidated way because there was insufficient space to dump the excavated earth. As Sanderson noted: '[i]t was a pity that the site could not have been lowered to its original level in the first instance as the sides of the channels were, after they were dug out, found to be in a *kacha* state and in need of considerable repair.'[34]

Some water channels and causeways of the charbagh were discovered in further excavations, including the large central tank of the Zafar Mahal and the subsidiary channels that originally divided each quarter of Hayat Baksh into four equal halves. Excavations under the floors that the British had made over the original floor levels in the Sawan, Bhadon and Shah Burj pavilions also revealed marble tanks, cascades and fountains.

Removal of later accretions to the surviving imperial buildings and the gardens was also commenced. The first buildings to be repaired with their details restored were Moti Masjid, Sawan, Bhadon and the imperial Hammam. New domes were provided to the small roof chattris in the Sawan pavilion, and those in Bhadon were reconstructed. Doors made by

Shah Burj, south facade before restoration (PD 1682/1907-8, ASI PL)

the military in the pavilions were closed up and marble dadoes restored. Modern window frames were replaced with marble ones. In the Shah Burj, the officer's residence with its modern additions was removed, and the marble channel that marked the beginning of Nahr-i-Bahist was reconstructed. However, in 1904, shortly after these efforts, an earthquake damaged Shah Burj, making it necessary to rebuild almost all of it.[35]

During this time, negotiations continued for the removal of the military road that ran through a part of Hayat Baksh, so that the length of the river-front terrace that it had interrupted could be restored to its termination point near Shah Burj. The Naqqar Khana, Rang Mahal and Mumtaz Mahal were also included in the archaeological area after 1908, and their conservation as well as removal of modern additions was begun.

In 1909-1910, the main entrance to Hayat Baksh was made at the Naqqar Khana, with another subsidiary entrance provided to the south of the Diwan-i-Am. In this year, a special military entrance was located near Shah Burj to enable the military to gain access to the gun-battery positioned on the east terrace. Thus, the removal of the military road, which ran through part of the garden, and the completion of the remainder of the pathways in Hayat Baksh could be achieved.

At the same time, work on the minor intersecting causeways in Hayat Baksh was completed, and the area of the garden was lowered to its original ground level. To irrigate it, electrical pumps were provided to lift water from the old wells. This water was stored in large tanks constructed for this purpose behind the Sawan pavilion. The reconstruction of channels and borders in Hayat Baksh and the Zafar Mahal tank is recorded by the ASI to have been based on old plans, and on fragments of ornamental kerbs and causeways found by the tank of the Sawan pavilion.

Grassed and planted in accordance with British concepts of pleasant settings for buildings, by 1911 Hayat Baksh was finally laid out in a way that it could fulfil some of its former functions, as well as be used for special occasions. Its pathways were repaired; the parapet around the tank restored; the main causeways, minor channels, pavements and ornamental beds reconstructed; and the backing of the retaining wall of its east terrace conserved. Thus, the bare bones of the garden—some of its boundaries and the positions of pathways, water channels and tank—were restored.

However, the filling in of plantation within the garden and the definition of its boundaries differed substantially from that of a Mughal garden. In the reinterpretation of Hayat Baksh by the British, the positions of the original Mughal colonnades on the north and south of the garden were indicated by dense masses of flowering shrubs. A screen of conifers backed by grauviilia trees was planted to mask the iron railing that demarcated the archaeological area from the military area, so that after full growth, these would screen off the modern barracks from the gardens.

Given the restrictions of the positions of military structures, such planting—as for instance in the Diwan-i-Am and Hayat Baksh—to convey the limits of an area was perhaps justifiable. This policy, however, appears to be essentially flawed. If the original limits of forecourts and gardens were to be accurately conveyed through shrubberies, then they would need to be planted on top of the foundations of the original boundary walls, colonnades and gateways, thus posing a grave danger to the foundations themselves.

If, on the other hand, the shrubberies were located sufficiently far to prevent the foundations coming to any harm, it would defeat the very objective of their plantation—namely, the delineation of the boundaries

The British barracks within Hayat Baksh (Photo: Author, 2000)

of Mughal spaces. This policy was unsuccessful even in areas where plantation was introduced to block out the barracks. In these cases, the new planting merely reiterated the effect of the high barrack buildings, echoing their vertical boundaries in a manner alien to a Mughal garden.

Sanderson, in this re-interpretation of the gardens, was perhaps largely following John Marshall's advice, recorded for posterity in his Conservation Manual.

> In laying out or restoring ancient Indian gardens, it is all important to pursue the essential character of the original, whether that character expresses itself in the symmetrical handling of the design as a whole, in the careful balance maintained between its component parts, in the schematic arrangement of parterres, causeways, water courses and the like, or in the formal treatment of other features.
>
> But it is not necessary to reproduce with pedantic accuracy the original appearance of the garden in all its particulars by banishing from it any trees, flowers or fruits etc. which were not grown by the ancients. Since the days of the Mughals, horticulture has made immense progress … In these matters concessions are rightly to be made to modern taste and the wishes of the community who frequent the garden. An officer should endeavour to observe the happy mean between antiquarian accuracy on the one hand and aesthetic beauty on the other.[36]

Such an intention reflected the views of the British community rather than the traditional inhabitants of Shahjahanabad. The methods of conservation adopted were dictated by the need to provide a setting for official receptions of the British establishment in India. Nonetheless, this ceremonial recreational use of the Fort did ensure its partial conservation, attracting more funds and attention than it would have, if meant only for the indigenous population. The climax of these conservation efforts, prompted by its stated use as a ceremonial venue, coincided with the revival of Delhi as one of the important cities of British India. In 1911, it was chosen as the site for another durbar—the third one. The choice of Delhi to mark the coronation of King George V was made by the king himself, who overrode the claims of Calcutta's persevering and vocal citizens to host this function. Among the many planned festivities for the durbar was a royal garden party to be held at the Red Fort. The Durbar Committee under Sir John Hewett visited the Fort some months before the proposed reception, and approved its suitability for the event.

The proposed garden party benefited the conservation effort in the Fort, the pace of which had been delayed by bureaucratic procedures. For example, the work in just the Hayat Baksh is reported to have entailed some thousand letters in addition to the setting up of a special military committee and numerous representations.[37] The desire for a substantially impressive effect at the reception for the coronation durbar resulted in more money being available for conservation. Thus, compared to only Rs 517 that had been listed as the expenses on the Fort in 1896-1897, or even Rs 6,842 in 1884-1885 and Rs 34,813 in 1908-1909, the amount increased substantially to Rs 81,240 in 1911-1912.[38] Sanderson notes that:

> Till 1908, the work was going on slowly, and its completion would have taken many more years, had it not been that the Coronation Durbar created a demand that the buildings which had so many years before, witnessed the similar ceremonies of the great Moghal, should be seen under more ideal conditions.[39]

The incentive of the garden party lent urgency to the demand for the removal of military structures in Hayat Baksh. A scheme to revitalise the water system and irrigate the garden by fixing pumps in the old wells and reusing them was also prepared. Trenching for shrubbery, removal of debris and provision of suitable earth for planting was undertaken. In the excavations that preceded the trenching, traces of buildings and of a retaining wall from the Hammam to Shah Burj were revealed. The backing of this wall was preserved up to the position of Hira Mahal.

In the excavations on the eastern terrace, the outlines of Nahr-i-Bahist were disclosed, and copper pipes of its fountains found. Further excavations revealed traces of a shallow basin, and a channel in front of Hira Mahal leading westward to connect with a minor channel of Hayat Baksh. A vaulted subterranean passage along the eastern wall is also recorded to have been discovered. The terrace was then grassed, and the profile of Nahr-i-Bahist was redefined by Mughal bricks on edge.

Though conservation efforts were largely concentrated in Hayat Baksh, work was also done in other parts of the Fort that would be visible at the reception. The upper floors of Chatta Bazaar, occupied by military menial staff even till 1911, were vacated; their closed arched windows were re-opened.[40] Of the extant pavilions, Mumtaz Mahal had been greatly abused under the British occupation by its use as a prison and then as a sergeants' mess. Walls, sinks and cisterns had been added on; its original roof and chajjas had gone and many coats of whitewash had been smeared over its original glasswork and wall paintings. Given this abuse and transformation of its original elements, it was decided to refurbish it as the local museum of archaeology to be on view at the durbar, rather than any attempt at its conservation.[41] The courts between the Rang Mahal and Diwan-i-Am, which had been filled up and crossed by a military road and drain, were also excavated. Traces of a central tank and a little square building reached by a small causeway were found here. The base of the causeway piers was preserved along with what remained of the building.

The excavation also uncovered remains of Rang Mahal's original awning system: a part of its old coping and an old stone ring. An original decorative feature of its forecourt—the carved marble basin—was brought back from the Queen's Gardens in Shahjahanabad. There appears to have been a lack of unanimity regarding its original position, and it is recorded to have been replaced as near its old position as could be approximately determined through old pictures.[42] A fountainhead was fixed in the marble basin in front of Rang Mahal.

In 1911-1912, conservation work on Rang Mahal itself was carried out. This included the installation of a false ceiling of asbestos sheets to hide the modern roof, re-laying of its floor to the old levels, removal of coats of whitewash to expose its wall paintings and repairing of its central tank. With the provision of water already in place, this fountain as well as the channels in Hayat Baksh, the Zafar Mahal tank, and a section of Nahr-i-Bahist from the Hammam to Rang Mahal were filled. The fountains in Zafar Mahal and Sawan, Bhadon and Shah Burj pavilions were also made to work. The amount of water required to operate the fountains and fill the channels and tanks was considerable—the pumps were run continuously for two weeks before the durbar to ensure the working of the water features.

In December 1911, for the first time, a ruling English monarch came to India to be crowned as emperor. Almost nine months before the visit, a proclamation about the forthcoming durbar was issued simultaneously in England and India.[43] The durbar was held on the ridge north of Shahjahanabad. Princes, chieftains and members of the governor general's executive and legislative council, as well as officials and military officers gathered for it. The ceremonial implication of the Red Fort is evident from the reinvention at this durbar of the ritual of darshan that the Mughal emperors had followed. The state entry of George V, king-emperor as he was termed, was over the new bridge (made at the time of the insertion of the railway) that connected Salimgarh to the Red Fort. The royal guests then displayed themselves to the public from the imperial terrace, surrounded by the sons of local princes dressed in regalia.[44]

The banks of the Yamuna on the eastern face of the Fort, where crowds used to gather each morning for a sight of the Mughal emperors, were again filled with people eager to see the visitors. Within the Fort, its imperial buildings, such as the Diwan-i-Khas, were used for the reception of the royal guests during the garden party. Furnishings used in the time of Bahadur Shah II were displayed in the Khas Mahal to indicate its original use and appearance.

The restored Mughal pavilions within the Fort drew admiration. However, the intended effects of the planting did not work as planned, as can be gauged from the reaction of C.M. Villiers-Stuart, who attended the durbar party.

> Looking across the garden from the river, a range of hideous barracks forms the background, towering over the exquisite little Bhadon and Sawan pavilions. The whole effect of the reception held there during the Imperial Durbar festivities was spoilt till the kindly dusk shut out the iron railings and the ugly red and yellow walls.[45]

At the coronation durbar, King George made an announcement that was to have momentous consequences for Delhi. Acting on the advice of the governor general in council, he proclaimed that 'on geographical, historical, and political grounds, the capital of the Indian empire should be at Delhi',[46] and announced the intention to build a new city for this purpose. The British government had contemplated shifting the capital from Calcutta to Delhi as early as 1869, for similar reasons as those of the earlier rulers of the sub-continent. With the spread and consolidation of British rule over the entire Indian peninsula, Delhi was seen to be more central than Calcutta. The practical advantages of its equidistant position to various parts of the empire, its proximity to the summer capital of Simla, its fine communication and many railway lines, as well as its comparatively better climate were reinforced by its historical associations with imperial power.

Political developments around the turn of the century made such a change urgent. The unsettled political situation in Calcutta after the partition of Bengal acted in Delhi's favour. Additionally, the presence of both the imperial and the Bengal government in Calcutta had begun to cause administrative problems. King George, in a bid to demonstrate his interest in the fate of his favourite colony, was in favour of personally marking the foundation of a new capital at Delhi. Thus, he and Queen Mary laid the foundation stones of the new city on a site in the northern Delhi ridge, and formally sealed the decision of transfer.

The year 1911 was therefore important both for the renewed importance of Delhi as a future imperial seat, and for the recognition of some of the Red Fort's attributes. Many public works were commissioned at this time, including the widening of some roads and the reconstruction of others, such as around Jama Masjid. New fire stations and over-bridges were also built. The effect of such activities was not always praiseworthy. In one instance, it resulted in the removal of the old bastions outside the Ajmere Gate of the city.[47]

A year after the durbar, on 1 October 1912, the British government took over an area of 528 square miles (1,367 square kilometres) of the Delhi *tehsil* and Mehrauli *thana* under its direct management. The rest of the old district was left in the hands of the Punjab government. However, the conservation impetus in the Fort does not appear to have benefited much from the decision to transfer the capital to Delhi, or the promotion in its special administrative status from being merely a part of Punjab, notwithstanding Sanderson's stated opinion that 'of all the Mughal monuments of Delhi which are now invested with so much interest owing to the city having become once more the Capital of the Indian Empire, the Fort of Shah Jahan will, to the majority, appeal the most.'[48]

In this year, the funds for the Fort's conservation dropped to a mere Rs 4,881. Though work slowed down, the gun-battery was finally removed from the eastern terrace in Hayat Baksh in 1914, which allowed excavations to take place. Despite this, the British military still had a total ordnance of six smooth box guns, seven 8-inch howitzers, four 8-inch mortars, and six field pieces within the Fort, as recorded in the *Delhi Gazetteer*.[49]

Work on the new capital at Delhi was actively commenced in 1913, with the appointment of Edwin Lutyens as architect. Though its construction was interrupted by disputes over the position of the site and by the outbreak of World War I, it was finally decided to site the capital on the south-central ridge of Delhi, with the Viceregal Lodge situated on the Raisina hill. In the meantime, the ceremonial use of the Red Fort continued, with the Duke of Connaught inaugurating a Permanent Chamber of Princes here in 1921. Ironically, at the same time, its function as a garrison fort became more prominent to control the increasing number of strikes and demonstrations in Shahjahanabad against British rule.[50]

Work continued on the British imperial capital, christened New Delhi, and its main parts were finished in 1929.[51] The viceroy occupied it the same year, though formal completion and inauguration ceremonies took place in 1931. Paradoxically, the construction of this capital, though it resulted in allocation of attention and funds in the larger geographical area of Delhi, reduced both the significance of the Red Fort and its conservation impetus. The main focus of the region shifted south to what is today

North wall, Red Fort, 1960s (Photo: D.N. Chaudhuri)

referred to as central Delhi. The importance of Shahjahanabad (that began to be termed as Old Delhi) as an administrative centre, and that of the Red Fort as a ceremonial area used for official receptions, declined.

The viceroy presided over the inauguration festivities held in New Delhi. While the formal events that marked the Delhi Week (with its balls, polo matches, garden parties and state investitures) were centred in the Viceregal House and the Princes' Place around it, the contractors who had worked on the construction of New Delhi organised a people's fete at the Red Fort. Thus, after appropriating it for their sole use for more than seven decades, the British now sidelined the Red Fort. Three years later, Connaught Place was completed, taking away a part of the retail business from Chandni Chowk and Shahjahanabad.

With New Delhi catering exclusively for the rich and powerful, Shahjahanabad began to be inhabited by the poorer sections. This deglamorisation was accompanied by a rise in population, leading to a decrease in amenities. To address this, the Delhi Improvement Trust was founded in 1937. However, instead of solving the issue, it further reduced the importance of Shahjahanabad. One of its most significant projects, the Delhi Ajmeri Gate Slum Clearance and Development Scheme, caused about 70 acres to be cleared in Shahjahanabad, including the demolition of the entire city wall in this area and the filling up of the moat around it.[52] These were replaced by multi-storey residential and commercial structures. This amputation of the urban and architectural character of the city echoed the earlier demolitions by the British within and around the Fort.

The discontinuation of even the ceremonial uses of the Fort resulted in a further decrease of funds and attention for its conservation. In the years that followed, the political and economic climate was such that the British centred their efforts on forcibly resisting the increasingly stronger demand for freedom within India, and for financing the war effort in Europe. It was also at this time that some of the military buildings in the Fort were the scene of the imprisonment and trial of important freedom fighters by the British. This period of the Fort's history is associated with the famous trial of the three Indian National Army (INA) officers, Shah Nawaz Khan, Gurbaksh Singh Dhillon and Prem Sahgal, who had to be released by the British government due to intense public pressure. Therefore, the attraction of the Fort for travellers and its occasional use for social celebrations of the Indian population was now superseded by its function of a military garrison. Conservation ceased to be a priority.

Thus, the actual conservation impetus of the Red Fort may be said to have been limited to the first three decades of the nineteenth century. Though the ASI did continue its conservation work within the Fort (as it still does), the impetus decreased with the lessening of the active interest taken in it by the British government. Nonetheless, the reputation of the Fort was too well-established to be greatly affected by the decrease in its ceremonial use. Even at this time, it was termed as 'the most famous non-religious monument of the city'.[53] The Fort and its surrounding walls still provided an urban space that was simultaneously serene and strong. In the larger context, the Red Fort played an enormous symbolic role for the Indian people throughout the country, both during and after the freedom movement. It was from this Fort that Pandit Jawaharlal Nehru, the first prime minister of independent India, addressed his countrymen on 15 August 1947, to commemorate a day that had been long sought for.

The heightened symbolic aura that the Fort was now invested with, was accompanied by a paradoxical decrease in its historical use. The partition

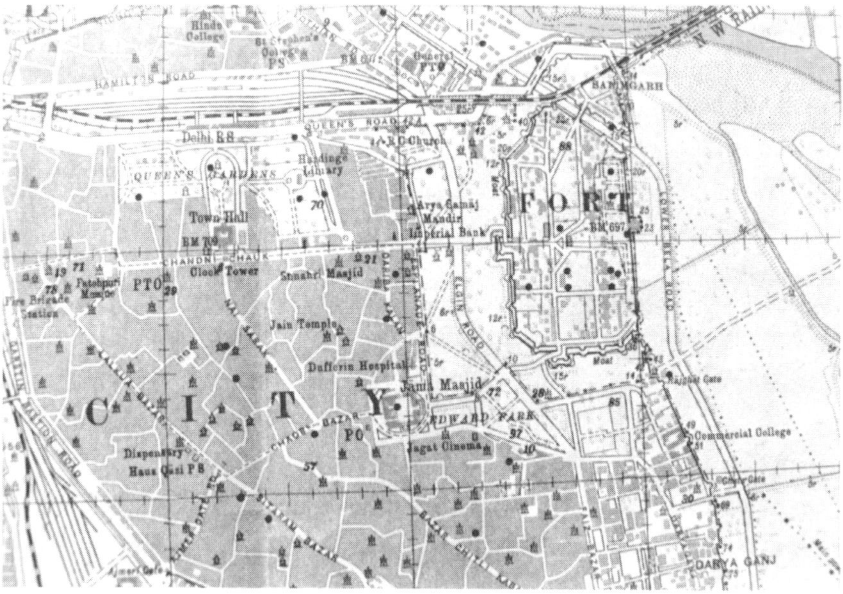

Red Fort and its environs, 1939 (Survey of India map, private collection of Anuj Mehta)

caused an influx of mainly Hindu Punjabi refugees from Pakistan into Delhi, and the migration of a large portion of the Muslim population of Shahjahanabad to Pakistan. The character of Shahjahanabad underwent another transformation. The task of resettling the migrant population implied a change in density and composition of its inhabitants. Burgeoning wholesale trade replaced cultural and administrative activities, at a time when the survival of displaced and desperate migrants was the key issue. These migrants were accommodated in existing buildings, as well as in temporary structures erected within available open space. The remaining older buildings and gardens were further transformed as a result of this increased need for built shelter.

From the mid-1960s, the population figures decreased, perhaps due to the increasing commercialisation which caused a migration of residents from Shahjahanabad to other areas of Delhi. Surveys indicate that in 1958, 74.5 per cent of the enterprises operating here were founded after 1947.[54] The change in the population and their primary occupation did not have a direct effect on the Fort. It, nonetheless, indirectly affected the manner in which it was perceived, and its surrounding environment. The new population did not have any historical memories or associations with the Fort. The emotional, symbolic and functional linkages between the Fort and the rest of Shahjahanabad grew weaker. However, the general public of Delhi continued to use the area around the Fort as a space for recreation till the middle of the twentieth century, as seen in photographs dating from this time, which show benches and seats amidst pleasant grassed stretches.

The immediate years after Independence were dominated by acts of rebuilding the country economically and politically. Conservation was only one amongst a wide range of objectives that the new Indian government needed to address. The most urgent of these objectives were probably seen to be the spread of health, education, and economic production as well as the alleviation of poverty and the defence of the country. During and since that time, conservation of the Fort has continued to be an extension of the early practices undertaken by the ASI when it was founded by the British. There has been little revaluation to assess its appropriateness in the Indian context. Meanwhile, immediately outside the Fort in Shahjahanabad, the residential functions of the buildings have been consistently replaced by commercial activity. To accommodate the growing pressures of commercialisation, many existing residential buildings have been either converted, transformed or replaced.

The residential population, which had reached its peak in 1961, has declined rapidly since then, and a great number of the original buildings even in the inner residential precincts have been and continue to be transformed for commercial use.[55] This includes industrial units using acids, inflammable materials, chemicals; trade in noxious and hazardous materials like plastic, rexine, leather and wholesale storage godowns. Such a use has changed the immediate and larger surroundings of the Red Fort in insidious and obvious ways, diluting its grandeur and its existence. Despite a continuing conservation effort that has now lasted for more than a century, the return of the Mughal attributes of the Red Fort has only been in parts.

9

THE PERSISTENCE OF GRANDEUR

'But whether born under divine guidance or the speculative urge, the pattern will dry up and even die, unless the people fuse within it a special, self sustaining life that can survive adversity and the turns of fortune.'

Sigfried Giedeon, *Space, Time and Architecture*

The handful of extant Mughal buildings within the red walls of the Fort exist as isolated events of a scarcely understood story rather than as parts of the coherent dramatic narrative they once were. The foundations of many Mughal structures still lie buried under British military barracks. Old and full-grown trees, incongruous with the original pattern of planting, dot various parts of the Fort. Many of Shah Jahan's imperial pavilions require urgent attention. Cracks have developed in their stone joints, a number of cornices have chipped off and their famed decorative details, as well as their sandstone and marble cladding, are steadily eroding.

The loss of stone facing, especially in those parts of the Fort that are vulnerable to overuse, pollution and water ingress, has subjected the underlying masonry to accelerated weathering, while the use of cement mortar for repair has caused adverse effects, such as cleavage of the building material. Efflorescence, staining, flaking and blistering are particularly visible in the ceilings and near the base of walls. In the pavilions designated as monuments, visitor pressure has damaged or worn

Screen of Justice, Khas Mahal (Photo: S. Mukherjee, 2000)

away the paving and floor plinths, as well as the delicate mirror-work on the walls and the dadoes and floors inlaid with precious stones. It is possible—but only barely—to discern some part of the unique pattern of craftsmanship, decoration and construction of the Red Fort under the layers of neglect and destruction.

The Fort may be likened to a large book, whose seemingly intact hard-bound cover is moth-eaten around the edges. When you turn the cover, you discover that most pages inside are missing. In the few that remain, the text has been so erased that only some scattered words of the original story are visible: in a half-familiar script that is not completely legible, crossed-out and overlaid by insertions in a different language and a different hand. How do we read such an incomplete document? To do so, it is evident that we must closely scrutinise the primary record of the extant original structures in the Fort: their explicit forms, as well as the entire canvas of implicit systems that gave rise to their architecture. It is then that we can spot some clues to what the iconic Red Fort may have

Degradation of the emperor's entrance into the Red Fort
(Photo: A. Chaturvedi, 2022)

State of extant imperial Mughal structures in the Red Fort (Photos: Author)

been, and answer the challenge posed by the erasure and reordering of so much of it—as demonstrated in the analysis in the foregoing pages.

The ASI, the custodians of the Red Fort—which is among one of the many protected historical monuments, sites and buildings identified within Shahjahanabad alone[1]—has traditionally concentrated on only its surviving built structures. The spatial relationships that characterised Mughal architecture, in which built structures and open space were intricately linked, do not appear to have been sufficiently considered in their conservation work. Therefore, the restoration of these spatial relationships has, thus far, been almost entirely excluded in the conservation process.

The lack of understanding of the spatial history of the Fort has also led to an inaccurate interpretation of its open spaces, and a transformation and misuse of the Mughal buildings within these open spaces. This may be observed throughout the archaeological area of the vast Fort. For instance, the paving that has replaced the triangular garden bordered by roads placed in front of the Naqqar Khana does not convey the majesty and the breadth of space of the Mughal forecourt which originally stood in this location. In a similar manner, the scale and feeling of the Diwan-i-Am's original forecourt beyond the Naqqar Khana is unfathomable, standing as it does in lawns marked by a central paved pathway and surrounded by shrubs. In the Naqqar Khana itself, the arcaded upper galleries once used by the musicians of the Mughal court, and later by the British military, and then as a museum, have been transformed into closed facades.

Further east from the Diwan-i-Am, the gardens in front of Rang Mahal within the Private Imperial domain, though regularly re-grassed and demarcated as a kind of charbagh, do not retain any hint of the original sequence or proportions of its garden courts. Within the Rang Mahal, ad-hoc provisions are made to discourage visitor access, such as horizontal metal rails around the central fountain. Wooden platforms are intermittently placed as bridges across the portion of the Nahr-i-Bahist channel within it. Further on, the lawns developed in front of the Khas Mahal and Diwan-i-Khas have fortunately been released from the intrusion of rows of seats for the 'sound and light show' held here,

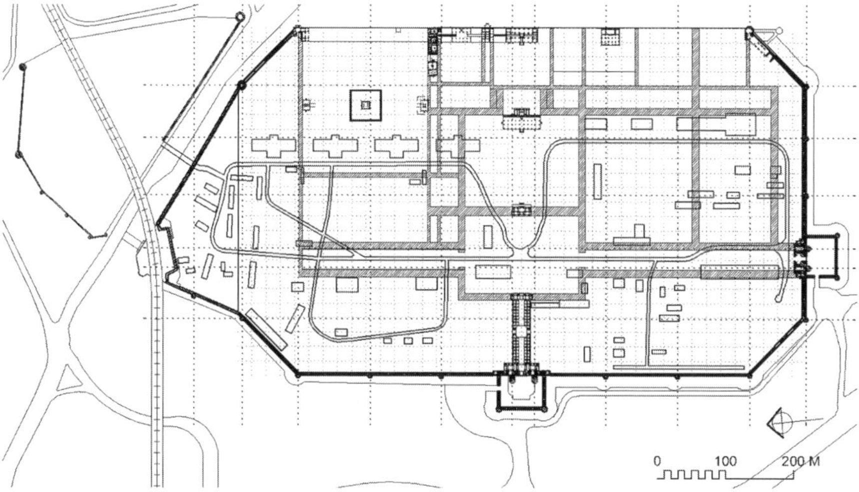

Plan, original colonnaded boundaries of main forecourts and gardens within the Red Fort, overlaid on colonial and post-colonial roads and buildings
(Drawing: N. Joshi, Author)

but there is no attempt to convey the scale of the paved courts that these pavilions were originally set within.

Similarly, the lawns in front of Mumtaz Mahal have still not been lowered to their original levels. These levels, it may be recalled, had been discovered during the very first excavations carried out in the Fort at the beginning of the twentieth century. There is also no visible indication of the Mughal charbagh that is depicted as being located here in old maps. The Mumtaz Mahal, reused as an archaeological museum for many years, with wooden panels fitted into its external arches, is the reverse of the characteristic airy pavilion of the imperial Mughal seraglio.

Large trees, planted along the junctions and corners of some of the garden paths in this part of the Fort, provide shade that is welcome in the very hot summers of Delhi. However, their scale and type are inconsistent with the kind of trees that the Mughal emperors would have got planted in their Forts. In fact, the lawns, paths and plantation tend to follow the early ASI interpretation of monuments and open spaces of the Fort—without even comprehending the intention of this interpretation in using shrubs and pathways to convey the boundaries of the destroyed Mughal courts and colonnades. Today, some pathways occupy positions that do not tally with any of these boundaries. Traces of these colonnades, even where they are visible, are not treated with the deference they deserve, as in the exposed portions of a plinth-high wall marking the line of the colonnades that would have originally connected the Bhadon pavilion and Moti Masjid. This wall still forms a tentative boundary to the open area in front of the Diwan-i-Khas, but is hidden by plants.

Ahead of the Diwan-i-Khas, Hayat Baksh does not communicate any of the essential aspects of an imperial Mughal garden in the Indian plains. Neither does it retain any of its erstwhile grandeur: its channels and tanks lie empty; many of its extant pavilions are weathered or vandalised and its layout and planting follows the same method initiated by the British during the early days of the ASI with trees lined in front of the barracks. These trees may be likened to a green wall across Hayat Baksh. They only partially screen the view of the barracks from the garden, and actually echo the effect of these tall buildings. The imposition of the barracks and trees has reduced Hayat Baksh to half its original size, and completely transformed its original design. Within the part retained as a garden, the trees and flowers appear dissimilar to a Mughal charbagh—both in the type of plantation and its positioning.

Thus, today, grassed lawns occupy the same ground level as the paths, instead of low plantation beds bordering the raised pathways recorded in archival documents and drawings of Mughal charbaghs,. In another misinterpretation of the attributes of a charbagh, large trees are scattered amidst Hayat Baksh, bearing no relation to the geometry of the garden, and substantially reducing its formal splendour.

The lack of understanding of the role of different built and open elements in forming the spatial sequence into the Red Fort has served to continue the effects of its past unhappy transformations. At one time, most of the souvenir shops located in Chatta Bazaar were under the control of the Municipal Corporation of Delhi, with a few of them under the Indian Army. This Bazaar—once the ceremonial Mughal promenade of Shah Jahan's court and a landmark in its time (as mentioned in the discussion in preceding sections)—is a unique constructional feat even in today's context. The uncontrolled insertion of services such as signboards, rolling shutters, electrical wires and fittings throughout Chatta Bazaar, in complete disregard of its original use and appearance, has now been

Hayat Baksh
(Photo: S. Mukherjee, 2000)

Traces of original court/garden boundaries between Moti Masjid and Hayat Baksh
(Photo: Author, 1997)

replaced by some attempt at rationalising the location of these services. However, this rationalisation is in the guise of a conjectural restoration into a Victorian-inspired arcade. This has not just reduced the significant historic value of Chatta Bazaar, but also altered its unique spatial and architectural characteristics.

The resolution of information facilities and other amenities for visitors to the Fort is still not satisfactory. Provision for public toilets is now within the barracks near the Naqqar Khana, but signage and information facilities continue to be inadequate in range as well as content, and show no understanding of the spatial sequence of the Fort. Neither does the newer paving and interpretation of open spaces communicate any of the attributes of these spaces, or even fulfil the needs of present-day visitors.

For instance, there are no clues as to how to move beyond the inner-gateway of the Chatta Chowk. Visitors may be seen drifting arbitrarily to the new museums housed in the barracks, or the boundary walls near Salimgarh, or the Delhi Gate, or Naqqar Khana. The Naqqar Khana, originally shaded and defined by colonnades and arches, was the space where visitors and residents could literally come together after passing through the entrance-ways from the Delhi and Lahori Gates, before being allowed entry into the inner Fort. The reinstatement of the spatial boundaries of the forecourt with its original qualities of repose has immense potential not just to orient visitors appropriately, but also to afford a space to reflect and relax. And to rediscover 'a certain kinship with my fellow human beings', an essential aspect of life that the Lebanese-French author Amin Malouf uncovers for us in his book *On Identity*.

The lack of sufficiently clear information has, in some cases, led to a completely inaccurate communication of its features. Thus, some visitors interpret the colour of the magnificent red sandstone pavilion, the Diwan-i-Am, as the reason for the name of the Red Fort. The paucity of information and the absence of any visual records make it almost impossible to visualise the original appearance of the Diwan-i-Am clad in shimmering white plaster and surrounded by colonnades—or indeed, to visualise the original appearance of any part of the Fort.

Apart from discrepancies in the understanding and communication of the spatial attributes of the Fort, there are other severe lacunae in its conservation. One of these is the lack of a systematic programme of

Aerial view, 2002: Red Fort (Courtesy VCOAS Sectt. and NRSA)

repair and maintenance. The absence of such a programme, coupled with insufficient documentation of the original methods of construction used in the Fort, has led to accelerated decay and, in some cases, to irreversible transformations of many of the Mughal monuments. The inappropriate intensive reuse of some of these has resulted in the insertion of facilities that they were not originally designed for, and further heightened their vulnerability. As an example, services for the 'sound and light' show, including bulky light boxes are placed in front of many of them; electric cables, conduits and appliances are inserted in floors and walls; audio equipment is housed within pavilions. In the name of making the Fort visitor-friendly, multi-coloured lights play on the facades of the fragile imperial pavilions, even as stains left by water seepage are visible on many walls and ceilings, and crudely designed modern grills are introduced next to exquisite carved screens. Seen throughout the Fort, this can perhaps be metaphorically summarised by the rusty iron nails tacked in between the beautifully decorated metal panels of the Moti Masjid door to hold its weathered wooden framing.[2]

Open spaces display the same treatment. The clumsily restored eastern end of Hayat Baksh bears little resemblance to the terrace which once celebrated its climax and housed delicate marble pavilions and fountains. Parts of Shah Burj—at one end of this terrace that marked the northern edge of the emperor's private domain—are still resplendent, such as its delicately carved pavilion, and the remains of mirror-work inset on the dome across a central chamber that may be glimpsed through its locked doors. Conversely, many of the openings on its outer walls are permanently open and look down steeply at the road circuiting its base. The Nahr-i-Bahist, celebrated as the 'river of paradise', has been remade with none of the original qualities of finesse and detailing characteristics of the imperial part of the Fort. The development of a municipal-style garden with ill-planned water drainage, thick railings and inappropriate plantation on the east face of the Fort, has caused water to stagnate, damaging its base and foundations and reducing the royal entrance to nothing more or less than a cesspool.

Such disintegration and abdication of beauty is especially visible beyond Rang Mahal. Here, the Nahr-i-Bahist disappears and so does the terrace. Asad Burj, which ends the east face of the Fort, though more or less intact in its overall form, bears unwitnessed marks of weathering. The stagnant water in its baoli is green, beautifully so, as seen from a distance. Closer at hand, its insidious effects are visible in the stain marks, salt deposits and cracks in the red sandstone.

The once-luxurious environs of the Fort are now stifled amidst growing numbers of people, traffic, noise and dirt. The pleasant views looking out towards the Yamuna no longer exist; neither do most of the other gardens of Shahjahanabad that used to lie along it. The river, which played such an important part in the design and location of Shah Jahan's Fort, has altered its course. It flows too far away to have any perceptible or positive visual or climatic effect on Shahjahanabad, now known as Old Delhi.

Increasing changes in land use here have caused a loss of its recreational areas, and a degradation of open spaces. A large percentage of the steadily decreasing residential component here is without municipal water supply or municipal sewage facilities. And the urban vista of Chandni Chowk, which even in its reduced form in the early 1900s was described by the British as 'probably one of the finest native streets in India',[3] continues to be transformed daily into a jungle of buildings and widening streets.

Though successive Master Plans of Delhi have designated Shahjahanabad as a heritage zone and devised special development regulations to recognise the Red Fort as one of its significant architectural features, in actual fact, these have not made any significant improvements.[4]

Proposals to provide water and sewage services to all the houses within Shahjahanabad, and a reduction of road traffic pressure proposed through a reorganisation of traffic with cycle tracks, have not been achieved.[5]

The remains of the city wall and entrance gates, Jama Masjid, Chandni Chowk vista and its streetscape of mohallas and katras have been considered as areas of special cultural value. Notwithstanding this, many decisions by the authorities are completely at variance with stated objectives of planning for the special historical and architectural features of this part of Delhi. The area originally occupied by the gardens in front of the Red Fort—already an intimidating sea of parked cars—was at one time planned to be developed as an underground parking, stretching in line with the Delhi Gate, Turkman Gate and Ajmeri Gate of Shahjahanabad. Countenancing or even contemplating such vast activity in the vicinity of the Fort, as much as constructing the metro railway line in Shahjahanabad, while it does serve to make this part of Delhi more accessible, shows how inconsequential its architectural history is considered.

It is a tribute to the strength of the design of Shah Jahan's architects that despite this litany of loss, and despite the absence of most of its original pattern of life and architecture, the Red Fort continues to be one of the most potent symbols of Delhi. Its image of grandeur draws in tourists from different parts of India and the world—reportedly over 1.3 million visitors in the fiscal year 2022—who trudge up its vast width as an essential part of their travel itinerary. Passengers waiting to catch trains from the Old Delhi railway station to different parts of the country use their time to visit the Fort. Historians and academics come to study aspects of Mughal architecture. Young people lounge in its gardens as a respite from the world beyond its walls. The ceremonial function of the Red Fort is celebrated each year when hundreds of men, women and children gather around the historic Lahori Gate ramparts every Independence Day, amidst fluttering flags, ceremonial guards of honour and the words of the prime minister.

In 1997, President Nelson Mandela of South Africa, on a state visit to India, was presented with the Nehru Peace Prize in the Diwan-i-Am. A concert of Indian classical music was held the same year as part of the celebrations, marking fifty years of Indian Independence, and attended, among others, by the then president and the prime minister of India.

Column capitals, Diwan-i-Am (Photo: S. Mukherjee, 2000)

Renowned exponents of Indian classical music performed to an audience seated in front of the Hall, reviving at least part of the activity that characterised its use during its heyday. At other, more recent landmark anniversaries of the Indian nation, the Red Fort has again been thrust into the limelight, with grand mega-events organised here.

However, this image of grandeur may not survive the many forces of decay at work in the Red Fort today. As discussed earlier, these range from those caused by natural weathering, to those inflicted by the impact of its urban environs as well as by the pressures from a huge number of visitors. Vandalism, the lack of a holistic repair and conservation programme, and short-term objectives that focus on only seeing it as a resource to increase visitor numbers or generate greater revenue by turning it into a Disney-land like spectacle only compound these pressures. Added to this is the confused perception and, therefore, an insufficient appreciation of the Fort caused by its large-scale destruction.

It is precisely because there are so many memories and layers embedded in a piece of heritage embodied as architecture that it is easy to miss its essential characteristics, and be led astray in understanding or interpreting it. With reference to the Red Fort, one of its essential characteristics arrived at through the analysis of its primary source—its architecture—is that it was created by a philosophy of coming together: of multiple skills, sensibilities and social strata. This coming together, was because of the patron and ruler, and his acceptance of varied ideas of beauty, technology and craft and also because of the inclusive values that influenced life in the subcontinent, over and above the individual religious philosophies of the emperor or those who worked to make the Fort.

On revisiting and examining the primary record of the Red Fort, we realise that its refined resolution of space was in many ways the grand finale of a tradition where buildings were not used as sealed objects sitting in space, but interlinked with open areas and with each other. Such an expression of architecture—permeable, efficient and adaptive to different seasons and use by a wide number of people across the spectrum—was the embodiment of the underpinnings of life in the subcontinent and its plural identities and multiple affiliations. Yet, despite this fact of an inclusive philosophy central to its creation and functioning, we paradoxically reinforce the appearance and use of the Fort set forth during its colonial occupation. It is now an exclusive, aloof and barred space, occasionally used as a stage-set and backdrop for celebrations that ironically dwell on its memory as a symbol of resistance to colonial British rule—while continuing colonial concepts of rigidly keeping people out.

Till some years ago, the Indian army occupied certain parts of the Red Fort for ceremonial duties and accompanying security implications. The ASI, as official custodians, even now continue to have offices and residences within many parts. Shops and retail functions in the Fort are under municipal authority, while the sound and light show conducted in front of the Diwan-i-Khas, as well as some other functions, have been taken over by corporate organisations. Immediately outside the Fort are other agencies—the Delhi Development Authority (DDA), the Municipal Corporation of Delhi (MCD) and the environmental agencies in control of the Delhi Ridge.

There is, in fact, no conflict between the historical role and use of the Red Fort, and the different organisations in and around it today. It was designed, and it functioned for a long period of its history, as a miniature city with manufacturing, retail and ordinary residential areas situated alongside its ceremonial, military and imperial areas. All the activities that these areas entailed were originally allowed to function with a fair degree of individual freedom.

The difference between then and now is that originally there was an overall regulating vision of the Fort's actual functioning as well as its symbolic role, which was clear to the emperor and all other inmates as well as to the inhabitants of Shahjahanabad and the rest of the empire. Today, there is no concerted overall perception, let alone a vision of the Fort, either in those responsible for its well-being or in the minds of the people who come to see it. It is difficult to achieve this unity of vision, while there is very little knowledge or coordination between the agencies managing different areas of the Fort.

For this, a holistic conservation plan is required that clearly recognises the historical and present context of the Fort; one that lays out and reorganises the responsibilities of the agencies operating in it as well as ties in its existing uses with the introduction of appropriate new ones. An important component of the effort is the resolution of the conflict inherent in the conservation of built elements belonging to different time periods—as, for instance, between the British barracks and the Mughal buildings they have replaced. In other words, should the British barracks located in the Fort be retained or removed?

The normal ASI method used to judge whether a structure is worthy of conservation is its age. By this logic, the British barracks should all be retained because they are more than 100 years old. The Australia ICOMOS Charter for the Conservation of Places of Cultural Significance (The Burra Charter, 1979) also reiterates: '[t]he contributions of all periods to the place must be respected'.[6] At the same time, it clarifies that 'revealing the fabric of one period at the expense of another can only be justified when what is removed is of slight cultural significance and the fabric which is to be revealed is of much greater cultural significance'.[7]

Therefore, any inferences with regard to the Red Fort based on the general advice of the Burra Charter would need to be preceded by an understanding of the relative cultural significance of the different parts of the Fort. In addition to standard methods of historical and architectural research, an essential tool in generating such an understanding is a process of spatial investigation. The preceding sections constitute such a spatial investigation in the history of the Fort. This investigation may be summarised as a study of the relationships existing between built and open space at the time of the Fort's construction, and at different pivotal periods of its history. It has already been demonstrated that the lack of such an investigation leads to conservation decisions that are inappropriate for a site.

It is, of course, true that a relationship exists between built and open space in any act of building and, therefore, the conservation of this relationship in culturally significant sites is necessary. However, it is important to recognise that the spatial relationship is of overwhelming importance in certain cultures—as in the Indic. If ignored in the conservation process, it results in a substantial reduction of the cultural, architectural and functional values of a historical site. While the necessity of a process of spatial exploration is universal, the application of its results must be tempered by the social, climatic and cultural needs of the societies that form the context of the conservation effort. Conservation, therefore, differs according to geography and culture. As an instance, in societies where traditional crafts have almost completely died out, restoration of decorative attributes, even if they are integral aspects of a monument's cultural value, may perhaps not be possible.

The relevance of the spatial investigation of the Fort's history in providing an appropriate set of guidelines to arrive at its cultural significance, as well as in weighing the conservation claims of its various architectural elements, may be demonstrated by a few examples. Thus, in the choice between the retention of the British barracks and the reinstatement of original spatial boundaries of various parts of the Fort, it would appear that the latter course would be more in keeping with their cultural value. Such an inference is justified by the fact that the architectural and spatial attributes of the extant Mughal monuments in the Red Fort can only be clearly communicated after the reinstatement of these boundaries. These monuments are the surviving components of the only urban palace to have been created in a period that may be designated the climax of Mughal architecture; a period, moreover, whose contribution is recognised as one of the most important in the history of architectural endeavours. Their cultural significance is immeasurable.

Naqqar Khana and Delhi Gate, amidst later interventions and plantation (Photo: Author, 2000)

The British barracks, on the other hand, are a utilitarian type of building created by engineers serving the British rule in India. Many examples of such a building type exist within the Fort as well as in other sites. The continuing presence of these barracks, especially in the imperial domains, greatly alters the perception of the more culturally significant extant monuments of the Fort. Thus, it appears appropriate to remove at least those barracks which interfere with the aspect and perception of the designed space of these Mughal monuments—such as in the Diwan-i-Am forecourt—and reinstate their spatial boundaries. At the same time, the fact that the barracks were constructed at a certain period in the Fort's existence means that they should not be hidden or removed from sight, since this would constitute erasure of history. One possible solution may be to retain the footprint of these buildings, whose intrusion into the limits of the original forecourt would achieve the dual purpose of conveying the limits of the Mughal space while also recording the takeover of this space by the later construction.

In pursuance of the understanding of cultural significance as related to spatial value, a similar conflict between the conservation claims of the remaining imperial gardens and the barracks may be resolved. An assessment of the cultural significance of the gardens, based on an understanding derived from their spatial investigation, leads to the conclusion that these were vital components of the Fort. The changes to the gardens, some of them deliberate interventions, have overwhelmingly reduced their design. This is especially so because most imperial Mughal gardens in the plains were devised to give predominance to the space they enclosed, rather than the views they looked out on. These views were, as compared to the Mughal gardens in the hills, always limited.

Thus, the loss of their internal designed features is more telling here than in the hill gardens where, despite internal transformations, the external views have generally remained impressive. Many of the changed features of the Fort's gardens—such as the course of the river Yamuna and the loss of the views towards the sequence of other riverine gardens of Shahjahanabad—cannot be reinstated. However, some unsuitable man-made interventions can be rectified. In Hayat Baksh, one such rectification would be the reinstatement of its original boundaries, reduced by the military barracks looming behind. The volume of the barracks has destroyed the illusion of spaciousness that an imperial Mughal garden in the plains was designed to convey. It has also altered the plan and topography of Hayat Baksh.

These features of original plan and topography of a garden are deemed to be 'intrinsic components of its architectural composition' according to the guidance devised for the conservation of historic gardens in the Florence Charter.[8] Based on the above analysis, it seems reasonable to say that the feel of Hayat Baksh can never be communicated if the barracks, positioned as they are, continue to intrude upon it.

The third major issue in the conservation of the Fort that needs to be addressed is the dilemma of built conservation versus nature conservation. Would it be justified to cut trees, many of them very old, to reinstate the original spatial quality of the Mughal monuments? The Burra Charter gives some general advice which may be considered with reference to such a question.

> Conservation requires the maintenance of an appropriate visual setting, for example form, scale, colour, texture and materials. No new construction,

> demolition or modification which would adversely affect the setting should be allowed. Environmental intrusions which adversely affect the appreciation or enjoyment of the place should be excluded.[9]

To reach a valid conclusion on whether the later plantation in parts of the Fort such as Hayat Baksh constitutes an 'environmental intrusion' or not, it is necessary to understand the reason for its introduction, and its effect on the attributes of the Fort. One of these reasons, as discussed in preceding chapters, was to demarcate the boundaries of original Mughal courts and gardens. The second reason was to screen the barracks.

In the first case, there is likely to be a danger to the foundations of the Mughal structures from the roots of the later shrubs or trees. Evidently, in the face of such a possibility, there would be a need to attach greater significance to built conservation over nature conservation. In cases where the plantation adversely affects the visual and spatial aspects of a particular part of the Fort, there seems to be a clear justification for the removal of this planting. However, forcible removal should be kept to a minimum and, wherever possible, achieved with the aid of the natural cycle of life-and-death of the plantation.

It may be useful to discuss here the suitability of using an ephemeral and changeable element like planting to convey spatial boundaries. As has been observed in the Red Fort, such a procedure is not very successful because of the long time taken by any plantation to reach a requisite growth. Even when there is an initial understanding of the objective of such plantation, its achievement is not actually realised for many years, by which time the objective itself may well be forgotten.

In the case of the Fort, a major proportion of the newer tree plantation is inconsistent with the tradition of plantation in Mughal gardens. It is appropriate to phase out this planting, since the architectural composition of a historic garden is recognised as including 'its vegetation including its species, proportions, colour, schemes, spacing and respective heights'.[10] A related conservation issue affecting all decisions, including those about tree plantation, is to do with the original and current uses of different parts of the Fort. Appropriate decisions can only be taken if there is an understanding of the way in which the entire Fort as well as its individual parts were designed to function.

A, B, C: Entrance Door, Moti Masjid in 1995, 1997, 2000 (Photo: Author)

For instance, Moti Masjid and the imperial pavilions are structures designed for private rather than community or congregational use. They employ expensive and fragile materials in their construction and decoration. The fragility and uniqueness of these monuments, as well as their cultural significance, calls for measures that regulate the number of people present in them at any one time. Thus, it seems valid to limit entrance to them to a sustainable optimum number of people. A similar logic is applicable for the imperial gardens. The Florence Charter specifically advises, '[w]hile any historic garden is designed to be seen and walked about in, access to it must be restricted to the extent demanded by its size and vulnerability, so that its physical fabric and cultural message may be preserved.'[11]

The decision to reuse Mumtaz Mahal as a museum is also one which may be debated. The reason advanced in favour of this decision was that the building had been so badly abused that it was not possible to restore its original attributes. While that may have been a valid observation, it is also a fact that the flow of large numbers of visitors to the museum results in increased pressure on what remains of Mumtaz Mahal as well as on the inner domain of the Fort that surrounds it.

In other areas of the Fort where the original spaces are not deemed to be culturally unique, some current functions could continue. For example, in the western sector, the planning was originally more amorphous than the eastern sectors. There was no regulated progression of spaces, and many structures were composed of unadorned masonry or thatch. The layout here was very similar to the public common parts of Shahjahanabad. Since this area did not display unique features of space or structure, the presence of the Indian military here may not be said to cause loss of cultural significance. I have argued earlier that the presence of the military is tied up with the Red Fort's present national role and the western sector is, in fact, the most appropriate place to accommodate it. It must also be remembered that the Mughal military was an integral part of the Fort even in Shah Jahan's time. Furthermore, the analysis of the Fort's history indicates that the Mughal military probably occupied part of the western area of the Fort. However, it is equally necessary to communicate the form of the original built structures in this area through maps, drawings and other interpretive material.

The content as well as the display of this interpretive material must be carefully thought over, since it will both inform and direct visitors. In fact, the presentation and interpretation of various aspects of the Fort—including its spatial elements—remains a subjective and thorny issue. It would naturally differ according to the cultural climate and the particular philosophy of the conserving body, but would also need to satisfy issues considered universally as part of good conservation practice. Despite the relative freedom of interpretation generally permissible, it is well accepted that the historical documentary function of a site is as important as its cultural, economic and recreational attributes. This documentary function, therefore, needs to be respected for an authentic conservation effort.

It is also true that our collective sense of history and pleasure are derived from the sense of 'time' that we perceive in a site—that is, through built interventions representative of different historical periods. To faithfully imitate the construction of a previous time would result in a removal of this sense of history and pleasure. In the Red Fort, for instance, the restoration of spatial boundaries of destroyed colonnades may be carried out in different ways. One way is to reconstruct newer interventions of the colonnades or arcades using column details or methods of roofing prevalent in Mughal times. Such reconstruction could cloud historical clarity because it might convey the idea that these colonnades had never been destroyed. This reconstruction would also be partly conjectural since the architectural details of these built elements are not available. Thus, a more truthful interpretation would be a restoration that succeeds in communicating the spatial characteristics of the Fort, while simultaneously clearly marking out its own time. This is not an impossible task. It is possible to design with contemporary methods and materials in a manner that highlights special aspects of a transformed historical site. The Burra Charter seems to endorse this view in its explanatory notes, 'New Construction work, including infill and additions, may be acceptable, provided: it does not reduce or obscure the cultural significance of the place; it is in keeping with article 8.'[12] Thus, the most appropriate method of spatial restoration in the Fort would be to devise systems of enclosure that provide similar qualities of space as the original, and yet are detailed and presented such that historical accuracy about the transformation of the site is maintained. Additionally, these enclosures need to be conceived in such a way that the foundations of the demolished Mughal structures are protected, and a regulated viewing of the monuments is made possible.

Other conservation issues in the Fort today are a lack of funds and accountability, as well as the exclusion of visitors from the conservation process. All these issues may be addressed by initiating steps that revive its erstwhile cultural importance and by disseminating accurate information about the many aspects of the Fort's personality. Thus, the Fort can function as a cultural centre containing museums, crafts display areas, interpretation centres, libraries, bookshops and performance areas for music and dance. Such a revival would not only help generate funds and facilitate the conservation of living heritage, but also build up an active association with the residents of Shahjahanabad and the rest of Delhi, and increase awareness about the history of the city. In keeping with the experience of historical sites worldwide, the international charters specifically mention that 'the conservation of a place of cultural heritage value is usually facilitated by it serving a socially, culturally or economically useful purpose'.[13]

Information on conservation work must also be in the public domain. An aware public can demand and, therefore, ensure responsible conservation from the custodians of their heritage. For such responsible and correct implementation, an active involvement of conservationists, archaeologists, historians, craftsmen, contractors, technicians and engineers is required—to all of whom the identified conservation objectives must be communicated. It is inescapably true that 'culture, which is the life of mind, can only be imparted through man to man ... Culture grows and moves and multiplies itself in life'.[14] It is not possible to achieve any significant improvement without the extraordinary presence, participation and potential contribution of ordinary men and women. It is their will and aspirations that will determine the form and fate of their city and its parts including, perhaps, its most famous monument.

For this, conservation efforts of the Fort must be linked with a larger vision for the area around it, of which Shahjahanabad is a vital component. This vision needs to look beyond conventional conservation. It needs to be combined with environmental upgradation of the area, in the interest of both historic clarity and sustainable long-term existence. It needs to integrate the economic well-being of the people who inhabit the environs, with efforts to conserve the physical and symbolic value of the Fort. It needs to plan for the flow of sufficient funds independent of bolstering through government financing, as well as ensure that the process of raising funds does not jeopardise the historical existence of the Fort. Only through such a holistic effort can we provide a real meaning of the Fort for all the people who visit it and live in its neighbourhood.

Finally, such an alternative must foster an association that connects beyond the purely materialistic to the identity and memory of the people whose ancestors or ancestors' contemporaries built so many beautiful parts of this city. If this is not done, even the shades of the most magnificent palace of the East may be lost to us. It was perhaps this possibility that moved one of the greatest poets of the world a century ago to interpret the then melancholic air of the palace[15] in words that sound even more poignant today.

You are gone today,
Emperor;
Your empire like a dream
is lost;
your throne broken;
The wind with the memories
of your soldiers,
whose march shook the earth,
flies away with the dust
of the streets of Delhi.

Singers sing no songs;
No longer
does the rhythm of the naubat
flow with the Yamuna;
The sound of the shattered anklets of
your beauteous women
dies away with the crickets' drone,
In the corners of

your broken palace
As the night-sky mourns.

Even so, your messenger,
Unsoiled, untiring,
Above the ruins of empires rising,
Above the turn
of life and death,
Through time and after
in a breath
Of bereavement infinite
Avers again and again
Beloved, I have not forgotten.

NOTES

OF TIME AND SPACE

1. Home Dept. Public A, June 1874, Proceeding Nos 10/13, p. 2, NAI.
2. 'For a parallel to the ardent, sustained and perceptive patronage of the Mughal dynasty, history may be searched in vain ... in none of these worldwide and historical instances does there appear to have been that effectively personal and intimate association, almost amounting to a collaboration between the Crown and the craftsman.' P. Brown, *Indian Architecture, Islamic Period*, p. 88.
3. 'Instrumental for this "Mughalization" of Indian architecture was Shah Jahan's new... architectural vocabulary which lent itself well to realisation in cheaper materials.' E. Koch, *Mughal Architecture*, p. 136.
4. This discussion on the court histories is primarily based on W. E. Begley and Z. A. Desai's introduction to their edited version of A. R. Fuller's nineteenth century manuscript translation of *The Shah Jahan Nama of Inayat Khan.*
5. The published account of the first two decades of Shah Jahan's rule by Lahori, is edited in Urdu by Kabiruddin and Abdur Rahim (2 vols. Calcutta 1867–8).
6. Published versions of Mohammed Salih Kambo's *Shah Jahan Nama* are the following: ed. G. Yazdani (3 vols., Calcutta 1923–46); ed. Wahid Quraishi (3 vols., Lahore 1972); Urdu trans. by N. H. Zaidi (2 vols., Lahore 1972–4).
7. For a discussion on the role of photographs as a means of record as well as representation, especially those of F. Beato, refer to J. Masselos, 'Beato's Eye, Imaging Delhi in the 1850s', *Beato's Delhi 1857–1997*, J. Masselos and N. Gupta, pp. 1–11.
8. Susan Gole, 'Plans of Indian Towns', pp. 100–6; in *Shahjahanabad/Old Delhi, Tradition and Colonial Change*, Eds. E. Ehlers and T. Krafft. See also Susan Gole, *Indian Maps and Plans*, p. 100.
9. This map, dated around 1850, is redrawn and translated into English with the help of the Department of Geography, University of Bonn. Prints of the map are available with the 1993 publication *Shahjahanabad/Old Delhi, Tradition and Colonial Change.*
10. Ibid., 'Islamic Cities in India, Theoretical Concepts and the Case of Shahjahanabad/Old Delhi', E. Ehlers and T. Krafft, p. 16.
11. ASI Delhi Circle Archives, Drawing No. 15/9, Site Plan.

12. Bichitr, fol. 50 v; reproduced as Pl. 2, *The Shah Jahan Nama of Inayat Khan*, Eng. trans. A.R. Fuller eds W. E. Begley and Z. A. Desai. A similar case is 'Shah Jahan Honouring the Religious Orthodoxy at a Banquet Celebration of the Prophet's birthday in the Hall of Public Audience, Akbarabad Fort on 12 Rabi I 1043 (16 September 1633 CE)', The Freer Gallery of Art, Smithsonian Institution, reproduced as Pl. 21, ibid.
13. 'Bahadur Shah II Enthroned', Delhi c.1839, Lib. No. 69.14; Linda Leach No. 8.58. Chester Beatty Collection, Dublin, Ireland.
14. Thomas Daniell and William Daniell's *Oriental Scenery, Parts I-V*, 1812-14; and Antonio Martinelli and George Michell, India, *Yesterday and Today, Aquatints by Thomas and William Daniell, Oriental Scenery*, 1998.
15. See also Nelson Goodman, *Ways of Worldmaking*, 1985, on the nature of perception and communication; Edward W. Said, *Orientalism*, and *Culture and Imperialism*, 1978, on the general perception and representation of the Oriental World; and Thomas Metcalf, *An Imperial Vision*, 2002, on the British perception of traditional Indian architecture in the eighteenth, nineteenth and twentieth centuries.
16. Add. Or. 1790, OIOC, British Library (B. L.).
17. Count Hermann A. Keyserling, *Indian Travel Diary of a Philosopher*, 1999, p. 109.
18. Rabindranath Tagore, *The Centre of Indian Culture*, 1988, p. 11.

THE MOST MAGNIFICENT PALACE IN THE EAST

1. G. Sanderson, *Delhi Fort, A Guide to its Historical Buildings and Gardens*, p. 4. Other sources claim that the Red Fort was called Urdu-i-Mualla in Shah Jahan's time and came to be called Qila-i-Mualla in Akbar Shah's reign. See also Maheshwar Dayal, *Rediscovering Delhi*, 1975, p. 4.
2. *The Shah Jahan Nama of Inayat Khan*, Eng. trans., eds Begley and Desai, 1990, pp. 406-7. The date of the Red Fort's establishment in different accounts varies between CE 1638 and 1639, due to the different dating systems and lengths of a year followed in the Muslim Calendar and in the (Common) Christian Era. The first Muslim year begins after 16 July 622 of the Christian Era — when Mohammad migrated from Mecca to Medina. The years of the Muslim Calendar are dated as AH, After the *Hijra* (Mohammad's migration), and each year comprises about 354 days divided into twelve lunar months. So, for any 30 solar years, 31 lunar years elapse, and a Hijra year may run into two successive solar years.
3. Survey of India, Delhi Guide Map 1939–42.
4. Francois Bernier, *Travels in the Mughal Empire,* 1996, p. 243.
5. The British established a new imperial capital at Delhi in 1931. The decision to found this new capital was announced at the State visit of King George V in 1911, when Shahjahanabad was still New Delhi in the minds of its visitors and residents.
6. Francois Bernier, *Travels in The Mughal Empire*, 1996, p. 245.
7. Originally, only the area approximately in the middle of the street's length, where it broadened into an octagonal court, was termed Chandni Chowk. This axis is termed 'the Lahauri Bazaar' by S. Ahmed, *Athar-al-Sanadid*, Eng. trans. 1979, p. 20.
8. Francois Bernier, *Travels in the Mughal Empire*, Eng. trans. pp. 210 and 243.

9. *Delhi in 1857, The Trial of Bahadur Shah*, ed. K.C. Yadav, p. 56, No. 53: The petition of Ahmad Khan and Muhammad Khan.
10. These names are given in the map 'Forts and Streets of Shahjahanabad' (Persian with some French) in Susan Gole's *Indian Maps and Plans,* 1981, p. 178.
11. As quoted by G. Sanderson in the *ASI Annual Report (1911–12)*, p. 4.
12. Francois Bernier, *Travels in the Mughal Empire*, 1996, p. 258.
13. G. Sanderson, *Delhi Fort, A Guide to the Historical Buildings and Gardens*, 1914, p. 45.
14. Francois Bernier, *Travels in the Mughal Empire*, Eng. trans. 1996, p. 260.
15. G. Sanderson, *Delhi Fort, A Guide to the Historical Buildings and Gardens*, 1914, p. 10.
16. National Archives of India (NAI), Letter from Ch. Secy, Fort William to F. Hawkins, Officiating Resident Delhi, Foreign Dept, Political Branch, Cons. 19 March 1830. See also Z. Hasan, *Monuments of Delhi (Vol. I)*, 1997, p. 11.
17. Z. Hasan, *Monuments of Delhi (Vol. I)*, 1997, p. 11.
18. Francois Bernier, *Travels in the Mughal Empire*, 1996, Eng. trans. p. 260. See also W. Irvine, *Later Mughals (Vol. I)*, 1964, pp. 280 and 390.
19. Abdul Hamid Lahori and Muhammad Waris, Badshahnama, Eng. trans.; eds. H. M. Elliot and J. Dowson, *The History of India, The Muhammaden Period (Vol. VII)*, 1964, p. 8.
20. J. Tavernier, Eng. trans. 1925, *Travels in India* (Vol. I) Book I, Chapter VI, p. 81.
21. Saqi Mustad Khan, *Maasir-i-Alamgiri*, Eng. trans. J. Sarkar, 1990, pp. 45–6.
22. *The Shah Jahan Nama of Inayat Khan*, Begley and Desai, 1990, p. 450.
23. James Fergusson, *The History of Indian and Eastern Architecture*, 1994, p. 312.
24. *Francois Bernier, Travels in the Mughal Empire*, Eng. trans. 1996, p. 12.
25. Ibid., p. 132.
26. The Khas Mahal, also referred to as the Bari Baithak and Khwabgah, is believed to have been begun in AH 1048 (CE 1639) and completed in AH 1058 (CE 1648) at a cost of 50 lacs, according to an inscription on its southern wall. Syed Ahmed, *Athar-al-Sanadid*, 1979, p. 15.
27. *The Golden Calm* ed. M. M. Kaye, 1980, p. 168.
28. According to Z. Hasan, translation of inscriptions on arches of Khwabgah, *Monuments of Delhi* (Vol. I), 1997, p. 16. See also Sir Syed Ahmed, *Athar-al-Sanadid*, Eng. trans. p. 16. Amir Khusro is the poet who is popularly attributed to have originally composed these lines.
29. *Francois Bernier, Travels in the Mughal Empire*, Eng. trans. 1996, p. 265.
30. Y. D. Sharma, *Delhi and its Neighbourhood*, 1990, p. 155.
31. *The Golden Calm* ed. M. M. Kaye, 1980, p. 208.
32. Mohd. Salih Kambo, *Amal-i-Salih*, folios 580–82; as quoted by G. Sanderson, *Delhi Fort, A Guide to the Historical Buildings and Gardens*, 1914, p. 38.
33. X/ 1659, BL OIOC.
34. *Punjab Gazetteer, Delhi District*, Ch.1, p. 11.
35. Mohd. Salih Kambo, *Amal-i-Salih*, folios 580–82; as quoted by G. Sanderson, *Delhi Fort, A Guide to the Historical Buildings and Gardens*, 1914, p. 38. It is not certain which of these pavilions is Sawan and which is Bhadon. In the absence of available confirmation, the nomenclature used in the discussion is the same as that followed by the ASI.

36. This is called the Chotta Rang Mahal or Khas Mahal in Sir Syed Ahmed's *Athar-al-Sanadid*, Eng. trans. 1979, p. 13.
37. *The Golden Calm* ed. M. M. Kaye, 1980, p. 168.
38. *The Shah Jahan Nama of Inayat Khan*, Eng. trans., eds. Begley and Desai, pp. 12–14. See also Abdul Hamid Lahori, *Badshah Nama*, Eng. trans. eds. Elliot and Dowson, *The History of India, The Muhammaden Period (Vol. VII)*, p. 5.
39. Muhammed Hadi Kanwar Khan, 'Tazkira-i-Chagahtai', as in Elliot and Dowson, p. 19.

LINEAGE

1. Constance Villiers-Stuart, *The Gardens of the Great Mughals*, 'Shahjahanabad, modern Delhi, as we call it', 1913, p. 92.
2. *Gazetteer of the Delhi District*, p. 1; geographical location given as N lat. 28 degrees 39 feet 40 inches and E long. 77 degrees 17 feet 45 inches, ibid. p. 181.
3. According to the broad classification of Geological eras and the periods they describe, the Pre-Cambrian continues from the earth's formation to about 570 million years ago. The Permo-Carboniferous dates to about 230–570 million years ago; and the Quartenary (the most recent geological period) to 3 million years ago. J. Gribbin, *Our Changing Planet*, p. 13.
4. The phases of the Stone age associated with a hunting–gathering economy.
5. B. R. Mani, *Delhi, Threshold of the Orient*, 1997, p. 8.
6. For a discussion on the choice of Delhi as the capital of successive empires, refer to R. E. Frykenburg, 'The Study of Delhi: An Analytical and Historiographical Introduction', *Delhi Through the Ages*, 1996, pp. xxi-xxix.
7. *The Baburnama*, Eng. trans. W. M. Thackston, ed., 1996, pp. 359-60.
8. Mohd. Salih Kambo, *Amal-i-Salih*, 2, pp. 471-2; as mentioned by Stephen Blake in *Shahjahanabad — the Sovereign City in Mughal India, 1639-1739*, p. 43.
9. E. Koch, *Mughal Architecture*, pp. 94-5; and *Mughal Art and Imperial Ideology*, 'The Baluster Column', pp. 38-60, and 'Shah Jahan and Orpheus', pp. 61-129. For a somewhat different interpretation, see R. Nath, *Some Aspects of Mughal Architecture*, 'Depiction of a Tantric Symbol in Mughal Architecture', pp. 68-77; 'Inlay Specimens at Akbar's Tomb', pp. 92-4; 'Augustin de Bordeaux and his Relation with the Mughal Court', pp. 112-19.
10. The *Mahabharata*, the longest epic in the world, is an important social, religious and cultural reference for the Indian sub-continent.
11. The layers excavated at this site are Sultanate, Rajput, Post-Gupta, Gupta, Saka-Kushan, Sunga reaching down to Maurya. Evidence of the Mauryan period is proved, among other evidence, by the presence of Northern Black Polished Ware. Y. D. Sharma, *Delhi and Its Neighbourhood*, ASI, pp. 1 and 8.
12. U. Singh, *Ancient Delhi*, pp. 36-7.
13. The successive dynasties with capitals at Delhi before the Mughals were:
    The Tomars (CE 1052–1164)
    The Chauhans (CE 1164–1192)
    The Mamluks (CE 1206–1290)
    The Khaljis (CE 1290–1320)

The Tughluqs (CE 1321–1413)
The Sayyids (CE 1414–1451)
The Lodis (CE 1451–1526)
The Mughals themselves had an interrupted rule, initially ruling from CE 1526–1540 and then from CE 1555–1857. The Sur dynasty ruled from CE 1540–1555.

14. Y. D. Sharma, *Delhi and Its Neighbourhood*, ASI, pp. 1 and 11.
15. This pillar, manufactured in the Gupta period and originally the standard of an unidentified Vishnu Temple of the fourth century CE; was believed to have been transported to Delhi in the tenth century CE. Ibid. pp. 11 and 13.
16. Recorded by A. Cunningham, in ASIR (Vol. XX) 1882–3, pp. 139–42; as mentioned by B. R. Mani, *Delhi, Threshold of the Orient*, p. 47.
17. Ibid. p. 4. See also R. Tagore, *A Vision of India's History*, p. 36; where he makes the point that 'though the Mahabharata may not be history in the modern western definition of the term, it is, nevertheless, a receptacle of the historical records which had left their impress upon the living memory of people for ages.'
18. B. R. Mani, *Delhi, Threshold of the Orient*, p. 44.
19. Ibn Battuta,*Travels in Asia and Africa*, p. 194. Muhammad Abdullah Ibn Battuta (1304–1377), a young man of learning, started on a pilgrimage to Mecca in 1325. He travelled across Persia, Asia Minor, the Crimea, Constantinople, India and China, to finally return to Tangier after some 25 years. He reached India in about CE 1333 during Muhammad Tughlak's rule, who appointed him Malikite *qadi* of Delhi.
20. Mahdi Hasan (tr.), *The Rehla of Ibn-Battuta*, Baroda 1953, as mentioned by B. R. Mani, *Delhi, Threshold of the Orient*, p. 44.
21. *Gazetteer of the Delhi District*, pp. 190 and 204.
22. W. M. Thackston, *The Baburnama*, 1996, pp. 328-30.
23. Ibn Battuta, 1952, *Travels in Asia and Africa*, pp. 131–3.
24. W. McNeill and M. Waldman, eds. *The Islamic World, Selections from Quran*, 1997, pp. 33 and 65.
25. The circuit of its walls is said to be about 1.2 km; originally protected by 19 bastions. After Salim Shah's death, the fort came into the possession of an Amir who is said to have built houses within it (in the reign of Akbar and Jahangir).
26. The baoli had a shaft 21 feet, 4 inches in diameter; 46 feet 10 inches deep; with an adjoining tank (20 feet by 20 feet). At a depth of 27 feet 5 inches was an arch in the north wall through which water from the well ran into the tank. Z. Hasan, *Monuments of Delhi (Vol. I)*, 1997, p. 28.
27. This mosque lies in the Khari Baoli area of Shahjahanabad.
28. E. Koch, *Mughal Art and Imperial Ideology*, 'The Delhi of the Mughals', pp. 166–72.
29. Abul Fazl, *Ain-i-Akbari*, ed. Blochman, p. 170, as quoted by Ahsan Jan Qaisar, *Building Construction of Mughal India*, 1988, p. 3.
30. The canal that bought water into the city, was originally activated in CE 1291 (AH 691) by the Tughlak ruler, Firoz Shah. He brought the canal from the Jamuna near Khizrabad to Safidun (his hunting lodge) from a point 30 'kos' higher up the river. It fell into disuse after his death. *The Shah Jahan Nama of Inayat Khan*, ed. Begley and Desai, 1990, p. 407

31. For a detailed general account of the architectural developments in Delhi during this period, see C.B. Asher, *Architecture of Mughal India*, The New Cambridge History of India. See also E. Koch, *Mughal Art and Imperial Ideology*, 'Delhi of the Mughals', pp. 163–79.
32. *Ain-i-Akbari*, (Vol. II) revised ed. J. Sarkar, 1997-8, pp. 283-4.
33. R. Nath maintains that the octagonal tomb form was used for Akbar's spiritual guide, Sadiq Khan in Agra and was neither abandoned wholly nor used only for courtiers who displeased the Emperor. See 'Tomb Firoz Khan at Agra', *Some Aspects of Mughal Architecture*, 1970, p. 123.
34. Abul Fazl, *Ain-i-Akbari* (Vol. II) p. 191.
35. *Fathpur Sikri*, A. A. Rizvi and V. J. A. Flynn, 1975, pp. 1 and 13.
36. E. Koch, *Mughal Art and Imperial Ideology*, 'Mughal Palace Gardens', p. 206.
37. Allahabad Fort was constructed by Akbar in 1583. Jahangir rebelled and declared himself the ruler here, during the last years of Akbar's reign. Only one of Akbar's structures is believed to survive within this Fort.
38. Thus, there are references to the location of the pleasure garden (orchard) and the flower garden in the royal palaces; as well as the flower pavilion; in traditional Indian building texts. See Prasanna K. Acharya, *The Architecture of the Mansara*, 1980, Ch. XL, 'Royal Palaces', pts. 119 and 120, p. 429; and pt. 102, p. 428.
39. See also David L. Lentz, 'Botanical Symbolism and Function at the Mahtab Bagh', pp. 43–54, *Moonlight Garden*, ed. E. Moynihan, for a discussion of the influence of Hindu garden concepts on Mughal gardens
40. 'The movement we know as Sufism began as a confluence of ascetic exercises, sharing much in common with Christian monasticism in Syria and gnostic attitudes towards the material world, and of mystical speculation fed probably by Zorastrian, Manichean, Buddhist and Hindu theophosical teaching.' Franklin D. Lewis, *Rumi*, p. 21.
41. Y. D. Sharma, *Delhi and its Neighbourhood*, p. 91. See also Abul Fazl, Akbarnama, (Vol. III) Eng. trans. H. Beveridge, p. 1155.
42. *The Shah Jahan Nama of Inayat Khan*, Eng. trans. eds Begley and Desai, Appendix, p. 567.
43. An inscription on the original bridge recorded its construction in the seventeenth year of Jahangir's reign, AH 1031/CE 1627; S. Ahmed, *Athar-al-Sanadid*, p. 55.
44. J. Jourdain, *The Journal of John Jourdain*, 1608–17, ed. W. Foster; as quoted by S. Blake, *Shahjahanabad, the Imperial City*, 1993, p. 28.
45. *Gazetteer of the Delhi District*, pp. 20–1.
46. Francois Bernier, *Travels in the Mughal Empire 1656–1668*, 1996, p. 280.
47. F. Paelsaert, *Jahangir's India*; as quoted by Ahsan Jan Qaisar in *Building Construction in Mughal India*, 1998, p. 4.
48. E. Koch, *Mughal Architecture*, 2001, p. 10.
49. *The Shah Jahan Nama of Inayat Khan*, Eng. trans. eds. Begley and Desai, 1990, p. 9.
50. Ibid., p. 15.
51. Ibid., pp. 262 and 404.
52. Ibid., p. 406. See also H. G. Keene, *Handbook for Visitors to Delhi*, 1906, p. 4, who states that in comparison to Agra, 'it is better situated in some other respects, nearer

to the hills for purposes of pleasure, nearer to the frontier for purposes of defence, and enjoying a milder climate'.

53. *Gazetteer of the Delhi District*, p. 10.
54. *The Shah Jahan Nama of Inayat Khan*, Eng. trans., eds: Begley and Desai, 1990, p. 571.
55. Abdul Ahmed Lahori, *Badshahnama*, Eng. trans. eds Elliot and Dawson, *The History of India, The Muhammaden Period* (Vol. VII), 1964, p. 45.
56. The construction of the Kali or Kalan Masjid is credited to Khan-i-Jahan Junana Shah, the prime minister of Firoz Shah Tughlak. Y. D. Sharma, *Delhi and its Neighbourhood*, 1990, p. 27.
57. Shams-ul-Aarifin, known as Shah Turkman Biyabani was a Sufi saint who died in 1347. He is believed to have inhabited the same place where his tomb is located. Dargah Quli Khan, *Muraqqa-e-Dehli*, S. M. Chenoy and C. Shekhar, Eng. trans. 1989, p. 12.
58. The mandala formed the basis for architecture and town planning in the Indic tradition. From this origin, it was incorporated into the planning traditions of other religions.
59. Attributed to Maharat Khan Isfahani, *Bahjat-al-alam*, and Mohd. Salih Kambo, *Amal-i-Salih*; in Stephen Blake, *Shahjahanabad — the Sovereign City in Mughal India 1639–1739*, p. 30.
60. Ibid. p. 32; and Prabakhar V. Begde, *Forts and Palaces of India*, p. 137-8.
61. Prasanna K. Acharya, Eng. Trans. *Architecture of the Mansara* (Vol. IV), 1990, Ch. IX, pt. 458, p. 88.
62. As quoted by A. K. Coomaraswamy, *Early Indian Architecture* 'Palaces', p. 1.
63. A. K. Coomaraswamy, *Early Indian Architecture*, p. 3.
64. *The Shah Jahan Nama of Inayat Khan*, Eng. trans. eds Begley and Desai, 1990, p. 4.
65. For a detailed discussion, refer to Nader Ardalen and Laleh Bakhtiar, *The Sense of Unity*, 1973, p. 89.
66. Stephen Blake, *Shahjahanabad — The Sovereign City in Mughal India 1639-1739*, pp. 193–8. See also N. Manucci, *Storia Do Mogo*r (Vol. I), 1907, pp. 36-7, for a description of Isfahan in the mid-seventeenth century.
67. For a detailed discussion, refer to Stephen Blake, *Shahjahanabad — The Sovereign City in Mughal India 1639–1739*, 1993, pp. 17–21.
68. J. Tavernier, *Travels in India*, Eng. trans. (Vol. I) Book II, Chapter II, 1925, p. 260.
69. *Gazetteer of the Delhi District*, pp. 2, 18 and 19.
70. The Shah Jahan Nama of Inayat Khan, Eng. trans. eds. Begley and Desai, 1990, p. 406.
71. Lt. George Wilby Eaton, 'The life, diary and adventures of Titleyupshebumpshe, A Manual, Delhi Palace, September 1, 1858', Chapter XI, (Vol. I), OIOC, British Library.
72. Prasanna K. Acharya, *Architecture of the Mansara*, Eng. trans. (Vol. IV) Ch. XXXIV, 1980, p. 340, pt. 37–43,
73. A. K. Coomaraswamy, *Early Indian Architecture*, 1975, p. 5.
74. ASI Central Photographic Library, Vol. 3A, 1911–12, Nos. 201 and 204. See also, E. Koch, *Mughal Art and Imperial Ideology*, Shah Jahani Painting, pp. 131–3.
75. *The Shah Jahan Nama of Inayat Khan*, Eng. trans. eds. Begley and Desai, Pl. 19 and 21 showing respectively: 'Shah Jahan celebrating the wedding of Dara Shikoh, Padshah

Nama; fol. 124 v, Windsor Castle Royal Library; and 'Shah Jahan honouring religious orthodoxy' Diwan-i-Am, Agra, 1633; no. 42.17 Freer Gallery of Art, Smithsonian Institution Washington D.C.

76. Abul Fazl, *Ain-i-Akbari* as quoted in *The Islamic World*, eds W. Mcneill and M. Waldman, p. 354.
77. Francois Pelsaert, *Jahangir's India*, ed. and trans. W. H. Moreland and P. Geyl (reprint), Delhi 1972, pp. 1-2; as quoted by Ahsan Jan Qaisar in *Building Construction in Mughal India*, p. 3.
78. Refer to 'Shah Jahan's Ceremonial Reunion with the Princes Dara Shikoh, Shah Shuja and Aurangzeb in the Hall of Public Audience, Akbarabad Fort, 1 Rajab 1037' (7 March 1628) signed by Bichitr, Windsor Castle, Royal Library, *Padshah Nama* fol. 50.v; ibid., Pl. 2, p. 16. See also E. Koch, *Mughal Art and Imperial Ideology*, 'The Audience Halls of Shah Jahan', pp. 229–54.
79. *The Shah Jahan Nama of Inayat Khan*, Eng. trans. eds. Begley and Desai, p. 25.
80. Nader Ardalen and Laleh Bakhtiar, *The Sense of Unity*, p. 47. 'In the Islamic tradition, colour is considered primarily from a metaphysical point of view, one which sees the duality of light and darkness as permanent possibilities latent in the Celestial archetypes.'
81. *The Shah Jahan Nama of Inayat Khan*, Eng. trans. eds Begley and Desai, p. 92.
82. Ibid., p. 567–8. See also J. Tavernier, Eng. trans. *Travels in India* (Vol. I) Book I, Chapter VI, p. 86 for his description of the elephant-fights and the reasons for siting the elephant ground next to the river.
83. Ibid., p. 497.
84. Ibid., p. 408.

THE CITY WITHIN

1. Shah Jahan's coronation took place on 8 Jumada II (14 February 1628 CE), but the first day of the Ilahi (which coincided with the Vernal or Spring Equinox in March) traditionally marked the beginning of each regnal year. *The Shah Jahan Nama of Inayat Khan*, Eng. trans. A. R. Fuller, eds. Begley and Desai, pp. xvii and 22.
2. Shah Jahan is reported to have occasionally inspected the construction work on site himself. Ibid., pp. 403-4.
3. *The Shah Jahan Nama of Inayat Khan*, eds. Begley and Desai; p. 408; and Syed Ahmed, *Athar-al-Sanadid*, Eng. trans. R. Nath, p. 11.
4. Z. Hasan, *Monuments of Delhi* (Vol. I), p. 2; the Red Fort's dimensions are given as 1.5 miles (2.41 km) in circumference, 1000 gaz long, 800 broad, 25 in height by Mohd. Salih Kambo, *Amal-i-Salih*, folios 576–2 as well as by Abdul Hamid Lahori and Mohd. Waris in the *Badshah Nama* in the Eng.tr. by S. A. N. Rezavi, p. 1111 in *IHC: Proceedings, 71st Session, 2010-11*. (The value of a gaz varies from about 31.5 inches (80 cm) to 32.8 inches (83.5 cm). The location of the Fort according to G. Sanderson, *Delhi Fort, A Guide to its Historical Buildings and Gardens*, p. 2; is 3100 degrees N and S by 1650 degrees E and W.
5. *The Shah Jahan Nama of Inayat Khan*, eds. Begley and Desai, p. 571.
6. Ibid., p. 205-6.

7. Francois Bernier, *Travels in the Mughal Empire*, 1996, p. 243.
8. As recorded in the translation of the 1850s map of Shahjahanabad, (X/ 1659) OIOC.
9. Laleh Bakhtiyar, *Sufi*, 1976, p. 43.
10. *The Shah Jahan Nama of Inayat Khan*, eds. Begley and Desai, 1990, p. 571. See also Francois Bernier, *Travels in the Mughal Empire*, 1996, pp. 261 and 263.
11. Ebba Koch, *Mughal Architecture*, p. 110. I. Habib deduces the *zira-i-padshahi* used in Shah Jahan's time to be equivalent to 31.464 inches (81.5 cm) or 32.818 inches (83.35 cms), *The Agrarian System of the Mughal Empire*, 1999, pp. 412-15.
12. See E. Koch, *Mughal Art and Imperial Ideology*, 2001, 'The Delhi of the Mughals', p. 172, where despite the attraction of Salimgarh for the Mughal emperors being duly noted on the basis of detailed surveys of historical texts, its strategic importance has not been recognised or discussed.
13. *The Shah Jahan Nama of Inayat Khan*, eds. Begley and Desai, 1990, pp. 554 and 560-1.
14. Francois Bernier, *Travels in the Mughal Empire*, 1996, pp. 258-9. See also J. Tavernier, Eng. trans. *Travels in India,* 1925, (Vol. I, Book I) Chapter VI, p. 79. and the 1850s Map of Shahjahanabad, (X/ 1659) OIOC, B.L.
15. *Padshah Nama*, fol. 122; 'Wedding Procession of Prince Dara Shikoh approaching the Akbarabad Fort'; Windsor Castle Royal Library; Pl. 18. See also *King of the World, The Padshah Nama*, Eng. trans. Wheeler Thackston, 1996, pp. 108 and 67, for descriptions of Prince Aurangzeb and Shah Shuja's weddings respectively.
16. *The Shah Jahan Nama of Inayat Khan*, eds. Begley and Desai, 1990, pp. 333, 452 and 496.
17. Translation of an inscription on the northern arch of the Khwabgah; Zafar Hasan, *Monuments of Delhi* (Vol. I), 1997, p. 16.
18. For a general discussion on space, its meaning and its manifestations in the context of Islamic architecture, refer to Nader Ardalen and Laleh Bakhtiar in *The Sense of Unity*. Also refer to *Shahjahanabad/Old Delhi, Tradition and Colonial Change*, eds. E. Ehlers and T. Krafft, 2003, for a discussion of the urban structure of Islamic cities.
19. Interestingly, the inferred areas of movement for different users of the Fort, is borne out by a map of 1812, Plan of Dehli, N.A.I. drawn by Ensign Peter Lawtie which shows only the part of the Fort that is accessible to a nobleman.
20. *The Shah Jahan Nama of Inayat Khan*, Eng. trans., eds. Begley and Desai, 1990, Appendix, pp. 567–73. Based on the assumption that two *gharis* were equal to an hour, the Emperor's day would begin at about 4 o'clock in the morning. This implied that he performed his prayers at about 6 a.m., proceeded to his balcony by 7/7:30 a.m., and reached his Hall of Public Audience approximately an hour later, finishing with the business there to move to the Hall of Private Audience at around 10:30, and went to the Shah Burj close to 12:00 p.m. His visit to the seraglio was shortly after this, followed by a meal and rest (at noon, in Fuller's translation, but probably a little later if Inayat Khan's time frame for each activity is adopted). In keeping with the demands of a hot climate, no major administrative business seems to have been transacted in the afternoon, with pending affairs in the Halls of Private and Public Audience Halls attended to after evening prayers. Administrative and state matters were attended to till the early part of the night, intermittently relieved by music sessions and spectacles of elephant fights or horse-riding feats.

21. N. Manucci refers to Shah Jahan gathering fruit in the garden with his favourite pages as a means of recreation in the morning. *Storio Do Mogor*, Eng. trans. (Vol. I), 1907, pp. 199-200.
22. *The Shah Jahan Nama of Inayat Khan*, eds. Begley and Desai, 1990, p. 91.
23. *Ain-i-Akbari*, as mentioned in *The Islamic World*, eds. W. McNeill and M. Waldman, 1973, p. 356.
24. *Padshah Nama*, fol. 124v, Windsor Castle Royal Library; Pl. 19 as reproduced in *The Shah Jahan Nama of Inayat Khan* eds. Begley and Desai, 1990.
25. J. Tavernier, Eng. trans. *Travels in India* (Vol. II, Book II), 1925, Chapter VIII, p. 302.
26. *The Islamic World*, eds. W. Mcneill and M. Waldman, 1973, Selections from the Quran, pp. 59-60.
27. *The Shah Jahan Nama of Inayat Khan*, eds. Begley and Desai, 1990, Appendix, p. 568.
28. See also I. Habib, *The Agrarian System of Mughal India*, 1999, p. 55-56; and David L. Lentz, 'Botanical Symbolism and Function at the Mehtab Bagh'. p. 43–54, in *The Moonlight Garden*, ed. E. Moynihan, 2000.
29. Francois Bernier, *Travels in the Mughal Empire*, 1996, p. 243.
30. G. Sanderson, *Delhi Fort, A Guide*, 1914, p. 56.
31. See also I. Habib, *The Agrarian System of Mughal India*, 1999, for a listing of different methods of drawing water from wells, p. 28.
32. R. Nath. Agra and its Monuments, 1997, p. 64. See also 'Waterworks and Landscape Design', James L. Wescoat, p. 63–5, *The Moonlight Garden*, ed. E. Moynihan, for an estimate of the water requirements at the Mehtab Bagh opposite the Taj Mahal.
33. In a letter of November 1830, from T. Metcalfe, In Charge of Palace Affairs. Foreign Dept, 1830; N.A.I. Political Progs, 10–31 Dec, S. No 636, Cons No 8, pp. 35–7.
34. The Yamuna entered the Delhi district at 710 feet and left it at about 630 feet above msl, traversing approximately 90 miles with an average fall of 10–11 feet per mile. *Gazetteer of the Delhi District*, p. 3.
35. R. Nath, *The Private life of the Mughals*, 1997, p. 70. See also *The Shah Jahan Nama of Inayat Khan*, eds. Begley and Desai, 1990, p. 553.
36. Gordon Sanderson, 'Shah Jahan' Fort — Delhi'; in *ASI Annual Report 1911-12*, p. 25.
37. Gordon Sanderson, *Delhi Fort — Guide to its Historical Buildings and Gardens*, 1914, p. 55.
38. E. Koch, *Mughal Architecture*, 2001, pp. 104-5.
39. R. Nath, *Private Life of the Mughals*, 1997, p. 3.
40. *The Shah Jahan Nama of Inayat Khan*, eds. Begley and Desai, 1990, p. 451.
41. Mohd. Salih Kambo, Amal-i-Salih, p. 41; as quoted by Ahsan Jan Qaisar, *Building Construction in Mughal India*, 1988, pp. 26-7.
42. Gordon Sanderson, 'Shah Jahan' Fort — Delhi'; in *ASI Annual Report 1911-12*, p. 3.
43. J. Tavernier, Eng. trans. *Travels in India*, Vol. I, Book I, Chapter III, 1925, p. 35. See also S. A. N. Rezavi, p. 1112 in *IHC: Proceedings, 71st Session 2010-11*
44. 1047 AH/ 1 July 1637 AD; S. A. I. Tirmizi, *Mughal Documents*, Vol. I, 1995, p. 61.
45. A list of the types of workers participating in the construction process, is given by R. Nath in *The Taj Mahal and its Reincarnation*, 1985, pp. 38–43.
46. Ahsan Jan Qaisar, *Building Construction in Mughal India*, 1988, p. 21.

IMPERIAL DOMAINS

1. *The Shah Jahan Nama of Inayat Khan*, Eng. trans. A. R. Fuller, eds. Begley and Desai, 1990, p. 407. Approximately another 50 lakh rupees (5 million) are recorded to have been spent on the ramparts, gateways and moat. Syed Ahmed, *Athar-al-Sanadid*, Eng. trans., R. Nath, 1979, p. 11. See also S. A. N. Rezavi, p. 1119 in *IHC: Proceedings, 71st Session 2010-11*
2. Zafar Hasan, *Monuments of Delhi* (Vol. 1), 1997, p. 5.
3. James Fergusson, *History of Indian and Eastern Architecture* (Vol. I and II), 1994, p. 309.
4. Zafar Hasan, *Monuments of Delhi* (Vol. 1), 1997, p. 10.
5. *The Shah Jahan Nama of Inayat Khan*, Eng. trans. eds. Begley and Desai, 1990, pp. 245, 251-2, and 255.
6. Francois Bernier, *Travels in the Mughal Empire*, 1996, p. 245.
7. Faiz Bazar, 1,050 yards in length and 30 yards in width, was laid out by Shah Jahan's Begum Akbarabadi Mahal in AH 1060/CE 1650. Chandni Chowk was laid out by Jahanara in the same year. Syed Ahmed, *Athar-al-Sanadid*, Eng. trans. R. Nath, 1979, p. 21.
8. Its dimensions are given as 200 yards long by 140 yards wide by Sayed Ahmed, *Athar-al-Sanadid*; Eng. trans. R. Nath, 1979, p. 11. The same dimensions are given in Lahore and Waris's *Badshah Nama*, Eng. trans. S.A.N. Rezavi, in *IHC Proceedings, 2010-11*, p. 1118. Gordon Sanderson in *Delhi Fort, A Guide to its Historical Buildings and Gardens*, 1914, p. 8, records the dimensions of the Naqqar Khana forecourt as 200 feet square and the map in the Jaipur City-Palace Museum, F 122 (c. 1750) also shows this as a square, while according to Zafar Hasan, *Monuments of Delhi* (Vol. I), 1997, p. 10. This court was 'some 200 feet in length by 140 feet in breadth'.
9. This geometrical analysis uses for its base map an aerial photograph of the Fort, and the derivations of external spaces have been reached after a study and comparisons of available maps and recorded dimensions. The proportions are close to those calculated from Lahore and Waris's dimensions of this forecourt.
10. Zafar Hasan conversely gives these dimensions as 107 feet 6 inches width by 68 feet 2 inches depth by 49 feet 4 inches height; *Monuments of Delhi*, (Vol. I) p. 11.
11. As quoted in the *ASI Annual Report 1911-12*, p. 16.
12. The OIOC map, and Gordon Sanderson's map in *Delhi Fort, A Guide to its Historical Buildings and Gardens*, show the Diwan-i-Am forecourt with rectangular proportions, while the Jaipur City Palace Museum map, shows it to be a square.
13. Thus, the approximate proportions of length: breadth work out to be: Naqqar Khana—1:1.55; Naqqar Khana forecourt—1:1.5; Diwan-i-Am—1:2.65; and Diwan-i-Am forecourt—1:1.3.
14. 550 feet width by 300 feet depth; Z. Hasan, *Monuments of Delhi* (Vol. I), p. 12, and Gordon Sanderson, *Delhi Fort, A Guide*, p. 10.
15. *The Shah Jahan Nama of Inayat Khan*, eds. Begley and Desai, 1990, p. 571.
16. Ibid., p. 495. See also J. Tavernier, Eng. trans. *Travels in India* (Vol. I, Book I), 1925, Chapter VI, p. 88, for a description of the jharoka at the Agra Fort Diwan-i-Am and the success of its design in ensuring the safety of the emperor.

17. S. Wheeler, *The History of the Delhi Coronation Durbar*, 1904, p. 151.
18. Kambo, *Amal-i-Salih*, 1923–39, fols. 583-84; as quoted by G. Sanderson in *Delhi Fort, A Guide to its Historical Buildings and Gardens*, p. 10. The hall's dimensions are given as 80 feet L x 40 feet B x 30 feet H above the plinth level by Z. Hasan, *Monuments of Delhi*, p. 12.
19. Drawing of the Diwan-i-Am, Add. Or 4668, OIOC, B. L.
20. J. Tavernier, Eng. trans. *Travels in India* (Vol. I, Book I) Chapter VI, p. 80. See also Mohd. Salih, *Amal-i-Salih*, folios 583–84; as quoted by G. Sanderson, *Delhi Fort, A Guide to the Historical Buildings and Gardens*, pp. 10 and 16.
21. In ASI measured drawings. Lahore and Waris give these as 67 zira by 24 zira.
22. However, the map reproduced in J. Fergusson's *History of Indian and Eastern Architecture* and by G. Sanderson, in Delhi Fort, shows only one court. Some historians have also followed this depiction. See Koch, 2001 and Blake, 1993.
23. Lahore Citadel Plan, N. A. I., Historical maps, folio 10, sheet 25.
24. G. Sanderson, *Delhi Fort, A Guide to its Historical Buildings and Gardens*, p. 7.
25. A. Shekhar, Unpublished Thesis 1998, 'An Approach Towards Spatial Conservation — The Red Fort, Shahjahanabad', p. 35a; De Montfort University, Leicester, U.K.
26. *ASI Annual Report 1911-12*, p. 14.
27. In ASI measured drawings. These are conversely given as 150 feet by 40 feet in *The Golden Calm, Reminiscences by Emily, Lady Clive Bailey and Sir Thomas Metcalfe*, ed. M. M. Kaye, p. 44.
28. In Syed Ahmed's *Athar-al-Sanadid*, Eng. trans. R. Nath, p. 11. However, Zafar Hasan gives these dimensions as 90 feet L by 67 feet W, with the central chamber as 48 feet by 27 feet, p. 20.
29. *The Golden Calm*, ed. M. M. Kaye, p.168.
30. *The Shah Jahan Nama of Inayat Khan*, Eng. trans. eds. Begley and Desai, p. 572.
31. Syed Ahmed, *Athar-al-Sanadid*, Eng. trans., R. Nath, p. 16.
32. *Inayat Khan, The Shah Jahan Nama of Inayat Khan*, Eng. trans. eds. Begley and Desai, p. 569.
33. Such an arrangement seems to have been in use even in earlier Mughal palaces: as discovered by excavations next to Akbar's Diwan-i-Am hammam at Sikri that yielded a bottle of *itr*. R. C. Gaur, *Fathepur Sikri, Excavations*, p. 12.
34. *ASI Annual Report 1911–12*, p. 12.
35. R.C. Gaur, *Fathepur Sikri, Excavations*, pp. 11–20.
36. Bakhtawar Khan, *Mirat-i-alam*, Eng. trans. eds. H. M. Elliot and J. Dowson, *The History of India, Muhammaden Period* (Vol. VII), p. 157.
37. According to Ebba Koch, 'Shah Jahan commissioned or initiated the construction of more mosques than any other Mughal ruler before him'. *Mughal Architecture*, p. 117.
38. *The Shah Jahan Nama of Inayat Khan*, Eng. trans., eds. Begley and Desai, pp. 490, 510 and 530. This mosque was probably the Moti Masjid (1648-54 CE), since the Nagina Masjid was constructed earlier (1631-40 CE), R. Nath, *Agra and its Monuments*, pp. 56 and 58.
39. Francois Bernier, *Travels in the Mughal Empire*, p. 265.
40. A description of the Hayat Baksh by contemporary historians of Shah Jahan as quoted by G. Sanderson, *Delhi Fort, A Guide to its Historical Buildings and Gardens*, p. 38.

41. Francois Bernier, *Travels in the Mughal Empire*, p. 280.
42. The OIOC Map X/ 1659 and the Jaipur map F. 122 (c. 1750).
43. Muhammad Salih Kambo, *Amal-i-Salih,* fols. 580-582 as quoted by G. Sanderson, *Delhi Fort, A Guide to its Historical Buildings and Gardens*, p. 38.
44. Zafar Hasan, *List of Monuments of Delhi,* p. 25.
45. *The Shah Jahan Nama of Inayat Khan*, eds. Begley and Desai, p. 571.
46. See f 7/9, N.A.I. and Add. Or. 540, OIOC, B. L.
47. *The Shah Jahan Nama of Inayat Khan*, eds. Begley and Desai, p. 499.
48. Francois Bernier, *Travels in the Mughal Empire*, p. 265.
49. 1850s Map, Cat. X/1659, OIOC, B. L.
50. Niccoloa Manucci, a visitor to Shah Jahan's court, mentions that Jahanara lived in a palace outside the Fort. *Storio Do Mogor* (Vol. I) p. 212 and (Vol. II), p. 30.
51. *The Shah Jahan Nama of Inayat Khan*, eds. Begley and Desai, p. 570.
52. Ibid., pp. 21 and 26.
53. Bernier, *Travels in the Mughal Empire;* and Tavernier, *Travels in India* (Vol. I) Book II, Chapter IX, p. 312. See also N. Manucci, *Storio Do Mogor* (Vol. I), p. 212 for a similar description of Jahanara's retinue.
54. 1850s Map, Cat. X/1659, OIOC, B. L.
55. Ibid.

UNPLANNED ASSAULT

1. *The Shah Jahan Nama of Inayat Khan*, Eng. trans. A. R. Fuller, eds. Begley and Desai, p. 3.
2. Ibid., p. 543, Epilogue by W. E. Begley adapted from Kambo's *Shah Jahan Nama*, Mohd. Kazwini's *Alamgir Nama*, and other sources.
3. Zafar Hasan, *Monuments of Delhi* (Vol. I), p. 8.
4. Ibrahim Shah, in *Quarterly Journal of The Pakistan Historical Society*, 'Major Architectural Remains of the time of Aurangzeb', pp. 45–7.
5. *Muhammad Salih Kambo, Amal-i-Salih*, as quoted by G. Sanderson, ASI Annual Report, 1911-12, p. 4.
6. Saqi Mustad Khan, *Maasir-i-Alamgiri*, Eng trans. J. N. Sarkar, p. 49.
7. As quoted by G. Sanderson, *Delhi Fort, A Guide to its Historical Buildings and Gardens*, p. 35. See also R. Nath, *Some Aspects of Mughal Architecture*, 'The Moti Masjid of the Red Fort, Delhi,' p. 14.
8. Saqi Mustad Khan, *Maasir-i-Alamgiri*, Eng trans. J. N. Sarkar, p. 4.
9. Ibid. pp. 14, 22.
10. Francois Bernier, *Travels in the Mughal Empire*, p. 261.
11. Saqi Mustad Khan, *Maasir-i-Alamgiri*, Eng trans. J. N. Sarkar, pp. 45–6.
12. Ibid., p. 77.
13. Ibid., pp. 47, 49, 73 and 77.
14. 'Kanzul Mahfuz' Eng. trans. Eds. Elliot and Dowson, *The History of India, Muhammadan Period* (Vol. VIII), pp. 38–9.
15. Saqi Mustad Khan, *Maasir-i-Alamgiri*, Eng. trans J. N. Sarkar, p. 55.
16. Ibid., p. 44.

17. Ibid., p. 61.
18. Khafi Khan, 'Muntakhabu-l Lubab', Eng. trans. eds. Elliot and Dowson, *The History of India, Muhammadan Period* (Vol. VII), pp. 283–4.
19. N. Manucci, *Storio Do Mogor* (Vol. II), pp. 5–6. Aurangzeb's conservative outlook seems to have struck a chord in England, which was going through a royalist revival after the disintegration of the Commonwealth. The least romantic persona of the Great Mughals, was eulogised and feted — ironically enough, in dramatic productions! Aurangzebe, a tragedy written by John Dryden and based on a recasting of accounts by European travellers to the Orient, was enacted at the Royal Theatre in 1675 for the King of England. Dryden exercised poetic license to the fullest, pushing in Mughal kings and queens from different eras along with fictional characters and portrayed Aurangzeb as a hero.
20. H. G. Keene, *Dehli*, p. 13. See also W. Irvine, *Later Mughals* (Vol. I), p. 306.
21. Syed Ahmed, *Athar-al-Sanadid*, Eng. trans., p. 14.
22. Muhammad Ali Khan Ansari, Tarikh-i-Muzaffari, Mss. in Government Library, Allahabad, Folios 115/116; as quoted by G. Sanderson, *Delhi Fort, A Guide to its Historical Buildings and Gardens*, p. 4.
23. 'Tarikh-i-Ahmad Shah', Eng. trans. eds. Elliot and Dowson, *The History of India, Muhammadan Period* (Vol. VIII), pp. 105, 112.
24. Ibid. pp. 104–5.
25. For a discussion of the state of Delhi in the last quarter of the seventeenth century and the first quarter of the eighteenth, refer to Satish Chandra, 'Cultural and Political Role of Delhi (1675–1725)', pp. 106–118. in *Delhi Through the Ages*, ed. R. E. Frykenberg.
26. 'Tazkira of Anand Ram Mukhlis', Eng. trans. eds. H. M. Elliot and J. Dowson, *The History of India, Muhammadan Period* (Vol. VIII), p. 88.
27. Rustam Ali, 'Tarikh-i-Hindi', eds. Elliot and Dowson, *The History of India, Muhammadan Period* (Vol. VIII) pp. 64–5.
28. 'Tazkira of Anand Ram Mukhlis', Elliot and Dowson, *The History of India, Muhammadan Period* (Vol. VIII), p. 88.
29. Dargah Quli Khan, *Muraqqa-e-Dehli*, Eng. trans. S. M. Chenoy and C. Shekhar, Introduction, pp. xxxiv and 82.
30. Ibid., pp. 19-20.
31. Ibid., pp. 21–5.
32. A map of 1789 shows the route from Agra to Delhi with many forts laid out next to the river, F. 12/31, National Archives of India.
33. J. Sarkar, *Delhi during the Anarchy*, p. 4.
34. Ibid., p. 4.
35. See J. Masselos and N. Gupta, *Beato's Delhi 1857-1997*, p. 50.
36. Y. D. Sharma. *Delhi and its Neighbourhood*, p. 90.
37. *The Treaty of Kora*, 1765.
38. J. Sarkar, *Delhi during the Anarchy*, pp. 2–5.
39. Francklin, *The History of Shah Alam*, p. 6; as mentioned by Antoine Louise Henri Polier, *Shah Alam and his Court*, Eng. trans. P. Gupta, p. 15.
40. *Gazetteer of the Delhi District*, p. 158.

41. Comte de Modave, from Antoine Louise Henri Polier, *Shah Alam and his Court*, Eng. trans. P. Gupta, Notes, pp. 87–8.
42. Z. Hasan, *Monuments of Delhi* (Vol. I), p. 20.
43. *Gazetteer of the Delhi District*, p. 23.
44. I. Habib, *The Agrarian System of Mughal India*, p. 15.
45. *Gazetteer of the Delhi District*, p. 9.
46. See 'Plan of the City of Delhi 1812' NAI, F 183/23.
47. Zafar Hasan, *Monuments of Delhi* (Vol. I), translation of inscription on arches of Mussaman Burj, p. 19.
48. Syed Ahmed, *Athar-u-Sanadid*, Eng. trans. R. Nath, p. 12.
49. Nawab Server-ul-mulk Bahadur, *My Life*, Eng. trans. p. 11.
50. *Gazetteer of the Delhi District*, p. 9.
51. The size of this orchard was recorded by Reginald Heber as 107 gaz by 115 gaz, *Narrative of a Journey through the Upper Provinces* (Vol. II), pp. 302–5.
52. Ibid., p. 297.
53. Fanny Parks, *Wanderings of a Pilgrim* (Vol. II), pp. 212–14.
54. *The Golden Calm, Reminiscences of E. Bailey and T. Metcalfe*, ed. M. M. Kaye, p. 142.
55. This was the tomb in Qutub, which he called Dilkusha; The chain of events that put this tomb in Metcalfe's possession, at least as recorded by Emily Bailey, begin from the impoverished owners' handing over of the tomb to a banker. Metcalfe purchased the tomb from the banker. The grounds around the Qutub ruins, were then laid out at his suggestion as a 'beautiful garden'. ibid. p. 146. This modified building is identified as the grave of Muhammad Quli Khan, in *Beato's Delhi 1857–1997*, J. Masselos and N. Gupta, p. 44.
56. In a letter from the King, received on 1st January 1830, National Archives of India, Foreign Dept, Political Proceedings, 8 January 1830, Cons. No.42, pp. 322–5.
57. National Archives of India, Foreign Dept, Political Proceedings, 8 January 1830, Cons. No. 45–7, pp. 333–6.
58. In a letter from Secretary to Governor General, Fort William; addressed to Agent, Governor General, Delhi; 27 October 1832, Political Department, National Archives of India.
59. Hawkins was replaced by W. Martin as the Resident of Delhi on 25 November 1830, Foreign Department, Political, Dec. 1830, Cons. 10, p. 1, National Archives of India. See also Percival Spear. 'The British in Delhi', *Twilight of the Mughuls, Studies in late Mughul Delhi*, pp. 137–166.
60. 1835, Foreign Dept, Political Consultation, 8 June, No. 10, pp. 2–5. National Archives of India.
61. Secretary to the Government, Fort William to F. Hawkins, Foreign Department, Political Consultation, 19 March 1830, pp. 52–3, National Archives of India.
62. Nawab Server-ul-mulk Bahadur, *My Life*, Eng. trans., Foreword, p. vi.
63. *Delhi in 1857, The Trial of Bahadur Shah*, ed. K. C. Yadav, pp. 56–7.
64. For a discussion of the urban Islamic institutions of Shahjahanabad as it appears in the 1850s OIOC map, refer to Jamal Malik, 'Islamic Institutions and Infrastructure in Shahjahanabad', pp. 42–64, from *Shahjahanabad/ Old Delhi, Tradition and Colonial Change*, eds. E. Ehlers and T. Krafft.

65. For a detailed account of life in Delhi from 1803 to 1931, refer to Narayani Gupta, *Delhi Between Two Empires*. See also P. Spear, *Twilight of the Mughuls, Studies in Late Mughal Delhi*.
66. Delhi in 1857, The Trial of Bahadur Shah, ed. K.C.Yadav, p. 205-6
67. Zafar Hasan, *Monuments of Delhi* (Vol. I), p. 28.
68. Syed Ahmed, *Athar-al-Sanadid*, Eng. trans. R. Nath, p. 19.
69. *The Golden Calm*, ed. M. M. Kaye, p. 98.
70. Syed Ahmed, *Athar-al-Sanadid*, Eng. trans. R. Nath, p. 15.
71. *Delhi in 1857, The Trial of Bahadur Shah*, ed. K. C. Yadav, pp. 144, 175 and 183.
72. *The Golden Calm*, ed. M. M. Kaye, pp. 168 and 162.

ASSAULT

1. Karl Marx, 'The British Rule in India', London, 1853, *On Colonialism*, Karl Marx and Frederick Engels, p. 37.
2. For a summary of major events during this period, see *A Companion to the Indian Mutiny of 1857*, pp. 355–6, ed. P. J. O. Taylor.
3. G. R. Hearn, *The Seven Cities of Delhi*, 1997, pp. 262–3. See also J. S. Sharma, *India Since the Advent of the British*, 1970, p. 81.
4. *Delhi in 1857*, ed. K. C. Yadav, pp. 62, 204 and 221.
5. This 'close' gateway had been opened a few years before 1857 according to J. Cave-Browne, *The Punjab and Delhi in 1857* (Vol. I), pp. 63-4. B. R. Mani gives this date as 1852, *Threshold of the Orient*, p. 27.
6. *Delhi in 1857*, ed. K. C. Yadav, 1980, p. 173.
7. *Two Native Narratives of the Mutiny at Delhi*, Eng. trans. C. T. Metcalfe, 'Narrative of Mainodin Hassan Khan', 1898, p. 60.
8. G. R. Hearn, *The Seven Cities of Delhi*, p. 263.
9. Nawab Server-el-mulk-Bahadur, *My Life*, Eng. trans. of his Autobiography, p. 26.
10. *Two Native Narratives of the Mutiny at Delhi*, Eng. trans. C. T. Metcalfe, 'Narrative of Munshi Jeewan Lal', pp. 86–7.
11. *Delhi in 1857*, ed. K. C. Yadav, p 38-39: no. 36, Order of the King to Mirza Moghal, 22 July, 1857
12. Ibid., p. 335, no. 16, Copy of an Order from the King to Mirza Moghal.
13. *Two Native Narratives of the Mutiny at Delhi*, Eng. trans. C. T. Metcalfe; 'Narrative of Munshi Jeewan Lal', pp. 92–120.
14. Herbert Strang, *Stories of the Mutiny*, J. E. W. Rotton, 'A Chaplain's Narrative of the Siege of Delhi', p. 60.
15. *Two Native Narratives of the Mutiny at Delhi*, Eng. Trans. C. T. Metcalfe, 'Narrative of Munshi Jeewan Lal', pp. 103-4.
16. Ibid., p. 190. See also Percival Spear, 'The Mutiny in Delhi', *Twilight of the Mughuls*, pp. 212–15.
17. Herbert Strang, *Stories of the Mutiny*, J. E. W. Rotton,'A Chaplain's Narrative of the Siege of Delhi', pp. 75–6.
18. From the Military Secretary to the Chief Commissioner, Punjab, 30 October, 1857, Secret, No. 83, National Archives of India.

19. 'Selimgurh shelled 17th and 18th, reoccupied 20th September,' Plan of the Siege of Delhi, Maps aa. 388.85.1, Cambridge University Library, Map Collection.
20. *Delhi in 1857*, ed. K. C. Yadav, p. 346.
21. Herbert Strang, *Stories of the Mutiny*, 'The Seige of Delhi', (From a Chaplain's Narrative of the Seige of Delhi', by J. E. W. Rotton, M. A.) p. 7.
22. J. Cave-Browne, *The Punjab and Delhi in 1857* (Vol. I), p. 7.
23. C. J. Griffiths, *The Siege of Delhi*, ed. Yonge, p. 193.
24. Sangat Singh, *Freedom Movement in Delhi*, pp. 3–4.
25. C. J. Griffiths, *The Siege of Delhi*, pp. 233-4.
26. C. J. Griffiths, *The Siege of Delhi*, pp. 245–6.
27. Ibid., pp. 8–199 and 237.
28. S. Wheeler, *History of the Delhi Coronation Durbar*, p. 3.
29. R. Nath, *Agra and its Monuments*, p. XVIII.
30. For photographic images of Delhi in the period 1858–60, see J. Masselos and N. Gupta, B*eato's Delhi, 1857–1997.*
31. D.C. Records, Delhi Archives.
32. *Punjab Gazetteer, Delhi District,* p. 183.
33. Narayani Gupta, *Delhi Between Two Empires*, p. 27.
34. Maj. Gen. Cunninghham, R. R. File 19, Memorandum regarding the old Mohammaden buildings of Delhi, p. 3B, Delhi Archives.
35. S. Wheeler, *History of Coronation Durbar*, p. 46.
36. C. M. Villiers-Stuart, *Gardens of the Great Mughals*, p. 113.
37. H. G. Keene, *Dehli*, p. 24.
38. Carr Stephen, Judge Small-Cause Court Dehli, to Comm. Delhi, 16 December 1872, Misc. File No 26, Delhi Archives.
39. Later amended to 450 yards, Narayani Gupta, *Delhi Between Two Empires*, p. 28; See also File No 72, Box-5, Chandni Chowk, 13 July 1869, R.R., Delhi Archives.
40. R. R, Box No-5, File No 48, Chandni Chowk, 28 March 1860, Delhi Archives.
41. 'Shah Jahan's Fort', Gordon Sanderson, *Archaeological Report, 1911–12*, p. 7.
42. Map, Cantonment, Civil Stations and Environs of Delhi 1867–8, Railways to 1905, National Archives of India.
43. Plan, Lahore Citadel, National Archives of India.
44. J Marshall, *Archaeological Society Annual, 1902–3.*
45. However, Capt. H. H. Cole in a report to Secy of State, mentions that these panels were at the India Office Museum, London. Jaipur, Political Agency, File No 4/1882, p. 9, NAI.
46. Gordon Sanderson, 'Shah Jahan's Fort, Delhi', *Archaeological Report 1911–12*, p. 7. See also Memorandum by Major General Cunningham, File Misc/19, R. R. Delhi Archives.
47. H. C. Fanshawe, *Delhi Past and Present*, p. 93. See also J. E. W. Rotton, 'A Chaplain's Narrative of the Siege of Delhi', from *Stories of the Mutiny*, Herbert Strang, p. 81.
48. Plan of Artillery and Infantry Barracks, Punjab Delhi Division and District, 1869; folio no. 178, National Archives of India.
49. Ibid. For a description of the Lahore, Delhi and Agra Forts at this time, see 'Report of Capt. H. H. Cole', (R.E. on special duty to the Secretary of Government of India,

Public Works Department) National Archives of India, Jaipur Political Agency, File No. 4/ 1882, pp. 7–11, 18–19.

50. *ASI Report, Punjab 1901–1904*, p. 4.
51. J. Masselos and N. Gupta, *Beato's Delhi, 1857–1997*, 'Saman Burj of Palace', p. 69.
52. Gordon Sanderson, 'Shah Jahan's Fort, Delhi', *Archaeological Report 1911–12*, p. 14.
53. File Misc/19, R.R., Memorandum by Major General Cunningham, Delhi Archives.
54. Jaipur Political Agency, File No 4/1882, Report from Capt. H. H. Cole to Secy. Govt of India, PWD, p. 8, National Archives of India.

A RETURN IN PARTS

1. H. G. Keene, *Delhi*, pp. 1 and 3.
2. W. S. Caine, *Picturesque India*, pp. 127, 143 and 144.
3. Gordon Riseley Hearn, *Seven Cities of Delh*i, p. 2.
4. *Gazetteer of the Delhi District*, p. 181.
5. S. Wheeler, *History of the Coronation Durbar of Delhi*, p. 61.
6. Gordon Sanderson, 'Shah Jahan' Fort, Delhi', *ASI Annual Report, 1911-12*, p. 13. See also Zafar Hasan, *Monuments of Delh*i (Vol. I), p. 23.
7. Major H. H. Cole, *Preservation of National Monuments in India*, Delhi, 1884.
8. The 1850s Map of Shahjahanabad, X/ 1659, Eng. trans. OIOC, B. L.
9. Maps of Delhi Division, Deputy Commissioner's Office, DO, 6/1895, Delhi Archives.
10. H. C. Fanshawe, *Delhi, Past and Present*, 1902, p. 20.
11. Gordon Sanderson, 'Shah Jahan's Fort, Delhi,' *Archaeological Report, 1911–12*, p. 1. See also *ASI Annual Report, 1905-6*; pp. 28–42.
12. Gordon Sanderson, *Delhi Fort, Guide to its Historical Buildings and Gardens*, 1914. p. 6. See also *ASI Annual Report, 1905-06,* Dr. J. H. Marshall, pp. 33–42; and Gordon Sanderson, pp. 1–28.
13. *Gazetteer of the Delhi District*, p. 102.
14. Jaipur Political Agency, File no. 4, 1882, From Capt. H. H. Cole to Secy. Govt. of India, P. W. D. p. 9, N.A.I. See also S. Wheeler, *The History of the Delhi Coronation Durbar*, p. 174.
15. H. C. Fanshawe, *Delhi, Past and Presen*t, 1902, Preface, p. xiii.
16. S. Wheeler, *The History of the Delhi Coronation Durbar*, p. 5.
17. Gordon Sanderson, in *Archaeological Report, 1911-12*, p. 20-21. See also *ASI Annual Report, 1906-07*, p. 2.
18. Gordon Sanderson in *Archaeological Report 1911-12*, pp. 7-8.
19. H. C. Fanshawe, *Delhi Past and Present*, Preface, p. xiii.
20. Compare the '1850s map, Cat. X/1659'; with 'Delhi — Cantonment, Civil Station, City and Environs, 1867–8 with addition of Railways upto 1905', Cat. X/ 9402, OIOC, B. L.
21. Photos 430/11, 430/12, 430/13, 430.16, OIOC, B. L.
22. John Marshall, *Conservation of Ancient Monuments*, 1922, p. 10. See also 'General Principles for ... Repair of Ancient Monuments', Jaipur Agency, File No.9/1903, pp. 1–4, National Archives of India.
23. *ASI Annual Report 1911-12*, p. 1.
24. Gordon Sanderson, in *Archaeological Report 1911-12*, p. 20.

25. Zafar Hasan, *Monuments of Delhi* (Vol. I), p. 6.
26. S. Wheeler, *The History of the Delhi Coronation Durbar*, p. 152.
27. *ASI Annual Report 1908-09*, p. 1; and *ASI Annual Report 1911-12*, p. 9.
28. Gordon Sanderson, in *ASI Annual Report, 1911-12*, p. 8.
29. Gordon Sanderson, *Delhi Fort, Guide to its Historical Buildings and Gardens*, p. 55.
30. Sanderson in *A.S.I. Annual Report, 1911–12*, p. 16.
31. Refer to John Martin Robinson, *Stowe Landscape Gardens, Temples of Delight*, 1990, The National Trust, for a detailed discussion on the concept of an English landscape garden.
32. Zafar Hasan, *Monuments of Delhi* (Vol. I), p. 13.
33. Gordon Sanderson, *Delhi Fort, Guide to its Historical Buildings and Gardens*, 1914, p. 53.
34. Zafar Hasan, *Monuments of Delhi* (Vol. I), p. 25. See also *Annual Progress Report*, Archaeological Survey, N. Circle, year ending 1909, p. 11.
35. John Marshall, *Conservation Manual*, p. 36.
36. Gordon Sanderson in *Archaeological Report 1911-12*, p. 8.
37. Gordon Sanderson, *Delhi Fort, A Guide to its Historical Buildings and Gardens*, 1914, p. 57.
38. Ibid.
39. Though the Lahori Gate continued to be occupied by the officers in the Fort, Z. Hasan, *List of Monuments*, p. 4.
40. Gordon Sanderson in *Archaeological Report 1911-12*, p. 22.
41. Ibid., p. 55.
42. Robert Grant Irving, *Indian Summer*, p. 5.
43. *ASI Annual 1911–12*. See also Photos 592 (2) 75 and 592 (2) 74, OIOC, B.L. titled 'Their Imperial Majesties showing themselves to the Public from the Fort walls'.
44. C. M. Villiers-Stuart, *Gardens of the Great Mughals*, p. 121.
45. Booklet of an Exhibition titled 'New Delhi, The Eighth City of Delhi, An Exhibition of Historical Records and Photographs', organised by Delhi Archives, Delhi Administration, 1979, p. 5.
46. J. Renton-Dennings, Delhi, *The Imperial City*, p. 29.
47. Gordon Sanderson in *Archaeological Report 1911–12*, p. 1.
48. *Gazetteer of the Delhi Distric*t, p. 158.
49. Sangat Singh, *Freedom Movement in Delhi*, pp. 268-9.
50. Robert Grant Irving, *Indian Summer*, p. 342.
51. T. Krafft, 'Contemporary Old Delhi, Transformation of an Historical Place', from *Shahjahanabad/Old Delhi, Tradition and Colonial Change*, eds. E. Ehlers and T. Krafft, p. 70.
52. T. G. P. Spears, *Delhi – Its Monuments and History*, p. 1.
53. T. Krafft, 'Contemporary Old Delhi, Transformation of an Historical Place, from *Shahjahanabad/Old Delhi, Tradition and Colonial Change*, eds. E. Ehlers and T. Krafft, p. 68.
54. Delhi Master Plan 2001, pp. 123 and 146

THE PERSISTENCE OF GRANDEUR

1. Delhi Master Plan 2001, p. 123.
2. These decorative door panels have been conserved and replaced of late.
3. *Gazetteer of the Delhi District*, p. 183.
4. Delhi Master Plan 2001, 'Conservation, Revitalisation, and Environmental Improvement' pp. 122–3. See also 'Conservation of the Walled City', p. 142; and 'Pedestrianisation', p. 144; 'Special Area', p. 145; and 'Urban Renewal Area — Walled City', p. 165.
5. Ibid., pp. 132-133.
6. Article 16, The International Council on Monuments and Sites (ICOMOS) Charter for the Conservation of Places of Cultural Significance at Burra-Burra, Australia, 1979 (The Burra Charter).
7. Ibid., Article 11.
8. Article 4, 'Definitions and Objectives', ICOMOS - IFLA International Committee for Historic Gardens, The Florence Charter.
9. Article 8, The Burra Charter, 1979.
10. Article 4, 'Definitions and Objectives', The Florence Charter.
11. Ibid. Article 8, 'Use'.
12. The work of the Italian architect, Carlo Scarpa (1906–78) illustrates such an approach.
13. The Burra Charter, Article 8, Explanatory notes.
14. The ICOMOS New Zealand Charter for the Conservation of Places of Cultural Heritage Value Article 20, Adaptation.
15. Rabindranath Tagore, *The Centre of Indian Culture*, p. 13.
16. Anisha Shekhar Mukherji, Eng. trans. from the original poem in Bengali, 'Shah Jahan', in the *Balaka* collection written by Rabindranath Tagore on 14th Kartik 1321 Samvat, Allahabad.

Credits Abbreviations

ASI PL	Archaeological Survey of India Photo Library
OIOC	Oriental and India Office Collection
BL	British Library
NAI	National Archives of India
VCOAS Sectt.	Vice Chief of Army Staff Secretariat

SELECT BIBLIOGRAPHY

Abul Fazl, *Ain-i-Akbari*, ed. J Sarkar, 1948-9, Oriental Books Reprint Corporation, 1977-8

Acharya, Prasanna Kumar: *Architecture of Mansara*, Translated from the original Sanskrit, Vol. IV, Oriental Books Reprint Corporation, New Delhi, 1980, first published by Oxford University Press, London, 1934.

Ahmed, Syed: *Atharal-Sanadid*, Eng. trans. R. Nath *Monuments of Delhi*, Ambika Publications, Indian Institute of Islamic Studies, New Delhi, 1979.

Alam, Muzaffar and Subrahmanyam, Sanjay, eds: *The Mughal State 1526–1750*, Oxford in India Readings, OUP Delhi 1998.

Ansar Zahid Khan, ed.: *Quarterly Journal of the Pakistani Historical Society*, January-March 2001; Vol. XLIX, No 1; Punjab and N.W.F.P.; Ibrahim Shah, 'Major Architectural Remains of the time of Aurangzeb', p. 45-47.

Archer, Mildred: *Company Drawings in the India Office Library*, HMSO, London, 1972.

Archer, Mildred: *Company Drawings, Indian Paintings of the British Period*, Indian Art Series, Victoria and Albert Museum London, in association with Mapin, Ahmedabad 1992.

Ardalen, Nader and Bakhtiar, Laleh: *The Sense of Unity — The Sufi Tradition in Persian Architecture*, Publication of the Centre for Middle Eastern Studies 9, The University of Chicago Press, Chicago, 1973.

Asher, Catherine B: *Architecture of Mughal India*, The New Cambridge History of India, l: 4, Cambridge University Press, 1992.

Ashurst, J and Ashurst, N: *Practical Building Conservation* (Vol. 1) Stone Masonry, English Heritage Technical Handbook, Aldershott: Gower Technical Press, 1988.

Ashurst, J and Ashurst, N: *Practical Building Conservation* (Vol. 3) Mortars, Plasters and Renders, English Heritage Technical Handbook, Aldershott: Gower Technical Press, 1983.

Bakhtiyar, Lalch: *Sufi. Expressions of the Mystic Quest*, Thames and Hudson 1976

Basham, A.L. ed: *A Cultural History of India*, Oxford University Press, New Delhi, 1975.

Beach, Milo Cleveland and Koch, Ebba, with translations by Thackston, Wheeler. M. : *King of the World, The Padshahnama, An Imperial Mughal Manuscript from the Royal Library Windsor Castle*, Azimuth Editions, Sackler Gallery.

Begde, Prabhakar V: Forts and Palaces of India, Sagar Publications, New Delhi 1982

Beglar, J. D. and Carlleyle, A. C. L., Assistant Superintending Archaeologists: *ASI Report 1871-72, Delhi and Agra*, Vol. IV, Indological Book House, Varanasi, 1966.

Begley, W. E. and Desai, Z. A. eds: *The Shah Jahan Nama of Inayat Khan,* the 19th century manuscript translation of A.R. Fuller (B.L Add. 301777), Delhi, Oxford University Press, 1990.

Bernier, Francois: *Travels in the Mughal Empire, 1656-68*, First Published London 1891; Reprint Asian Educational Services AES, New Delhi, 1996.

Beveridge, H: Eng. trans. *Akbarnama of Abul Fazal,* The Asiatic Society, Calcutta, 1907.

Blake, Stephen, P: *Shahjahanabad, the Sovereign City in Mughal India, 1639–1739*, Cambridge University Press, Delhi, 1993.

Bredin, Hugh and Santoro-Brienza Liberato: *Philosophies of Art and Beauty*, An Introduction to Aesthetics, Edinburgh University Press, Edinburgh, 2000

Brookes, John: *Gardens of Paradise*, The History and Design of the Great Islamic Gardens, Weidenfield and Nicholson, London, 1987.

Brown, Percy: *Indian Architecture (Islamic Period)*, Fourth edition, Taraporevala Sons & Co. Pvt. Ltd., Bombay 1964, First Edition 1956.

Cameron, Sonja, Uruquhart, D. C. M., Wakefield, Rachel and Young, M. E.: TAN 10, *Biological Growths on Sandstone Buildings — Control and Treatment*, Historic Scotland, Edinburgh, 1997.

Carr-Stephen: *The Archaeology and Monumental Remains of Delhi,* (Ludhiana and Calcutta), 1876; Kitab Mahal, Allahabad 1967.

Cave-Browne, J.: *The Punjab and Delhi in 1857* (Vol. I and II), Deepak Reprints, 1993, Gurgaon, Haryana; first published 1861.

Chaudhuri, Sashi Bhusan: *Theories of the Indian Mutiny (1857–59)*, The World Press Private Ltd. Calcutta, 1965.

Chenoy, Shama Mitra; *Shahjahanabad: The City of Delhi 1639–1857*, Munshi Ram, New Delhi, 1998.

Clark, Roger, H: *Analysis of Precedent: An Investigation of Elements, Relationships and Order*: Raleigh (N.C.) Student Publication of the School of Design, North Carolina, 1979.

Coomaraswamy, A. K.: *Early Indian Architecture, Palaces*, Munshiram Manoharlal Publishers Pvt. Ltd., 1975, First published in *Eastern Art* (Vol. III) 1931.

Coomaraswamy, A. K.: *Christian and Oriental philosophy of Art,* Dover Publications Inc., New York 1956.

Crowe S., Hayward S., Jellicoe S. and Patterson G: *Gardens of Mughal India,* Thames and Hudson, 1972.

Dal Co, Francesco and Mazzariol, Giuseppe: *Carlo Scarpa, The Complete Works,* Electa/The Architectural Press, 1986.

Daniell, Thomas and Daniell, William: *Oriental Scenery, Parts I-V,* each containing 24 views of the architecture, antiquities and landscape scenery of Hindoustan by Messrs. Thomas and William Daniell, 2 volumes, Longman, Hurst, Rees, Ovme and Brown, 1812-1814.

Dayal, Maheshwar: *Rediscovering Delhi* (Delhi, 1975).

Delhi Coronation Durbar, Coronation Durbar Illustrated, Delhi, Madras, Vest & Co., 1903.

Delhi, Imperial Committee Proceedings for November 1916, Delhi, Suptt. Govt. Press, 1915.

Delhi Master Plan, Akalank Publications, Delhi, 1990.

Delhi, Residency and Agency, Punjab Govt. Records, 1807-57.

Dix, Gerald and Tarn, John Nelson eds.: *Design and Conservation in the City*, Liverpool University Press, 1985.

Ehlers, Eckart and Krafft, Thomas, Eds.: *Shahjahanabad/Old Delhi, Tradition and Colonial Change*, Erdkundliches Wissen 111, Franz Steiner Verlag, Stuttgart, 1993.

Elliot and Dowson, eds.: *The History of India By its Own Historians, The Muhammaden Period (Vol. VII & VIII)*, Kitab Mahal Pvt. Ltd. 1969.

Fanshawe, H. C.: *Delhi: Past and Present*, 1902 AES Reprint, New Delhi, 1998.

Fass, Virginia: *The Forts of India*, Collins, London, in association with Oberoi Hotels International, 1980.

Feilden Bernard: *Conservation of Historic Buildings*, second ed. London, Butterworth Heinemann Ltd, 1982.

Fergusson, James: *History of Indian and Eastern Architecture*, Revised and Edited: John, Burgess, reprint, Low Price Publications, Delhi, 1994, first published 1910, London.

Fonseca, Rory: 'The Walled City of Old Delhi', *Shelter and Society* ed. Paul Oliver.

Forrest, C. R.: *A Picturesque Tour Along the Rivers Ganges and Jumna in India*, R. Ackermann, London, July 1824

Frykenberg, R. E. ed: *Delhi Through the Ages*, Essays in Urban History, Culture and Society, Oxford University Press, New Delhi, 1986.

Gaur, R. C.: *Excavations at Fatehpur Sikri*, Aryan Books International, Darya Ganj, New Delhi, 2000.

Gazetteer of the Delhi District, 1883–84, Punjab Govt., second edition, 1989.

Gideon, Sigfried: *Space, Time and Architecture, The Growth of a New Tradition*, Cambridge, Massachusetts, Harvard University Press, 1941.

Goodman, Nelson: *Ways of Worldmaking*, Hackett Publishing Co. Indianapolis, 1978, fourth printing 1985

Gole, Susan: *Indian Maps and Plans, from Earliest Times to the Advent of European Surveys*, Manohar, New Delhi, 1981.

Green, Bryn: *Countryside Conservation—Landscape, Ecology, Planning and Management*, 3rd ed. E&FN SPON, An imprint of Chapman & Hall.

Gribbin, John: *Our Changing Planet*, Wildwood House London, first published 1977.

Griffiths, Charles John: *Siege of Delhi*, ed. H. J. Yonge (London 1910), Mittal Publications, New Delhi, 1995.

Gupta, Narayani: *Delhi Between Two Empires 1803-1931, Society, Government and Urban Growth*, Oxford University Press, Delhi, 1981.

Habib, Irfan: *The Agrarian System of Mughal India 1656-1707*, Oxford University Press, 1989, first published 1963

Hambly, Gavin and Swann, Wim: *Cities of Mughal India, Delhi, Agra and Fatehpur Sikri*, Elek Books, G.P. Putnam's Sons, New York 1968.

Harvey, Paul, ed: *The Oxford Companion to English Literature*, OUP, Oxford, 1934 first published 1932,

Hasan, S. Nurul: *The Morphology of the Medieval Indian City, A Case Study of Shahjahanabad in the 18th and early 19th Century,* Occasional Paper Series: 4, urban History association of India, 1982.

Hasan, Zafar: *List of Monuments of the Delhi Circle (Vol. I) Shahjahanabad*, ASI, Published 1916, ed. J. A. Page et.al. Reprinted as *Monuments of Delhi (Vol. I)*, Aryan Books International, New Delhi 1997.

Head, Raymond: *The Indian Style*, George Allen and Unwin Publishers Ltd. London, 1986

Hearn, Gordon Risley: *Seven Cities of Delhi*, 1997, S. B. W. Publishers, New Delhi; first published 1906.

Heber, Reginald: *Narrative of a Journey through the Upper Provinces of India from Calcutta to Bombay 1824-25, an account of a journey to Madras and the Southern Provinces and Letters written in India,* third edition, 3 volumes, Murray, London 1828.

Herdew, Klaus: *Formal Structure in Islamic Architecture of Iran and Turkistan* first edition, Rizzoli Int, 1990.

Heyman, J.: *The Stone Skeleton: Structural Engineering of Masonry Architecture,* 2nd ed. Cambridge, Cambridge University Press, 1997.

Hodges, William, *Select Views in India Drawn on the Spot (1780-83)* Printed for William Hodges.

Hooper-Greenhill, Eileen: *Museums and their Visitors,* Routledge, 1994.

Ibn-Batutta: *Travels in Asia and Africa 1325-1354, (Vol. II)*, translated and selected, H. A. R. Gibb. London, Kegan Paul 1952.

Irvine, William: *The Later Mughals*, Vol 2, Oriental Books Reprint Corporation, New Delhi 1971

Jain, Nalini and Richardson, John, eds.: *Eighteenth Century English Poetry, The Annotated Anthology*, 1994, Harvester Wheatsheaf, Hertfordshire.

Kaye, M. M. ed.: *The Golden Calm, An English Lady's Life in Moghul Delhi, Reminiscences by Emily, Lady Clive Bailey and her father, Sir Thomas Metcalfe,* Viking Press, New York, 1980.

Keene, H. G.: *Dehli,* M. N. Publishers and Distributors, New Delhi; first published London, (1874 and Calcutta 1906).

Khan, Dargah Quli: *Muraqqa-i-Delhi,* The Mughal Capital in Muhammad Shah's Time, Eng. trans. Shekhar, Chander and Chenoy, Shama Mitra, Deputy Publication, New Delhi, 1989.

Khan, Saqi Mustaad: *Maasir-i-Alamgiri*, Eng. Trans: J. Sarkar, The Asiatoc Society 1947, reprinted 1990.

Keyserling, Hermann Von: *Indian Diary of a Philosopher,* Bharatiya Vidya Bhawan.

Koch, Ebba: *Mughal Architecture,* Pretzel, Munich, 1991; Oxford University Press, New Delhi, 2002.

Koch, Ebba: *Shah Jahan and Orpheus, The Pietra dura Decoration and the Programme of the Throne in the Diwan-i-Am,* GRAZ, 1988.

Koch, Ebba: *Mughal Art and Imperial Ideology,* Collected Essays, Oxford University Press, 2001 New Delhi.

Lal, P: *The Mahabharata of Vyasa,* 1980, Vikas Publishing House Pvt. Ltd, New Delhi

Lapidus, Ira: *Muslim Cities in the Later Middle Ages,* Harvard University Press, 1967.

Leyden, John and Erskine, William; Humphrey: *Baburnama — Memoirs of Zehir-ed-din Muhammad* (Vol. I and II), Milford, Oxford, 1921-2.

Lewis, Franklin D.: *Rumi — Past and Present, East and West*, One World, Oxford, 2000.

Los, Sergio: *Carlo Scarpa, An Architectural Guide,* Arsenale Editrice srl, Verona, Italy, 1995.

Majumdar, R. C. ed.: *The Mughal Empire, History and Culture of the Indian People,* (Vol. VII): Bombay, Bharatiya Vidya Bhawan, 1994.

Manganuakar, K. T. *Delhi Durbar,* 1911.

Mani. B. K.: *Delhi, Threshold of the Orient, Studies in Archeological Investigations,* Aryan Books International, New Delhi, 1997.

Marshall, J.: *Conservation Manual for the Care of Ancient Monuments* (1902–3), Indological Book House, Varanasi, 1973.

Marshall, John, Ed.: *The ASI Annual Report,* 1911–12; Calcutta, Superintendent Government Printing, India, 1915.

Martinelli, Antonio (Photographs) and Michell, George (Text): *India, Yesterday and Today, Aquatints by Thomas and William Daniell*, Oriental Scenery, Swanhill Press, England, 1998.

Marx, Karl and Engels, Frederic: *On Colonialism,* Progress Publishers, Moscow, 1978.

Masselos, Jim and Gupta, Narayani: *Beato's Delhi 1857, 1997,* Ravi Dayal Publisher, Delhi 2000.

McNeill, William H. and Waldman, Marilyn Robinson, eds.: *The Islamic World, Readings in World History,* (Vol. 6) Oxford University Press, New York, 1973.

Metcalf, Thomas, R: *An Imperial Vision,* Faber and Faber, London, 1989.

Metcalfe, Charles Theophilus, ed.: *Two Native Narratives of the Mutiny in Delhi, Narrative of Mainodin Hasan Khan and Narrative of Munshi Jeewan Lal*, Archibald Constable & Co. (London 1898).

Mundy, Peter: *The Travels of Peter Mundy in Europe and Asia, 1608–67* (Vol. I–V) Edited by Richard Carnac Temple and Lavinia Mary Anstey, Hakluyt Society Second Series, no. 78, Printed for the Hakluyt Society, 1936.

Murphy, Richard: *Carlo Scarpa and Castelvecchio,* Butterworth Architecture, 1990.

The ASI Annual Report, 1905–6; Calcutta, Superintendent Government Printing, India, 1909.

Nath, R.: *Colour Decoration In India,* Taraporevala, Bombay, 1970.

Nath, R.: *Agra and its Monuments*, The Historical Research Documentation Program, Jaipur 1997.

Nath, R.: *The Private Life of the Mughals,* The Historical Research Documentation Program, Jaipur 1997

Nath, R.: *The Taj Mahal and its Incarnation, Original Persian Data on its Builders, Materials, Costs, Measurements, etc.*; The Historical Research Documentation Program, Jaipur 1985.

Nawab Server-al-Mulk Bahadur: *My Life,* Eng. Trans. Nawab Jawan Yar Jung Bahadur, Arthur H. Stockwell Ltd., London.

Nicholson, Louise: *The Red Fort, Delhi,* Taurus Parke Books, London, 1989.

Noe, Samuel V: 'Old Lahore and Old Delhi, Variations on a Mughal Theme', *Ekistics*, Vol. 49, No. 295, July/Aug 1902.

Noe, Samuel V: 'Shahjahanabad: Geometrical bases for the Plan of Mughal India', *Design India Quarterly*, Vol 27, No 37, Apr/June 1903.

Page, J. A.: *A Memoir of Kotla Firoz Shah, Delhi*, Memoirs of the ASI No. 52, ASI Janpath, New Delhi 1999, Original Edition 1937.

Page, J. A.: *A Historical Memoir on the Qutb, Delhi*, Memoirs of the ASI No. 22, ASI Janpath, New Delhi 1998, Original Edition 1926.

Parks, Fanny: *Wanderings of a Pilgrim in Search of the Picturesque during four-and-twenty years in the East* (Vol. I and II), Pelham Richardson, London 1850.

Pelsaert, Francois: *Jahangir's India*, ed. and trans: W. H. Moreland and P. Geyl, reprint Delhi 1972

Petruccioli, Attilio: 'The Case of Fatehpur Sikri', *Environmental Design:* Journal of Islamic Environment Designs and Research Centre.

Polier, Antoine Louis Henry: *Shah Alam II and his Court*, ed. Pratul. C. Gupta, The Asiatic Society Calcutta, first published 1947, Reprint 1989.

Qaisar, Ahsan Jan: *Building Construction in Mughal India - the Evidence from Painting*, Aligarh Muslim University. Oxford University Press, Delhi, 1988.

Renton-Dennings, J.: *Delhi, The Imperial City*, J. Renton-Dennings, Times Press Bombay 1911.

Rizvi, S. A. A. and Flynn, V. J. A.: *Fathpur-Sikri*, D.B. Taraporevala Sons and Co. Private limited, first published 1975, Bombay.

Said, Edward W.: *Culture and Imperialism*, Routledge and Kegan Paul, London and Hneley, 1978. Sanderson, Gordon: *Delhi Fort, A Guide to its Buildings and Gardens*, Archaeological Survey of India, Calcutta, Suptt. Government Printing, 1914.

Sarkar, Jadunath: *Delhi during the Anarchy 1749–1788*, as told in contemporary Records, Calcutta, Suptt. Government Printing, India, 1921.

Sarkar, Jadunath: *A History of Jaipur, c. 1503–1938*, Orient Longman, New Delhi, 1984.

Sarkar, Jadunath: *Fall of the Mughal Empire 1789–1803* (Vol. 4) First Published 1950, Second Edition 1992, Orient Longman.

Seminar papers and proceedings, Visitor Management: 1993, Stratford-upon-Avon, English Historic Towns Forum, Publication no. 25.

Shaffer, R. J. : *The Weathering of Natural Building Stones*, BRE Sp. Report No. 18, 1985.

Facsimile of 1932 edition, Building Research Station.

Sharma, Y. D.: *Delhi and Its Neighbourhood*, 1990, ASI, Government of India, first published in 1964.

Sharma, Jagdish Saran: *India Since the Advent of the British*, A Descriptive Chronology, From 1600 - October 1969, S. Chand and Company, New Delhi, 1970.

Spear, T. G. P.: *Twilight of the Mughuls, Studies in Late Mughul Delhi*, Munshiram Manoharlal Publishers pvt. Ltd. New Delhi, 1991, first published 1951.

Strang, Herbert: *Stories of the Mutiny*, Mittal Publications, New Delhi, 1990.

Tandon, Banmali: *The Architecture of Luckhnow and its Dependencies, 1722–1865;* A descriptive inventory and an analysis of Nawabi types, Vikas publishing House Pvt. Ltd, New Delhi, 2001

Tagore, Rabindranath: *A Vision of India's History*, Visva Bharati Publishing Department, Calcutta 1988, First published 1951

Tagore, Rabindranath: *The Centre of Indian Culture*, Visva Bharati Publishing Department, Calcutta 1988, First published 1919

Tavernier, Jean-Baptiste: *Travels in India* (Vol. I and II) second edition of the Eng. translation by V. Ball from the original French edition of 1676, ed. William Crooke, Oxford University Press, London 1925; first edition 1889.

Thackston, Wheeler. M. ed.: *The Baburnama, Memoirs of Babur, Prince and Emperor,* OUP New York, in association with Freer Gallery of Art and The Arthur M. Sackler Gallery, Smithsonian Institute, Washington DC 1996.

The India Collection, Catalogue of a collection of over 2,200 books concerning the British Period, The British Council, AIFACS Building, New Delhi 1982.

'*The Eighth City of Delhi*', An Exhibition of Historical Records and Photos organised by Delhi Archives, Delhi Administration, New Delhi, October 1979.

Tillotson, G. H. R.: *Mughal India,* Viking, London, 1960, 1990.

Tirmizi, S. A. I: *Mughal Documents (AD 1628-59)* (Vol. II), Manohar Publishers and Distributors, New Delhi, 1995.

Topsfield, Andrew: *Indian Paintings from Oxford Collections,* Ashmolean Museum in association with the Bodleian Library, Oxford 1994.

Torraca Giorgio: *Porous Building Materials, Material Science for Architectural Conservation,* 3rd Edition, ICCROM, Rome, 1988.

Upadhyay, Raju: 'Conservation and Revitalisation of the Physical Environment, Katra Neel, Shahjahanabad,' Thesis Report 1985, S.P.A. Library (29245-UF) 09.711.163 (545.5)

Villiers-Stuart, Constance M.: *Gardens of the Great Mughals,* Adam and Charles Black, London, 1913.

Volwahsen, Andreas, ed. Steirlin, Henri: *Architecture of the World (Islamic India),* Benedikt Taschen.

Watt, David: *Journal of Architectural Conservation,* No.3, Vol.3, Donhead, Dorset, November 1997.

Weaver, M. E. *Conserving Buildings: A Guide to Techniques and Materials,* New York, John Wiley and Sons, 1993.

Webster. Robin G. M. ed. *Stone Cleaning and the Nature, Soiling and Decay Mechanisms of Stone,* Proceedings of the International Conference held in Edinburgh, UK, Donhead Publishing, London, 1992.

Wheeler, Stephen: *History of the Delhi Coronation Durbar,* London, John Murray, 1904.

Wollaston, Arthur, N: *English-Persian Dictionary,* Cosmo Publications, New Delhi 1978, first published 1842.

Woolf, Virginia: *A Room of One's Own,* Penguin Books, 1945.

Yadav, K.C. ed.: *Delhi in 1857, The Trial of Bahadur Shah* (Vol. I) The Academic Press, Gurgaon, 1980.

GLOSSARY

abad	inhabited, populated, prosperous
aiwan	palace, chamber, hall
Asad	lion, Leo, the fifth sign of the zodiac
bagh	a garden, orchard
bagheecha	a small garden
burj	tower, turret, dome
chaddar	carved stone surfaces, generally set at an incline to form a surface for water to flow down
chajja	overhanging eaves
charbagh	a garden divided into quadrants by running watercourses
chattri	a domed kiosk supported on pillars
chowk	literally a square; a market; a public area
chuna	lime plaster, usually highly burnished
dado	the finishing of an interior wall from the floor to about 3-feet height
dargah	a saint's shrine, often the centre of pilgrimage
dhalan	verandah; lobby
Diwan-i-Am	Hall of Public Audience
Diwan-i-Khas	Hall of Private Audience
diya	lamp

ganj	market place
garh	fort
ghat	an embankment, usually stepped
ghazal	ode, short poem
hakeem	physician practising one of the traditional systems of medicine of India
hammam	a bath with hot, cold and warm chambers
haram	sacred, forbidden; a sanctuary, the sacred territory of Mecca, wife
haveli	home, dwelling, a large and spacious building
hayat	life, existence
hayat baksh	life-giving
hasht-bahisht	eight paradises
Imtiaz Mahal	literally Hall of Distinction; the pavilion in the Red Fort, Delhi, today known as Rang Mahal
jali-gavaksha	latticed window
jali	pierced carved stone screen
Jami Mosque	a congregational mosque
jat	an agricultural group found primarily in certain parts of north India and modern Pakistan
jharoka	a window, a balcony, a throne from which the emperor displayed himself to his subjects
jalash	literally urn; in architecture, the curved ornamentation in this shape that surmounts the top of a spire or a dome
karakhana	workshop or centre of production
katra	locality, market
kotwal	chief of police in a town
kucha	a narrow street, lane
kuuhna	old, ancient
mahal	palace, a palatial building, a mansion
maidan	open grassy field, a congregational area

mansab	rank in the Mughal administrative system
mansabdar	rank-holder
masjid	mosque
Nahr-i-Bahist	canal of paradise, the canal that runs through the Red Fort
Naqqar Khana	chamber within a palace where ceremonial drums are played at stated intervals
padamkosa	lotus petals
pandan	betel-leaf holder
raja	king
rang	colour, dye, paint, enjoyment, merriment
Rang Mahal	a place for festive enjoyment
shamiana	tent
squinch	an arch or system of gradually projecting and wider arches placed diagonally at the internal angle of a square structure, thus allowing it to be surmounted by a dome
sufi	a mystic
tehsil	district
thana	police station
trabeated	construction on post and lintel system
vastushastras	ancient Indian texts with rules for architecture
zenana	women's quarters or dwelling place
zill	shadow, shade, protection
Zill-e-Soobhani	form of addressing a king; (lit.) shadow of God